GEORGIE!
MY GEORGIE!

GEORGIE!
MY GEORGIE!

George Dilboy

THE FIRST GREEK-AMERICAN
TO WIN THE MEDAL OF HONOR

America's Highest Military Award

An Incredible Love Story

A Novel

EDDIE BRADY

To order additional copies of this book, contact:
Xlibris Corporation
1-888-795-4274
www.Xlibris.com
Orders@Xlibris.com
22905

CONTENTS

PART III

PART IV

OTHER BOOKS BY EDDIE BRADY

Last In My Class—How humor Helped Me Survive Alcoholism (a Serious—Humorous Memoir).

Good Grief! About Relationships.—And Other Short Stories That Make You Wish They Were Shorter.

FOREWORD

The heart of this story is true. George Dilboy was a Greek immigrant who became a U.S. Citizen. He was born in 1896. His first twelve years were spent surviving the incessant fighting between Greeks and Turks in Asia Minor, present day Western Turkey. He immigrated to America and lived in Somerville, MA at age twelve in 1908. He went back to Greece to fight in the First Balkan War in 1912 and stayed to fight in the Second Balkan War in 1913, to help the Greek cause. He returned to America and volunteered to fight for the U.S. Army in the Mexican Border War in 1916-1917 and was honorably discharged. He answered the call to the colors and joined the U.S. Army once again later in 1917, entering World War I, after the U.S. declared war against Kaiser Wilhelm's Germany.

He fought with the newly formed 26th "Yankee" Division throughout France in 1917 and 1918, on the Western Front. He won the then called Congressional Medal of Honor, America's highest military award. He was the first Greek-American to win the now called, Medal of Honor.

There has never been a book written about George "the hero" Dilboy, as the Greeks call him, to my knowledge. There have been many newspaper articles, however. I was born and brought up in Somerville, MA and played on Dilboy Field and Stadium. One day I stopped and read the wording on the plaque beneath a bust standing on top of a monument dedicated to George Dilboy in front of City Hall. I was intrigued. When I looked further into his background, I was startled. It was so unique, so different, so remarkable, so inspiring, I was fascinated. Hopefully, so won't you.

Many newspaper articles were written about his heroic behavior under fire during the last few hours of his life, but very little was known about his early life. I was fortunate to be able to locate living descendents and relatives of the "hero," who were most helpful in furnishing me with documents about his family history in Asia Minor, Greece and here in America, from Massachusetts, and New Hampshire to California. The following acknowledgement section is more specific.

The advantage of the Novel approach in telling this story is that it allows the author to infuse a breathing, pulsating, throbbing, human being that was George Dilboy into its telling, that a dry recitation of historical facts lacks. In writing this Novel, I made what I thought were reasonable inferences from known facts to create characters to connect the dots or fill in blanks, in the same way juries work in reaching their verdicts.

Written comments, descriptions, characterizations, and public quotes from some of George Dilboys fellow soldiers and superior officers who served with and alongside him, helped me to create George Dilboy's character and others around him, both real and fictional. It was like painting portraits of people from photographs taken by others.

Arguably, the comments of other individuals who knew him were presumably more objective than the words of George Dilboy himself. The only words of Dilboy that are direct quotes from him are:

"I'm going to get that gun!" **and**
"Some day my name will be etched in stone."

Ultimately, both became true.

A written history of the 26th Yankee Division, U.S. Army, in France entitled, "*With The Yankee Division In France*," by Frank P. Sibley, a newspaper reporter on the city staff of the Boston Globe, who accompanied the Yankee Division throughout France, was very helpful to me in following its actions. Sibley was an eyewitness to that which he wrote about. Mr. Sibley was given a special assignment by his employer, The Boston Globe, to report on the New England troops.

Sibley went "over there" to France with only a letter of
introduction from George Creel, Chairman of the Committee on
Public Information, an agency set up by President Wilson to sell
the nation the Governments view of the war. Sibley was initially
accredited by General John J. Pershing, Commander of the
American Expeditionary Force in Europe. Sibley returned after
the Armistice, authored this book, and had it published in 1919.

A second publication that was instrumental in helping me to
write about the background of the World War was Floyd Gibbons
book entitled *And "They Thought We Wouldn't Fight,"* which was
published in 1918. Mr. Gibbons was an official newspaper
correspondent of The Chicago Tribune, and accredited to the
American Expeditionary Force. While serving with the Doughboys
on the front lines, he had an eye shot out by machine gun bullets
at Belleau Wood. He was awarded the coveted Croix de Guerre
Medal by the French Government.

Unfortunately, "the hero's" letters from France were buried
with him. As to his social life, I could find no indication that he
ever married. However, his extraordinary good looks, which even
a crude 1917 photo can't hide, his happy-go-lucky attitude, his
ability to get along with others, his sensitivity, his fun-loving spirit,
his adventuresomeness, his fortitude, demonstrated time after time
over a period of years, all of which was commented on by others in
writing, made it inconceivable to me that he didn't have a girlfriend
or a special lady in his life, human nature being what it is. So I
created a fiance to fit his circumstances. I believe someone like the
storied Angelika to be entirely possible and even probable in his
real life.

Literary license was taken in the timing, but not the true fact,
of the United States Grand Fleet taking a fifteen month world
goodwill tour from 1908 to 1910. It's sailing into the
Mediterranean was advanced a few months to fit the story line,
but otherwise it could well have happened as related in this novel.

The New England National Guard troops, including George
Dilboy, who served during the Mexican Border War, were generally
held to duties guarding the U.S.-Mexican border, leaving the

invasion and interior fighting to regular Army soldiers. However, exceptions were made for demonstrated skilled marksmen and sharpshooters, who were used as scouts, reconnaissance and snipers for special assignments.

Since Dilboy had early exposure, informal training and frequent use of rifles with his father for defense of home, for sport and recreation in Asia Minor, as well as formal training in the U.S, Army, it is inconceivable to me that these easily identifiable shooting skills were not used by savy superiors in Army pursuits in interior Mexico. I assumed this happened to Dilboy and had him experience the fighting of the troops that penetrated five hundred miles deep, into the largest Mexican Province of Chihuahua.

Copies of still photographs of core events in the life of "the hero" Dilboy exist, that I have gratefully come in possession of:

- His Army photograph taken in 1917, on this book's front cover.
- His first burial site in Belleau Wood.
- His casket being carried by the villagers in Alatsata in 1922.
- His white gravestone in Arlington National Cemetary.
- His letters being buried beneath the foundation of his statute, in front of the largest veterans hospital in the world in Hines, Illinois in 1942.
- Daniel Rozakis, relative of "the hero," placing a lei at the USS Arizona Memorial, Pearl Harbor, HI to honor the men of the USS Arizona, and in memory of George Dilboy, August 27, 2000.

In summary, and in my view, this necessary weaving of fact and fiction to color the rich fabric of this amazing story, is too enthralling not to be perpetuated in a Novel form. I hope you agree, or are at least inspired by the tale.

AKNOWLEDGEMENTS

I owe a huge debt of gratitude to Richard Rozakis, of California, and formerly from the Brickbottom section of Somerville, second cousin to George Dilboy. He made available to me material containing the history of the Dilboy family back to the year 1800, and an oral history passed down by Dilboy descendents of the unique Greek experience of the people of Alatsata, Chios, Crete, Athens and America. His mother, Georgia Dilboy Rozakis, was a first cousin of George Dilboy. She was born near the time Dilboy immigrated to America in 1908. She passed away at age 93 in 2002, while residing in California. She instilled in her son Richard the passion to keep the memory of George Dilboy alive for the benefit of future generations.

Special thanks is also extended to Evangeline Dilboy Alexis, First Cousin to George Dilboy, who kept the "hero's" memory current with many attendences representing the Dilboy family at public events, and bringing along her son George.

I tip my hat to George Alexis, of Massachusetts, son of the aforementioned Evangeline Dilboy Alexis, and thus a second cousin to George Dilboy, who is working to help veterans to this day. He also was born in Brickbottom, and made time from his busy schedule to meet with me and share memories of his youth there.

I would like to thank Angie Doukas, originally born in Brickbottom, who passed away in 2004, at age 81, and who personally knew the members of the original twelve families that immigrated to Brickbottom from Asia Minor, and related to me his experiences. George Tsirigotis of the Demosthenes Greek-American Political Club in Somerville, MA, who is related by marriage to the Dilboy family, was helpful with information, including a picture on the wall of this club showing the port city of Alatsata when it was a thriving community of Asia Minor Greeks. The priests and employees on the beautiful campus at Hellenic College in Brookline, MA were very helpful in guiding my research there. My heartful thanks for them going out of their way to assist an inquiring Irishman.

I would also like to recognize former three term Governor and 1988 Democratic Presidential candidate, Michael Dukakis, now a Distinguished Professor of Political Science at Northeastern University in Boston, MA, for his encouragement and suggestions that helped inform this three year project.

By one of the quirks of history, Governor Dukakis's Professor's office is feet away from his deceased father's office on Huntington Ave in Boston, where the father practiced medicine as a physician for fifty years. This dovetails with George Dilboy because descendents of the original twelve Alatsata families that immigrated to Brickbottom told me they took three trolley cars into Boston during the 1940's and 1950's to be treated by Doctor Panos Dukakis, because he was Greek, spoke Greek fluently, and was an excellent physcian. Dr Dukakis continued to treat his patients until he was eighty-two years young.

Dr. Dukakis himself immigrated to America in 1912, not speaking a word of English and worked his way through Harvard Medical School, graduating in 1924. He did his own general surgery, was a Fellow of the American College of Surgeons, was an Obstetrician, delivered 3,000 babies, and was a Family Practioner who made house calls. Surely, he was another inspiritional immigration success story.

A special note of thanks to Christine Cook, Office Manager and Secretary of the George Dilboy Veterans of Foreign Wars Post in Davis Square, in the heart of Somerville, MA and the first and oldest Dilboy Post in America, for making their records available to me, and thereby assisting my research.

Others who shared their interest and encouragement were Michael Canavan, born and brought up in Somerville and a sports participant on Dilboy Field; Jean Flanagan, Instructor of Literature at Middlesex Community College, Bedford, MA, who has her own published works in historical poetry, and Frank Flanagan, Esquire, now deceased, who spent his formative years on Dilboy and other playing fields of Somerville, and had a lifelong interest in the Literary Arts.

Also, thanks go out to Mary Flanagan, Esquire for sharing her experience in crossing the Atlantic Ocean at an early age, that resulted in chapter 6 in this book. I would like to salute Jack Canavan, Joe Connelly and Connie McGrail for enobling Dilboy field and other playing fields of Somerville with the formative honing of their athletic skills, that subsequently transitioned into their respective career successes.

PART 1

CHAPTER ONE

THE OLD MAN

The old man was unnoticed in the crowd

It was a chilly, dreary day. His overcoat collar was pulled high to protect his neck from the piercing cold. The front of the collar covered his face up to his red nose, like a mask. His black hat tilted down to reveal only his eyes, glistening and watering from the stinging late winter weather. High on his chest was a glistening gold and blue military award, fluttering in the wind. It had been pinned on him earlier in the day during ceremonies on the Boston Common.

It was early April, 1919, almost five months after the end of the Great War, so-called. The Kaiser had fled Germany for exile in Holland and would die there forever in exile. Though hundreds of thousands of American troops still remained in Europe, some had come home, as many as reversed planning and readied troop ships could allow. They came back, that is, those not buried in mass graves in European soil and those not ravaged by the killer Spanish Flu.

The old man seemed mesmerized by the passing parade. He was celebrating, with our beloved marching doughboys, their victory in the war to end all wars. But he was especially saluting the return of one of the war's most heroic soldiers. And George was marching by, that is, his spirit, rather than his body. The distraught old man was silent, but his mouth was trembling.

Through biting cold, the sky was bright blue and the sun was radiating down on this excited and happy holiday parade crowd. Fathers held their children astride their shoulders so they could see the passing marchers. American flags waved, Battle flags of Belleau Wood and Chateau Thierry fluttered and snapped in the whipping winds. Thousands crowded the sidewalks at the bottom of Boston's historic Beacon Hill, in spots five and ten rows deep. The gloriously colorful marching bands were playing and serenading the air with World War I patriotic songs, now that the surviving boys were safely back from *"Over There."* Happy, beaming throngs nodded their heads, tapped their toes, and spontaneously waved their arms in tune with the music pacing the braced bodies of the smartly dressed soldiers strutting by.

Now the heroic United States Army, 26th, Yankee Division, was passing by—*his* division, *his* buddies, George's boys. The proud survivors of this honored unit stepped in tune with the blaring band with admirable precision. These foxhole buddies were the same ones who went over the top with George, and together finally stopped the rampaging hoards of Huns at Belleau Wood, and saved millions of civilians in panicked Paris.

As the leather skinned, physically fit and magnificently attired veterans tramped past, the old man's eyes never wavered. He sat in the stands still as a stone, except for the uncontrollable quivering of his lips. The boys of the Yankee Division were now directly in front of him and the remainder of his body began to stir. He mumbled something barely audible. He started to rise, but, off balance, fell back. He rose again and muttered something. He gestured and uttered, more sharply, in broken English.

Nearby parade viewers cast puzzled looks and annoyed glances at this odd sounding foreigner. Now, among the tumult and excited masses, the tiny old man could be seen moving and pushing his way down the main review stand for the invited honored politicians. An alert Boy Scout helped the tottering old man to regain his balance, as he stepped unevenly off the bottom step of the reviewing stand. Governor Calvin Coolidge was there, as was the Greek Ambassador to the United States. Army brass, impressive in their highly decorated uniforms, stood tall. Also present were elderly U.S. veterans of the Spanish-American War, and a few veterans of the Grand Army of the Republic, from the American Civil War, the deadliest war in U.S. history, where up to 620,000 Americans died.

But this increasingly emotional old man was only interested in one death, that of his son, George. He pushed his way down and through the crowd toward the street, his foreign voice mindlessly chanting in an accented cadence, "My Georgie! My Georgie!" He became more upset, as he shouldered his way to the front, hesitantly reaching out to the distancing troops, as if to plead with them not to leave. Tears staggered down his wrinkled, craggy face, worn by worry and time. Reaching the street, he was stopped only by the white wooden barriers.

Up to three million American soldiers had crossed the Atlantic Ocean to the fighting fields of France to make the world safe for Democracy. They had responded with patriotic fervor to the exhortations of President Woodrow Wilson. Now these deserving veterans had returned home and once again wore their uniforms for the adoring citizenry, who were shouting their appreciation for their sacrifices made to protect the future of their families in homeland America. They had come home, as best they could, the lame, the halt, the crippled and the dead. That is, those that could march did. As the music faded in the distance, the tramp! tramp! tramp! of their marching feet rose to a collective thud! Some invalided soldiers saluted and sat tall, while sitting in wheelchairs. Other soldiers stood up ramrod straight with crutches and canes, having paid for their patriotism with missing arms or legs. And, in one occasion, both.

It's the closest he could get to his son's spirit. The old man clutched in his tight fist, the colorful, decorative medal pinned to his chest, the Congressional Medal of Honor, this country's highest military award. He bent his head down in convulsive sobs, racked with grief. When he looked up again, seeing the soldiers of the Yankee Division disappearing around a turn in the street, he sputtered, "Georgie! Georgie!" His eyes went blurry as his thoughts went back in time.

CHAPTER TWO

ALATSATA

The old man's name was Antonios Dilboy. In Greece he was also called Antone, Antoni or Anton. His last name has also been spelled Dilvoi, Dilvois or Delevois. He was born in the village of Alatsata, near the State of Smyrna, Asia Minor in 1858. He was part of a family of eight brothers and sisters that survived birth. That was not something taken for granted then, as other brothers and sisters didn't survive, or if they did, not for long. Maria was born in 1853, Nicholaos in 1855, Antonios, as stated, in 1858, Dimitris, 1860, Kostas, 1866, Evangelos and Zenovia, whose exact, later dates of birth are unknown.

Today Alatsata is called Alacati, State of Izmir, Western Turkey. Alatsata is located on the Erythrean Peninsula, 45 miles west of Smyrna, now named Izmir. It sticks out into the Aegean Sea like a thumb. Antonios was given its oral history by his parents. Originally, Alatsata was owned by two Turkish Aga's. One was named Touriyout, who owned the upper village; the other was Memis, who owned the lower village. They did not like to farm, but needed people to cultivate the land. To solve this problem, they first went to Chios, (now called Khios), a nearby island further west on the Erythrean Peninsula, and hired Greeks to till the soil. It worked out so well that other Greek settlers were sought and induced to migrate from as far as Karistos and Kimi, located one hundred miles directly west across the Aegean Sea on mainland Greece, and others from that part of southern Greece called the Peloponnese. Further migrants sailed from various Aegean Islands near and far, including north from Lesbos and south from Samos, the Cyclades Islands and Crete, the largest Greek Island.

As part of the family's oral history, Antonios learned growing up that in 1688, the long island of Evvoia, generally northeast of Athens, was occupied by the great Italian businessman from Genoa, Francisco Morosini, with whom the Greeks got along well. That changed when the island was taken over and put under strict Turkish rule. Afraid of reprisals from the Turks because they had aided the Italian, a lot of the Greeks fled. Many of these sailed across the Aegean Sea over the one hundred miles to Alatsata. The Dilboys were among the early settlers who fled from Karistos, which is located on this island of Evvoia, to the lower village of Alatsata.

The Greeks sailed to Alatsata and made a new home there because they received favorable reports that the Turks owned huge properties there that they could not or would not work. They would lease out parcels of their land to willing Greeks, who would clear the land and plant crops. The Turks would then collect one tenth of the product produced, as their payment. The Greek settlers proved to be productive farmers and prospered. Eventually, they were able to buy the land they had leased and expanded their holdings.

At first, the farmers raised wheat, corn, barley, beans and all kinds of vegetables for food. In the 1700's they brought grape vines from the surrounding areas, and grew "Rozakia," black and "Sutana" grapes, which were dried as raisins. When production increased and their exports expanded, they built warehouses in Agriglia, by the sea, where they packed and shipped raisins to all parts of Europe.

Another important crop was Alatsata's sun-dried Oriental tobacco. This was especially valued for its quality and was shipped to England to be blended with the milder European tobaccos. Kostas Dilboy grew, bought and sold tobacco in Alatsata in the late 1800's and early 1900's. Together with his older brothers, Nicholaos and Antonios, he went into the interior of Asia Minor (that is, Central Turkey) to buy lamb and beef, which was butchered to supply the people of the lower village. They were also into cheese making.

Alatsatian Greeks enjoyed some freedom of religion and were able to live according to their own morals and standards. Four churches were built in Alatsata. These included the Holy Trinity Church, the Church of St. Constantine, the Cathedral Annunciation of the Virgin Mary, and the Church of the Presentation of the Theotokos. This last church was the one attended by the Dilboys.

With respect to education, at one time, as in many countries, only boys went to school. In the early 1800's in this area, girls started attending school. The education system was comprised of grammar school and high school. Beyond that, many of the boys went to Halki, Turkey and to the Theological School of Stavrou in Jerusalem to become priests. Others went to different schools such as the American College in Smyrna and the Evangilicou School on the nearby island of Samos, south of Alatsata. In the 1860's twelve promising young men from Alatsata went to Athens to study to become Medical Doctors. In 1871 *Constantinos Antonios Molakidis* became the first Doctor in Alatsata. In the 1880's, all Greek males under Turkish rule, upon becoming eighteen years of age, were required to join the Turkish Army. Most of these males rebelled by leaving their homes and migrating to America and other countries before reaching draft age. For many, this meant they would never see their families again.

In the early 1900's, the city's central location made nearby Smyrna the most cosmopolitan city in that part of the world. It was an eastern mecca for business and trade, and drew very strong interest and influence from England, Italy, France and America. At one time, there were more Greeks in Smyrna than Athens.

ANCIENT GREECE

This family oral history passed on to Antonios put the Dilboys, Alatsata, and Asia Minor (todays Turkey) in a broader perspective, and helped him to understand how Greece and Turkey overlap and intertwine.

As a young boy, from his earliest years, George listened to his father as he described Greece as a country divided by mountains and united by the sea. He regaled George with the fact that Greece is composed of over two thousand islands.

"What other country can say that!" He boasted.

Antonios continued as if he was in a trance. They both were proud descendants of an ancient nation that was the first to develop a democratic way of life, because they started the idea that every citizen should take an active part in government. Historians regard them as the founders of Western civilization. Greek civilization was far more advanced than any that had existed before. The Hippocratic Oath for Physcians was of Greek origin. The Greeks began the first popular elections, the first jury system, and were the first to give high value to education. They gave us brilliant minds, such as Plato, Socrates and Cicero. Ancient Greece brought the Western world the dramatic and visual arts and crafts. The world's first great orators, philosophers, historians, dramatists and poets were Greek. The ancient Greeks were the first people to study geometry, medicine, botany, physics and zoology on a scientific basis. They also held the first athletic games, predecessors of the Olympics.

"And don't you ever forget that, George!" Stated Antonios. He felt honored by its history. Though not overly educated in a formal sense, Antonios lectured George like a classical professor: He felt strongly about Greek history and tradition.

"Greece's unique heritage goes back to 2000 BC when a civilization was traced to Crete, the largest Greek Island. It lies south of the Greek mainland. On Crete, a Minoan civilization thrived with busy city citizens and stately palaces. It's trading empire sailed across the Eastern Mediterranean. This civilization is generally considered to be the earliest discovered in Europe. Four hundred years later its population had expanded to the southern mainland part of Greece, known as the Peloponnese. There, in Mycenae, King Agamemnon and his army launched their attack on the ancient city of Troy. However, by 1200 BC, the Mycenaeans were conquered by Dorian armies from the north, using their new iron weapons." George's attention was focused as much on his father's intenseness, as he was by the story itself. This legacy was a pet passion of Antonios passed on to him by his own father. By continuing this oral history, Antonios was honoring his own father's request and family obligation.

Antonios went on to describe how the Pellopannesean Greeks protected themselves from future invasions:

"Scattered villages grouped together into walled fortresses for self-defense. This is believed to be the origin of the Greek city-states. Colonies and trading partners were established around the Mediterranean and across the Aegean Sea, where Byzantium was founded in the 6th century BC. Trade prospered, for the most part, for the next three centuries. However, rivalries among the principal city-states so weakened them that Philip of Macedonia came down from the north and conquered them in the 3rd century BC."

Only seven years old, George interrupted his father: "BC? What's BC?"

Antonios seemed irritated and impatient:

"Your mother must have told you! In the time *Before Christ*! Before Jesus Christ! Our Lord and Savior! May he have mercy on your soul! Now heed what I say."

"Where was I? Oh, yeah. Thereafter, Philip's son, Alexander the Great, crossed the Aegean Sea and founded Smyrna, the port city on the western coast of Asia Minor. He then spread Greek culture across Asia as far away as northern India. In the 1st century BC, the stronger Rome sent its legions and took over the area from the Greeks. In 330 AD, now called the Common Era (CE), the Roman Emperor Constantine changed the name from Byzantium to Constantinople. He also made it the capital of the Eastern Roman Empire for the next thousand years. From the 11th century CE onward, Asia Minor was invaded and controlled by the Muslim Seljuks, a mounted Army of Central and Eastern Asian nomads that eventually conquered Asia Minor and became Turkic rulers. The name Seljuks transposed into and became a shorter version of the name Turks. In 1243, however, the Mongols invaded Anatolia(Western Turkey) and defeated the Seljuk Turks. When the Mongolians left, this area was broken up into small semi-independent kingdoms and ruled by Turkish Emirs."

"Is that why you drink Turkish coffee?" Asked a curious George?

"We drink *Greek* coffee. It's similar, but they have their coffee, and we have ours."

"Let me finish, George. This will be the shortest summary of Greek history you will ever hear. This is my family obligation, you must understand."

Antonios forged ahead with his message and mission:

"In the 13th century, Ottoman Tribes, descendants of the Seljuk Turks, joined forces and, under Osman I, took over ruling Anatolia. He is traditionally believed to be the founder of the Ottoman Empire. He is one of their hero's, not ours. Under his son, Orkhan I, this Empire connected both sides of the Dardanelles. Fearing Islamic zealots, who were increasingly moving into the Smyrna-Alatsata area, and now in the thirteenth and fourteenth centuries, most of the Greek Christians in the area fled and went to Chios, Lesbos, Rhodes and other Aegean Islands. This scattering to safer islands would be repeated often in the future. At one point in the sixteenth century, it reached a stage where there were only Turks, and some very hardy, scattered Greek Christians in the area."

"George, are you still with me? I can continue now or later. What's your choice?"

George would have preferred later, as it was too much to absorb at once, but instinctively knew that his father wanted to continue. So he told his father what he wanted to hear. "I'd like to hear it now, please."

"Good! It's important that you know this. And I don't often have the time to go over it."

"More specifically, in 1453, Constantinople fell to Mehmed II, and nearly all of Greece was absorbed into the Ottoman Empire. They changed the name from Constantinople to Istanbul, and made it their capital. The Ottoman Empire then extended their conquered territory over most of Asia Minor, the Balkan countries, as well as land north of the Black Sea. The word '*Balkan*,' by the way, means '*mountain*.' Later rulers, particularly Suleiman the Magnificent, stretched the boundaries of the Ottoman Empire still further into the Middle East, Northern Africa and even Europe. Thus, the Ottoman Empire reached the height of its power in the 16th century."

"Now pay special attention to this part, George. Due to corruption, poor government and inept foreign relations their Empire steadily declined for the next two centuries. After nearly four hundred years of oppression, the Greeks rebelled. Their War of Independence began on April 6, 1821, when the Greek flag was first raised in defiance against Turkish rule. This war raged for over ten years, until 1832, when the Greeks declared itself to be an independent state. But they lost the lands in Asia Minor, including Alatsata. The Turks, having had enough of fighting and war, let the matter stand. As you should know, the Greeks still today celebrate their Independence Day yearly on this date, April 6."

Summarizing the barbarity of the Ottoman Turks against the Greeks, during the Greek War of Independence, an American diplomat wrote in 1842:

'No war, ancient or modern, was ever carried on with such unrelenting fury and such cruelty as the war against the Greeks by the Turks. It is a matter of astonishment that the Christian nations of Europe could have so long remained silent spectators of its atrocities.'

"However, over the decades, during the life of your great grandfather and grandfather, it was an uneasy peace, with clashes breaking out, periodically. Further fighting broke out again in 1870, during my youth, when I was your age. After they had fought to a stand-still, hostilities ceased, and the Greeks maintained their independent status. Thereafter, territorial clashes and border skirmishes and island disputes perpetually threatened the fragile peace. Some Greeks lived in Turkish territories and some Turks lived in Greek territories. Because of these overlapping occupations, tensions and frictions were continually close to a flash point. In 1897, the northern Greek city-state of Thessaly revolted against the iron rule of the Turks on the European side of the Aegean Sea.

After about a month of fighting, the Turks asked the Germans to intervene, and together the Germans and the Turks were able to put down the local rebellion before it spread."

And now we come to your time and our current tensions. You cannot escape your heritage, George. Thousands of Greeks have given their yesterdays for your today. Never forget. Forgive, yes. That's the Christian way. But never forget. Do you hear me, George? Do you?"

George sat motionless and silent. Then he realized that his father expected an answer.

"Yes. Yes. I hear you, Dad. I hear you."

CHAPTER THREE

ANTONIOS AND YIASEMI

After taking enough schooling to read and write, Antonios got involved in the family farming enterprises producing and selling milk and cheese, beef and lamb, and growing and selling tobacco. He also developed a fondness for woodworking and carpentry. He felt confident with his hands and liked to build things. Along with his farming and business skills, in time he became a self-taught skilled carpenter. When the inevitable family business tensions accumulated and clashed with his willful nature, he would work off his accumulated stress by sawing wood, knocking down a wall, or repairing a barn or fence. It also got him into projects for villagers willing to hire someone who was skilled and handy doing odd jobs. He was popular with the villagers, and favored with a fine reputation as a reliable and adept woodworker. Other villagers, who heard of his craftmanship, sought him out. After a while, he had earned enough and saved enough to be able to get married, but he did not want to rush into anything.

While working at repairing a schoolhouse in a neighboring village, he met a teacher. Her name was Yiasemi Kotari. He liked her at first sight because she was pretty and friendly. Antonios was quiet and reserved. In addition, he wasn't one to use a lot of words, when he did speak. But she would. She chatted with him while he was having his lunch on one occasion and she asked him if he would mind if she joined him.

"No, not at all," he replied.

He welcomed her company because she frequently said "hi" to him and was easy at words, while he was not nearly as fluent. She liked to talk and he liked to listen. Being a man of few words, her chattiness complemented his reticence. In time, their casual greetings turned into a friendship. They talked, took walks and enjoyed each other's company at village get-togethers. She had a way of making him feel good. She taught him to dance and he fixed things at her parent's home. Antonios felt awkward at social functions, but not when she was with him. A relationship naturally evolved over the next year into an expectation of getting married.

Months passed and since both were in their late twenties, Yiasemi became impatient with Antonios's slowness in proposing. She let him know that she had other men seeking her company who were serious in their intentions, and she didn't intend to waste her time on someone who couldn't make up his mind. Antonios had no doubt that Yiasemi was the girl for him, but he resisted being pressured. On the other hand, he didn't want to lose her, either.

One beautifully bright and sunny day, during a walk after a church service, they stopped to sit in the shade under an olive tree. Antonios took Yiesemi's hand, as they discussed their hopes and the future. Suddenly, Antonios turned serious and asked:

"What do you think of marriage?"

She hesitated, looked Antonios in the eye and asked him:

"Are you asking me to marry you?"

"Yes!"

"Why?"

"Why? Because I love you! I want to spend my life with you. I want to have children with you and raise a family. Aren't those reasons good enough."

"The first reason's enough. But I like the others, too," she responded.

Then she smiled, took Antonios's hand in both of hers and pulled him towards her. Antonios slowly put his arms around her shoulder and waist, embraced her and kissed her tenderly.

"Yes! I'll marry you, Antonios Dilboy. Because I love you, too."

They hugged each other without another word and this time kissed passionately. Then Yiasemi suddenly pushed Antoni away and heatedly asked:

"What took you so long! Did you think I would wait forever?"

"No, of course not! I was just trying to read you better. I wanted to make sure you would say, 'yes.' Nobody likes to be rejected, you know."

"Well, you better learn how to read me better, if you are going to be my husband!"

"Yes, I'll just have to learn how to read women better."

"Not women! Just me! I'm the one you are marrying."

"OK, Yiasemi. You'll just have to teach me. After all, you are the teacher."

With that, they squeezed each other tight, kissed again and started to walk out into the glorious sun, swinging each other's arms. They walked back happily to her home.

Now they had to break the news to their parents. They wanted to get their parents' blessing. Antonios's parents quickly consented, thinking they would make a good match as a couple. They liked Yiasemi's pleasing personality and thought she would make a wonderful mother.

However, Yiasemi's parents were a little more hesitant. They asked Yiasemi if she was sure this was the man for her. She assured them she was sure. "After all," she reminded them, she was "well into her twenties and knew when she was in love." After Yiasemi told them that they planned to get married in a year's time, they realized she wasn't rushing into anything, and would have more time to think about it. Thus reassured, they consented.

A year later, they married in a typical village ceremony. Because they married later than most, they combined their savings and planned to buy property when they found something they liked. Besides being a school teacher, Yiasemi was quite a seamstress, who made most of her own clothes. She also had a passion for flowers, and liked to talk about the different varieties. Antonios faked an interest, but had little. It was just something else to use up Yiasemi's nervous energy, he thought. She was fortunate to come from a good family that wanted only the best for her.

Her father was a civil servant for the local government, and as an administrator working in an office, wore a tie at work. Her mother was a housewife, like most Greek women. She had an older brother who was unmarried and worked in the port city of Piraeus, located on a promontory beside Athens. He was an administrator for a shipping company in Smyrna. Because Yiasemi's parents were initially cool and distant to him, Antonios got the impression that Yiasemi's parents thought she could have done better. Antonios got this impression because of the differences in their education, and background, even though the Dilboys were financially better off.

Her family was well schooled and interested in books. His family was peasant farmers and business hustlers. The Kotaris worked with their heads; the Dilboys worked with their hands. But what matters this? Antoni asked himself. He was a hard worker, caused no trouble to the villagers, and an acclaimed carpenter and businessman whose industry and fine reputation was well known. He loved Yiasemi, could provide for her and would win them over. They would see.

Antonios's parents may have only been peasant farmers and rough edged business types, who worked the hardscrabble land to earn their living, Antoni thought, but they were happy and made the best of their rough circumstances. He would do the same. He didn't know too much about feelings or emotions, but he knew when he was happy with someone and felt strongly about her. He was determined to show them that his hard work and good intentions would be enough to establish him as worthy. Antonios's family was industrious and worked long hours, as everyone could see. If his family needed extra money for special needs or desires, like a new barn or for a wedding, his mother would sell her home baked goods, take in wash or weave baskets for sale at the village market.

Antonios's family liked Yiasemi especially because she was the opposite of Antonios, her being more flexible and talkative. She seemed to soften Antonios's stubbornness. Like Antonios, Yiasemi was thin, and dark haired, but a little taller. She would make Antonios a good wife, they thought. Antonios and his other brothers made a **family** business possible. Antonios had an older Sister,

Maria, and an older brother Nicholaos; and younger silblings named Dimitris, Kostas, Evangelos and Zenovia. Yes, they had their disputes, but what business didn't? Yes, they were tough, but you had to be tough in business to survive. Antonios's mother had a miscarriage that they never talked about. A baby sister was stillborn and his mother survived, but had been very sick. This was why there was a six year gap between the births of his brothers Dimitris and Kostas. His mother was told that, thereafter, she should not attempt to have any more children, because it would endanger her health. But she did anyway. She had two more healthy children. Medical doctors don't know everything, the family believed. It was God's will.

CHIOS

With the sentimentality of youth and as a tribute to their ancestors, they decided to get married closer to Greece. Though Chios is on the Turkish side of the Aegean Sea, it is an island that would be annexed by Greece in 1914. In time they settled in and Antonios went about working at the family farm and tobacco business. He also took occasional work as a self-taught carpenter. He believed he could take that skill wherever he went.

Yiasemi found employment again as a teacher of young children. She also indulged her passion for beauty in flowers by nurturing the tall and majestic tulip. Their allure was enhanced by it growing in every color except blue and black. Their height and stature seemed to impress her as a sort of compensation for her and Antonios's lack of such grandeur, at least in terms of height. She discovered that the morning sun opened its petals and the dusk closed them. It was as if the colorful flower were spreading its love by wishing them a good morning to start the day, and a good night to wish them pleasant dreams. Though she knew that the country of Holland was credited with cultivating and popularizing the mighty tulip, she was also aware that it was originally found in the Middle East. And its Middle Eastern roots fathered its botanical name, tulipa, derived from tulbent, the Turkish word for turban. She would cut them from her flower garden and place them in her window. She then noticed in fascination, as her baby tulips stood tall, the cold water kept the stems straight, and they grew straight up toward the light.

But then her nurturing instincts took a motherly turn when she discovered that she was blessed with child. She looked forward with pride and anticipation to starting a family. Antonios was delighted with the wonderful news and seemed to walk a little taller. While waiting for the blessed day of birth, they made all the necessary preparations, including selecting a name for a girl or a boy.

Dimitri was the first born in 1885. He was a healthy and robust baby and introduced into the world a new generation of Dilboys. Dimitri had his parents all to himself because Yiasemi did not have another successful birth until 1893 when she had Marianthe. She was a delight to her parents because they now had a boy and a girl.

Thereafter, Kostas was born the next year, John the year after that, and Yiorgos, the Greek name for George, on February 5, 1896. Following George, Evangelos, Zenovios and Stamatia completed the family. Children, in these times, were considered an economic asset because they became extra hands to help out on the farm. Thus, the more children you had in the family, the better.

George was a handful because he was an energetic child and very curious. He was so active and impulsive that his mother was heard to say,

"There's the devil in him!"

This young colt of a baby was a chore to keep up with, impetuous, even as he charmed you with his impish smile. He was of average height and weight, with jet black, thick hair. Even as an infant, he was so strikingly handsome that the other women in the village chided Yiasemi about how she was going to keep the girls away from him when he was old enough to leave home.

"Oh, the girl that gets him better have her papers in order!"

Thus warned the protective and proud mother. Yiasemi marveled that children from the same family could be so different.

And Yiasemi noticed that these different personalities became more prominent as they grew and developed. Antonios didn't seem to notice his children's unique differences, or, if he did, he didn't mention them. But he did express his appreciation that they were all healthy, though a handful. A handful for her, anyway, because Antonios would leave the care of the children in Yiasemi's good hands. His main concern was work and activities outside the home. At times, however, he would infuriate Yiasemi with his flip comments that there was nothing to bringing up children; she "only had to pour water on them, like her flowers, and they would grow," he quipped. Though she knew he wasn't serious, such comments irritated her, because it seemed to belittle her considerable efforts caring for all these eight children, as well as all the family washing and cooking.

George was of particular concern to his mother because he was adventurous and a risk taker. He loved the water and frequently pestered his father to teach him to swim. Alatsata, was right on the water, next to a tributary that led to the Aegean Sea. It's location gave George ample opportunity to sail, fish and swim. He had to be constantly reminded by his parents not to swim or sail alone, for safety reasons. When scolded for venturing off alone, he said that he couldn't always get someone to go with him. He pouted, looked at his mother with those big brown eyes and she would melt. She couldn't stay mad at him. She would hug him and then push him away to go play.

She was teaching her own children at home now. Of course, as much as she had liked to teach children at school, she felt obligated to quit that job to concentrate on the full time requirements of raising a family. Besides, Antoni had insisted on it, and earlier than Yiasemi would have preferred.

"You cannot risk the healthy birth of a child by continuing to work," he remonstrated.

For the sake of peace in the family, Yiasemi had quit half way through her first pregnancy, when she started to show. And now, after many years of an agreeable marriage, there were ten adults and children in the Dilboy family that itself was a full time job. For the time being now all was well within the family.

But all was not well outside the home.

During this time, local disputes erupted between Greeks and Turks, and were a constant concern in certain areas. An uneasy peace was restored. Nevertheless, hostilities were never far below the surface and continued to threaten the peace, as it had in their long history of strife.

GREEK DISPERSION

Antonios knew from the many family discussions that over the centuries, many adventurous Greeks took to their boats, rowed and sailed to and occupied many of the offshore islands near the coasts of Greece and Western Turkey. The nomadic Greeks treated the Aegean Sea as their own large lake, with settlements on both sides. Whatever peace there was in common areas became tentative and temporary. It was a risky situation for a young, vulnerable family. Now, in Alatsata and Smyrna, as the Greek minority increased its population to a claimed majority, smoldering resentments simmered up and territorial skirmishes broke out persistently, with little pretext between the two feuding peoples. It kept many peaceloving villagers on edge.

George would never forget the morning he opened the front door and was startled to see a dead body on his front doorstep. His mother, who was holding his hand, suddenly screamed: "Antonios! "Antonios!" She slammed the door shut and blessed herself, mumbling prayers to the high heavens. She then herded the children into their bedroom, closed the curtain and told them to stay there until she came back. George could hear much outside commotion going on. The village police were called and the body was taken away. George pulled the curtain aside and sneaked a peak to see what was happening. Neighbors and police were talking excitedly in the front room and outside. George noticed that his father seemed angry and was pacing back and forth. They talked about increasing the village night patrols. George's mother went outside to wash the front door area with soap, water and a scrub brush to wash away the blood and smell of a dead body as best she could. George had to shush Marianthe's crying because she was scaring the baby, Zenovios, who was also crying.

When their mother later came for them, she rushed in and picked up the infant from his crib and ushered George and Marianthe, who burst into tears again when she saw her mother, into the kitchen, rocking the baby to comfort him and running her other hand through Marianthe's hair and weakly smiling at George, as she tried to reassure them,

"It's ok, kids, it's ok."

"Momee, who was that man on the ground? What was the matter with him?" asked George.

"He was a dead Turk from another village," answered a still upset Yiasemi.

"But why did he come here?"

"George, the Turks throw dead bodies on our doorsteps to spread disease among the Greeks."

"But why, Momma?"

"They want us to leave, to go back to Greece."

"Why, Momma?"

"They want this land for themselves. Oh, George, stop with the questions. Go ask your father."

George ran out of the house and saw his father talking with some neighbors. He reached up and pulled at his sleeve to ask him, "Why don't the Turks want us to live here?" But his father shooed him away, "Not now, George! Later, later!"

Angered by these type of outrages, Antonios was determined to fight back. He roared: "The Greeks have been settlers here for hundreds of years. We have a right to be here!" He was proud to be Greek and entitled to raise a family, free of these raids. And his growing family would be his contribution to carrying on the family lineage and legacy to the Greek homeland. At five feet, five inches in height, he was a wiry, fiery little man, with a swarthy complexion, and a full head of black, wavy hair. He passionately yearned for freedom for the Greek people, *his* people, from four hundred years of persistent harassment and continuing oppressive interference by the more intolerant Turks. He became part of the Greek resistance working underground as part of a guerilla force to intercept and fight the Turks that were harassing them. Some Turks were good neighbors and were quite friendly, others were tolerant, but they seemed indifferent toward this fanatical fringe element that was a constant threat.

George had another particular, youthful memory of his father having an argument with his mother. Generally, they did not argue much, but lately they were having disagreements with increasing frequency as the problems with the Turks escalated. In this instance, he saw his father sneaking out the back door armed with his rifle and disappearing into the black, stifling hot, night. On other occasions, he, more than his younger siblings, innocently and quizzically watched armed, tense men having secret meetings in his home.

He would later realize that armed resistance fighters and their father were going off in the night, carrying their crude weapons, leaving their mother, fretful and worried. When very young, George could sense his mothers anxiety and anguish, and it would frighten him and he would cry. She would scoop him up, hug him and sing to him until he stopped fussing. She squeezed him tight, and he could feel her trembling body, rocking him to sleep. In this way, she attempted to reassure him that everything would be all right.

But everything was not all right. Things got more intense when marauding Turks would infiltrate their village, attack with their slashing, bloody knives and swords, injure, kidnap and kill wantonly, as they plundered, and set fire to Greek homes. It was not unheard of for a family to discover blood splattered on their front door as they left in the morning. One day, Yiasemi stopped to catch an errant soccer ball rolling in the dust. George and the neighborhood kids were in the middle of a noisy soccer game. She stooped down to pick up the ball when she yelled and jumped away as she realized that the ball was a human head! Another ghoulish gift from the pillaging and murdering Turks in the black of night. The Turks wanted to get the Greeks out of their major port cities on the Aegean. Even the names, Smyrna, Alatsata, Greek names, were a continuing insult to the Turks, because it was on the land, territory and peninsula of Turkey. Greece was on the continent of *Europe*; Turkey was on the continent of *Asia*. Greece was largely *Christian*; Turkey was *Islamic* and therefore, almost exclusively *Muslim*.

Because of these continuing raids by the Turks, the Greeks of Smyrna-Alatsata rallied in righteous fury and vowed vengence. The senior members of the community counseled caution and a night home guard of Greeks was organized and maintained to safeguard their homes and villages. But there was tension and trouble when the older and wiser village members tried to control the younger, quick tempered, men and boys, who would, with little discipline, rush out on their own night hunts. They would retaliate impulsively, wrecking havoc with their own indiscriminate destruction of properties and retaliatory killings. Too often, innocent people were caught in the crossfire and injured. This arguing within their own ranks, as well as fighting the Turks was a constant struggle to corral a cohesive protective militia, rag tag as it was.

Frightfully, in the Greek villages in and around greater Smyrna, these seasons of long nights were illuminated only by the foggy blur of gas lights, sitting uncertainly on top of their posts. The rutted dirt roads looked forbidding and ghostly, eerily deserted and forelorn, except for the occasional piercing meows of hungry or feuding cats and the barking of howling dogs foraging for food. Most people could not afford to feed or own dogs, so there were packs of hungry dogs roving around going through garbage and swill barrels and baskets. The only compensation was that the barking dogs, and the painful screeching of cats, acted as warnings against lurking Turks sneaking about in the night waiting to strike. But these sounds became so familiar, they also masked their movements.

However, the animal noises of the night were not something you could rely on because sometimes the Turks would bring raw meat to feed the animals to keep them quiet. Sometimes the meat was poisoned. If that failed, they clubbed the animals to death. To counter this, the Greeks resorted to concealed or camouflaged trip wires attached to bells, to complement armed patrols. The more rural outlying Greek villages were especially at risk with their herds of goats and sheep slaughtered and left to rot under their back windows and rear doors.

CHAPTER FOUR

ALATSATIAN EMIGRATION

Although most of the Greeks had hardened their minds to endure the current hardships, as they had done so often before, others wanted a better life. Word had reached Alatsata that a number of families in Smryna were moving to some offshore islands, back to mainland Greece or going on to America to escape the turmoil. Each destination had its own unique risks. The Greeks from Alatsata and Smyrna had their own customs, culture and dialect, different from mainland Greece. And each of the Greek islands had their own way of doing things. Nevertheless, some still decided to move, thinking it a lesser evil. The Greeks who could adapt, assimilated easier. Over the past four hundred years, similar migrations had taken place depending on the then current deprivations, and according to their level of tolerance.

When Yiasemi's health started to suffer under the strain of a large family in a roiling, hostile atmosphere, Antonios and Yiasemi reluctantly started to think about leaving Alatsata. She was having tension headaches, feeling queasy and having trouble sleeping, worrying about her family. Antonios's brothers Kostas and Nicholaos talked about moving to the nearby island of Chios. They would try to run their business from there. If it didn't work out, they would sell out. They were determined to make the best of it. At Chios, they would be on a nearby island, although still on the eastern side of the Aegean Sea. However, other Alatsatians, seeing the trend, didn't just want to move locally, but wanted to emigrate to more distant islands, mainland Greece or to America, to be further away from all the harrassment and danger in Alatsata.

In particular, a group of twelve families finally decided to send some family members to America in 1906. They were expected to find work and send money home. If their experience was positive, other family members would follow. The Dilboys listened, watched and discussed their own options, as this group of selected family members left for the Greek mainland. Then they made their way across Greece, and could either go to Patras, a port in northwest Greece, on the Ionian Sea, or to Pireaus, a large port outside of Athens. There, they would board a steamship for their ultimate destination, America. This group of twelve went to Pireaus because it was closer. They decided to go to Boston, Massachusetts, because they heard there was a successful Greek Community there that had built a new, beautiful, Cathedral in the Back Bay section in 1903. Wages in America were reported to be three to four times what could be earned in Alatsata.

Months later, letters back to Alatsatians told how the twelve families had arrived safely on the East Coast of America, and on to Boston. They reported that the energy, hustle and bustle in Boston was confusing, at first, but invigorating. Because of overcrowding in Boston, they moved around Boston's North End and across the Charles River to adjacent Cambridge and Somerville, MA, where jobs were to be had. There, in the brickbottom section of East Somerville, they settled in multi-family homes close to each other, and found work immediately in nearby meat packing companies, slaughter houses and warehouses. The neighborhood was mostly Irish, and they were too busy to do anything but look at the new Greek arrivals curiously, but didn't bother them, for the most part.

The Greek immigrants were able to start their own businesses in this highly congested, three and four family dominated area. They proudly talked about fruit peddlers, Coatas Fecas's Bananas, self-employed bootblacks, Nick Jakis and Steve Girdis, public spirited neighbors like Costas Alexis and John Finitsis of Poplar St., a corner bar and bakery owned by Greeks. Though independent, the Alatsatian Greeks fit in among the strange sounding American mix of businesses and neighbors, like Fuch's Bakery and Giroux Milk on Linwood St., Ward's Tip Top Bread outlet on London St., where they could buy discounted day-old bread, Towers Wood Yard, Callahan's Goats, Maroney's Express, Rosenberg's Rags and Bottles Place, McCarthy the printer, Gene Gormly's Ponies and Wagons on Chestnut St., and Jimmy Welch's Charcoal and Coal Yard on long, Linwood St.

The Greek immigrants dazzled the folks back home with their letters sharing a dizzying display of nicknames so easily adopted by Americans, such as Bullet's O'Leary, Tootsie O'Kane, Gyp Garvey, Knuckles McCoy, Biddy Doyles Grocery Store, Corky Cochran, Buck Foley, Wa Wa Corbett, and Happy Hourihan. Not all Irish, there was Schultz the German born butcher, and Max's pies on Linwood St., Robitaille's Horse and Buggy Garage, a Frenchman, on Joy St., and Fisher, the Jewish Ragman on Joy St., English Ian Blair's news and cigar shop, Polish Kid Curmisky's carpentry shop, and Guiseppi Forgetti's Italian Bakery. And generally, nobody was shooting at anyone else. And yes, the pay was indeed up to four times what one could earn in Asia Minor. To the Greeks back in Alatsata and Smyrna, this sounded very promising.

These pioneering Greek immigrants, who traveled thousands of miles over seas, oceans and by land from Asia Minor to America, were to be the beginning of the largest group of immigrants from Alatsata ever to immigrate to the United States. They could neither speak English, nor be understood, initially. They had little formal education. It was to them a strange land with different customs, but they were free. According to the census takers of the day, who displayed little patience in trying to get their names spelled correctly, they were listed as:

Niglis Alexopoulos, age 38; John Dimitrakis, 30; George Papeas, 22; Peter Papeas, 23; John Adas, 30; Peter Arvanitis, 22; Dennis Arvantis 24; Dennis Suris, 23; John Makanos, 25; John Braion, 22 and a John Grristes, 23, all of whom were listed as laborers. The twelth member of the group, John Petropoulos, 25, was listed as a shoemaker.

The following year their numbers rose to forty and over the next couple of years, they numbered in the hundreds. Over subsequent years, three hundred Greek families would settle in this Brickbottom settlement in Somerville. To them it was an endpoint to an exodus, their escape to a new and exciting life.

In 1907, Antonios's brother, Kostas, age 41, decided to emigrate. He took the same route as the original group of twelve. He joined the Alatsatian group in the Boston suburb of Somerville. He sought and readily obtained employment and sent word and money back to his family. George, more than any of the other children, became excited and haunted his mother with chants of:

"I want to go! I want to go, too!"

"Stop it, George! You are too young and you have to finish primary school!" reprimanded his mother.

Finally, his father put a halt to it by harshly scolding George, "Enough George! Enough! I don't want to hear any more of it!"

But the matter was revisited the following year, after George periodically pined for the sea, traveling to America and adventure. He was becoming very willful. After much discussion, and the situation with the Turks becoming more intense, with more neighbors leaving, Antonios and Yiasemi, made a joint decision. Antonios would follow Kostas to America, along with five sons and one daughter. They were at an age when all could work. Yiasemi would stay behind with the two youngest children, Zenovios, age three, and Evangelos, age eleven. Evangelos would be able to help her with the baby.

In case Antonios and the others of working age couldn't get jobs in America, or it otherwise didn't work out, they would have a place and people to come back to. But with them leaving, she would feel better if she knew most of the family were safe, despite her reluctance to break up the family. She would live on what resources she had and on the money they would send back from working in America. It would give her a break from caring for a large family and to regain her health. She didn't feel up to making a long journey, just then. The Turks weren't forcing children or women to join their Army. Her boys would be saved from this forced servitude.

The related Delevois (whose name was changed to Dilboy on entry to the U.S.) would later immigrate to the West Coast of the

United States. Nicholaos would run the family farm and business from Chios. Yiasemi would stay in Alatsata, for the time being, or retreat to Chios with Nicholaos, if necessary.

A fellow Alatsatian carpenter, Spyros Stratis, was also immigrating to America and would stay with relatives in Chicago, by way of Boston. Because they would travel in steerage, the lowest cost fare, and each cabin had wall bunks for four people, Spyros agreed to join their group to make it an even eight. Then they could take two adjacent cabins. Because of George's stubborn habit of going off on his own, Spyros was asked to keep an eye on George during the trip. In exchange, part of the cost of his fare was paid by the Dilboys. This would free Antonios to concentrate on the others in the family during the trip.

Part of the reason for the current problems with the Turks was the fact that the Greek farms were doing well, according to the standards of the area. Also, the tobacco business was established, and the Turks, seeing this, wanted to take over. To do that, they had to move the Greeks out. To accelerate this design, they passed rules and regulations to further distress the Christian Greeks. Lately, for example, in order to stop the spread of Christianity, the Islamic Ottoman Empire declared that Greek churches, in the future, could only be built on ancient Greek Orthodox Church sites where mosaics could be found. This, of course, reflected a style of a certain time, and effectively stopped the building of new churches.

Due to the constant consternation and emigration trend, the times became chaotic, exciting and fearful in Alatsata and Smyrna. The young were energized, the old reluctant and the rest resigned and fatefully looking forward. Properties were sold or leased out. Some enterprising Greeks exchanged properties with Turks on islands in the Aegean Sea, that is, with Turks who wanted to move back to mainland Turkey.

Besides, more Turks were flooding into the thriving port of Smyrna from inland Turkey. To the Dilboy family, the trek across the Aegean Sea to Greece would initially seem to relieve some of the strain, even as it added some in the transplantation, uprooting and resettling of the family.

Disturbing as it was, Western Turkey was not the area in most turmoil, at the time. Even more than the Greek mainland, the occupying Turks seemed to be more concerned with the rebelling Northern Balkan States of Serbia and Montenegro, as well as Bulgaria and Rumania. Like Greece, these peoples wanted their independence, and were agitating to break away from the last vestiges of the strangling grip of the Ottoman Turks. But the Turks brought over more soldiers and imposed additional strictures against them and the Greek citizens in their territories on the Northern European side of the Aegean Sea. They were determined to put down these rebellions against Turkic rule. The Turkish Army created havoc in their march on their way north to the Balkans. They randomly and forcibly dragooned Greek civilians in Turkish territories into their Army as they went along, and used them to control their own countrymen. It was an impossible situation for the suffering Greeks in Turkish territories. As concern about the growing war murmurs increased, Antonios sped up his plans to move west to America.

They had the advantage of the experiences of Kostas and the Alatsatian settlement in the distant Boston area. Correspondence back and forth educated them about what they could expect during their trip and on their arrival. They made inquiries to the American Consulate in Athens as to current emigration requirements.

At this time, as part of the general harrassment, the children's schooling was too often interrupted by bomb scares and other disrupting events that acted as an additional impetus to emigrate. Yiasemi wanted her children to continue their schooling in America away from all this turmoil.

Neither Greece nor America had any quota limiting the number of immigrants. But they would have to all pass medical examinations administered by United States health physicians. Though Yiasemi was a worrier, she was also a thinker. It all seemed so complex because she thought ahead. She continued to discuss the matter with Antonios, relatives, friends and neighbors listening carefully to their thoughts and feelings. It made her feel like she was not helpless, but was doing something to control their lives.

But the pressures continued to mount. Antonios was now fifty years old. It was not easy to uproot your family and move to a different part of the world at this age. Although Antonios was only one year older than Yiasemi, he had a more rugged constitution. He was concerned about her health, her nervous nature and how he could get her relief from her worries. Fortunately, the children were well and strong, but who could count on this continuing with the feuding and fighting going on all around them? Antonios had repeatedly refused to sell some of their Alatsata property to scavenger Turks offering insulting money. However, at Yiasemi's urging, he finally agreed to compromise, a characteristic alien to his nature, and sell some of the land to a Greek neighbor, who suggested the partial sale of land and property. Though contrary to his all or nothing style of doing business, he begrudgingly went along because he and his relatives worried about Yiasemi's health and how it might hurt her future chances to pass the American doctors immigration health examinations.

But even this he did reluctantly, and only after Yiasemi broke down in tears from frustration. At worst, his friends reassured Antonios, such a partial sale would minimize a loss and, at best, it would maximize a partial gain. It would get them needed money, calm Yiasemi down and maybe increase the chances of selling the house and the rest of the property by requiring a lower price affordable to more potential buyers. To get everyone off his back, Antonios threw up his hands and said OK, but only because it would be sold to a trusted Greek who offered a fair price. Now they had enough money to pay for passage; but not for all. Again, the gain was partial, but it was progress. Yet with all this they were still property owners in Alatsata, Western Turkey or Asia Minor, as the Greeks preferred to call it.

The main reasons that convinced them to immigrate to America was the pleadings of most of their relatives and friends to think of the welfare of their children and their future. Would they be better off in a freer country, where there was no war and better opportunities for a young family? And if they didn't go at this time, how long would it be before they could save the increasing fare cost, and how much longer would they have to wait to be called from the lengthening wait list and the limited capacities of the ships? Besides, Yiasemi was upset every time she saw George coming in from playing with dirt all over his face. He was playing night patrol with the village boys, again. He was forbidden to use his father's bootblack to blacken his face, as his father did before his night patrols, so he used dirt from the ground. He was seeing all too much of the incessant fighting, rifles and the carrying around of weapons. And now that they had decided to move most of the family, it would be better to do it when they were younger and in better health, rather than older and in poorer health, which might well be their future, the way things were going around there.

While preparing to emigrate, the situation with the Turks continued to fester and erupt. Yiasemi and Antonios watched events unfold ominously; he with anger and she nervously. The tension grew as irregular fighting persistently broke out. Mainland Greece was supposedly an independent nation for nearly one hundred years now. But this meant nothing to the ever lurking Turks, menacingly surrounding their borders. Night raids and blatant daytime border raids were all too frequent. If the Turks needed food, shelter or mules, no Greek fishing net, goat heard, sheep corral or home was safe. Roving gangs of Ottoman raiders thought nothing of silently terrorizing the countryside and cared not a wit for borders. Stealing and plundering was their wanton way and the devil to those who got in their path.

Retailatory raids and counter attacks were often launched by the avenging Greeks. And woe to the Turks caught from behind! Not infrequently the old testament justice of an eye for an eye was stricken instantly in the heat of pursuit. It seemed the only way to strike fear into the undisciplined rabble. The Christian new testament turn the other cheek preaching often fell on deaf ears in the wake of revenge. It made for an unsettling atmosphere, keeping everyone on grim alert.

It was also frustrating and frightening to hear neighbors talking about joining their Greek relatives and friends in Turkish territories to fight the Ottomans. Sooner or later, it looked like mainland

Greece would be sucked into a war against the Turkic Ottomans, as so often happened in the past.

This cycle had to end, vowed Antonios.

SPYROS STRATIS

Something else bothered Yiasemi; George's growing fondness for guns. Going hunting with his father, shooting birds and small animals was one thing, but George was now agitating to help his father pack for his night patrols, and it wouldn't be too long before he would want to go out on these dangerous searches himself. This fondness for the rifle and adventurous nature was why Yiasemi implored Antonios to have George watched on the trip to America by a trusted neighbor, Spyros Stratis. He was a twenty seven year old, unmarried, and a skilled carpenter. Spyros was a neighbor well known to them, who had returned the year before to his family in Alatsata from the island of Lesbos, lying off the coast of Western Turkey, near Smyrna.

CHAPTER FIVE

TRAVEL ROUTE TO AMERICA

The Dilboys and Spyros Stratis would take a ship from Athens-Pireaus, the port of embarkation. The route was across the Mediterranean Sea, stopping at Taranto, Italy, and then entering the Atlantic Ocean and stopping at Lisbon, Portugal to refuel and to pick up and drop off some more passengers and cargo, and then on to their ultimate destination, the United States, at the major port of New York City, and then on to Boston.

Since Antonios tended to be careless about details, except when it came to his carpentry trade and trimming his mustache, Yiasemi looked to the making of lists and planning the particulars for the big trip. They studied the written instructions from the Greek and American authorities and got the medical shots necessary. Adults were limited to two travel bags of a maximum size and weight each, and one for each child. It was suggested that they buy their tickets early to assure themselves a place on board.

They were advised by Uncle Kostas to sew spare money into their clothes to foil thieves and pickpockets. There will invariably be a minority criminal element who abuse their freedom, he cautioned. This precaution was contained in a letter he wrote to them after he heard that Antonios was definitely coming to America. He reminded them that he lost some of his savings to a pickpocket in New York City after he passed through a place called Ellis Island. His desire to see America's biggest city cost him. This and the fact that the waiting lines and delays in Boston would be shorter because of fewer immigrants being processed, made Kostas suggest they sail through and disembark in Boston. Kostas cautioned further that, though Boston was smaller, every big city had its hooligans, so everyone should be careful.

Spyros believed his chances of passing through customs and passing inspection and being allowed into the United States was good, because he was healthy, had an established occupation to obtain gainful employment, as well as resident relatives already in the United States. Antonios, also healthy, a skilled carpenter and businessman, had a waiting brother and other Alatsatian Greeks to vouch for him. And all the Dilboy children were healthy, as far as they knew. Thus, the immigrants had US residents waiting for them so that they would not become traveling vagabonds that might be tempted to steal to eat and thus run afoul of the law. They thus would be less likely to fall prey to the lurking hustlers and petty con men. All these factors were in their favor to impress the Immigration authorities sufficiently to get Spyros and the Antoni led Dilboy family the final approval to get by the Immigration Officials in Boston. Of course, all this assumed that once in country, they would pass through customs and inspection. Thereafter, for most of the immigrants, they only had to worry about their physical examinations by the American doctors.

ANCHORS AWAY

In 1908 George was twelve years old. He was so excited about going on a big steamship for a cruise on the high seas, he could hardly sleep. Whilst traveling with his father to Smyrna to cart goods back, George had sneaked over to the port of Smyrna to stare at the boats in the harbor. He anticipated with awe and wonder at some day sailing on a big ship to take to the high seas and to travel the world to America. It was during the summer, so he hoped to start school anew in America to finish his primary school. He would be leaving during the summer months and the best sailing conditions. But it was also more expensive because it was a popular time to travel by sea. Though taking a gamble by emigrating, Antonios and Yiasemi were hedging their bet by not spending all their money on the big trip, saving something for a possible return to Greece if things didn't turn out as they hoped it would. They had heard that when jobs were scarce during American recessions it periodically had, many immigrants returned to their home countries. Not everyone who went to foreign countries stayed there. If they adapted well, Yiasemi and the two children could follow along when, and as they chose.

In helping George to prepare for his long sea and ocean journey, Yiasemi entreated him to take along a hydrangea plant. It was a plant that bloomed naturally in the summer. George resisted this because, like his father, he did not care about flowers and thought it a bother. But his mother said that she had a dream that it would bring them luck on this journey. Yiasemi had this quirk; she used flowers the way other people read tea leaves.

Although found in the Far East, Yiasemi knew from her readings that it was native to the United States, especially along it's eastern seaboard where they would disembark. Besides, the name hydrangea comes from the Greek word meaning vessel. She was not superstitious, but was a faithful believer in the Greek Orthodox religion and its myths. And according to folklore, if a witch put a curse on an unlucky person, the hydrangea would break the spell, just as the crucifix could be used to chase away the devil. She had heard from other villagers that Salem, just up the coast, north of Boston, had a history of burning witches at the stake. Though long ago, her fears gave it unwarranted currency. She even had George promise to have the plant face the sun in the morning because it helped it grow and the shade in the afternoon because it helped stabilize and strengthen it.

"But what if the sun doesn't come out?" pleaded George. "Then you can place it near an oil lamp," replied his mother. "And if it's sunny all day, you can let the night provide the shade naturally. And stop trying to find excuses, my talking-back son." George was not happy with this mandate and complained to his father:

"Dad, Mom says I have to take a plant to America. Do I have to?"

"Yes, you have to."

"But why? It's such a bother."

"Because your mother says so. It'll make her happy. And she thinks it will bring us luck, so just do it."

Resigned, George sighed and said, "Oh, ok. I guess I have to, but I don't have to like it!"

"George, I don't want any back talk. Just make your peace with it", said his father with finality.

George comforted himself with the thought that he couldn't have it all his way. He was just thrilled thinking about the upcoming trip and new adventure opening up before him. He just wanted to get going. His mother kept pestering him with endless directions and instructions. The closer his departure date, the more she smothered him. She was also approaching Antonios with many cautions, and inplored Spyros to keep an eye on George, "who doesn't know enough to be careful." Antonios and Spyros sought to continually reassure Yiasemi. They had their own private anxieties about this long voyage, but kept them to themselves.

To his dismay, however, the village kids made fun of George and mocked his dreams. "It's stupid! They taunted. "Americans speak a foreign language, you won't be able to get a job, such a long trip on the ocean is dangerous and you can't swim to America." Hurt and angered by this constant heckling, George snapped back:

"Ships have safety boats! And I can learn to speak English at school!"

Then George threw stones at his tormentors and ran home. He burst through the front door, and impetuously blurted out:

"Mom, the kids say I'm stupid going to America because the ship will sink, I can't speak English and stuff like that!"

"Oh George, why do you listen to them. They are just jealous."

Then Yiasemi, ever the teacher, couldn't help instructing George with a history lesson of life in America. She told him the story of the discoverer of the steamboat there. Robert Fulton, she said, was an artist, engineer and an inventor. One day he announced that he would launch the first steamboat from a levy. The following week thousands of curious onlookers crowded the shoreline to look at this large monstrosity of a boat that was to be powered by the new method of steam. At the appointed time, the boat started to sputter, cough and to make strange sounds, but it didn't move. Smoke started to come out of a large funnel above the vessel that shuddered, but didn't move. At this point, someone shouted:

"He can't *start* it! He can't *start* it!"

Slowly, almost imperceptibly, the huge, wide-bodied boat drifted away from the pier. As the steamboat slowly chugged-chugged its way down along the river and was about to disappear around the far bend, the same critic shouted:

"He can't *stop* it! He can't *stop* it!"

His mother continued: "The point of the story, George, is that there will always be critics. If you believe you are doing the right thing, just go ahead and do it. Let the critics make fools of themselves."

ALL ABOARD !

The big day finally arrived. They made their way to Smyrna to the departure port. They were accompanied by bright blue skies and a sparkling sun, wonderful sailing weather, thought Antonios. Splendid weather for a growing plant, thought Yiasemi. Both Yiasemi and Antonios had mixed feelings. Antonios was eagerly looking forward to the long voyage, which could take anywhere from three weeks to three months at sea, depending on the weather, which could knock them off course, and the number and length of stops at the intervening ports. But their excitement was anchored by sadness about breaking up the family. Bigger, heavier and more powerful steamships had taken much of the danger out of long voyages on the high seas, but it was still dangerous. Mainland Greece was a peninsula country surrounded by the Ionian Sea to the west, the Aegean Sea to the east and the Mediterranean Sea to the south and its dangers were well known all along its many miles of inlets, coastlines and offshore islands. Some Greeks fishermen referred to the Mediterranean Sea as the "maker of widows," because of the number of fishermen who drowned from sea storms and fishing accidents.

They walked toward the huge, multitiered ship, named the *Saturnia*. It was a large, two funneled Italian steamship. The name of the ship was painted in big block letters across the front side of the bow. Long runways lead up to the entryways to board the ship. While waiting to be allowed to go aboard the ship, Yiasemi kissed and hugged Antonios for the longest time, then warned George not to fall asleep in the sun or get too close to the railing. Now even Antonios was beseeching Yiasemi to "leave the boy be."

Everyone was a little on edge with nervous tension and anxiety, except George, who was enthused with anticipation. The ship was the largest George had ever seen in his life. It seemed bigger than the ships he had secretly seen in Smyrna, but maybe that was because he had never gotten this close before. He looked up in awe, hardly believing this huge ocean vessel was going to take him to a new world. He was looking forward to this trip ever since he heard his parents discussing it on many occasions over the past few years. They thought he was asleep, but he listened to their serious conversations with keen interest and it fed his imagination.

And what a magnificent ship it was! He had to put a hand above his eyes to block the glare of the sun bouncing off the bright white of this ocean going behemoth. The other hand was holding his precious suitcase. It was a cardboard rectangular box that held all his worldly possessions. George wanted to carry his own suitcase like an adult would. The repeated blaring of a loud horn was followed by bullhorn announcements for all passengers to board! The turmoil and the chaos of the crowd increased as the final goodbyes, farewells and Godspeed's were exchanged and the passengers lined up to board the ship.

As if by signal, Yiasemi burst into tears as she grabbed and kissed Antonios again, longingly and lovingly, knocking her hat off in the process. She then hugged and kissed each of her children and tried to get them all huddled together in a big bear hug and kept saying, "My babies! Oh, my babies!" Antonios was not one to easily show his feelings, so he hid his emotions and started to move the children along, asking Spyros to lead them and he would follow along, making sure all were accounted for. Everyone briefly hugged each other for the last time, while Yiasemi implored Antonios and Spyros not to take their eye off George, her most spirited child.

"He's curious about everything! Watch him!" she implored.

"I will, I will, he'll be fine. Don't worry about a thing," reassured Spyros.

With that, Spyros playfully urged George to follow him and they both sprang forward and walked up the long plank stairway. Then the rest of the Dilboy family followed behind; Dimitri, age 23, Marianthe, age 15, Kostas, age 14, John, age 13, George was age 12, and Stamatia, age 8. As Spyros surged upward, he pulled George back to stay with the family and not go ahead. George kept looking behind at his remaining family getting smaller in the distance and then fading into the waving crowd. Antonios let himself go enough to have his chest swell with his own private surge of grief, lamenting the loss of his wife and two of his children. But he comforted himself with the belief that Yiasemi staying behind was backup security in case they decided to return to the land of their roots. When Spyros and George reached the passenger deck they attempted to stop for a final wave, but were pushed along by the crowd and the ship's crew, who were barking into their megaphones. They urged the passengers to move along to their assigned decks.

When Spyros and George disappeared from view, the remaining Yiasemi, with Zenovios, age three on her hip, and Evangelos, age eleven, at her side, were all waving their final goodbyes and blowing farewell kisses to their loved ones. Eventually, they lowered their arms and watched the ship make its final preparations for departure. After what seemed like a long while, the ship started drifting away, pumped by it's straining and noisy power, as it left the pier, with accompanying tugs to guide it out of the harbor and away from other ships. Yiasemi, blotting her eyes with her handkerchief, lagged behind, until the *Saturnia* disappeared over the horizon. They walked away, Yiasemi sniffing and sobbing into her handkerchief as they mounted their cart and the hired driver took the reins in his hand. With a snap of the whip, he urged the donkey back home.

Meanwhile on board the ship, Antonios, Spyros and the six children were all working their way down the stairs below decks, along with most of the passengers down to the second class level and down further into the third class level, also called steerage, where they were quartered. They were on the same level as the cargo. When they reached their assigned rooms they saw small rooms with four bunks hanging from the wall by diagonal chains in each room. Two bunks were on each side with a small sink in the middle. The sink would prove to be a problem because when John threw himself on the bed to try it out, he banged his head on it when he jumped up. He learned the hard way to sleep with his feet next to the sink, not his head.

The "That's using your head!" comment by George, was met with a cold stare, as John tried to rub the pain away from his skull.

There was no porthole in either room. A bare bulb hung down on a wire from the ceiling. It was very stuffy and smelled of oil. The rooms shook with the droning sound and vibrations of steam engines.

To avoid any arguments, Antonios assigned who would bunk in each room and worked out conflicting requests for lower or upper beds. He suggested they rest for a while, but the boys seemed too excited. They wanted to tour the deck. So they went about their exploration, with a warning from their father to return when they heard the announcement to pick up their luggage. And woe to those if he had to send Spyros out after them, he warned them.

Spyros and the other boys were quartered in one room and Antonios and the rest were assigned to the other. Lavatory facilities were located in one common bathroom for males and another for females. Antonios then fell into his bunk to rest and try it out. He and Spyros waited for the anticipated announcement to come to reclaim their luggage from the central hold area. Within the hour, a bullhorn announcement instructed them to come for their belongings. As instructed the boys came running back. Then they turned right around and followed Antonios and Spyros to go and reclaim their suitcases. Antonios had to yell at the younger ones racing ahead to slow down and wait for them. Marianthe and Stamatia stayed behind to watch their hand carried personal items.

After a wait and some confusion in the crowded central hold area, they displayed their luggage tickets and retrieved their suitcases. Dimitri was muttering to himself because the handle on one of his suitcases was broken. Spyros showed Dimitri one of his suitcases that had a gouge in it.

"What can you do," he shrugged. "They are made of cardboard and don't hold up through rough handling."

Kostas wanted to know when they would eat. John retorted:

"That's all you think about is food! Don't complain so much."

"I wasn't complaining about anything! I was just asking!"

Antonios turned and snapped:

"Boys! That's it! Enough!"

The boys sulked and, grim faced, they leaned forward, dragged and carried their suitcases along.

George looked around at other passengers and thought, at least they spoke Greek, although different dialects and pronunciations from Macedonians, Cretans and Albanians made it more difficult to understand. Nearby mingled a family of Bulgars from Bulgaria. Their suitcases and canvas duffle bags were so marked. They must have felt even stranger than he felt, thought George. He also noticed that it was pretty warm and stuffy this far down in the bowels of the ship, even though he saw some fans spinning. Eventually, the heat made him feel sleepy. But he was more hungry than sleepy, so he forced himself to look around for some sort of canteen where he might buy food. He looked in vain.

After a while, George heard Spyros snoring loudly. Spyros, he knew, had partied his last night in Greece and the wine and lack of sleep combined to rob him of lasting energy. George went over and took a closer look to make sure he was asleep. Now so assured, George decided to walk around and satisfy his curiosity, while "Spy," appropriately named, couldn't spy on him. George had overheard his mother express her concern about George's independence and wanderlust. In response his father promised her he would recruit Spyros and have him keep a special eye out for George. Thus the eighth roommate of their traveling group would have this dual purpose.

People were so engrossed in their own selves that they paid little attention to the wandering boy. There was one exception, however. A girl who looked his own age stared at him and followed his movements, at the same time she grabbed her apple and doll. She made George feel like he was a thief to be wary of.

When George realized he had drifted beyond sight of Spyros, he used the watchful girl as a marker to return to his bunk area. On his way back, a careless man had dropped his suitcase on a boy's foot and the boy yelped out in pain. His yelling and crying above the din startled Spyros awake and he sat up and rolled out of his hammock and sat on George's cot, while running his fingers through his hair and rubbing his eyes open. He spotted George standing there, not realizing George had already put one over on him, touring the ship while he fell asleep.

Suddenly, a ships bell pealed out in a repetitive ring. "Hungry, little one?" Spyros asked George. "I wanted to ask you when we ate, but you fell asleep on me," said a pouting George. "We can eat right now, as a matter of fact," remarked Spyros, as he stretched his arms to more fully awaken himself. "Where do we go?" asked the ever questioning George. Spyros merely smiled, pointed his finger, and said, "Just follow the crowd, little one. You'll have to learn to follow more than one of your senses. Then you won't have to ask so many questions." With that, Spyros bounded up, nudged George forward and joined the rest of the family and the crowd flowing to the main passageway to the other end of the deck.

There they entered a massive cafeteria. They got in a long line at the near end where the food was distributed and took a tray. It was self-help. Spryos asked George what he wanted from the long tables of food and filled his tray. George followed Spyros lead as he selected an empty space at one of the long tables in this huge room full of chattering noises. Spyros directed George to go around and sit directly across from him, so "I can keep an eye on you. Your mother's orders, you know."

"But you didn't keep an eye on me when you fell asleep. *I* kept an eye on *you*," riposted George.

"That's right. And now that you are becoming a world traveler, you'll grow up fast, and we will have to keep an eye out for each other, fair enough?"

"Uh, huh," said a pleased George.

"Now eat up! It will make you grow taller. Some day, if you eat well, you may be able to eat peanuts off my head . . . . Boy! Not only do you have questions, but you have answers. Now I know why your mother said you would be a handful."

"But I'm not a boy! My Dad says that I can shoot a rifle like a man. Can I have my own rifle in America?"

"Not for a while, but you'll have to take that up with your father. Now, stop talking and eat your fill."

While gazing around the table, everyone was quiet, engrossed in eating their fill. George suddenly stopped his looking around when he noticed that one family was stuffing knives, folks and spoons into their pockets. "Look, Spyros! Why do they put their forks and things in their clothes?"

"Gypsies stealing," snapped Spyros. "Do not heed them. If caught, they could be put off the ship. We will give back what we got. Understand, little one?"

"Why do you call me "little one? I've grown up as far as I can. And I'm as big as I need to be!"

"Of course. But don't be so sensitive. What would you like me to call you, Yiorgos?"

"That was my given name at birth, but, as you know, my family calls me George, so that's what I am."

"Then that's what I'll call you. And another thing, while we're talking about names. My name is Spyros, not Spy. Agreed?"

With that, Spyros stuck out his hand and they shook hands, smiling at each other.

Despite their agreement, George didn't agree that the kitchenware thieves were Gypsies, because they didn't look like any Gypsies he had seen back home.

When they had finished eating, Spyros took George to the lavatory, so he would know where the toilet was. They had all returned to their bunk area, and variously talked, read and settled down until lights out. They heard the blast of the fog-horn from the top deck, warning away any other ships that might be near and the ship's bells announcing the time. The ships swaying was beginning to make some people sick. Buckets could be obtained from the hose areas hung and strung out against the inside wall of the ship.

The swaying of the ship and the alternating roar of the powerful engines could be heard through the walls and after a while segued into a rhythm that disappeared to the point of no longer being noticed. It lulled some people into a hypnotic-like trance that sent them into a twilight and blissful sleep. Others got sick. A few passengers couldn't sleep because they were scared; this was their first trip on an ocean going vessel. They would eventually fall asleep, some sitting up until they couldn't keep their eyes open any longer. Some passengers on this overcrowded ship didn't have rooms, but slept on the floor or slept sitting up on long benches set up along the walls in the hallways. To prevent them from falling onto the floor, the ships' crew tied ropes from one iron pillar to another at their chest level.

Spyros whiled away the evening whittling wood with a jackknife, making George a toy rifle, while sitting on the floor against a post. Now exhausted from a long, exciting day, George lay on his side on his cot watching Spyros. George was motionless for the first time since he had awoken early that morning. Suddenly the lights went out. George hardly noticed as he slumped into stillness, falling numbly into a peaceful sleep.

The next morning after breakfast in the huge hall, George and his siblings wanted to go on deck to see the great sea. Antonios had to warn them to stay on the steerage deck. They were not allowed to go in the first class or second class areas.

"Why?" asked George.

Antonios answered, "Because the first and second class passengers paid more for their cabins and decks. And their cabins are bigger because there were fewer passengers and more space in both first and second class, than steerage, where we are."

"Well so what," quipped George, "we're closer to the water!"

Spyros was impressed with George's spirit and his youthful recognition that every status has its advantages. Once on deck, George breathed in the fresh air, and was pleased to feel the warm sun's rays shining brightly down from above, accompanied by a pleasant, soft breeze. While dawdling here, he suddenly remembered his mother's hydrangea plant and his promising her to make sure it was put in the sun so that both of them could grow. He pushed himself away from the railing and ran down the stairs, taking two at a time, whizzing by startled passengers coming up the other way. Reaching the bottom of the steps, he leapt the final three steps in his youthful zest and landed on his two hands and feet. Leaping up from a crouched form, he ran all the way down the hall, rounded a corner and crashed into a young girl! Both went tumbling to the floor.

"What the heck!" sputtered the stunned girl, glaring at George. A woman with the girl, picked her up, brushed off her backside and scolded George:

"Watch where you're going, young man! This isn't a racetrack!"

George sat there speechless and embarrassed. He got up and stammered:

"I'm, . . . I'm sorry," and hastened away. But not before he waded through a surprised crowd and an irritated man yelled after him:

"Go on with ya! Ya scattering scalliwag!"

George realized, as he quickly ran away, that the girl was the same one that was chewing an apple that stared at him, like he was a thief, on his first day on board ship. What she must think of him now! He wondered.

Though chastened into slowing down, he still hurried back to his cot with a fast walk. There, he retrieved his belongings and pulled the now limp hydrangea plant from his backpack. He then went to the lavatory to water the wilted plant and took it back up to the open-air deck and held it on top of the railing to give it some sun. After a while, he swore he could see it growing. But maybe it was his imagination, maybe it relieved him of guilt or maybe he needed to think that to make himself feel like he was fulfilling his promise to his mother. When he took it back, he left it out so he could see it and remind himself to bring it to the sun every morning. He did this conscientiously for the next few days. He was pleased to see that the plant did come back to life and proudly showed his father, who gave it a cursory look, nodded acknowledgedly, but without George's enthusiasm. At least he would be a witness to his efforts, in case his mother asked, as she surely would, George thought.

While faithfully holding the plant to the sun one morning, a passing couple stopped to admire the plant. They asked him where he got it, what kind of plant it was and what he was going to do with it. George had not thought what he would do with it when he got to America, so with boyish confidence he said:

"Oh, I'll plant it in the ground and have a whole tree of them. Then I'll send one back to my mother so she could grow her own bunch. She likes them because they kill witches and bring luck."

The woman and man looked at each other with indulgent smiles and wished George well with his adventures. George then waved at them as they walked away. He turned back to grab the plant from the top of the rail, but not before a gust of wind quickly blew the plant off the railing! George lunged for the falling plant, throwing himself against the railing. But he could only watch helplessly as the hydrangea flowers plunged down into the churning sea and disappeared into the white topped whirling waves. George exclaimed in frustration:

"Oh, No 0-0-0!"

He pounded the rail to vent his wrath. He spun himself around in exasperation and found himself saying:

"Now what do I do?"

He ran away looking for Spyros. He didn't want to tell his father. When he finally found him, he breathlessly interrupted him talking to another passenger:

"I lost my mother's plant! The wind pushed it off the railing and it drowned in the sea! Now what do I do?"

George looked like he was about to cry. But Spyros didn't seem to be bothered. He said casually:

"Well, since your mother said the Hydrangea plant originally came from America, you can buy another one there and start over. And since you have already practiced growing it, with this experience, you will be more careful, and even better at it next time."

George was taken up short by this idea. He had not thought of it that way. It didn't seem to be any big deal to Spyros, so George decided that maybe it was all for the best. And it made him feel better. As he walked away lost momentarily in his own thoughts, he further rationalized that maybe the plant would float onto an island and grow into a big tree there. He could then name the island after his mother. She would like that. Besides that, by the time his mother wrote to him in America, he would have another Hydrangea plant and could tell his mother all about it. Now George smiled to himself and felt real good. He began to realize that thoughts can control feelings.

This energized George. He developed the habit of leaning on the railing and staring down at the roiling waters as the big ship plowed through the sea. He noticed that when he looked at the land in the distance, the ship seemed to be almost standing still; but when he looked at the bottom of the ship cutting through the dark water, the ship seemed to be speeding. He would later learn that this observation was originally formulated a couple of years before in 1905 in a more complicated way by a German physicist by the name of Albert Einstein. He would inform the world of his observation and he called it his Theory of Relativity.

CHAPTER SIX

ANGELIKA

George liked to rove around the deck to see what was going on. He would deliberately go the other way from his brothers and sisters. After all, he could talk to them anytime. He was looking for boys his own age that he could play with. But so far the groups he tried to join were clannish and were not overly friendly. One day he saw the apple-chewing girl that he knocked down. He was still embarrassed by the incident so he looked away as he passed her. But she didn't. She said:

"Hello."

George stopped in surprise and said nothing. After a pause, he said, "Hi."

"You want to be my friend?" She asked.

"I got friends. Boys," said George.

"I'm a girl."

"I already know that," said George.

"Boys and girls sometimes play together. I played marbles and jacks with boys back home. You hit me and I didn't cry. So I can play with boys if I want to."

"What's your name?" asked George.

"My name is Angelika. But my mother calls me Angel."

"Your mother doesn't like me. She yelled at me."

"She's not mad anymore because I wasn't hurt. And if I tell her you're my friend, she'll like you."

Want a peanut?" asked Angelika.

"Where did you get the peanuts?"

"It's a secret."

"What do you mean, it's a secret! Why is it a secret?"

"Because."

"That's dumb. Don't friends tell friends secrets?"

"Ok, I'll tell you. But you have to promise me that you won't tell anyone. Promise?"

"Yup."

"Down stairs where they drink on those high stools," said Angelika.

"But that's a bar! Kids can't go in there!"

"Yes, they can. I sneak in and get all the peanuts I want!"

"Oh yeah! How do you do that?"

"Follow me. I'll show you how."

George followed Angelika up the steps to the first class level. They walked down a long hallway on a soft carpeted floor and entered a lounge area that was crowded with well-dressed people. If anyone noticed them, they merely glanced at the two children and carried on with their conversations. Angelika quietly worked her way to the bar area where the crowds were even more congested during this late afternoon "happy hour" time, when drinks were half price. Instead of people sitting in chairs as in the lounge, most were standing and milling about. All seats at the horseshoe shaped bar were full with men and women chatting in a loud buzz. A cloud of white smoke hung in the air from cigarette smokers exhaling and gave the room a foggy atmosphere. Angelica told George to stay there in the corner behind some long drapes hanging from the ceiling and then she whispered:

"Watch this."

With that Angelika slithered in back of the bar stools to the near end of the U-shaped bar. For a moment she crouched there under the lip of the bar and impishly waved back to the wide-eyed George peeking around the curtain. With people moving back and forth George caught long and short glimpses of Angelika. He saw her reach up her hand and slowly bend it like a question mark and clamp her tiny fist into a peanut bowl, pull her peanut full hand down and start eating the peanuts now clinched in her small fist. When she finished she reached up again.

From the inside of the bar, one of the bartenders came to that end in response to a request to refill some drinks for a couple sitting and chatting at the bar. While doing so he was startled to see a small wrist rise up above the bar. The bartender watched the tiny wrist reach in and clutch a fistful of peanuts and then disappear. The couple on either side of the mysterious wrist was too busy gazing into each others eyes to notice. Puzzled, the bartender lifted a counter section and walked around to the customer side and spotted Angelika sneaking away between unsuspecting patrons.

"Go on with you, you little snitch! Get out of here!"

Angelika squealed with delight as she caught up to the fleeing George, and they both ran out of the lounge without looking back. They didn't stop running until they got down to the third class deck. Once safely there she threw herself onto a deck bench and offered George some peanuts. She was breathing heavily and giggling. She was exhilarated with her daring escape!

"Wasn't that fun?" enthused Angelika. "The peanuts are free, but kids are not supposed to be in bars."

"Now you can't do it anymore because you're found out."

"Oh, yes I can. I'll just wait until there's a different bartender."

"I'm ten years old and I'm not going to wait all those years until I'm big enough to go into a lounge to have free peanuts."

"I'm twelve and I'm already a head taller than you."

"So what. When it rains out you'll get wet sooner than me."

"Your mother may call you Angel, but I'm going to call you peanuts, not because you like them, but because you're small as one."

"Oh, I don't care. I like being little."

"Well, thanks for the peanuts. I got to go. See ya."

George couldn't wait to see Spyros to tell him about the free peanuts. But Spyros was not happy with him going up to the first class deck.

"You'll get us in trouble. Stay here where you belong. We could lose our deck privileges and be stuck down here, he warned."

"You won't tell my Dad, will you?"

"Not this time. But you have to stay out of trouble or I'll get in trouble."

With his youthful energy, George couldn't seem to stay in one place, as he bounced from one rail section of the ship to another. Spyros, tired of following the frenetic George, found an unoccupied chair and told George that he would be there, while George continued to move around the ship. While sitting down, Spyros looked at his passage ticket and noticed that their first stop was at Taranto, Italy. He had heard that this was a large port city at the foot of Italy, between the heel and the toe. It was in the middle of the Gulf of Taranto and was the home-port of the Italian Naval Fleet.

Since they would only be there a short time to disembark some passengers and cargo and to take some on, they would not be allowed to leave the ship. He would make sure George understood that. George was turning out to be a special care, ruminated Spyros. He was very impulsive like his mother. One just never knew what he would do next, or get himself into. He hasn't lived long enough to know fear, Spyros mused.

When they eventually pulled into Taranto, George was disappointed because the Italian Fleet was out to sea and he got to see only the smaller vessels. He wanted to see the big war ships, look at their bristling guns and to watch how fast they could go. The only thing he saw going fast was the passengers disembarking. Then he watched as some fast talking Italians boarded. They were very chatty and gestured wildly. When George started to mimic and imitate their grand gestures and speed-talk, Antonios noticed with displeasure, and, alarmed at causing offense, told George to stop.

"Why?" asked George.

His father shot back:

"It's not nice. They may think you are making fun of them."

"But I am," said George, innocently.

Retorted Antonios, "That could cause trouble and they might get angry and retaliate or complain to the Captain. He might then confine you to below decks. Then you would have to answer to me. Think on that!"

"Ok, Ok, I won't do it anymore."

Back out to sea again, George complained about how bored he got just looking at the endless water, and he couldn't find any boys his age to play with. He saw Spyros talking to other big people and he frowned. This wasn't as exciting as he thought it would be. While sunk down in a canvas chair swinging his restless legs, back and forth, Antonios beckoned George to come to the rail and see the giant rock the ship was passing. It was the biggest rock George had ever seen. It was called the Rock of Gibraltar.

"Can you climb up and dive off the top?" asked George, suddenly excited.

"No. You would kill yourself," answered his father.

"Why? Wouldn't you land in the water?" George's questions were unrelenting.

"No. You would land on the rocks below. The angle we're looking at is deceiving. In school you will find out. But even if you could dive out far enough to hit the water, at that height, the force would probably kill you. If not, you would break your arms and legs, not be able to swim and drown."

Adamantly, George argued back: "Then I would use one of those big balloons to come down slower."

George was showing his argumentative nature, just like me, thought Antonios, somewhat guiltily. There is nothing like seeing yourself in somebody else to give yourself an education, ruminated Antonios.

The next day, as they rounded the tip of Spain, coming out of the Mediterranean Sea into the giant Atlantic Ocean, Antonios related to George what a passenger, a history student from Italy, told him to watch out for. The *Saturnia* was passing outside the Gulf of Trafalgar.

"Here, nearly one hundred years earlier, in 1805," said Antonios, "the legendary British Admiral, Horatio Nelson, and his fleet of twenty seven warships fought and defeated a larger thirty three ship Armada of Spain and France. But, just when victory was won, he was killed directing his ship, the Victoria, when shot by a French sharpshooter. This, effectively, destroyed Napoleon's Naval Fleet, and left him with only an Army to terrify Europe and Western Russia for the next ten years. History always has lessons for us, George, so pay attention to it."

"So, what's the lesson there?" Asked George.

"That bigger numbers don't always win battles," said his father, with a little impatience.

As dispassionate as Antonios seemed to be in passing on this information, George listened with interest, imagining the exploding cannons and exciting runs of the ships of the line roaring by each other and blasting away through billowing gunsmoke. Antonios was almost sorry he brought the incident up, because it awakened George's curiosity, and he couldn't answer the flood of questions George threw at him for more details. He told him he could learn more, like the Italian student, in school. Some people are book learned, while he preferred to work with his hands. America was a big country where a lot of building was going on and jobs were many. But he was sure there was room for both book learners and laborers.

The next day, George was staring at a wide expanse of gunmetal gray waves undulating across the Atlantic Ocean. The low swells were so monotonous and endless, they lost their initial allure. George ignored the horizon to look around the ship to satisfy his ranging curiosity and craving for excitement. He walked the deck, watched others play cards and deck games, and listened to their conversations. He stopped and listened to a group of older boys. He tried to break in and have a say, but they just stared at him; then they continued while ignoring him. George shrugged and moved on. Then he saw scattered groups of people rushing to the rails and pointing enthusiastically out across the ocean. He too ran over and looked. What he saw took his breath away!

A large fleet of ships could be seen in the distance, but fast approaching. Could this be the Italian Fleet he had missed in the Gulf of Taranto? George wondered. Spyros came up behind him, shielded his eyes and gazed out at the arriving spectacle. He whistled in amazement as the flotilla came clearer in view and the enormity of its size became evident.

What is it, Spyros. What is it?" demanded George, with his usual youthful impatience. Spyros could only guess: "It looks like a naval task force. England's? Germany's?

"No," said a man, standing along side with his wife, next to them, and peering through binoculars. "It's a United States Fleet. I can see the flag."

He said that he had heard back in Greece that President Theodore Roosevelt was sending his prized fleet around the world on a goodwill tour. Others claimed, more cynically, that the US was showing off after defeating Spain in the Spanish-American War of 1898, putting down the Philippine Insurrection in 1899 and the Boxer Rebellion in 1900 in China. And here it was, sixteen white ships, crossing the Atlantic to enter the Mediterranean Sea. Battleships were the pride of the fleet and couldn't help but impress all who saw the grand floating armada during its fifteen month world tour over a three year period.

One nation in particular it was to impress was Japan, whose Imperial Fleet had destroyed the Russian Fleet in the Sea of Japan during the Russo-Japanese War of 1904-05. President Roosevelt was instrumental in brokering a peace in that war of attrition. Not only was this American Fleet going to impress the Japanese military, but more importantly, it would make them fear their naval might as a threat to the expansion of their Empire. In the long reach of time, some historians believe that this grandstanding of the American Naval fleet planted the seed in the Japanese Naval Command that would culminate in the attack and attempted destruction of the American Fleet at Pearl Harbor, Hawaii on December 7, 1941, thirty three years later.

"Look at those big guns!" shouted George. "Will we see them shoot, Spyros?"

"No, he answered, They are not at war; they are on a public relations trip."

"How many soldiers can they carry? How can they sleep when the guns shoot? What happens when they run out of fuel, asked George, in rapid fire order.

"They carry sailors, not soldiers," related Spyros. "And I don't know how many. But you can be sure that there are enough sailors to run the ship properly. And they refuel the same way our ship refuels; they pull into a port and buy more fuel. And that's enough questions for now, thank you."

When the grand fleet steamed out of sight, George ran into Angelika again. This time George saw her first and greeted her with a haughty:

"Hi there, peanuts!"

"Oh, ... I recognized your voice. I don't like the nickname "peanuts," said a peeved Angelika. "I like Angel, even though I'm not one."

"Want to have some more fun? teased Angelika.

"Doing what?" asked George.

"Lets go up to the top deck and I'll tell you on the way."

"See, it's like this. We both climb up on top of some deck chairs that are piled up underneath a stairway. And when people walk by we jump them like Geronimo-o-o! And knock their hats off," confided Angelika. She clasped her tiny hands over her mouth, as she tried to stifle her high pitched, hushed voice. She was anticipating the caper with delicious delight!

"Then I go back and look for ribbons, barrettes and hat pins that fell off."

"Geronimo? Who's Geronimo?"

"He's the big Indian Chief in the American desert who rides out of the hills and steals horses and stuff and the American cavalry can't catch him."

"But what do I get out of this?" asked George.

"Fun," answered Angelica.

"Ok, I'll try it. But I better not get in trouble."

Sure enough, once they worked their way up to the first class section, there were the chairs piled up beneath the stairs. They both climbed up and sat on the chairs, innocently sunning themselves waiting for people to go by.

"What happens if someone wants a chair?" Asked George.

"We give them one. And they think we're here to help them, see?"

"Look!" said Angelika. "Here comes two ladies. All dressed up and wearing big, fancy hats, too! After we knock off their hats, you run one way and I'll run the other, Ok?"

"Yup."

As the ladies passed beneath them, Angelika leapt, yelling "Geronimo-0-0!" knocked off the nearest lady's hat and ran away around the corner. George leapt also, but missed the second lady's hat and just ran the other way. The women called out in surprise and anger:

"Oh! Those kids! Don't they have anything better to do? It's those rascals from steerage. Why don't they stay where they belong!"

The other woman merely pinned her hat back on and muttered, "Really, those devils!"

George decided that he had enough excitement for the day and went back down to his room. A while later, he saw Angelika jauntily walking back to her area and saw that she was putting a barrette in her hair. She saw George, smiled and waved at him, as she went on her way. George just shrugged, went back into his room and lay down to rest. Watching the American Fleet steam by was much more exciting, he thought.

The next day the *Saturnia* turned landward and entered Lisbon, the chief port and capital-city of Portugal. Like Greece, it had a seafaring history, a ship's officer explained to George, as they approached landfall. Pointing to the main harbor, he said that Lisbon is located in a river estuary that empties out into the Atlantic Ocean. The river, named the Tagus River, divides the upper half of this tiny country from the lower half. As the ship entered the port, he swept his hand in a semi-circle and showed how villages were strung out like a necklace spread across the circular, rising coastal plain, expanding the city of Lisbon inland. Then George saw something that made his mouth water. He could see yellow mellons, oranges, apricots, almonds, grapes, olives and other fruits and vegetables spread out in colorful displays on tilted carts in a nearby market square.

The Ship's First Mate stopped while passing by, and mentioned that:

"Arabs, then called Moors, brought their Islamic religion and invaded southern Spain and Portugal in the 8ᵗʰ century. Coming from North Africa and its desert, they brought with them irrigation systems that helped the hot, dry climate of Spain and Portugal grow the many fruits and vegetables you see now displayed. Resistance to Arab rule started growing from the 11ᵗʰ century and increased with help from the opposing Roman Catholic Church and Northern Spain and Portugal", he continued.

"By 1492, when Columbus discovered America, the Moors were driven out of all of Spain and Portugal. Now, as you can see, most work is in agriculture among peasant farmers and landless laborers, as in Greece."

With that, the First Mate, waved himself away to attend to his landing duties. Spyros, listening nearby, then vented his resentment.

"Why do these traveling sailors show off their knowledge of these passing countries? What makes them think we care? But George thought to himself that he liked the friendly talk and cared to know these things.

While docked at Lisbon, George knew he was forbidden to leave the ship but he wanted to get to eat one of those delicious looking oranges he could see piled up on those carts. He wondered whether he should ask his father, but decided to just do it. He would get him one also. He worked his way behind the departing passengers to the main down ramp. He hesitated at the top of the ramp, making believe he was waiting for someone. Then he took one last quick look around and bolted for the down ramp. But he didn't look well enough or fast enough. He was yanked back by his collar. Spyros had him in his grip:

"And just where do you thing you're going, on my watch?"

And he wasn't smiling. "Go back down to your bunk and stay there until I talk to your father! And I don't want to hear any back talk; you'll just make it worse." George knew he was caught and didn't argue. He lowered his head and walked below deck. Spyros was angry. He would see Antonios later and fill him in on this attempt. But he would wait until the ship left the dock and was away from the shore. Meanwhile, Spyros would let George fret and think about what he had almost done. It would also give Spyros time to cool down.

When the ship was well out to sea again, Spyros went down to steerage and informed his father. Antonios whirled around and instantly confronted George:

"Just what did you think you were doing?" He asked.

George answered: "I was only going to buy oranges for you and I. I wasn't going to steal anything."

"Buy? Buy with what? You have no money!"

"Yes I do. Mom sewed some money into my clothes. See?"

"But that's Greek money and this is Portugal. They have their own money," said a simmering Antonios.

"Why would Ma give me money that's no good?" said George.

Somewhat exasperated, Antonios sputtered,

"You have to go to a bank and change it for local money. Don't do that again! You could have been left behind. Then I would never hear the end of it from your Mother. From now on you stay in my sight or Spyros's at every port. Do you understand me? I don't want to have to talk to you like this again!" George merely nodded and reprimanded, turned his head away, and walked back up on deck.

CHAPTER SEVEN

OCEAN STORM

Early evening the following day, as the sinking orange sun was spreading its golden rays across the rising ocean, George found himself on the top deck, avoiding his siblings on a venture of his own. Suddenly, Angelika rounded a corner and almost ran into George.

"Oh, it's you!" She said, almost startled. "What are you doing?"

"I'm trying to get rid of my brothers. They're been following me, to spy on me. It's bad enough with Spyros tailing me." So complained George.

"I just saw Dimitri and John downstairs. I'll bet when they don't find you there, they will use it as an excuse to come up to the top deck after you," warned Angelika.

Thinking they were on the way up, George looked around and motioned Angelika to follow him:

"Quick! Over here!"

With that, he lifted a canvas covering for a rescue boat and told Angelika to climb up and get into the lifeboat. He then jumped in after her.

"Lets hide in the dark here under the canvas and see if we can turn the tables and spy on them!"

A little later, while they were peeking out from one of the corners of the canvas covering, a man and a woman, who were holding each others hands strolled over, leaned dreamily on the rail, and admired the sun disappearing on the far horizon.

"Isn't it beautiful, Cosmos?"

"Yes, it certainly is! And now I have two beautiful sights to enthrall me. You and the horizon."

"Oh, Cosmos, you make me feel so special."

Angelika had to stifle her giggling and covered her mouth. George squeezed her arm and shushed her to be quiet. But Angelika, seized by a daring impulse, blurted out:

"Go ahead, kiss her!"

Not to be outdone, and almost at the same time, George shouted:

"Boo!"

The couple were startled speechless out of their romantic interlude. Recovering from the surprise, the woman pulled Cosmos away, while protesting:

"Oh, can you believe it. Those young urchins! Where are their parents!"

Meanwhile Angelika and George were howling with delight at their prank. They thought it was hilarious.

"What fun!" guffawed Angelika.

"Let's get out of here before they complain to the crew," said George. Then they both scrambled down below decks before anyone could catch up to them.

"It's getting dark, I have to go," yelled Angelika, as she disappeared around the corner. George then went back to his room to see what everyone else was doing.

Some days later, George was on deck leaning over the rail watching the churning waters below when he felt a wind sweep by and blow his hair up. Looking out on the gray ocean, he noticed that waves were getting white caps and the ship started to sway widely. The sky also darkened, even though this was early afternoon. He crossed his arms to cut down the chill he felt. A passenger walking by suggested he might want to go and get a jacket. George just nodded and did nothing. But then Antonios came up on deck and told George that he had heard that the ship was approaching a storm and that he should get below. Reluctantly, George moved to walk downstairs, but stalled because the waves were getting higher and he wanted to see the ship ride the waves up and down.

He liked getting sprayed by the wind blown mists. It was fun watching the waves crash against the bow and the swells surge over the deck. His father quickly lost his patience and yelled at George above the noise of the storm:

"I told you to go below! And that means now!"

Letting go of the rail, George stumbled across the swaying deck and made for the stairs below. Antonios followed directly behind him. At the same time a deck hand was walking the deck with a bullhorn announcing that they were entering a storm.

"Attention all passengers! Attention all passengers! There is a storm approaching! Return at once to your cabins, rooms and assigned areas until further notice!"

By the time they reached their bunk area, the ship was rolling violently and pitching sideways. The ship was rising to the top of huge waves and then plunging violently down to its depths. People started yelling and getting sick. Children cried from fright and hugged their mothers. People were holding on to anything that was bolted down. Some others were flung across the floor screaming in panic. Cots started to snap up and down, people had to sit on them. Luggage slid wildly from side to side. Lights flickered on and off. George was alarmed, but remained silent, hanging on to a post outside his room. He was watching his father who was hanging on to his bed, with one hand on the chain, and the other on the bed frame. His brother Dimitri shouted and motioned for George to come in and sit on his own bed to stop it from banging up and down. When he did, he promptly hit his head on the upper bunk. So Dimitri motioned for him to lie down to prevent it happening again.

George tried to roll with the ship, and hoped he wouldn't sprain his wrists holding on to a shaking cot. George tried closing his eyes to see if he could sleep past this nightmare. It was no longer fun. But he kept opening his eyes and felt reassured looking at the silent, but pale looking Spyros. George could hear the ocean waves crashing against the hull. He looked up at his older brother, John, lying on his bunk above and across from him, and he looked terrified. George, to distract himself, called out to Spyros:

"Can the water break through the side of the Ship? Will the ship sink? Are we ok?"

Spyros pointed to the wall and said:

"The rivets. Those big bolts make the ship watertight and keep the hull together. This is a big, strong, ship, George. It is safe."

George wondred if Spyros was trying to reassure himself as well as George, because what he said didn't square with how he looked. The storm went on into the night and people, who were crying and yelling, were now moaning, groaning and praying. Many got sick. The sour stench of vomit was in the air. Occasional megaphone announcements attempted to calm the passengers. But because of the violent swaying of the ship, the announcements were abruptly interrupted and had the opposite effect. It was announced, however hesitantly, that the Captain was attempting to find a way out of the storm and that, in any event, they would ride it out. In the meantime, they were warned to stay below decks and remain with their families. Anyone who was seriously injured should call the bridge for medical assistance. Those with medical training were encouraged to help their fellow passengers.

The storm raged all through the night and those that could sleep, did so. Others were too terrified to sleep and fought it. Still others finally fell asleep from exhaustion. George fell asleep in his bunk when he stopped trying to force himself to sleep. Much later, Spyros fell asleep, though he woke, off and on, throughout the pitch and roll of the night. Some didn't sleep at all. Some time before sunrise the storm broke and the ship leveled off, though some complained that they still felt off balance. That morning many passengers moved around with haggard looks from loss of or interrupted sleep and sickness. Some thanked their God for surviving the storm.

When the announcement finally came that passengers would be allowed to come on deck, there was a rush of people to get away from the stinking and suffocating smell of sickness. They wanted to breathe fresh air. The Dilboys and Spyros joined them.

On deck, they heard of some passengers who panicked during the night and ran up on deck because they thought that they would drown if they stayed below. They refused to believe they would be safer below deck. Those who refused to go below were given the choice of returning to their bunks or being taken into custody and thrown in the brig. The few that refused to go below were seized, confined below and released once the storm was over. The ship's crew claimed that the storm was the worst one they had experienced in years.

The rest of the voyage across the Atlantic Ocean was calm and anti-climatic. Many expressed relief and were thankful. Some railed at the *Saturnia's* officers, as if they could control the raging ocean.

Next stop was New York City. George was anxious to see the most celebrated city in the United States. Uncle Kostas had entered the United States there the prior year. Some of his fellow Greek passengers had gotten off the ship in New York City to see the sights, stay a few days with some fellow Greeks, and then took a train to Boston. There was a Greek community in Boston in their Back Bay and Mission Hill sections. Some Greek immigrants stayed in rooming houses near the Huntington Ave grounds where one of Boston's professional baseball teams played their home games. In 1903 they had won what American's called their World Series beating a team from Pittsburg City in a coal mining state called Pennsylvania. Some Greeks opened shoe-shine stands that they could carry with them. Others sold fruit from pushcarts. They earned a lot of money at these games, at least compared to their meager earnings in Greece on farms and shops. Up to twelve thousand people went to these games. They learned to pick up and to practice their English talking to their customers.

That same year a huge Greek Cathedral church was built on Ruggles St. nearby. It was named the Annunciation Cathedral and Greeks came from all over Boston to attend this beautiful Cathedral. Some Greek immigrants did much business shining shoes and selling fruits outside this church. Then they would go in for the service, and rush out afterwards to do more business.

A few years later, word got around Boston that Swift, Armour and Squires Meat Packing Companies in East Cambridge, across the Charles River, were hiring at more pay, so some of the Greek immigrants went over there to work. The Swift's plant was right on the Cambridge/Somerville city line. The Armour Company was in the same general area. As were other such companies and slaughter houses. The Greek immigrants were ready to take whatever jobs were available to allow them an honest living. They would send money home and save what they could. To be near their places of work, they lived in nearby multi-family tenement houses. Many moved into the Brickbottom area of East Somerville, a densely populated area of multi-family houses on the border with equally crowded East Cambridge.

It was called the Brickbottom section because it had some brickyards in the area and over by the nearby Mystic River, and its sidewalks were mostly made of brick, if they weren't made of dirt. Since many Greeks couldn't get housing in crowded Boston at the time, they came around the heavily Italian populated North End of Boston and walked or took a trolley car the short distance across the crossway and a small bridge over the Charles River into the city of Somerville. There Uncle Kostas joined a bustling Greek Community that was building up in the area. In this community, the Greeks combined their money to rent a building and turned it into a local Greek Church. With further contributions, they proudly ended up buying a nearby building years later in 1916 and owning their own church. Also, in the area was a Grammar school named the Bennett School that they could walk to and learn American English at night.

NEW YORK CITY

When it became certain that the Dilboys were coming to America, Kostas's letters became more frequent and longer. He told them what they could expect and what to get ready for. He had many suggestions for them, including sticking together and learning key English words like food, bathroom, doctor, police. All this George was thinking about as the ship pulled into the docking area in New York harbor. George marveled at the tall buildings that to him looked like uprooted trees. He couldn't see any streets because the buildings seemed to be on top of each other.

"Where are the streets, Spyros?" he asked.

"They are there; you just can't see them at this angle and distance, responded Spyros."

"Well they must be pretty skinny," said George.

Some of the buildings were cut off by a low lying fog. He was barely able to make out the tall lady that they called the Statue of Liberty when they passed by her. Spyros said that he was older that this statute. "It was made in France and shipped over as a gift to the United States in the 1880's," he said.

"Wow," said George. "It sure must have been a big ship for that size statute to fit in."

"It came in sections in large boxes," replied Spyros.

George could hear a newspaper boy on the pier shouting out a headline that the first fleet of metered taxicabs arrived from France!

Spyros and George both rushed down to their section to "guard their things," because most of the immigrant passengers got off the ship at Ellis Island in New York Harbor and he wanted to make sure none of their belongings were taken by "mistake." They were ever on the alert to protect their few belongings. Another stop for U.S. citizen passengers and cargo was made further up the harbor at Batterypark in New York City. This stop wasn't as long as the other, and they still weren't allowed off the ship. When the ship made its way out of the harbor, Spyros and George went on top to watch the New York skyline get smaller and then disappear in the fading sunlight and distance from shore. They were off to the short voyage to Boston.

The *Saturnia* moved northeast for the last leg of their voyage into international waters, but within sight of the distant shore. The weather was clear and bright, with the sun glinting off of the dark waters and low waves. Later, the ship rounded the furthest tip of Cape Cod, off Provincetown, Massachusetts. Cape Cod was a peninsula that stuck out into the Atlantic Ocean like Italy stuck out of Southern Europe, though on a much smaller scale, according to their map. This is how it appeared to George, as Spyros showed him a navigational map lent them by a deckhand that befriended them. Neither Spyros nor George had any idea what all those little numbers and letters meant scattered all over the map. But it showed them how the *Saturnia* traveled on it's long voyage. Antonios looked on with a distant interest.

As they approached Boston Harbor, the *Saturnia* blew it's horn a number of times to announce it's arrival. The ship passed a number of small islands as it entered the harbor and houses all along the shore could be seen, made mostly of gray clapboard wood, Antonios noted with his carpenter's eyes. The bright late afternoon sun gave the houses a blue tinge, reflections from the shallow waters and the green grass above the sandy shores. The ship eased its way against the pier and its cushioned sides to avoid damaging the ship and the pier. People were bunched at the end of the pier anxiously awaiting the passengers.

Immigrants, of course, had to go through the Immigration section and it's officials. Bullhorns told the second class passengers to wait for the disembarkation of the first class passengers, before they could leave. Steerage passengers were told to stay below decks until a further announcement and to make sure they took with them all their belongings.

When they finally got on deck, all the Dilboys were leaning over the rail scanning the pier for Uncle Kostas. Antonios gave Spyros an old photograph showing a younger non-smiling Kostas, so he would be able to spot him. It was not an especially flattering picture of Kostas, but it would have to do. Peering over Spyros's arm, George wondered why someone didn't think to bring along a more recent photograph of Uncle Kostas. As much as they looked at the excitedly waiting receiving parties on the pier with raised signs calling attention to the names on them, they didn't see any for Dilboy. Maybe they were too excited or maybe Kostas hadn't arrived yet. They would have to wait anyway, until after they had gone through customs and immigration. The Buildings they could see in Boston weren't as tall or as mysterious as those they saw in New York City, thought George.

BOSTON

They finally walked down the plank into a huge building. Antonios was cautioning everybody to "Stick together now! Stick together!" After getting their suitcases, they lined up behind others to have their passports and luggage checked by the customs officials. It was very confusing to George, with excited utterances from the assembled people, some of whom were talking in strange languages. After about an hour or so, they were passed through into another long line.

"What's this line for, Spyros?" asked George.

"It's to register at the immigration desk. They check our names against their passenger list."

Once this line was passed, they all had to line up again to be examined by a medical doctor. George watched as his father had his mouth, ears and eyes checked and they had him open his coat and shirt for any kind of skin rash or disease or heart problem, George would later be told. When the doctor finished with Antonios, the Nurse assistant called for George to come forward. She compared George to his passport photograph.

"You are George Dilboy?"

"Yes, M'am," he replied, as polite as he could, just the way his mother had instructed him to. They did not take as long to examine George. He wasn't old enough to develop any chronic medical problem. He was passed through and the Nurse smilingly said to him:

"Welcome to America, young man."

George hurried over and joined the waiting Dilboys, all having smiles on their faces. They had all passed the medical tests. He couldn't wait to write and tell his mother! They walked together through another door and saw a crowd waiting behind a roped off area. Through the tumult and the rushing bodies, they heard a man shout:

"Antonios! Dimitri!" He had no sign.

Dimitri saw Uncle Kostas first and waved quickly back at him: "Here! Over Here!"

The group broke into a sprint and ran up to Uncle Kostas hugging and excitingly surrounding him, knocking his derby hat off. A short heavy-set man finally emerged from the circle and grabbed Antonios's hand, shaking it happily and giving each other an enthusiastic brotherly hug. Kostas ended up slapping Antonios on the back. He then pointed at his nieces and nephews and exclaimed:

"Marianthe! Come to your Uncle Kostas! I come all the way into Boston to see you!" He joked.

Then he lifted her up in the air and swung her around and put her down, saying :

"My Marianthe! Let me take a good look at you! Yes, yes, you have grown into such a fine young lady. What a difference a year makes!" So, how was your long journey, huh?"

He then dotted on eight year old Stamatia and twisted her hair playfully.

"You will grow taller than your sister, eh? All that sun and ocean, she make you shoot up like a tall tree."

And Spyros! It is so fine to see my old neighbor! You looked after George good, did you? Welcome, my friend. Welcome!"

He heartily grabbed hands and greeted all the family, then did it again, as if he hadn't done it before. He thereafter loudly proclaimed:

"Let us all go outside now. All come now, just follow me."

He took Stamatia's suitcase out of her hand. But she wanted to carry hers like everyone else, so Kostas relented, trussing her hair affectionately.

"So Antonios, tell me, how was your ocean voyage?" Asked Kostas.

"Except for a bad storm in the Atlantic, it was a good voyage, Ko."

With that they all made their way to the street. Everyone seemed to be rushing. Outside what they called Commonwealth Pier, it was busy with traffic and people. Horses clip-clopped along pulling carriages over cobble stoned streets. Trolley cars with long rods attached to overhead wires rolled along sounding a low roar. Clanging bells told pedestrians that a trolley car was approaching and to get out of the way. Uncle Kostas warned them all to watch out for the horse dung that had plopped in the street. Horseless carriages were honking their way along, competing with people and horse drawn wagons and trolleys for limited space. The energy and vitality could be felt in the salty air, breeze and wind blowing in from Boston Harbor.

Everything seemed to be in motion. George wondered if he didn't move along he would get run over. It was overwhelming at first. Men in round derby hats and flat scalp caps and black, high buttoned shoes hustled by. Women in long dresses and huge hats moved swiftly along wooden planks laid across the muddy sidewalks. George stared at a newspaper vendor because the boy didn't look to be much older than him. He was yelling out headlines that a female British novelist's book was banned in Boston!

He thundered : "British female novelist chronicles a Balkan Queen's adulterous steamy affair and refers to sex as 'IT.'"

"They did IT again! Outraged censors won't stand for IT!" he yelled as he vigorously waved the newspaper in the air! George thought a job selling newspapers calling out the latest headlines might be a job he could do. It looked so exciting!

The three of them crossed the street and joined a crowd waiting for a streetcar rolling along on loud iron wheels. When one came along clanging its bell announcing its stop, Uncle Kostas led the way on board and the rest of the group followed him and the crowd surging up the steps. He also paid the fare for all of them, as they had no American money yet. George was impressed with the tall buildings. They didn't look so high from a distance. Police officers directed the rushing traffic at the busier intersections. George held on to Spyros clothes because he wasn't tall enough to reach the overhead nooses that hung from the roof of the trolley car. A conductor walked down the aisle collecting paper slips from riders who transferred from another streetcar.

When a woman passenger got up to get off at the next stop, Uncle Kostas nudged Stamatia to sit in her place. She then got to sit on the wooden slatted seats and noticed the many signs advertising corsets, cigarettes and other ads for goods on the side of the car. George liked the ride in the car, especially when the car lurched and swayed when the brakes were used. He also liked the low roar of the trolley car as it traveled along, before it came to a squealing stop. After about a half dozen stops, Uncle Kostas signaled them to follow him off the trolley car.

They crossed the street and went down some stairs into a dark underground tunnel to now get on a train. It was cooler than the hot, sunny ground surface. But the sound of the train was louder. This was a sight of wonder for all in the much-traveled group. It was the first subway tunnel ride they had ever been on. It took a while for their eyes to adjust to the dark subway after coming down from bright sunshine. Uncle Kostas told them to hurry as their train was just then coming into the station. George thought it was strange to call the station Park St. when he didn't see any park. Uncle Kostas said it was above them. It wasn't noticed because of the surging crowds pushing and hurrying them along.

Again the car was full and George had to stand, hanging onto a pole. George thought the train would crash into the wall because it seemed so close to it. It seemed amazing that this swaying and speeding car only inches away from the wall could whiz by disappearing posts and columns that held up the tunnel.

After a few stops the subway train came out of the tunnel and rose to the surface. The sun smarted his eyes again. He had to blink often to get use to the bright sun after the dark underground. They got off the train at a stop in the northern section of Boston. Many Italian, Polish and Irish immigrants lived here, said Uncle Kostas. Kostas's Greek neighborhood was less than half a mile away in the city of Somerville. They boarded another trolley car and rolled along across a bridge going over the Charles River that separates Boston from the nearby cities of Cambridge and

Somerville. By now it was late afternoon and they were running into plants and factories disgourging people from the work buildings and adding to the already overcrowded streets.

Uncle Kostas pointed out the window and told us that a tall stone structure was called the Bunker Hill Monument celebrating a great battle that occurred at the beginning of the American Revolution. Like Greece, the Americans lost some battles but won the war. In the opposite direction, the Charles River, separating Boston from Cambridge, wiggled its way west, around a curve and tailed away until it disappeared. About a mile down the winding river, out of sight, was Harvard University, the oldest University in the United States. They arrived, after a short ride, at their final stop, Linwood Street in East Somerville. Number 77 was the address of their new home. It was a tall, multi-family, wooden tenement house. They would occupy the six-room basement apartment and Uncle Kostas had the first floor. They would also share some of his flat, so called. Above them were two other Greek families. Although there had been a small Greek settlement there for two years now, this city was mostly Irish, with Italian being the other notable ethnic group. When the Greeks could not get more living quarters in heavily populated Boston, nearby East Cambridge and East Somerville was within easy distance by trolley car.

Kostas had told them that he had to put an extra month's rent down to hold their basement flat because four months earlier, on April 12, the nearby town of Chelsea had a catastrophic fire that caused the deaths of nineteen people and destroyed one quarter of its properties. Dislocated people flooded the surrounding cities and towns looking for flats.

While the Dilboys were getting settled, Spyros stayed a few days to rest from the long voyage and to try and acclimate himself to his new country. The first thing George did when he got a good night's rest was to write his mother that they arrived safely, because he knew she would want to know and because he knew his mother would worry. He also told his mother in the letter that he named an island in the middle of the Mediterranean Sea after her, because he buried her Hydrangea plant there, where it would get much needed sun and water. Therefore, he continued, some day she would be famous.

Now that he had safely arrived on the East Coast of America, George was anxious to survey his local surroundings. However, Uncle Kostas told him to stay near the house in this Greek neighborhood as there were Irish gangs about just a street or two away and they were very territorial. He was not to be caught alone as the new kid on the block. George confined himself to the front steps of the four family house, including a basement flat, watching the traffic go by and the public trolley cars and the high stacks of barrels over the back fence of a barrel company. He also got to see the fellow Greek residents of the second and third floors. Initially, he merely nodded to them because they spoke to him in broken English and he didn't want them to know he spoke almost no English. Little did he know that Uncle Kostas had already told them that he was bringing relatives to America from Greece. He would later find that when he smiled and was friendly to them, they would do the same to him.

Three days later Uncle Kostas took Spyros to the nearby trolley car stop and they went into Boston's South Station to put Spyros on a train to Chicago. Uncle Kostas had a group of friends over the night before to welcome Spyros and to thank him for helping the Dilboy family on the great voyage and to wish him godspeed to his further trip to his own relatives in the big midwestern cow city of Chicago.

CHAPTER EIGHT

SCHOOL DAZE

Within a week, Antonios and Dimitri were able to get jobs as laborers. Antonios would work in an East Cambridge Slaughter House and Dimitri would unload trucks at the nearby Swift Meat Packing Company. Next, Uncle Kostas had Antonios make arrangements for him to register the five school age kids for school for the following month of September. Marianthe was entered into the local Somerville High School. The local Bennett School Principal, John Smithers, had John, George and Stamatia in for an interview with his father Antonios to determine their suitable grade classes for their entrance.

Principal Smithers told them that:

"We have had other Greek immigrants here in prior years, but with a recent fire at the school and a limited budget, our records are not complete. And they did well here. In any event, you will probably run into them in the schoolyard and the neighborhood."

At their ages, Principal Smithers told them that would normally enter classes with students of the same age. However, given the fact that they were recent immigrants, literally, just off the boat, with a very limited understanding of the English language, he determined that they should enter one grade level lower, at least for the time being. He reasoned that it would make it easier for them to catch on and to catch up with their fellow students, because each grade was progressively more difficult. Their progress beyond that level would depend on their application of lessons, industry and developed abilities. Principal Smithers thought it helpful that they would be staying with a relative, Uncle Kostas, who already spoke passable English and encouraged Antonios to have them speak English at every opportunity and to avoid the natural habit of speaking Greek.

George, in particular, was not happy that he might be among the older students in the lower, fifth grade. However, he was somewhat mollified by his father promising that if he took to his lessons as well as his mother and father seemed to think he could, then he would ask Principal Smithers to advance him to a higher grade to catch up to his natural grade level. Antonios, Dimitri and Uncle Kostas, additionally, would undertake to help them all with their lessons, they assured them. In the meantime, Uncle Kostas had them meet other Greek children at the neighborhood school who would accompany them to school and look after them until they felt settled. Some bullies at school were known to make fun of and pick on new kids, especially foreign kids, struggling to learn English.

It didn't take long for George to be targeted. Within the first week, George found himself isolated in the school yard and surrounded by four menacing looking Irish kids:

"Hey Greeceball! Said Knuckles McCoy, the ringleader. He was a thick necked, older teenage tough. He had a wide body, a flattened nose, gum chewing, with wild looking black hair. He stood with his feet apart, in a confrontational stance, staring at George sideways, as if he stopped short, while passing by. "Just off the boat, huh! Stay off our Streets, got it? Yeah, that's Joy and Linwood streets! That's our turf! 'Cause if ya don't, ya could get hurt! Consider yourself lucky, Pal, this is just a warning!"

"Hey—, leave him alone!" Barked a burly, broad shouldered blonde kid, who stood taller than everyone. He had with him three Greek looking boys from nearby Poplar St. and Somerville Avenue, as they pushed their way through the threatening gang and surrounded George in a protective circle of their own. He's with us—so keep walking!"

"Oh, yeah, well we wuz just talk'n to him, is all. What's the big deal! Let's go guys, I don't like the smell around here!"

George watched his taunters swagger away. The ringleader spun around and gave them an insulting finger gesture.

The big kid, named Walt, returned the gesture with one of his own, a thumbs down motion and a derisive smirk. Then he turned to George, smiled and extended his hand in friendship, saying: "How ya, Pal. This is Alex Constantine, Jim Sakris and Nick Yeomarkis. And I'm Walt Wozlowski, Woz, for short. I'm Polish. My family moved here from the West End of Boston last year. These guys intervened for me when another gang hassled me, so I teamed up with them. We don't like bullies turning on anyone. What I learned is that the lone wolf is prey to the pack. So the answer is to join a pack of lone wolves. Like us. They're not likely to bother you if you're part of a group. You know, be part of your own gang."

"Thanks guys. My name's George Dilboy. My Uncle Kostas warned me about the street gangs. I just didn't see them coming. I have to be more alert, that's all." George gestured as much as he spoke, but the Greek boys translated back and forth for George and their meanings were made clear.

Alex Constantine was wisp of a kid, thin and wearing eyeglasses. He chatted freely, more like a nervous habit. He had a little stutter that became more pronounced as he tried to talk faster. But then he would make fun of his own stammering, as if to beat anyone else to it. George couldn't help liking him.

Nick Yeomarkis was a little above average in height, handsome, dark haired and complexioned, with a poker face. George would later realize that he didn't talk much, which made George wonder what he was thinking. But he was friendly enough.

Jim Sarkis stood out because of a large scar across his left cheek. He later told George that after he tried to mount a horse from the wrong side, it reared up, threw him off and kicked back, hitting him in the face. Though not as big as Woz, he was solidly built and mean looking. He was actually mild mannered, as George would eventually realize. His menacing looks seemed to make others not want to cross him. He greeted George warmly and with a firm handshake.

After this first schoolyard confrontation, George kept a heads up, picked up more English words and learned the neighborhoods. He noticed that this area of the city was heavily Irish, and they seemed to fight amongst themselves, as much as they did others. The other major ethnic group in this Boston border city was "Eyties," in the local lingo, Italians. But it seemed less threatening or dangerous here than back in Asia Minor or Greece, because here fisticuffs were more the norm than rifles or swords. George was learning fast.

The Dilboys had heard that the Bennett School was offering lessons in English for those interested. George was encouraged by his father and Uncle Kostas to take the course, because it would allow him to get a higher paying job. George was amused that his father wanted him to take English lessons, but he himself would not. It made him think that his father might be thinking of returning to Greece to rejoin his wife and George's mother. Antonios wouldn't say and George knew better than to ask him.

George had taken a job as soon as he could and walked his way the one mile to work in the laundry room at the Mass General Hospital. There the work was physical and he could watch and see what had to be done. His limited English was not such a problem, and getting less so as he picked up common words at night school and on the street. He was assimilating and learning the English language fairly quickly, like his Uncle Kostas, he was told.

After a while, in less than a year, his English had improved to the extent that he was hired at a higher paying job as a busboy at the Georgian Café in Park Square, downtown Boston. Being on his feet built up the strength and stamina of his young legs. His hustle and quick service earned him the respect of his manager and generous tips from the customers. Though this job involved him incurring the cost of a couple of short train rides to work, he still earned more money. As expected, being frugal, he gave some of his earnings to his father to send home to his mother and saved what he could above his expenses.

In fact, the Dilboys were such quick studies of the English language that within a year and a half, Principal Smithers, on his own, called in Antonios and the children and promoted the children to the more age appropriate class grades. Not only were they exceeding expectations in their school subjects, but their friendly, affable natures, made them many friends among different ethnic groups. In time they were able to relax more and be themselves. For the most part, their outgoing, pleasing personalities stood them in good stead, even among the Irish and Italians.

CHURCH

Many of the Greek immigrants associated themselves into clubs, groups and churches according to where they came from in Greece. Uncle Kostas brought them to the Alatsata chapter of the local Greek-American Club in Brickbottom. He also took them to the local Greek Orthodox Church that met on the second floor of rented space above the Woolworth's Department Store at the intersection of Bow and Warren Streets in nearby Union Square. They had asked the Greek Patriarch in Boston to send them a priest from Alatsata, which he did. Forty nine year old, Constantine Kaooyianis, became the first prelate. He performed their marriages and baptised their children. Union Square was named after the Union Army that had a recruiting office there during the American Civil War. George's interest in things military caused him to take note of such landmarks of history.

In getting them acclimated to this new neighborhood, Uncle Kostas pointed out the nearby Lincoln Park that was named after Abraham Lincoln, the American President who kept the states united and freed the slaves. But George, in particular, was more interested in seeing the Prospect Hill Tower where the American flag was first flown in defiance of the British Empire. It was also the hill to which the young American Revolutionary Army retreated from Bunker Hill, after running out of ammunition. The defiant flag raising reminded him of his father's pride in Greece's similar action in raising their own flag in defiance against the Turkish Empire.

Antonios especially, and George and his brothers liked to go with Uncle Kostas when he went to the two year old Sons of Ionia Greek-American Political Club on Somerville Avenue. There the men met to play cards, board games and to talk and drink coffee. It made them feel more at home with their own kind. And there they could speak Greek freely without being made fun of or given strange looks. They had pictures of Alatsata and other pictures of the homeland on the walls. The guys there always asked how his mother and family were doing back in Asia Minor and reminding them to write to their mother often to let her know how they were doing, so she wouldn't worry. But Uncle Kostas said:

"They also want you to write back to Greece so that you can be another line of communication with the folks back home, and they can get to hear additional news. They can never hear enough about their home country and their keen interest in the safety of their friends and relatives still there. That's why they keep asking if you received any letters from your mother and what the folks at home said about what was happening back there."

DAUGHTERS OF IONIA

George was also interested to see Angelika attending the same church with her parents. He didn't know she had moved into the area after she initially had lived in Boston's Back Bay section. She enthusiastically waved at George, who nodded back in recognition. Angelika was brought frequently to activities sponsored by the Daughters of Ionia, a social club also located in the Brickbottom section of East Somerville. Ionia is a section of Greece located in the northern areas, above and across the Ionian and Aegean Seas.

Angelika, though petite, was growing into a little lady. She was just a shade under five feet tall. She enjoyed dressing up for church and she had a keen interest in the latest fashions. She still liked to cut cloth and make dresses for her dolls. She cut out her own doll clothes from bolts of cloth remnants that her mother didn't use. She was her own consultant and best customer. She thought of it as practice for designing and making her own clothes, as did her mother. She thought of George as a future customer, because he was so handsome. However, George took little interest in clothes. Maybe he could be her first adult male customer, she thought to herself. He would make a good model to showcase her creations. This fed into her dreams of one day becoming a world class fashion designer, who would open up her own shop in New York City, Paris, Milan or some other fashion center.

Unfortunately, for Angelika, George thought of her as a prank-prone Buccaneer who helped him bridge his boredom on the *Saturnia*. He was more interested in rifles, war and adventure, and thought often of his family, especially his mother, back home in Asia Minor. He also missed his brother and sister, much as he thought of them as pests following him around in their village. George also thought often of getting a better job so he could earn more money, ride the trolley cars and go to the movies at the new Orpheum Theatre at the corner of Cross St. and Fountain Ave and the Strand Theater in Union Square. Often times he would stand outside these silent screen movie theaters and bellow out:

"Shoe shine! Shoe shine! Get your shoe shine here!"

Too often, however, he would earn some coins and then run into the movie house and spend his earnings to see the latest film. It helped him learn more English from the measured flicking of the English sub-titles and stirred his imagination. The piano playing accompanying the picture shows was also entertaining. On rare occasions, he would see news segments on the rising tensions and border skirmishes in Greece, the Balkan Countries and Asia Minor. The combatants were Turkey, on the one hand, and Serbia, Montenegro, Bulgaria, Greece and other Balkan countries, on the other. It made him wonder about the safety of his mother and what she was doing.

Back in Asia Minor, the Greeks had to be very careful that they didn't promote Hellenism. Helena was an old name for Greece. Despite letters from his mother saying she was doing fine, he couldn't help worrying. It was a well known Turkish policy at the time to eliminate all foreign culture and influence in an effort to

"Turkify" the entire populace of Asia Minor. To the Turks, the Greeks were foreigners on their peninsula.

In America, George was not interested in sports, as much as he was in sneaking off and practicing with an old rifle bought for him by Uncle Kostas. George would walk down the street in a long raincoat with the rifle hidden inside the raincoat and held onto by his hand hidden in the coat pocket, where the bottom had been cut out. He would practice near the brickyards, stacks of barrels piled up in barrel-yards, and wharves on the Mystic River. There he would hunt and shoot water rats thinking he was doing the neighborhood a favor by getting rid of disease carrying health pests. When these rodents couldn't be spotted, he would shoot at loose tin cans or debris thrown in the water. He was careful to keep a look out for stray people and Officer Donovan, who walked the area on foot patrol. The noise of the commercial traffic, passing trolley cars and new motor cars backfiring and put-putting covered his sporadic shots. He told himself that he was just practicing for his return to help his father hunt down the menacing Turkic raiders. He thought of it as fun and exciting!

At the movie houses, George laughed at the cartoons. He ever was on the lookout for a higher paying job, so he could save and send more money back to his mother. He was impatient with not growing taller, and kept marking his height against a wall in pencil to see if he was growing taller. He looked forward to getting older, so he could afford to go back to Asia Minor on his own. George also worked as a paper delivery boy, but had to be careful on certain streets that crossed into other gangs territories. One day he ran into Knuckles McCoy and a few of his boys:

"Hey you! Greece ball! You working my street? You gotta pay us. You saw in the movies dat Lewis and Clark hadda pay Indians to cross their river. So you gotta pay us to cross our streets. Unner stand?"

"I know," said George, but they gave them rifles to hunt buffalo. I don't make enough money to give you money, but I can show you how to shoot a rifle, how's that?"

"A real rifle?"

"Yeah, a real rifle. My Uncle got it for me."

"Can it shoot real bullets?"

"Yeah, real bullets. I kill rats with them."

"Ha! We got some rats we'd like to blast away, too!"

"Say, you gotta license for it, so it's legal and we don't get inna trouble wit the cops?"

"Yeah, my father gave me my license, though it was back in Asia Minor, but it's still good."

"Well, if it's good enuf for ya Pop, it's good enuf for us."

"When we goin huntin rats, huh?"

With that negotiated ploy, George, all five and a half feet of him, became a big man in the neighborhood and gained the favor of the numerically dominant Irish gang, as well as the Greek boys. The other boys now looked at him differently, with a mixture of awe, wonder and interest. George was pleased with his new status and together with his pleasing personality, it gave him the advantage of a nice guy-nasty guy potential, at least in their perception. In other words, as Woz explained it later:

"Now you can say, 'Be nice to me, and I'm nice to you. Be nasty to me, and I'll be nasty to you. But I've got a lethal back up, the wow weapon!'"

"Way to go! Georgie boy! That's usin the old noggin!" cheered Nickie Yeomarkis.

It didn't take long for the word to get around Brickbottom. Rifles were not common in Brickbottom, but they were in the part of the world where George came from. There, they were an everyday reality and a life necessity. Every so often, George would be approached by one of the Irish or Italian kids asking to watch him practice shooting. Invariably, he would be asked to let them fire it themselves. Depending on the individual, sometimes George would, and sometimes he wouldn't. It also depended on how George thought this kid could be trusted to be careful. George had them aim the rifle out at the water in the Mystic River. He would have them aim at a floating piece of branch or wood in the water. George shot to practice in order to maintain and improve his marksmanship. His training under his father made him a skilled marksman and was a point of pride with him. But some of these kids didn't appreciate its dangers.

For example, one day Butchy Shaughnessy suddenly turned toward a couple who were walking along Somerville Beach, a public beach on the Mystic River, and aimed the rifle at them. George grabbed the rifle out of his hands and yelled:

"Hey! What in hell do you think you're doing?"

The rifle blast startled both of them and knocked Butchy down. The couple turned around and stared at them with puzzled looks on their faces. A moment later they hurried off the beach, appearing scared and angry.

"I was just practicing drawing a bead on someone, is all, for Christ's sake, George. What ya getting so heated up for?"

"Hell, you don't do that with your finger on the trigger, you idiot! Let's get outta here before they set the cops on us. Damn you, Butchy, if the cops find out it was my rifle, they'll take it away from me and get my Uncle in trouble! That's it for you! You are not getting your hands on this again!"

"Oh, let's just get outta here! They ain't gonna find out. They were too far away to get a good look at us."

But they did find out.

The next day, Officer Donovan came to the house and asked to talk to the parents of George Dilboy. Fortunately, Uncle Kostas was also there when Antonios answered the door, and they both listened:

"Top of the morning to you, me boyo's, but we have received a complaint at the station that a teenage boy was seen discharging a rifle by the Mystic River yesterday. Upon investigation, we have determined that a George Dilboy, of this address, has been seen shooting at tin cans in the river. Would you, now, be the boy's father?"

Antonios turned to his brother with a puzzled look on his face. Kostas without interpretating for his brother, answered:

"Mr. Policeman, Antonios here is the boy's father. He does not speak the English, too well. I am the Uncle and I bought the rifle. Sometimes, I let the boy use the rifle, like I did in Asia Minor."

"Is that a fact, now? Well, Sir, in this country you need a license to own a gun. May I see it, please?"

"License? License? What's this license?"

"Well now, without a license, I'll have to take possession of the rifle and store it at headquarters. You can apply for a license, pay a fee, and get it back. May I have the rifle, please?"

Kostas turned to a puzzled Antonios and interpreted the problem. Antonios nodded, then walked away to George's room and returned with the unlicensed rifle. Officer Donovan took the rifle and checked it to make sure it wasn't loaded. Then he looked at them both and said:

"Because you co-operated and are recent immigrants, I will recommend that no complaint be issued. But you must learn our laws. You can become properly licensed and learn when and where you can properly discharge a firearm. Then you can reclaim your rifle at Police Headquarters on Bow St., just on the other side of Union Square. Do you understand that, now do you?"

Kostas nodded his understanding, and Officer Donovan left. Antonios threw up his hands irritated that George would scare people with the rifle. But Kostas rebutted:

"No, NO, Antonios! George is only doing what you and he did back in Alatsata. Here, you must get permits and licenses for such things. It's supposed to make things safer. I will find out what to do and get my rifle back. But we must caution George to be more careful. He is now fourteen and almost a man."

The following week Kostas did just that. Then he lectured a chastened George about the limitations on the piece of paper he received about where and when he would be allowed to shoot the rifle:

"This is a new country, George. They have their ways."

To establish some type of control, and to have George think about it, Kostas got Antonios to refuse George use of the rifle again until he became age fifteen. Since that would be in two short months, George didn't mind. It also gave George an excuse to keep the other kids from using it, since he couldn't use it himself.

Still George found other ways to have excitement in his life. One of the thrills for teenagers at this time was to jump on the back of trolley cars and be taken for a ride. Invariably, a conductor or a patrolman would spot them and chase them off. In the same spirit, teenagers liked to hop on the back of horse pulled ice wagons, hanging from the tailgate. The one who hung on the longest, without getting caught, was the winner. Horse drawn milk trucks were also fair game, where they would jump on the rear running board and duck down. To counter this, side and rear view mirrors were put on the wagons and trucks. This may have reduced the length of the mischievous ridings, but not the number, as it seemed to inadvertently up the risk of discovery and increase the thrill.

Angelika, around the corner and a street away took a dim view of these Irish shenanigans, to use their word. Though younger than George, she liked to lecture him to "grow up" and stop acting like a juvenile adolescent. Irritated, George would taunt back at her:

"Oh, OK, Miss know-it-all! You're such a big shot woman. You, who dresses dolls, who sneaks putting on her mothers lipstick, is a goody two shoes, now?"

Angelica would tighten her mouth and haughtily hurry away, as if she couldn't be bothered with these street ruffians.

His friend Woz would remark:

"George, why do you bother with her; where does she get off lecturing you? Does she thinks she's something special?"

"Ah, she's all right. She thinks she's my mother. We had some fun pulling pranks on passengers on the ship over, but sometimes she's a pain."

But she wouldn't be a pain for long. Though a little thing heightwise, she was developing into a full figured little woman, drawing longer looks from the growing boys in the neighborhood, including George.

On a particularly hot summer day, she saw George hurrying along the sidewalk by her house while she sat on her front steps, bored, and wondering what she could do with herself. She had finished her household chores, her dance lesson was cancelled because the teacher was sick and her mother told her to go out and play. Her girlfriend Despina was away with her family at the large public beach in the nearby coastal city of Revere, and her best friend, Tami, was visiting relatives in Boston.

"What's the hurry, George? You look like you're chasing the wind."

"I wish I could find one. It's so hot, you could fry an egg on the sidewalk."

"So, what's up?"

"I'm meeting the boys over at the railroad yards. We have fun climbing on top of the trains. If there's a breeze around we'll find it. Besides, there's fruit trains with juicy mellons in them!"

"But how can you get in the trains?"

"They open the cars between deliveries, and air out the cars. We just wait until they're open. Then we sample them. We're doing them a favor."

"Can I come?"

"No!"

"But I can be a lookout. They won't think a girl's doing anything!"

"Well, I suppose . . . . Ok, but you have to be quiet. Otherwise, it'll bring the railroad dicks, you know, detectives on us."

They walked across the street and down through a short tunnel beneath a railroad crossing above them to the Somerville-East Cambridge line. There they saw a big railroad yard covered with tracks and train sections. To the far side were slaughter houses where pigs and cattle were delivered to be slaughtered for market. The squeals of the animals being slaughtered could be heard, and the sickening, suffocating smell of the carcasses were inhaled with difficulty. This was the same head-turning and nose suffocating smell they could detect on some of their neighbors who worked there.

When George couldn't find any of his friends, he told Angelika to stay put, while he climbed up the iron ladder on the side of the train to the top to get a better look around. To escape the wilting heat, Angelika stood in the shadow of the train and watched George.

The top of the train had a two-foot wide wooden walkway along its middle for the train workers to walk from train to train. George put his hand up to shade his eyes and looked around for signs of his friends. When he didn't see them, he decided to have some fun with Angelika. He yelled down "Watch this!" and proceeded to run along the top of the train and leaped across to the next one, staggering when he landed, but keeping his feet.

Angelika, on seeing this, yelled:

"George! Don't! Are you crazy! What if you fall?"

"It's only fifteen feet!" He yelled back. Then he turned around and took another run back to where he came from and leapt across. This time he stumbled, staggered forward and fell off to the side, yelling:

"Angelika! Oh h h h, I'm fall-l-ling!"

"Oh, my goodness! Oh, my, . . . Oh, no! No-O! screamed Angelica, as she ran around the car to the other side. Panicky and out of breath, she raced around, almost tripping over a rail, straightened herself up and saw George, hanging onto the ladder, laughing his head off!

She was furious!

"George Dilboy! You are an idiot! You're a show off! One of these days you are going to kill yourself! See if I care!" Then she abruptly turned away and strode back toward home!

"Angelika! Wait a minute! I was only fooling! Hold up!"

"NO! I don't like your joking! It's dangerous!"

"But you'll miss the surprise. Wait up and I'll show you. You've come this far. Look. It's right here."

With that, George, hurriedly climbed down the ladder and added:

"Just a minute. Lighten up, will you? I didn't mean to scare you, I was just having some fun. Here, look at this."

"Look at what?"

"In here."

"George pointed inside an open door, jumped up and twisted himself inside, and rolled a huge watermellon to the door.

"Look at this!"

"What are we going to do with a watermellon?"

"Eat it, said George. Here, watch this."

With that, he reached into his back pocket and pulled out a jackknife. Then he plunged it into the watermellon and cut it in half. Then in quarters. From that, he sliced a piece off and handed it to Angelika.

"Here, take a bite. What could be better on a hot day, I ask you? It'll quench your thirst."

"But it's not ours."

"If they abandoned it, it's ours. If they didn't, we're doing them a favor testing it, to make sure the rest are ok. So we're helping them. Eat up."

They spent the next few minutes quietly eating additional slices of the juicy red fruit, that watered their mouths with it's rich, sweet, delicious taste. But after a while, when Angelika had her fill, she complained:

"But now my hands are all sticky and gooey!"

"That's ok. We'll just go to the rail yard water pump over by the water tower down the tracks some and wash our hands. But make sure you don't touch your clothes, because you'll get them sticky too."

As they were washing their hands at the water pump, a loud voice hollered out at them from far down the tracks:

"Hey you two! Get outta there!"

"Go on, scram! You damn kids! Wasting our water! Get going, before I run you in!"

"It's a train dick! Run!" said an alarmed George.

With that, they both bolted and broke into a headlong dash across the tracks away from the chasing detective, who was waving a stick at them and cursing away. They didn't stop running for the near quarter mile it took to scramble out of the railroad yard and on the other side of the tracks. They stopped under a tree on Somerville Ave, whilst a crowd of people were hurriedly walking along in each direction. George and Angelika were huffing and puffing heavily, and stopped to catch their breath. Neither talked until their breathing slowed down. And when they saw that no one followed them, they breathed easier. Then George broke into an exhilarated smile and started to laugh, now that they were safe.

George burst out: "Wasn't that fun?"

"For you, maybe. But I don't want to be arrested! You've got a dangerous sense of humor, George Dilboy! And I don't even know why I even care!"

"Oh, Angelika, ease up. It was no big deal. It's as big or as small as you want to make it. You better go home and wash the rest of your hands, before you mess up your clothes. Let's cross over the street."

When he left Angelika, George turned the corner onto Linwood St. and ran into Woz, Jimmy, Alex and Nicky. George hailed them:

"Hey, you guys, where were you?"

"What do you mean," said Alex, where were YOU? We found an open watermellon car and brought the watermellon over here to eat. What happened to you?"

"I came in the other end with Angelika. She was my reluctant lookout. I found an open car, too, cut open a watermellon with my jacknife, and we ate it there. But along came a dick and we ran for it. We must have just missed you."

"Well, it serves you right, almost getting caught, bringing a girl along. You getting sweet on her, George?"

"Naw. I told you. She was my look out."

"Sure, George, sure, said Nicky.

"She's growing out, you know. Not up, just out. And in the right places, too, in case you hadn't noticed," teased Jimmy.

"Well, she's going on fourteen and her folks won't let her go out yet, so you hound dogs will have to wait," riposted George. "I'm looking for something more mature, anyway."

CHAPTER NINE

SWIMMING THE CHARLES RIVER

When the boys wanted to swim to seek relief from the hot summer days, they would walk to the nearby Somerville Beach to dive off the piers on the Mystic River. This was the closest water, but the river at this point wasn't particularly deep. To go to deeper water, they would sometimes go in the opposite direction and walk a greater distance, but still less that a mile, to the Charles River Basin. There they were more likely to meet their fellow Mediterranean compatriots, the Italians from Boston's North End. There, the water went down to about a twelve foot depth, generally, there were fewer people diving in the area, and they could dive off a steeper ledge along the road.

In the winter, boys and girls would walk over to the Prospect Hill Tower and slide down the hills on ripped up cardboard boxes, curved wooden barel slats or barrel covers. From that vantage point, they could also see the nighttime lights from Cambridge and Boston, especially around the Christmas Holiday Season. In the summer, many a romantic evening was spent picnicking there, or just lying on the grass, admiring the blue sky and the moving white clouds. Evenings could be spent dreaming, while staring up at the glittering, star filled sky. Sometimes George and Angelika would walk up to Prospect Hill after Sunday church services, to sit and admire the countryside and wonder about their futures. Their in and out comings and goings over the years grew into a relationship of deepening interest and desires, as they both developed toward adulthood. It was now 1912 and George was sixteen and Angelika fourteen. Family and religious strictures kept them at arms length.

One sultry, early summer evening, the sting of the hot sun had died down, and a refreshing breeze was coming in from the Charles River. George, ever restless, decided to take a walk to the river to look at the sail boats and to catch more breezes coming across adjacent Boston Harbor and the Atlantic Ocean. The Charles River reminded him of the river estuary running from Alatsata to the Aegean Sea. As he walked along Poplar Street, Angelika was skipping rope with a couple of younger girls. Spotting George on the far sidewalk, she hollered:

"George! Where you hurrying off to?"

"To the river, the Charles. I'm going to watch the sailboats and catch the sea breezes!"

"Want some company?"

"If you like. It's a good walk; you up for it?"

"Yoanna, Katina; I got to go!"

"Well, Mr. George Dilboy, I can stroll along as fast as you. I may have a shorter stride, but I walk faster than you."

"Don't strain yourself, Angelica. I'm just bored and I felt like going to sit on the grass by the river. I've got to think."

"Think? Think about what? You've already got two jobs and you're going to school nights to study English, how can you be bored?"

"You don't understand, Angelika. You're only fourteen."

"Maybe so, but I'll be fifteen before you reach seventeen."

"I wouldn't be too sure about that."

"What do you mean?

"Easy. I just add a year to my age, by changing my birthdate to 1895. Then, since it's 1912, I'm seventeen. Simple as that."

"But why would you want to do that?"

"Didn't you hear about the upcoming war in the Balkans? It's in the news. Greece and others will be fighting the Turks. I want to go back."

"To fight or visit your folks?"

"Both."

"But what if the Authorities question you?"

"What's to question? They're so busy at the departure port, when they see an official document listing 1895, they won't question it. Besides their real concern is immigrants coming into America, not leaving it."

"But you're still taking a chance."

"A chance about what? What are they going to do, turn me around? So what? In a matter of months, I would try again anyway, when I would be really seventeen. So I'll just be getting an early start. Besides, if you don't take chances in life, you'll never get anywhere. Where would you be now, if your family didn't chance sailing half way around the world?"

"You had better think about this, George."

"I am. Isn't that what I'm doing talking to you?"

"Well, have you talked to your father, or your Uncle Kostas?"

"They aren't the ones going back to Greece! I am! The one I have to convince is myself. It's my life, you know."

"You better make sure you visit your mother, Evangelos and Zenovios. You haven't seen them in four years. Though your mother has moved to Chios, is she still afraid that she won't pass the immigration medical test? I thought she got over her sickness?"

"She did, but Zenovios is still only seven years old and Evangelos is now fifteen and is sweet on some girl."

"But wasn't Stamatia only eight when she came."

"Yes, but she was a mature eight. Besides, she wanted to come with Marianthe."

Because of their spirited discussion, they walked the short mile quickly and reached the banks of the Charles River sooner than expected.

"Two shorten the trip," said George."

"Well, how long will there be two? After all, you're thinking of going back."

"I've got my reasons."

"What reasons? Did you come all the way to America only to go back? Your life is here, now. Your future is here with your family. The rest of your family will come in time. Who needs all that fighting over there?"

"That's just it, Angelika. Things are happening in the world, not just here. My mother writes that Serbia and some other Balkan countries are talking war against the Turks, and Greece may be asked to join them. We could get our Alatsata land back. You're from Smyrna, Angelika. Don't you want to get your home back?"

"But I'm here, not there! I was born there. I don't have to die there, too!"

"Oh, Angelika, don't you have any sense of history? Aren't you proud of what Greece and the Greek people have done for the world? Don't you want to see justice done? We were in Asia Minor for hundreds of years. We have as much right to be there as they do! Are we trying to kick the Turks off the parts of Greece they live in? Why can't we live together in peace?"

"George, if you nurse old grudges, or try to right all the wrongs in Greek history, you'll never get on with your life."

"Yes, but to what kind of life? If a wrong is committed and you don't correct it, then you have committed a second wrong. If I were only thinking of myself, I'd never go back. I've had to look at the pain in my fathers eyes as he was forced out of the land of his birth, and had to uproot and split his family to survive. My mother hangs on to a lost dream that she will get her home back. I watched her fret and wring her hands wondering if my father would come back from his patrols alive. I can't forget him taking off in the night protecting us from nightraiders who were killing, robbing and destroying our property just because we are Christians or Greeks. Why couldn't they leave us alone? Am I supposed to forget, to make believe it never happened?"

"No, George; forgive. They will get their reward in the life hereafter, on Judgment Day, when we all have to account for our earthly conduct."

"Yes, I believe that they will get their punishment in heaven, but I want justice on earth, too. Even the old testament calls for an eye for an eye."

"And so it does. But the Bible also states: 'Revenge is mine, sayeth the Lord.' If we literally took an eye for an eye, everyone would be blind."

"'Justice is blind.' Isn't that what this country's Lady of Justice says?"

"Oh, George. You're just twisting meanings. That refers to even handed justice. We're just going to disagree, that's all. And I suppose you're going to do what you want to do in the end, anyway."

"I will. You got that right. But we can still meet half way."

"What do you mean? Half way where?"

"See the Boston side of the river on the opposite shore?"

"Yes."

"You take the bridge across and I'll swim across. Here, take my clothes and shoes."

As he jumped up spontaneously, pulled his jersey over his head and threw off his socks and shoes, he continued: "If I can swim in the sea in Alatsata, I can swin in a river here."

"George, are you crazy? That's farther than you think it is! It's dark now and they'll never see you in the water. A sailboat or rowboat might run over you!"

"It's nighttime. There are no boats. Get going! I'll meet you over there. I may even beat you over there."

George then dove head first into the dark night waters, twisted around in the water to face the shore, smiled and waved at Angelika, then spun around again and continued swimming across the river.

"George! This is stupid! What are you trying to prove! This doesn't make any sense!" Angelika's protests tailed off as George disappeared into the dark night, with the light from the street lamps glistening off the water like sparkling diamonds.

Exasperated, Angelika, turned abruptly and walked with angry purpose toward the bridge. As she hurried along she kept looking back and followed George's progress across the river, muttering to herself. However, as he swan further from the shore and what little lighting there was, he faded into the night. Angelika quickened her steps, but got more frustrated as she occasionally had to stop to pick up a dropped shoe or his knickers. After about half an hour, she had crossed over the river by land and headed toward the shoreline where he had pointed.

To make it more galling, George was sitting on the shoreline waiting and smugly smiling at her.

"What kept you?"

"Oh, you! Look at you! You're dripping wet!"

"Of course. I just finished a swim; what would you expect."

"And I'm sunk! I'm going to catch it, for sure! I'm supposed to be home before dark!"

"Aw, just tell them you helped someone out of the Charles River. Give me my clothes. See that, I just made you a hero. Come on; let's head back."

"Your impossible! I don't know why I get so mad."

"I like it when you get mad. It makes you taller."

"What are you going to tell your father? He won't want you to go off to fight in a war?"

"I'll tell him that I want to see my mother. I'm paying my own way, from four years work savings. Maybe I can convince my mother to brave the hazzards of ocean travel and bring all three back with me. How can my father disagree with that?"

"But what about the war?"

"Oh, we'll come back, after the war. With all those Balkan countries fighting the Turks, it shouldn't take long. This is my big chance to fight for Greece; I don't want to miss it."

"You've got it all figured out, haven't you! But what if you get shot or killed?"

"Hey, if it's my time, there's nothing I can do about it. I'm not going to run away from life."

"That's exactly what you'll be doing, because you'll be facing death."

"Well, it's my life, isn't it?

"All right. If you don't care about your own life; then I don't! And I don't want to talk about it anymore."

Angelika pouted and looked as if she was about to cry, but she kept control, with some difficulty. They continued their walk home, with Angelika giving George the silent treatment, and George periodically looking and smiling at her. He thought she was cute when she got mad. When they reached Angelika's house, she hurried in without saying goodnight and slammed the door.

Later in the week, George felt guilty when he heard that Angelika's parents grounded her from her dancing lessons for a week and she was told to stay away from that rascal, George Dilboy!

CHAPTER TEN

THE BALKAN WARS OF 1912-1913

"But if you go back, you face being forced into the Turkish Army!" argued Antonios.

"I want to fight the Turks, not join them. If they try that, they'll soon know their mistake!"

"I had a rifle in my hand when I was younger than you. I know the feeling. But I suppose you'll end up going anyway, since you will turn seventeen next February and can go off on your own. And I'd rather you go back in good summer weather than chance winter storms at sea. It's your life, your money and your decision."

"Thanks, Dad. I'll get to see how Mom, Evangelos and Zenovios are doing and be better able to judge how the situation is there. With a war coming, she may want to consider coming to America. We may never get our lands back in Alatsata. She's moved to Chios; she can move here."

"The messages from home we are getting back at the club say that a Balkan League is now being formed to fight the Turks," said Antonios. "The internal revolt of the young Turks four years ago has split their government and weakened the Ottoman Empire. Greece has been asked by Serbia, Montenegro and Bulgaria to form this Balkan League. They have been talking about it since Austria-Hungary forcibly annexed the Turkish provinces of Bosnia-Herzegovina in '08. The Ottomans are vulnerable; it's the time to strike! I just wish I were young enough to go back and fight!"

"What was that old Greek saying you told me, dad? Come back *with* your shield or *on* it. I will do just that!"

One last long walk with Angelika to new the Somerville Boat Club along the Mystic River the day before he departed provoked heated exchanges between George and her. Finally, Angelika resigned herself to George's determination and exclaimed: "Oh, I suppose I should make peace with the inevitable. You are going to do what you want to do, no matter what I say," sighed Angelika.

That night a raucous bon voyage party was held at the Sons of Ionia Club, where friends and family toasted their farewells to a returning patriot. Hugs, handshakes and slaps on the back were in order all through the festive evening.

THE VENETIAN

The following morning Uncle Kostas accompanied George and they took the trolley into Boston. There they made their way across town to the pier where the transatlantic steamship was waiting. Over the following weeks the Italian two funneled steamship, *Venetian*, would dock at New York City, where it would pick up most of its passengers. Then it would sail on to Lisbon, Portugal, then to Marseille, the major port in southeastern France, Taranto, Italy, it's home base, and then on across the Ionian Sea to the Greek port of Patras. Being four years older, he noticed more, was not as bored in the open sea, as he contemplated seeing his mother and siblings in Chios, and the excitement of a possible war. Besides, he wanted to keep a low profile, so that his "enhanced" travel documents showing his age as seventeen, wouldn't be questioned.

Landing at Patras, he thumbed a ride on a donkey-pulled cart into the center of town. With the enthusiasm of youth, he pumped the elderly driver for information on the Greek status with the Balkan League and rumors of war with the Turks.

"It's more than rumors, son," replied the old man, who said his name was "Theo." He shook his head from side to side, as he said: "They are already secretly recruiting volunteers for the coming battle. God help us all." George felt his blood pressure rise as he thought of the exciting coming battles. This contrasted sharply with the dread reaction of old man Theo.

"If the Turks would just let us be, all would be well," he lamented.

"Where can I sign up?" Asked George.

"Be careful, young man. The Turks have resurrected their old military order and are forcing Greek boys aged eighteen to men of forty five into their Army."

"But I'm not yet age eighteen!"

"That doesn't matter to them! Whatever it is, you are close enough. Since when did the Turks pay attention to Greek law, or to their own, for that matter."

"They won't take me into their Army; I can tell you that!" snarled George.

"Be on your guard then, young man, or it's the hell of a Turkish jail for you. Or worse."

They parted somewhere along the road to Athens, where the old man turned off to his local village of Aiyion, having sold his vegetables on this market day. George walked along the road for a couple of hours, then left the dusty road to seek shelter from the hot sun in the shade under an olive tree. The sun had drained the energy from him and the sweat was stinging his eyes. After a while, reflexively wiping the sweat from his face, he cooled off and faced toward whatever direction the wind was blowing, even though it was a warm wind. After about half an hour, and while resting and cooling off as much as he was going to, he noticed a wagon being pulled along by a mule headed in his direction. It was rounding the bend in the road about half a mile away. Picking up his suitcase, he walked up to the road again, hoping he could hitch a ride.

The empty wagon was being driven by a middle-aged man. George thought that he would hail him down, ask him some questions and at least get some information from him, if not a ride. The driver was smoking a pipe and returned George's wave as he reined up the mule. He greeted George heartily:

"Howdy there, young fella; where you bound?"

"Athens, if I can get a ride," answered George.

"Well now, I'm headed in that direction. I can get ya part way there. I'm going home to Korinthos. I've got plenty of room and wouldn't mind the company. So hop on up."

He said his name was Philo. He was full of good cheer as he had delivered and sold his load of local olives, raisins and grapes, he told George. As they clattered along the long dusty road, under the heat of the glaring sun, they followed the jutted coastline of the Gulf of Korinthos. It is a very beautiful narrow fiord with chains of mountains on either side, through the gaps of which you can see far. As a continuation of the Gulf of Patras, it nearly cut Greece in half, West to East. George told him he was returning from America to see his mother in Chios. He was crossing Greece to visit his ancestral home in Karistos, before sailing on across the Aegean.

"Well then, if you are interested in ancestry, you might like to know that my home town of Korinthos is the same town as ancient Corinth mentioned in the Bible. They just spell it differently today."

George mentioned that he was interested in current events, also. After George determined the man's loyalties, and that he could be trusted, George told him of his interest in enlisting in the Greek Army. He was eager to join the fight against the Turks to continue his father's grim efforts that he witnessed growing up in Alatsata, he told Philo.

"My mother and father wouldn't let me fight then, saying I was too young. But that was then; this is now. I want to do my part."

Philo looked hard at George, not saying anything. He then took out a pencil and wrote on a torn piece of paper an address in Athens where George could go to make contact with elements of the Greek Army being formed. George nodded his thanks and stuffed the paper into a pocket, unable to contain a smile. His timing was lucky, he thought to himself; he was going to be there at the beginning.

In Korinthos, George said he wanted to use the rest of daylight to get to Athens. Philo recommended an inexpensive but nice place to stay the night in Athens. He could take George to a omnibus depot, where he could take a canvas covered omnibus that only made two stops before reaching Athens. George jumped down from the wagon and waved his gratitude to Philo. George then walked up to the ticket office and bought a omnibus ticket to Athens. It would leave in half an hour. While waiting, he bought a lemon to suck on and tide him over until getting to Athens. At the same time, he looked out and watched the boats coming in and out of the harbor. This Gulf of Korinthos was long and busy. It was the place where the ancient city of Corinth was resurrected from centuries of neglect and abuse after being conquered by Julius Caesar's Roman Legions and later Turkic rule. Besides, it was the place where the biblical preachings of St. Paul took place, as recorded in the Christian Bible.

George was one of the first passengers to board the omnibus for Athens. Like the other transports he saw on the roads, it sounded and looked as if it was being run into the ground. And true enough, the two stops were made, as Philo said. But what he didn't say was how long the stops would be. At Megara, the omnibus driver had to eat and feed the horses pulling the rickety, old, wheeled transport. And he didn't hurry. At the second stop, Elevsis, the slow omnibus driver rushed into the men's outhouse to seek relief for his bursting bladder. It's amazing what motivation can do, thought George.

With these delays, George wondered why it was, that when you are in a hurry, the rest of the world isn't. Eventually, the bus driver came out of the outhouse looking relieved and they were off again. For all its sputtering and coughing, the leather faced driver seemed to get the horses to respond to his whipped lashings of the reins and his gutteral urgings up hills and around curves, overcoming the hesitant horses.

At last, Athens!

But unfortunately, it was dark by then, and George did not get a chance to see much of the capital city. Now, he only wanted to put up for the night and rest his weary bones. It was amazing to George that just sitting in vehicles that did almost all the work in traveling could be so tiring to the traveler. The mental and emotional effort in traveling seems to create, in time, a desire to stop and rest. It must be our need for balance, George mused. Whatever, he just wanted to bite into something solid to eat and then sleep. He would sort out his racing thoughts in the morning. He checked in to an older hotel and was able to get something to eat before the kitchen closed for the evening. He went to bed with his feelings all jumbled up. But his exhaustion overwhelmed him and he fell into a deep sleep.

The following morning George awoke refreshed. He bounced out of bed and stretched, while spontaneously gasping:

"Aah, there's nothing like a good night's sleep to refresh the body."

He stretched out his arms further and stood up on his toes. Spotting a tall porcelain container of water standing on a table, he poured it into a bowl and splashed water on his face and washed up. Quickly, he dressed and went downstairs to breakfast. He was famished and eagerly ate a full breakfast. Then, eating his fill and sating his hunger, his energy surged back with blazing fury. Where to go and what to do? He asked himself. While he was unconscious in heavy sleep, his subconscious must have been working overnight because his confusion was gone and his thoughts were now clear. He so wanted to see his mother and family. The war could wait.

George checked out of his hotel and got directions to Karistos, a city on a long island off the eastern coast of mainland Greece. Growing up, he was constantly reminded by his father that it was their ancestral home where his forbears had crossed the Aegean Sea and sailed the one hundred miles to Alatsata. He was curious to see his family origins, though his eagerness to see his remaindered family would not allow much time to sightsee. Last night while tired and hungry, he felt torn in many directions, but today he knew his priorities. Family first.

On the run, he bought his ticket and boarded another time and travel worn omnibus, whose wobbly wheels made it look like it was ready for the junkyard. He looked up and stared in wonder at the famous Acropolis, the Greek word for "High City," and whose Parthenon Temple ruins stood majestically on a high plateau overlooking Athens, like a sentinel protecting its people from its enemies. Heading northeast of the city, the omnibus made its first stop at the ancient city of Marathon, where the first Olympics were held to commemorate a Greek battle victory where the messenger ran twenty six miles to Athens to deliver the victorious news and died from the effort.

As if to tax his patience, the omnibus made a number of other local stops to drop off and pick up passengers and mail bags. This increased his anxiety and George found himself trying to push the groaning transport along. When he wasn't with other people, George would sometimes talk to himself and ask questions. Thus, he wondered why older people, who had less time to live, seemed more at ease than he was, who presumably had a longer lifetime ahead of him. Maybe he would figure that out as he got older.

What he did know is that if the wind was blowing past the omnibus the wrong way, he got unwelcome dust in the face. And it was too hot to close the window by dropping the canvas dropcloth down from the rickety roof. That turned out not to matter, because it suddenly got dark, a cloud burst, and thunder and lightning struck, launching a heavy downpour of rain, and the dropcloth when pulled down was ripped and flapped, failing to fully block the rain. After trying futilely to tie the loose, flapping canvas to a window post, George's let go and watched his dusty clothes gradually turn heavy with dirt and mud. All he could do was lean in toward the inside, crowding his seatmate, as the bus was full and all seats were taken. The rain struck the roof of the bus with a strong pattering sound that was swept away with gusts of wind. Then, just as suddenly, the rain stopped. The sun also returned. At least it broke my boredom, thought George. It was a strange feeling swinging from anxiety to boredom. Maybe it had something to do with the whimsicality of youth.

The omnibus reached a crossing point where it was ferried across to the elongated Island of Evvoia, where the omnibus turned south to Karistos. There George got off the transport, and wandered around until he found the transit office to buy a ticket for the boat that would carry him across and over the hundred miles of the Aegean Sea to Chios and his family. Then he found a food stand and bought himself some lunch. He had a few hours to await departure and wanted to eat on level land. He had heard that some of these crossings could be rough and he wanted his food to be well digested by the time he boarded the boat. Though he had not yet gotten sea sick, there was no sense in taking a chance. He wanted to look his best for his waiting family. That is, if they were waiting. All he could do was give them his scheduled departure date from Boston, because all arrival dates were estimates subject to the perils of the sea, oceans, weather and other travel risks. Their guess as to when he would arrive was as good as his guess. He could send a telegram, but it was expensive and George thought it was to be used only in an emergency. On Chios, they knew the daily schedule, but not the day he would arrive. So he would surprise them, that's all. To his delight, the crossing was uneventfull and went relatively smoothly.

CHIOS

They were there!

"YO! Evangelos! Evangelos!

Shouted George. He was waving his hands excitedly and they were jumping up and down! While the boat was docking, George was unable to wait and yelled:

"How did you know I would be on this boat?"

"We didn't. You are a week later than we thought you would be. The ferry comes once a day, so one of us would come down each day."

Looking at his little sister, he yelled: "Wow! Zenovios! You're grown so much! Four years and you've shot up so!"

Zenovios looked shy and self-conscious. She was now seven years old and clearly didn't seem to remember George. But that's ok, thought George; she was only three when they left and they would make up for lost time. The other passengers, seeing George's excitement, motioned him to the front of the off ramp. George leapt on to the ramp and ran toward them. He dropped his suitcase and hugged his fifteen year old brother who had run up and grabbed his shoulders and they clinched in a bear hug and some hearty back slaps. George pushed him roughly back and messed up his bushy hair. He protested:

"Ah! Leave me be!"

"Oh, some day you'll be bald. Then you'll have nothing to worry about. Now let me see my little sister. Zenovios, come to your older brother!"

Zenovios was hesitant and slowly came forward. George lifted her, hugged her warmly and kissed her cheek. Then he spun her around and asked:

"How's my little sister! Have you been taking care of Evangelos for me? Sure you have! And your mother, too, I'll bet!"

Zenovios nodded her head yes, shyly.

"All right everybody. Let's go home and see our mother!"

With that, they all walked to their waiting cart and mule to drive back to George's new home. The drive to Yiasemi's home was less than five miles and over a sandy white dusty, dirt road. George had only visited Chios half a dozen times growing up across the water and the short distance from Alatsata. The road was strewn with white loose rocks on the side, near low lying trees that were swept back by the winds breezing in from the Aegean Sea. Tall thin poles strung along telegraph and telephone lines. Turning off the main island road he could see his mother waiting outside the front door with her hand covering her eyes to shade them from the sun. She was outside a two story white stone house with faded old gray storm shutters framing the front door and windows. The second floor jutted out over the first, held up by diagonal support posts. She looked thinner than he remembered her.

As the cart pulled up to the front door, George jumped down and ran to his mother, thrilled into delightful whooping. She opened her arms and George hugged her tightly as she mumbled:

"Georgie! My Georgie! You made it!"

"Yes! Yes! I made it fine."

"And how's your father. He writes, but never enough for me. I wonder how he is."

"He's fine. He really is. He's having trouble with the English, but he's getting along. He sends us to school to learn the English, but he won't go. He says he'll learn from us. You know Dad, he's stubborn."

"Just like his son, Georgie."

"Oh, Mom. I'm like you too. Don't give Dad all the credit."

"Come in. Have something to eat. We have much to talk about. Evangelos, bring in George's suitcase. Now tell me, George, how goes the boys and girls?"

"They are all doing swell. Everyone has a job as you know and Marianthe has a boyfriend named John. A fine Greek boy."

George and his mother talked late into the evening. George thought that his mother had aged in the intervening four years. Her mouth and eyes had radiating lines that he hadn't noticed before. But her weight loss may have caused that, as well as normal aging. Nevertheless, she sounded good and she claimed that she was feeling good and that her health had improved after she moved from Alatsata. The Turks had forced them out and taken their lands. They let them continue their business work until they got the hang of it, then took that away too. They were promised payment, but nothing has been received yet and the Turkish government is still considering their claims for compensation.

"Meanwhile, we have had to start over here, George. It's not so bad. At least they are leaving us alone here in Chios. It could be worse. If it does, we can always join relatives in Athens or Crete."

"Or America," said George.

"What do you hear about the Balkan League arming to fight the Turks? Asked George."

"Oh George, I try not to pay too much attention to that military stuff. Rumors are everywhere."

"Well, what are the rumors saying?"

"I just hear bits and pieces. I don't understand it all. They say the Russians want access to the Mediterranean Sea, but the Turks control the Dardenelles and won't let them through, except for much money. So the Russians have been encouraging their fellow Slavs, the Serbs, to form a League of Balkan Countries, including Greece, to rebel against the Turks. Then, even if the Turks continue to block the Dardenelles, the Russians will have access to the rich trading ports in the Mediterranean Sea through a Greater Serbia that reaches to the Adriatic Sea, with Albania as part of Greater Serbia."

"I have an address of a recruiting station in Athens for the Greek Army."

"But George, it doesn't have to be your fight. You are American, now."

"Yes, but I am a Greek-American. And I will always be Greek!"

"You're so young, George. You're got your whole life ahead of you. You should get married, have children and have a good life. You are in a land of freedom now. Why risk your future?"

"I have to do what I got to do, Mom. Dad and you have lost your whole life's work. I have to look at Dad struggling to keep a split family going when his best years are behind him. Everything he earned and worked for over his prime years has been wrongly taken away from him. Where's the justice? I've argued this out already and I want justice. Why was it all right for Dad to fight, but not me?"

"Please George, I don't want to argue with you. You're my son. I love you and want only the best for you. You have to live with yourself. It's your life to live. I will stand behind you as I did your father. I can only pray that God will protect you."

Then she dropped her head into her hands and sobbed. George went to her and hugged her tightly:

"It's going to be all right, Mom. With God on our side we have nothing to fear. Come on now, give me a smile. I didn't come all the way out here to see you cry. All will be well. As you said to me as a little boy, you've got to have faith."

"OK George, you win. You could charm the devil out of hell, I swear it! Now go to your bed; you must be exhausted after that long journey."

GOOD MORNING CHIOS

The next morning George was called down to breakfast by his little sister, Zenovois. He had slept almost twelve hours. The strong smell of coffee filling George's nostrils helped George rise from a full and satisfying slumber. He did his usual stretching exercises and faced the rays of a strong sun, streaming through the upstairs bedroom window. Curtains were the rule in America, but not here.

Yiasemi kidded him about sleeping his life away as she fed him more than he wanted to eat. "Mom, I'm full. That's fine, thank you. How about I fix that hanging shutter outside my bedroom? If I wasn't so tired last night, it would have kept me awake."

"Leave that be, George. It'll wait. I want to show you off to the relatives. The neighbors, too, have been asking for you. We're been predicting your arrival for a week."

After meeting with the relatives and curious neighbors all day and attending a welcoming party that evening, George found himself itching to return to Athens and see about joining the Greek Army, now that he saw that his Mom and brother and sister were safe. Ironically, he had to dissuade Evangelos from trying to also join the recruiting Greek Army. He found himself lecturing:

"Someone has to stay with Mom and Zenovios. I know you are only a year younger than I am, but you have protected your mother the past four years and she needs you now more than ever. Your service is to stay and protect the home."

"Why should you get all the excitement," argued Evangelos.

"Your time will come, but not now," said George, with finality.

After two weeks, and rumors of the coming conflict intensifying, George couldn't contain himself any longer. He was tired of hanging around doing boring, domestic chores and staring at the Aegean Sea, wondering what he was missing across the water. He wanted to be in from the beginning. He didn't want to be left behind when they started marching. There's a war to fight!"

He went home and announced that he was leaving for Athens the next day. He could see that his mother was disappointed. She was hoping that George's war ardor would cool off in time, but it had the opposite effect. She just turned her head and controlled herself, seemingly resigned to the inevitable. Evangelos looked on in envy, but he too said nothing. Zenovios seemed the least concerned and asked if he would get a smart looking uniform and if he was going to become a General. At seven years old, George humored her:

"Well, in time maybe, but not right away. They make older guys Generals."

She persisted: "Will you send us a picture of you in your uniform?"

"If they give me one and I have the time, I'll mail it straight to you! How's that, Zenovios?"

"Oh, yeah! That would be grand!"

Early the next day, they all piled into their own farm wagon, urged the draft donkey on and trotted down the dirt road to the landing dock. George carried the conversation with his upbeat pep talk about when the Greeks, the Serbs, the Bulgars and the other allied Balkan countries had given the Turks the defeat they deserved, they could get their lands back and they would all be reunited as a family. Yiasemi listened with a mature tolerance to George's youthful enthusiasm and could only hope that the reality matched his bravado.

They reached the dock early, so there was nothing to do but wait. Of course, the ferry boat was late, to George's consternation. He used his anxiety by pacing back and forth, while engaging in desultory small talk about Evangelos and Zenovios's schooling, the weather, and food prices. But the unspoken worry of his mother was what was George getting himself into. Though George had experience shooting a rifle, his father had seen to that, he had never been in a shooting war. And he had no military training. Oh, well, it was out of her hands now, she thought. All she could do was to make the best of it. God be with us, she silently prayed.

The ferryboat ultimately arrived and they all huddled together as a family, hugging and kissing George. He hugged his mother the longest and then kissed her on both cheeks and was off. She kissed him on both eyelids, as was a Greek custom. As he hurried to the boat, he turned and yelled that he would write when he could. They all hung around until the boat pulled up the anchor and pulled away the ropes holding it to the posts standing up through the dock. They kept waving to each other until the boat became smaller and smaller on the horizon. To George, they became tiny specks that merged with the dock and then disappeared. He then turned around and faced the endless Sea with the blinding sun glistening off the deep blue water beckoning him to his future.

Back in Athens he went right to the address he had been given. He thought it would be a secret place, but it wasn't. It was right in the open with a large sign announcing it as an Army Recruiting Office. Officers in uniform were going in and out of the building greeting each other. He entered the two story white stone building and was asked to produce some form of identification. When he produced his passport, the uniformed officer examined it. Then he asked George why, if he was living in America, he wanted to join the Greek Army.

"I was born a Greek, in Alatsata, Asia Minor. The Turks took our property. They threw us off our land. If I went back, they would force me into their Army or shoot me. If I have to join any Army, it will be Greek first."

The officer looked at George with a slight smile on his face. He had George fill out an enlistment form and then had him sign it. Then he told George to stand, raise his hand and to swear under oath to follow the lawful orders and to defend the country of Greece. George did so. He then instructed George to come back tomorrow morning, 8 am sharp, sign in and he would be taken by transport with other recruits to a nearby training camp. When George asked if there was a place nearby where he could stay overnight, he was directed to a rooming house two blocks away where he could rent a room for the night.

George thanked the man, and took his leave. As he left, he noticed three other men had lined up behind him. The desk officer was a dark haired swarthy, middle aged, weather-beatened man with a mustache, in a uniform with a two striped patch on his shoulder. George wondered whether that made him a Sargeant. He also wondered that he never questioned his age, or if he even cared. Deciding not to take any chances, George determined that he would grow a mustache to make himself look older.

He walked down the cobblestoned street amid the clutter of traffic and people hurrying by and walked the three blocks to the rooming house. Either he counted different or the Army Sargeant's familiarity with the area made him see three blocks as two, George thought to himself. George checked in, was asked for and paid for his one night's lodging, and was directed to his room. When he asked about a key, the man just shook his head and told him to put the chair against the door knob. George shrugged and went up the creaking stairs to look for his room number. Finding it at the end of a long, dark corridor, he entered his home for the night. It was a sparsely furnished room about twelve feet long and eight feet wide, a big closet. He dropped his battered travel weary suitcase on a small bureau. Aside from a small trash basket and a wobbly chair that he wouldn't sit on, the room was bare. A lone bulb hung from a pealing ceiling. He plopped himself in the bed to test the thin matress. He looked up at a ceiling with paint chips curling down and surrounding the lone bulb, hanging from a taped wire.

"Well," George said to himself, "I can put up with anything if it's temporary." It would do.

But it wouldn't do to remain hungry. So he jumped up and went downstairs, asking the desk manager where he could find a place to eat. It was now early evening and George noticed the orange sun going down against the black, far horizon, telling him that it would be a hot day tomorrow. He intended to get to bed early so that he could get up early and arrive well in time for his first day in the Greek Army. He was anxiously looking forward to finally getting his chance to fight back.

PART II

CHAPTER ELEVEN

A SOLDIER AT LAST

George was one of the first recruits to arrive in the morning. He was told to sign in and report outside, which he did. But when he went outside, there was a horse drawn wagon at the side of the building, but nobody to report to. He saw a scruffy looking soldier, smoking and talking to another man beside the wagon. When he went up to the soldier and asked who he was supposed to report to, the soldier blithely waved him away and told him to stay in front of the building until he was called. This is one hell of a welcome, thought George. But he kept his mouth shut and leaned against the building watching and waiting.

Soon he saw other young and middle aged looking men flowing into the building and doing what he did. Their searching and quizzical looks on coming outside made George feel good, because it affirmed his own feelings. He spoke up and said that he was told to wait there. When he introduced himself, they were no longer strangers. This was repeated with others and soon there was a buzz of friendly and exciting conversations that helped pass the time. George felt like a veteran already. There are advantages to being first, he thought to himself, with some sense of satisfaction.

Finally, an Officer with a clipboard strode out of the Office, stood in front of them up to his full height, short as it was, and called them to attention. When not everyone heard, he indignantly pulled a whistle out of his pocket and blew it into a high piercing shrill whistle:

"Tweeeet!"

That did it! All eyes turned toward his now ruddy face.

"Attention everybody! When I call your name, shout out, line up and board the transport."

With that, the lorry, an open flat bed, roofless wagon, with ropes for sides to hang on to, backed out and clip-clopped to a noisy stop in front of the recruiting building. The Army Officer, irritated, stopped his calling, until the noisy racquet quieted down, to the extent it could. He started the call again, only to be interrupted again by the restless horses rearing up and loudly pulling forward wanting to go, until the straining wagon driver pulled them back to a halt. The Officer glared at the wagon driver, who was valiantly trying to calm the still stirring, six-horse lorry. Some of the recruits thought this was funny and started laughing. Seeing this, the officer, eyes widened, yelled out:

"Attention! Attention! You're in the Army now! Nothing funny here. The only thing I want to hear is my voice and the sound of your feet boarding that wagon!"

As he intoned this command, he was pointing with authority at the temporarily quiescent horse wagon. Since there were more recruits than seats, some had to sit on the edge of the wagon with their legs dangling over its side. It didn't bother Sargeant clipboard, as the men flippantly began to refer to him, none too loudly, because the rougher ride would "toughen you up," said Sargeant Clipboard. As the lorry roared off, one of the recruits yelled:

"Where are we going?"

"To an Army camp, Mr. Field Marshall!" yelled back the sarcastic Sargeant clipboard. And for good measure he added:

"God help this country, with this bunch!"

"Yeah, you too! Sargeant zero!" shouted a recruit, who got bolder with his expletives, as Sargeant Clipboard shrank in the distance. Laughter broke out. On the road out of the city, someone started to sing and most of the rest joined in. Not any professional voices here, thought George. But he enjoyed the camaraderie, anyway. People on the road acknowledged the Army transport as it sped by, waved and shouted "Good Luck!", "Go get them!" and other such entreaties in the spirit of the moment. One of the young recruits wondered out loud:

"Who of us will be the first to become a General?"

"General?" answered another. You mean Field Marshall; didn't you hear Sargeant Clipboard?"

George was loving this! He couldn't wait to get his uniform and rifle. The lorry, full of rambunctious recruits, disappeared north into the mountains and George was enjoying the moment with a light heart. They lumbered through the mountain roads singing as a group, as if they were going to an outing at the ocean. In time, the lorry pulled up to an Army Camp that had no name. It was supposed to be part of their secret build up. But that was a joke because it was common knowledge on the street. The party wouldn't last long. The transport was waved through the guarded front gate. A tall pole in the center of the campgrounds flew the blue and white Greek flag. The shaky, overloaded lorry bounced across a large parade ground where soldiers were practicing drills that had a loud drill instructor, in full uniform, barking orders at some recruits. The recruits had no uniforms or weapons. They looked like civilians. But shooting could be heard, so there was a firing range somewhere off post.

The lorry stopped in front of a long, white stone, single story building. Waiting was an Officer, in full uniform, standing ramrod straight and he didn't look happy. The truck driver pulled the rope from the tailgate and called:

"Everybody out!"

He then casually saluted the Army Officer and said:

"Sir. Reporting with today's recruits from Athens!"

"Take your leave, Sargeant. I'll take over."

"Fall in! Line up in a column of threes! Move it!" growled the Officer. George moved to the front and faced the Officer. The initial confusion was gradually smoothed out, accompanied by loud, sharp taunts:

"I said fall **in**, not fall out, you bungleheads! Straighten up and straighten out those lines. Wipe that smile off your face, soldier! The only joke here is you trying to be a soldier. No talking in the ranks! Save your energy; you are going to need it."

"Now listen up! Because I don't repeat myself. You are in the Army now. Your mother, your girlfriend, your family can't help you here. The only one who can help you now is your fellow soldier. Listen and learn. The life you save may be your own. You will line up single file and enter that door right behind me. You will check in by stating your name. You will then be given directions to pick up your gear. Then you will go directly to your designated barracks and await further orders."

"First line! Right face! Turn right, you idiots! **Your** right, not mine! Forward march! Left face! Forward, march!"

George was in the middle of the first line and followed the line of march into the front door of the receiving building. He stated his name and was told to follow the others into the supply room. There each recruit was handed underwear and socks, towel, soap and marching boots. He was asked if he wore small, or large boots, his only choices. The first recruit stood there dumbfounded and asked hesitantly:

"Where's my uniform?"

"Uniform? You're wearing your uniform! When you become Regular Army or an Officer, you will have **earned** a uniform. You get food, shelter, laundry, arms and pay; and the honor to fight for your country; what more do you want? You should pay **us** for training **you**! Now move on!"

George kept his mouth shut, fearing that they might take a close look at him and reject him because of his age. But no one said anything yet. He followed along and crossed the parade grounds, as moving wagons, marching soldiers and a few ordnance flatbeds kicked up dust and rattled across the grounds. The cavalcade didn't give ground and would have run over George if he didn't jump out of the way. He wobbled into his stone barracks building. He saw a long room with double bunk beds lining each wall. The room was bare, except for a wash pump at each end of the barracks and three light bulbs hanging down from the ceiling. The windows had no shutters. He threw his clothes on his bunk because there was nowhere else to put them. The latrines were outside in wooden outhouses. Right behind him came another recruit who asked:

"Do you want to go up or down?"

"Oh, hi there. I'm George. George Dilboy." They shook hands and a Chris Papps introduced himself. "'*Pappy*' my friends call me," he volunteered. "But I answer to both." Pappy was a huge body, both tall and wide. He wore both a mustache and a beard. His face was pocked marked and fierce, but he sounded friendly enough. He was well over six feet and two hundred pounds. George sensibly suggested that Pappy take the lower bunk because:

"If you ever fell on me, I wouldn't have to worry about the Turks. Be my guest."

With that Pappy playfully lifted George up with one hand to the top bunk and said, "Thanks." Others were introducing themselves to each other in their areas. One recruit asked the Sargeant accompanying them why they didn't have their rifles yet.

"Because you have to march and drill and be instructed in arms-use first. Besides, some of you aren't going to make it. We'll see if you can keep up. Rifles are kept in a locked storage area. Otherwise, arguments happen and we don't want weapons around."

"Everybody out! Out! Out! Line up outside! Move it! Move It! Let's go!" shouted the same Sargeant. When outside, they were told that they were going on a five-mile trek in the mountains and to form a column of two for the march. The surprise announcement was met with grumbles and groans.

"No talking in the ranks! You are going to earn your supper! Left face! Forward, march! Left! Right! Left! Right! Let's go! Move out! The quicker we move out, the quicker you get back! Get in step, soldier!"

"Company, halt! Listen up, you sorry excuse for soldiers! Stay in step with the cadence! Start up with your right foot and stay up with the group. If you fall out of step, get yourself back in. If we keep having to stop, I'll make you trot and run to make up for lost time and you'll make more work for yourself! Now let's try it again! Forward! March!"

"That's better! That's better! Move out!"

They marched, more or less, in sync, out of the campgrounds. When they were ordered into a trot or run, it didn't count toward the announced five miles, so they ended up almost doubling their planned distance march. They returned to base exhausted. Some would have to help others to the dining room. Then they collapsed into their bunks. How their day had changed! Pappy looked dead on his feet, and George not only had to help Pappy into his lower bunk, but also had to take off his boots. George didn't want to rest too long, because he was afraid he would nod off and miss supper. After a while, he had to really prod Pappy who didn't want to get up. He asked George to bring him back some food, but the Sargeant overheard him and shouted out for all to hear that:

"No food is allowed in the barracks! Wash up! You have one hour to eat! Lights out at ten o'clock!"

George and Pappy staggered up and splashed cold water on their faces to revive themselves and lurched out to the eating room. They ate their full, too tired to talk much, went back to their barracks and crashed into their bunks craving sleep. The next day, George swore that he was asleep before his head hit the pillow. The loud snoring by some of his soldiers, especially Pappy, didn't matter. He was just too exhausted to care.

The next morning they were blown out of their bunks by a loud blast of a bugle for morning wake up call. This noise was reinforced by a Drill Sargeant with a high decibel voice shouting and cursing everybody to:

"Get up! Get up! Everybody up and at 'em! Let's go! Shake a leg! This is the Army! Move it!" The groans and curses of the soldiers added to the chaos. They were told that each soldier was responsible for getting his bunk mate up and out on time or they would both face discipline. The Sargeant kept heaping abuse at the sluggish soldiers and singled out the slower risers. They washed up and hustled outside to answer the morning roll call. Thereafter, they marched over to the canteen for what passed for a breakfast. For the first week they were put on forced marches, drilled incessantly and ran through obstacle courses. The second week they were given rifles to disassemble and reassemble until they could do it blind folded. Then they were taken to the shooting range to practice their marksmanship. This was where George shined. He was one of the first to win his marksmen's medal and consistently outshot the rest of the company. He owned up to being taught how to shoot by his father since he was seven years old, which was a secret between George and his father, as far as his unknowing mother was concerned. This gave George instant respect among his company and his superior officers. He was quickly made a squad leader, though he probably was the youngest in the company. True to his word, George wrote with this good news to both his mother and father, who looked forward with great interest to his letters.

Back at the barracks, the rifle training brought up the merits of the rifle they were training with. Here it was 1912 and they were practice shooting with an 1897 Gras, single shot rifle, weighing slightly less than ten pounds. This irked the troops because the shooting range instructors were using the more modern 1903 Mannlicher-Schoenauer rifle made in Germany, that held five rounds, and weighed over a pound lighter.

While playing cards in the barracks one night, the talk about rifles made some of the guys curious as to what the other allied countries in the Balkan League were using. They wanted to compare arms. Even of greater interest was what the Turks were using. They made a point of asking a superior officer.

The range instructors, in a question and answer session, told them to stop griping. The Turks were using two rifles both older and less effective than what Greece had. The enemy Turks were fielding an 1874 style Peabody-Martini rifle, a single shot, ten pound weapon. Their latest rifle was almost twenty years old; an 1893 Mauser made in Germany, which held five rounds and weighed ten pounds. As for Greece's allies, Serbia was using ancient 1881 and 1883 Mauser rifles! The Montenegrins were using Russian rifles made in 1891 and the Bulgars were using 1886 and 1895 Mannlicher German rifles.

This had the effect of mollifying the company. They were told that when they had completed their training and mastered the use of their older rifle, they would be given the best rifle in the Greek Army. They had to earn it. George held up well throughout the rigors of the training regimen. They only lost two out of their company. The transferred two were just too clumsy in handling firearms and would have been a danger to their own soldiers and ineffective against an enemy. No-one wanted their life to depend on an incompetent rifleman. They both were moved out of the infantry and given a military support role.

In the next bunk a pipe smoking Athenian named Nikos "Niki" Nikitis, looked long at George, and casually asked him a question that apparently was bothering him:

"Hey, George, how does a Greek get a name like Dilboy?"

"It's Dilvois. But when we emigrated to America our Greek accent was misheard by an Immigration Official and he recorded it as it sounded to him, Dilboy. To help us become American, we kept it that way. Simple as that."

"So now that your're back in Greece, why still Dilboy?"

"Because that's what my passport says. Besides, after we take care of the Turks, I may want to return to America. That make sense to you?"

"If it makes sense to you, it makes sense to me."

CHAPTER TWELVE

SERBIA IS MARCHING!

After only two weeks in camp, George awoke to a special buzz of excitement at morning reveille. Neither Pappy, George nor anyone else knew what was going on, and the company officer wouldn't answer any of their questions. But it was obvious that something unusual was afoot. Too many officers were running around gesturing emphatically. They went through breakfast asking each other what all this meant. Had the Turks attacked? Was the war on? What the hell is happening? Finally, they were herded into an assembly hall and joined a cacophony of loud and excited talk. Shortly thereafter, the Camp Commander strode in briskly with his entourage of officers following behind. A loud piercing voice rendered the air:

"Attention!"

They all all jumped to their feet. The Camp Commander, General Eraklis, a tall, swarthy looking bull necked man, with a mustache, motioned us to sit down. He waited until he had their full attention; an eerie silence permeated the large hall as he finally spoke:

"Soldiers of the Army of Greece. Two days ago our ally, the Montenegrins attacked the Turks and their Albanian mercenaries. Yesterday, the Serbs marched against the Turks in Macedonia. As an ally of Serbia, Montenegro and Bulgaria in the Balkan League, we are now at war. We have no time for further training. Each of your units will be briefed with mobilization orders this afternoon at 01400 hours. Get ready to march. We move out tomorrow! Return to your barracks and await further orders. Dismissed!"

With that brief announcement, the Commander strode out as purposely as he had come in. The buzz of heavy conversations burst out as they moved their way out and back to their barracks. Some of them whooped it up and others seemed stunned at the startling announcement. But everyone was soon animated. It is one thing to deal with rumors, but quite another when faced with a real war. The first thing George wanted to do was to write his parents. However, back at the barracks he was told that no mail would be permitted for reasons of security. Nobody would be permitted to announce the moves of any unit, to unwittingly alert enemies to their positions. His squad was part of Karkis Company, 3rd Battalion, 2nd Division. So George put away his pencil and was told to obtain his rifle and allotted ammunition. He was an infantry soldier, and a squad leader with mobilization orders. As he had dreamed, he was in at the beginning of the Balkan War against the Ottoman Turks!

By the afternoon assembly word had filtered down that the Serbs had already attacked the Turks in Macedonia and routed the surprised Ottomans! The Turks had fallen back to Southern Macedonia. But the Serb Army failed to pursue the defeated Ottomans, preferring instead to occupy the fortifications abandoned by the enemy and regroup before any further advance. This incurred the barely concealed scorn of the Greek Generals. George's company was given the official briefing at the 01400 assembly.

"Soldiers of the Army of Greece. Let me have your attention," barked General Eraklis, the Camp Commander. Remember as I show you this map that eighty percent of Greece is mountains. We had you marching and hiking through the mountains and passes to strengthen your legs. Now hear the latest report from the front. There are two battlefronts, east and west."

A large map was unfurled down the front wall. It was October 8, 1912.

"We are contributing two field armies to the Balkan League's war effort. In the west, the Army of Epirus, led by General Zachary Sapountzakis, will guard the Epirote frontier and when reinforced will commence offensive operations. The Montenegro Army and some Greek irregulars have already engaged the Turks and their Albanian lackies.

We will be part of the Army of Thessaly, in the east. We will assemble in Central Greece at Larissa, the major city of the Province of Thessaly. The primary mission of our ground forces is to capture Thessalonika and drive the Ottomans back over the Turkish Border. We will be under the command of Crown Prince Constantine. You will all now report to your barracks, be issued full combat gear, and immediately mount your transport vehicles. We will go directly to our Army assembly area. God be with you! Dismissed!"

"At last! At last!" shouted George. "Action! Let's move, guys! I've been waiting all my life for this!"

"Ha! Listen to the Alatsatian. You would think he was an old man, instead of a green teenager!" scoffed barrack mate, Gregory Kapos.

"If you add my fathers fighting years to mine, then I am an old man," riposted George.

"Calm down, old man." You sound like you're bucking to become a General!" snapped Chuck Galatis, of their company.

"Maybe I will. Who knows?"

A special early call was made to eat at the canteen before moving out. They were given only half an hour, so they gulped and hustled back to barracks. In front of the barracks, the military transport wagons with hitched horses were already snorting and restless, just like them. They grabbed their gear and they rumbled off in a wagon caravan; they had no time to lose. There was a war waiting. As the noisy wagons clattered off into the barren mountains of the Attica peninsula, the adrenalin was flowing through the bodies of these happy warriors. They exchanged playful comments, peppered with barbs and ribald scoffs as to who would fire the first shot, who would win the first medal, who would capture the first prisoner, all in good natured mock-serious banter. But further remarks along this line ended abruptly when someone asked who would be the first to be killed.

An older, regular Army soldier listened on, in martyred silence at these neophyte Army greenhorns. He leaned in toward a fellow soldier and groused:

"I was there in '97 when Greece battled the Turks in Thessaly and the Germans interferred and put down our revolt. These foolish youngsters will find out soon enough what it's really like."

This naïve enthusiasm spent itself out and devolved into an awkward smattering of small talk. After a couple of hours bouncing along on the curving mountain roads, things quieted down, some soldiers lost in their own thoughts, while others were starting to nod off. The convoy of horse pulled wagons bounced their way up, around and down the mountains. They passed through the ancient city of Thebes to the waved hands and well wishes of the town folks. Others just stared at the passing troops. They drove through the Amphissian Plain and through the pass at Thermopyae.

"So this is where Leonidas and three hundred Spartans fought to the death against the invading Persians in 480 B.C.," said George in wonderment to nobody in particular.

"And just how do you know this, Professor Dilboy?" asked Pete Marvoulas sarcastically, but without rancor.

"In school. Besides, my father taught me a lot about Greek history. We may have lived on the Turkish coast in Asia Minor, but we are very interested in what happened on the mainland. But I thought the Pass at Thermopylae would be narrower."

"It was back then," chimed in Panos, but over the years, coastal silting has widened it into a broader plain."

The clattering troop convoy bounded through the fertile plains and rolling mountain ranges of Thessaly to the peninsula port town of Volos. Then they clippidy-clopped inland toward the west, and it was evening by the time they reached the assembly site of the Army of Thessaly in Larissa, and entered a massive Army encampment.

Tents, flatbed wheeled supply transports, wagons, donkeys, carts, lorries, soldiers dotted the hills, valleys and grounds as far as one could see. Organized confusion prevailed. They were ordered out of the wagons and assigned to an open field on a hill and ordered to set up their tents. Having set up their canvas tents, they lined up to join a feeding line for chow. They were to eat their grub and turn in by twenty two hundred hours later that evening, that is, 10 p.m. The military used a twenty-four hour clock. Reveille would be at first light.

The next morning after breakfast, their company was ordered out of the camp to march into the mountains toward the frontier. The Army artillery, ordnance wagons and troop transports would follow after more supplies and animals were brought up and maintenance on broken rolling stock vehicles was completed. Because of the rough roads, something was always breaking down. An infantry had to march to stay in fighting condition. Alternatively, the soldiers would march on foot to give the horses a break, and then board the lorries and flatbed hay wagons to feed the horses, in order to make better time. Scouting squads were sent ahead to reconnoiter. They didn't want to be surprised by an enemy sneak attack.

George volunteered to lead his squad to scout ahead. This angered an older member of his group, John Halachis, a heavy chested, angry man, with a double chin, in his late thirties, with hooded eyes, like they were slits. He resented the taking of unnecessary chances because of an inexperienced recruit's eager search for personal glory, as he saw it. George was aware of his hostility because Halachis didn't hide his grumbling, but George ignored it for the moment. Even at his young age, he had learned to let the first critical wise-crack go by, for the sake of group harmony. They were there to fight the enemy, not each other.

Nevertheless, despite some griping from Halachis and his cohorts, George's offer was accepted by the Company Commander, Captain Safiol, a clean-shaven, tall, thin blonde, with a stern countenance, from the Ionian Island of Corfu. The guys called him the "Viking," because of his light skin, blonde hair and reputed early ancestors. George's squad of four were sent ahead. George was given a pocket paper map, oriented and ordered to canvass to a certain point and to report back. If the enemy were spotted, he was not to engage with them, but to immediately report back.

Only if their lives were in danger, were they to shoot. George called his squad together and relayed their orders. Then he volunteered himself to lead and take the point. He designated the rest to follow along behind him. They were to proceed in single file and to keep each other in sight. They were to avoid any unnecessary talk and to use hand signals, because voices carry with the wind, and especially in narrow gorges. The Greek Army wanted to hide their approach as long as they could. The Serbs were to the northwest of them and the Greek Army was to protect their eastern flank. Right now the Turks were well aware of the position of the Serbs. But the Greeks had no reason to believe that the Turks were aware that the Greek Army was within striking distance.

Actually, the company "Viking" commander didn't expect any Turk incursion this far south, but wanted to send out his patrols to get them some field experience. The visability ahead was excellent because of the clear weather and the sparsity of trees in the area. However, low lying clouds developed and then it started raining. After about an hour out, suddenly, a single shot rang out and George automatically threw himself to the ground and motioned:

"Down! Down!"

Private Marvuoles exclaimed: "What was that? What the hell was that?"

"Shut up and stay down! Stay Down! Snapped George, as he scurried down the trail back toward John Halachis, who was protecting their rear. John was crouched down in a defensive firing position, with his rifle pointed toward some large stones up the side of a hill.

"Over there! Someone's hiding behind those boulders! Watch out!" spat John.

George motioned for Nick Panos, the fourth squad member, to circle around to the left and he himself would go around the right. He then whispered back to Pete Marvoulas and Halachis to cover them. George worked his way steathily in a wide arc around to his right. After moving around to get a better sight angle, sure enough, George saw scrub brush moving beside a boulder and brought up his rifle at the ready! He could now hear as well as see sounds of movement behind the large stone. Creeping up to the front of the boulder, he slowly slid around the side. He then leaped in back ready to fire and stared into the eyes of a goat!

"Damn!" He exploded, half-angry, half-relieved.

"Oh, for heaven's sake, a goat?" said Panos, breathing heavily, having then arrived just after George.

The black Goat looked up with its mouth chewing on some scrub grass. The animal hesitated, then bolted away.

George put his arm through his shoulder strap and hung his rifle on his shoulder and thumbed Panos to head back. Reaching the still crouched Marvuoles and Halachis, he glowered at Halachis:

"Can't you tell the difference between a Turk and a goat, you idiot? Your trigger happy nervousness, may have given us away, numbskull!"

"Marvoulas! Take the point! I'll bring up the rear. And I'll be staring at your back, Halachlis, to make sure you don't screw up again."

"Well, how was I supposed to know? The sun got in my eyes, but I knew I heard something. At least I was alert."

"Let's move on. We've got another mile to go to reach our end point." Said a disgusted George.

As they descended the next hill, a sudden barrage of explosions was heard to the east. Everybody froze and looked up. Artillery shells!

"What the hell?" yelled Panos.

"Looks about five miles away," said George.

"Is it friendly or hostile?" asked Marvoules.

"I can't tell." Said George. "I'm aborting this scouting patrol. If it's the Turks, we should rejoin our company; if it's friendly, I want to know just what in hell is going on."

"Which way" asked Halachis?"

"Let's go east toward the sound of the guns. Our objective is that way, anyway. Panos, rotate into the lead. Keep your pacing; five yards apart. OK, let's move out."

"But why toward the guns? Why not head back?" complained Halachis?

"Because we're scouts and that's our job. Move!"

The puzzling barrage continued intermittently, and just as quickly stopped, as did the rain. But the men pressed on until they ran into another patrol that was also heading toward the guns. But they were also confounded. Staying together, so they wouldn't end up shooting each other, they both headed generally east, in single file, one behind the other. When they finally reached a forward column of the Second Division, George had his squad rejoin their company, while he went looking for the Company Commander.

"You're back, Dilboy. What's to report?" asked Captain Safiol, the Viking.

"Nothing unusual, Sir. We broke silence because one of my men mistook a goat for the enemy and fired a shot. I was within a mile of my destination when I heard the artillery. So I changed direction and here we are. What was that artillery fire all about?"

"That was us. A courier from the Serb First Army asked us to open up an artillery barrage. Their Commander, Crown Prince Alexander, was stopped by the Ottaman Army of the Vadar, under Zekki Pasha. Our barrage was meant to draw away part of the Turk Army. The Turks fear being surrounded. Besides weakening the Turk defense against the Serbs, our barrage and drawing off the Turk troops will give the Serbs time to bring up their Second and Third Armies. The Serbs are also asking the Bulgars to attack from the North and cut off any Turk retreat across Trace. Sorry we surprised you. But there will be a lot of surprises before this war is over. Your report tells me we don't have to worry about our left flank. We have new scouts out, so rejoin the column, Dilboy. Good job."

While the Viking reported, in turn, to General Eraklis, George went back into the line and brought the others in the squad up to date, feeling good about helping avoid an ambush, but not everyone was happy.

"Our own guns? Are we in the Serb Army or are we fighting for Greece? Damn it, we could have been killed! Those idiot Generals tell us to keep quiet, and then they announce to the world that we're coming!" Griped Halachis.

"Shut up, Halachis! You fired the first shot, remember?"

"There's a difference between a bullet and an artillery shell, Sir!"

"Yeah, and either one can kill you." George fired back.

"I'll kill you, you friggin jerk!" Halachis lunged for Dilboy and threw a wild punch that missed. They both grabbed each other and fell to the ground. Before anyone landed a punch, Pappy came over and lifted Halachlis off the ground to his own tall height and growled:

"Halachis, I'm getting tired of you bellyaching. Get back in formation before something happens to you." With that Pappy lowered him to the ground and pushed Halachis away. Halachis left muttering and cursing under his breath.

"Thanks Pappy, but I can fight my own battles," said George, as he brushed himself off.

"Oh, I wasn't protecting *you*; I was protecting him!"

Pappy then winked and walked away with a smile on his face.

There's a reason Halachis has been in the Army fifteen years and hasn't made Sargeant, thought George. He's either been busted down or he was never put in for a promotion. I'll have to watch him. He's trouble.

After two hours, the column stopped and the Supply Sargeant was passing around some yellow peaches. Niki Panos jibed the Sargeant with the quip:

"Hey, Sargeant! Any ouzo served with this? I could use some booze."

"I'll give you some ouzo, wise guy! It's in your canteen; it's called water!"

A chorus of hecklers chimed in:

"Give him hell, Sargeant!"

"Let him boil some wild herbs, like the rest of us, if he wants something different to drink."

"Ha! He doesn't know how to boil water. His girl friend did all the cooking."

"All right, Guys. You're had your fun," riposted Panos.

"Hey, Sargeant. How'd you get so ugly? Your craggy face looks like a crumpled paper bag."

"You must be looking in a mirror, grunt!" retorted Sargeant Sardonis.

They marched on trying to cover as much territory as they could, before it got dark. They eventually bivouacked in the mountains that night off the road. The following days turned into weeks of slogging ahead with monotonous regularity. Rumblings of gunfire could be heard in the far distance. One morning the Greek Army was assembled in various groups and updated on the latest developments on the western Macedonian front, as opposed to the Thrace eastern front being fought by the Bulgars against Ottoman forces. General Eraklis stood like a tall tree before a hastily hung sheet and a rough map was displayed. With a sword he used as a pointer, he showed where the Serb First Army battled the Turkic Army of the Vadar in a two-day clash at Kumanovo. The Serbs broke through the Turkish defenses early last week, he related. Then he said that the Serb Second and Third Armies arrived and joined forces to rout the Turk Defense. The Ottoman Army withdrew toward Skopje, he showed. This was all happening north of their advancing Greek Army.

Three days later, he told us, the Serbs took Skopje and the Turks fell further back south to Stip. But the Serbs again failed to pursue the retreating Turks, preferring to regroup, snarled the acid voice of the General, in obvious disapproval about the Serb failure to follow up again.

The troops were then ordered to grab their gear and to mount their transports to immediately move out. They drove north into the valley of Aliakhmon, then marched along the Aliakhmon River to the northeast toward the Kampania plain and the Axios River, that the Turks called the Varda River. There, they met up with the smaller General Sapountzakis's Greek Army of Epirus. The total troop strength of the Balkan forces approached 500,000 soldiers, outnumbering the Turk and Albanian forces of about 400,000.

Included in this total, the Greek Armies numbered up to 100,000. Crown Prince Constantine's Army of Thessaly included seven infantry divisions, one calvary brigade, and four highlander battalions.

General Eraklis's Second division, including Dilboy's company, stopped for the evening between the two rivers Aliakmon and Axios(Varda). George was sitting against a bent olive tree and resting, when the giant, Pappy and Panos sat down beside him. Halachis also dropped down to rest. George was rolling up a cigarette when he asked a question that was bothering him:

"What's this I hear that the Turks don't take prisoners?" He threw the question out to the group, looking for any information.

"They don't? "Why not?" asked Panos.

"That's right, said Halachis. Back in '97, we captured a Turk and we asked him why we shouldn't just kill him, like his Army did our prisoners. But he begged us not to kill him. He could give us valuable information. When he told us helpful information, we let him live."

"But that doesn't tell us why the Turks don't take prisoners," said George, plaintiffly.

"Just hold your horses, Dilboy. I haven't finished. Their Army Commanders claim they can't afford to feed them. Besides, they say, why should they care for any captured soldier who is trying to kill them. That's war."

"So what is *our* policy?" asked Panos.

"We grill them for information. If they don't co-operate, we let them know that they would be better off escaping, and then we shoot them when they try. I don't know if that's official policy, but I've seen that happen."

"Well, I don't expect to be captured, but if I am, I will shoot my way out or die in the attempt," said George.

"We should all be shooting any day now. I'm itching to get into it," exclaimed Pappy.

"Aren't we all?" said George.

"No. I'm not. I've been there. It's not fun, as you'll find out." Snapped Halachis.

"Tell me, Halachis. Why do you stay in the Army? You have nothing good to say about it."

"Hey, it's a job. And I hold up my end. I'm a proven product. You aren't General Dilboy!" thrust Halachis, in a voice dripping with sarcasm.

"Well then, Halachis, we are going to be expecting great things from you, once hostilities begin. Then you won't be shooting at goats. I can't wait."

With that George stood up, rubbed his eyes with his fingers and stretched his arms out, saying:

"It's that time, Guys. We've got to turn in. Tomorrow awaits."

CHAPTER THIRTEEN

GREEK-TURKS CLASH

The Turkish Eighth Corps, under the Command of Hassan Taxim Pasha, were dug in at defensive positions awaiting the Greek Army of Thessaly at the border of Thessaly and Macedonia. Scouts reported that the Turkish Eighth Corps included three infantry divisions, one separate infantry brigade, and one cavalry regiment.

The Greek offensive began with whistles and commands of "Char-r-r-ge!" riffing the air. George's company jumped to their feet and ran forward. Running ahead with his company in line, George surged ahead across the field with the troops yelling "yo-o! yeah-h! and ch-a-rrge!" They were running toward the town of Elasson. After a long run, and leaping over the barricades, to their surprise, they found the town abandoned. The Turks had withdrawn from the town the night before and they captured it unopposed. George and his fellow soldiers were busy going from house to house where some villagers were waving white flags, saying the Turks were gone and not to shoot them. Some random shots were fired, but nothing organized. George believed the scattered firing was from nervous Greek soldiers whose imaginations made them see enemy ghosts. George thought cynically that Halachis was probably one of them.

They settled down for the night, exhilarated from their first attack with only one casualty from a careless soldier who tripped and broke his arm. They took shelter in an abandoned house and ate their rations, supplemented by local food. Grape leaves and rice never tasted so good. Nearby fig trees were plucked to supplement their food rations. They ate off the land as much as they could, because the Army portions were so meager.

"The Ottoman Commander, had retreated ten miles south of the Aliakhmon River and at the entrance to the Porta Petra Gorge. It's a strong natural defensive position," said George, as he rested against an interior wall of the abandoned and partially damaged house, the victim of a Greek artillery shell. "That's the word being passed down from Command Headquarters."

When Halachis walked in, George jumped up and grabbed his rifle from his hands. Halachis was startled and spouted:

"What the hell are you doing?"

George rubbed the barrel of his gun, felt that it was not hot, smirked, and threw it back at Halachis. He caught it reflexively.

"Don't worry Dilboy," stressing the pronunciation of "*boy*" of Dilboy, "I wasn't firing at ghosts!"

"Hey, Halachis, don't let him get your *goat*!"

"Oh, that's funny, real funny, Panos. You're a scream," said a flippant Halachis.

"Say, Marvoulas, where did you say you were from?" Asked Pappy.

"I didn't, but since you ask, I'm from Missolonghi."

"Where the hell is that?" inquired Panos.

"It's in West Aetolia, on the Ionian Sea, across from Patras and the Gulf of Patras."

"Isn't that where they poisoned Lord Byron, a hundred years ago?" smirked Halachis.

"Lord Byron caught an infectious disease and died of the fever. Why would we poison him? He was helping us fight for our independence. And it was in 1824, you dipshit; but you were close."

"Ok, guys, out with the candles. Time to turn in. The only light we're allowed is the moon or we'll have the night guards hassling us," remarked George, as he turned on his side to sleep. The night passed uneventfully until 500 hours, 5am, to the non-regular Army guys. Then all hell broke loose. Artillery shells were exploding all around the town. Mountains of dirt and rocks were flying in the air. Yelling and shouting marked the confusion and chaos of men blown out of a deep sleep! George jumped up with a start and grabbed for his boots. He threw them on, but didn't have time to tie them. He grabbed his rifle and ran for the nearest window to see what the hell was going on. Bugles blew "To arms! To arms!" Orders were barked to "Move out! Move out!"

Horses were furiously attached to lorries and troops were quickly ordered to abandon the town! The town was targeted for bombing while all slept. The Turks had abandoned the town to lure the Greeks in and to give the Ottomans one big condensed target! The Greeks had been suckered. The building they had just left was suddenly demolished by a direct hit! The town was being cleared. Soldiers who didn't get to their wagons, lorries or horses, had to run on foot to get out of the range of the Turk gun emplacements. Body parts were flying in the air, screams of the wounded shrieked through the dark night. "Get out! Get Out! Shouted the Officers.

George ran to a hastily horse drawn lorry and jumped on the rear end. He was pulled on board by other soldiers, who were cursing and filling the air with oaths. Some wounded were thrown aboard and they were moaning and crying out. All sense of order was forsaken; it was a wild scene of pandemonium. Soldiers scattered in all directions to get away from their targeted, fixed position. Some soldiers were shooting their rifles. But there was no enemy in sight. They were firing in frustration and felt they had to do something and fight back somehow. They were finally controlled by officers who ordered them to cease-fire, but not before one soldier in a mad firing spree shot a fellow soldier.

"Cease fire! Cease firing!" bellowed George, as he took up the cry. "You're shooting your own men! And don't waste bullets. George had to pull a rifle out of a boy's hands. He had panicked and was shooting wantonly. He had to slap him hard to stop him from screaming.

The shelling slowed down as they had out-run the guns range and the Turks had to pause to move them forward. But some of the scattering Greeks actually ran *toward* the Turk guns and were coming beneath their range. Thus, those Turk guns became ineffective. Seeing this, some of the Turks hitched their guns to horses and fell back. It was total chaos with some Greek troops moving forward *and* backward, while some Turk guns did the same. Surprise and confusion was rampant.

No organized response could be undertaken, until the troops were reorganized. The soldiers that ran ahead, seeing their isolation, worked their way back to the main group in scattered bunches. The Officers regained control and, gradually, some semblance of order was established. Ahead lay the entrenched lines of the Turk Army at Sarandaporon. George and his core group were told to stay where they were and to take cover. They were then ordered to chow down, since they had had no time to eat on this still early disastrous morning.

"Hell, we don't need an order to eat," remarked a soldier.

"Yes, we do. Some of us are too nervous to eat. But we have to. Who knows when we'll have a chance to eat again?" Countered another.

The Generals and the Officer Corps then went about the task of seeing to the wounded and reorganizing the soldier-groups and Army Command.

Crown Prince Alexander rode around with his Officer Command to help calm things down. However, the comments of the soldiers were not reassuring. George saw that the Crown Prince was much given to lecturing, solemnly stressing his views with stern gestures and oratorical flourishes that inevitably invited mocking and mimicry. The troops were upset that they were duped and trapped into a confining town while sleeping. Sure, Scout squads were sent out to reconnoiter, but where were they last night? So grumbled the rank and file soldiery.

Gradually, the rest of the morning the command structure was re-established and the Army of Thessaly was reformed, battered and "blooded," but again a fighting force. The supply lines and communication lines were restored and the troops were cautiously moving forward. Word had filtered down that the Bulgars had run into a cholera outbreak and had suffered three thousand casualties at the Thrace front up north. That's tough, thought George; but they've got their problems, we've got ours. He asked Captain Byzas, the leader of Karkis Company, if that rumor was true.

"So I've heard. Let's hope that the scourge doesn't spread south. We'll have enough problems with the Turks."

The columns were halted while the Generals conferred with the hastily returning scouts, who rode up in their sweating horses. The Officer Corps were hyper-vigilant; they weren't going to be caught asleep again. The Generals then hurried to their headquarters tent, where they studied their maps. Meanwhile, the Viking Captain, Safiol, had Sargeant Sardonis order the Company to get packed, with a battle supply of ammunition and to have their rifles to the ready. Karkis Company was shortly to move out as part of an attack formation. Close combat was expected. The Turks were standing to fight!

Greek scout squads had already made contact and exchanged shots with the entrenched Turks. The Viking alerted them to expect enemy artillery fire anytime. Crown Prince Constantine, surrounded by his Generals, stood atop a lorry and spoke to the hastily assembled Division:

"Soldiers of the Army of Thessaly! The Eighth Army Corps of the Ottomans are up ahead and blocking our advance. They are deployed across the Elasson-Kosanie Road that runs between the villages of Viglia and Glycovo. Our task is to attack and destroy them!"

"I have ordered the First, Second, and Third divisions to launch frontal attacks against the main line of the entrenched enemy's defenses. Simultaneously, our Fourth Division will launch a flanking turn around the Turkish right, through Metaxa, and capture the road junction at Kaldades to block any attempted retreat of the Turks."

"To the left of our main thrust," he continued, "Major-General Soutsos's calvary brigade, followed by the Fifth division backing them up, will swing wide to outflank the Turks and race ahead to seize the Aliakhmon Bridge between Kosanie and Servia. By this pincer movement, we will trap the Ottoman Eighth Army."

"God be with us. Division Commanders, take over!"

Immediately, with that, orders were barked to report at stations and rendezvous with their Commanders to form up in attack formations. They were herded onto horse drawn wagons, and lorries and a few loose, side-slated flatbed transports, followed by the foot infantry. Horse drawn cannons trailed behind. They moved deliberately ahead to the next hill, where they were ordered to jump off the vehicles and proceed on foot. They hadn't marched a mile when the Turks opened up on them. Long range artillery shells were the first to explode on them. Mounds of dirt flew up in an arc, raining rocks and debris down on their heads. Some of the men started to fall. Some cried out, others were knocked to the ground by the concussions of the exploding shells without uttering a sound. Rifle fire started to kick up the dust around their advance. George crouched down to be less of a target, but kept moving forward. To his right, Nick Panos cried out:

"Aarggh! I'm hit! I'm hit! Damn!"

George looked back and yelled: "Nick! Nick! You all right?"

"Keep going, Dilboy! Medics will get to him. Move on!" shouted Captain Safiol.

George couldn't help glancing back, and was relieved to see a medic run over and tend to him. General Eraklis called for their heavy guns to be called up. The horses galloped up and turned around to face the guns forward and were hastily set up to return fire. Cannon fire commenced as soon as they could be loaded. Greek barrages returned the fire. George would stop to steady his aim and fire at the dark figures behind the Turk defenses. Then he would move forward. Part of his boots left heel was shot away, but he felt no wound. But he couldn't be sure in all the explosions and shooting. It was getting dark and harder to see.

The Company was ordered to stand to. They stopped, and dropped to their knees and stomachs to steady their fire. After a certain advance, they were ordered to stop, so they wouldn't run into their own artillery and mortar-shell fire, being launched from behind them. Sporadic fire continued into the darkness of full night. As the lull grew, orders came down to dig in and set up a trench line for protection from snipers. George satisfied himself that his foot was uninjured. He pulled off the rest of the heel to give him a more even walk. He mentioned it to Sargeant Sardonis, who laughed and told him that he was lucky that was all that was hit. The Sarge continued:

"Panos got it in the shoulder. It looked pretty bad. He was carried back to the medevac field station. No other word yet."

"Looks like that's it for tonight," said Marvoulas. "There's no sense shooting at what we can't see. But how are we supposed to sleep after all this excitement?"

"Oh, you'll sleep when the adrenalin stops flowing. You'll drop from exhaustion. Wait and see," opined Halachis.

"Your probably right, Halachis. Your experience counts for something," said George.

"Damn right it does." Responded Halachis.

"Dilboy! Shouted Viking Captain Safiol. "You're on guard duty. After four hours, switch with Pappy. Report to Sargeant Sardonis, he's in charge of our sector."

George grabbed his shovel and rifle and went looking for Sargeant Sardonis.

"Dilboy! Over here! This is what happens when you're our best shot. You get to pull guard duty first."

"But what if I don't have the best eyes?" quipped George.

"Just how do you become a crack shot without good eyes?" replied the Sarge.

"Now I know why they made you a Sargeant," smiled George.

"Just keep your eyes open. Anything looks funny out there, give me a holler. Just remember, we got some night patrolers out there. We don't want to shoot our own guys. The password is 'Helene,' got it?"

"Very good, Sarge. I got it."

George took his post. Guard sentries were supposed to be separated about half a soccer field apart, dug into their slit trenches. It was eerily quiet. All candles were supposed to be extinguished. It was dark and noiseless, except for the sounds of the night. George looked back at the outline of the tents for reassurance that a quarter of moon allowed. He had to bestir himself to stay awake. Fear of the unknown helped. Two hours into his guard duty, he heard a rustling as if someone was crawling towards him. He snapped to alert and listened intently, rifle to the ready. After a bit he heard: "Dilboy!" A pause; then again: "Dilboy!" It was a loud whisper. "Password! What's the password!" George hushed back tensely. Silence. Then a hurried, "Hellene! Hellene! Don't shoot!" "Sargeant Sardonis, here! Don't shoot!" "Oh, it's you, Sarge." "Just making my rounds. Anything out there?" "Not that I can tell. It's too damn quiet. It's weird." "Well, that's the way we want it. The sneaky Turks like to do things in the middle of the night. Stay alert. I'm out of here."

George watched him crawl away on his hands and knees. It was a comforting visit, but then again, it reminded him of his isolation. He knew his sleeping brethren we're relying on him to protect them. It firmed his resolve. Every time his head dropped into drowsiness, he snapped it up! He couldn't even smoke; it was forbidden. He eyed his tobacco pouch, enviously. Ironically, it was Turkish tobacco. He pinched himself with his fingernails to stay awake. Surprisingly, it became easier as he entered his last hour, the toughest, he was told. So he steeled himself. He played mind games to stay alert. What he would do if something happened. Still, it was so still. He didn't hear anything.

But then he began to get uncomfortable. Something was bothering him. He couldn't see or hear anything unusual. But he sensed something. He peered ahead, straining to pick up any clue. He became restless and moved his head side to side; then he kneeled up on one leg and froze. He knew something was out there! He just knew! Then he heard something, a sliding sound. He raised his rifle and leaned forward, poised to shoot. Then he heard another sound, a crunching sound. But he still couldn't see anything.

Then he saw it.

Something moved in the dark! It stopped. Then it moved again. For a second he almost panicked, but caught himself. Finally, he spoke out horsely:

"Password! What's the password?"

Silence.

"That you, Sarge?"

"Yup, it's me. Don't shoot!"

"Bang!"

George had fired his rifle! The report startled George into a frozen pose, as he heard an immediate "Arraaggh! Then groans. George didn't move; there could be others.

Within a short time, George heard Sargeant Sardonis and some other soldiers come running up. They jumped into his slit trench or foxhole, as some called it.

"Dilboy! What is it? What happened? Rasped the Sarge!"

"I don't know", said a still stunned George. I heard something. I called for the password and nothing came back. I shot at something. It stopped moving! I heard groans. I just don't know!"

"All right, George. All right. Calm down! Galitis! Go check the other sentries. See if they're all accounted for. Ok, George, where did you shoot?"

"Straight out, about forty meters!"

"Kapos! Nakitis! Circle around left and right and meet me out there. And don't shoot *me!* Remember the password! Move out! The rest of you cover us. George, come along and show me!"

They all crawled out of the foxhole and dragged their elbows and knees along the dusty, desert like ground. Then they got up into a low crouch and continued on, every nerve taut. George and the Sarge were breathing heavily, but took shallow breaths, as they guardedly made their way forward. George eventually pointed to a small scrub tree.

"It was around here, somewhere."

They moved beyond the scrub tree, when the Sarge yelled:

"Here! Over here!"

Sarge saw a body with its left hand still clinging to a leafy tree branch. He turned the body over and exclaimed:

"Jesus Christ, Amen! A Turk. Dead as a stone."

"A sniper?" asked a bewildered Dilboy.

"No. An assassin."

"Huh? How do you know." George asked.

Sarge had quickly gone through the pockets of the still warm body and threw its contents on the ground.

"Look at this." He picked up a dirty photograph of Crown Prince Constantine, with its outer top corner bent, and fluttering in the light breeze.

"Looks like you got between an assassin and our leader. Should be a medal in this for you, Dilboy."

Still confounded by this sudden, lethal encounter, and not being regular army, George wasn't thinking of any medal. He was overwhelmed by his first killing; a soldier he never even saw! He fired on instinct. The good Lord above had protected him, he gratefully thought to himself.

Other soldiers, who couldn't contain their curiosity, ran up and surrounded the dead Turk, staring down at the body. One soldier kicked it in the leg to make sure it was dead. It didn't move, at least on its own.

"Oh, it's dead all right," quipped another. "Look, there's a bullet hole at the top of his forehead." A thin streak of blood ran down the middle of the forehead.

"Was he alone?" Galitis asked, pulling at his own ear, as was a nervous habit of his.

"Who knows? Did you hear any other shots? If there were others, they're gone, because we would have heard from them by now." Remarked Sargeant Sardonis.

"And, oh, by the way. It's not a man; it's a woman." Continued the Sarge.

"What? Huh? It's a what?" Shouted a cacophony of astonished voices. With that, Kapos bent down and broke open the shirt, popping buttons and exposed a bulbous set of mammary glands.

"Well, I'll be damned! Sarge, how did you know?" asked an admiring Pappy.

"Short hair, small bones and smooth skin. All you need is experience, something you guys don't have. Think of that next time you babies want to give me crap!"

"Sargeant Sardonis! Sargeant Sardonis! General Eraklis and the Crown Prince want an immediate report," shouted an excited courier who had run at them.

"All right, you guys. Back to your tents. Pappy! You and Galitis carry the body back to the medical wagons. Dilboy, come with me!"

Sargeant Sardonis and Dilboy, accompanied by the Viking Captain Safiol, who wanted to shine in the afterglow of his Company's prize kill, all hustled over to the Headquarters tent, where Crown Prince Constantine was completing the buttoning up of his uniform jacket. General Eraklis thought the Crown Prince should be informed of this deadly development and dared to have him awakened. General Eraklis's sense of urgency was rewarded with a pleasing reception from Constantine, when he took it upon himself to advise him of this incident. In fact, Crown Prince Constantine was so pleased that a soldier of his Army had intercepted an assassin, whose sole purpose was to kill him, that he immediately conferred on the not yet seventeen year old private, a double field promotion to Sargeant! Dilboy was delighted and tried unsuccessfully to hide his ebullience behind a mask of humility.

"I don't understand it," said George to his admiring comrades. "All I did was shoot in the dark."

But his prior marksman's medal, squad leaders appointment and scouting accomplishment gave his field promotion a quality of inevitability. The only damper on the occasion was the lament of Sargeant Sardonis, who gave George some perspective when he felt compelled to comment:

"Do you know how long it took me to earn these Sargeant stripes, Dilboy?" as he ruefully pointed to his shoulder.

"War creates opportunities for promotion, they tell me. Besides, it helps to be lucky, Sarge. I could have been the one to die out there."

"You know, Dilboy, with that attitude you might yet make something of yourself." The Sargeant then walked away, leaving George suffused in his own thoughts.

George walked back to his tent, and was either congratulated or stared at by his fellow soldiers. Those that were up, that is. It still wasn't 0600 hours yet and the daybreak ritual of shaking the troops awake by irasible Sargents was still to be done. Reaching his tent, he wanted to rest and lay down, but was too excited to sleep. He lay down trying to take in the full significance of it all. Besides, others kept approaching him and wanted to know, first hand, what happened. It's amazing how a life can turn so quickly, his or someone else's, George mused.

The rough shaking by the reliable but perpetually annoyed Sargent snapped him to full consciousness and he rushed out to breakfast. He was met with a fusillade of good-natured ribbing:

"Hey, Sargeant! Where's your stripes?" He hadn't had time to put them on.

"Yo, Hawkeye!" said a stranger, while pulling his rifle back, like he had just fired it. It was a wordless way of saying: "Nice shooting."

George just smiled and walked on. The morning was to see them briefed to renew the attack, at the same time they wolfed down their gulp and gallop breakfast at their division assembly. The buzz and excitement of the looming battle built up to a crescendo. Some soldiers quickly devoured their food, others were too nervous to eat much, knowing they were going to resume the battle.

CHAPTER FOURTEEN

BUGLER SOUND THE CHARGE !

They immediately moved out and lied on their stomachs and waited the command to attack. George and his fellow patriots were told to check their weapons and be at the ready. They stared ahead straining to see the enemy, to see what was waiting for them. They reassured each other with a thumbs-up sign, a nervous nod of the head or a tense smile.

Suddenly, the relative quiet was broken by the booming of cannon and artillery fire. The Greek Army batteries opened up with the preliminary barrage meant to soften up the entrenched enemy defending the horizon. It was music to Greek ears, since if they did their job, it would make the infantry's easier and would save lives. George silently cheered them on. Others weren't so silent:

"Give 'em hell!"

"Yeah! Pour it on them, you guys!"

"Take that, you bastards!"

After a half-hour of this deafening and unceasing roar of the guns, the commands came that they were waiting for:

"Army of Thessaly! First Company! Attack!

Up and at 'em! Let's go!" George heard the soldiers roar. He knew they were next.

"Second (Karkis) Company! Charge!" Hollered Captain Safoil!

As they got up on their feet and ran forward yelling for all they were worth, to give vent to their pent up rage, they could hear distantly:

"Third Company! All ahead! Ch-a-a-a-r-r-ge!"

Attack bugles could be heard above the din. It was 0700 hours and it started to rain, giving an unreality to the madness. The Turks could be seen scurrying around on the hill firing their own cannon and artillery into the Greek ranks. Exploding shells and dirt sprays showered the field; blood curdling screams shouted out, men fell to their deaths, and the injured cried out for help. Soldiers dropped to their knees to steady their aim, some fell on their stomachs to be less of a target. Officers pulled out their sabres to direct charges forward. It was hell on earth. The rain got heavier and turned the dirt to mud.

George had kept going to get as close as he could to get a better shot on the enemy. He looked for Turkish Officers on top of the redoubts to down the Ottoman leaders. He saw some fall, but he didn't know if it was from his shots or some other rifleman's. He shot in clips of five. He reloaded with rushed intensity. He was breathing heavily and in short gasps. Every so often he had to stop to catch his breath, as he dropped his head, turned over on his back and reloaded. He was fighting by instinct; he had no time to think. He felt the ground shake from under his feet, his ears hurt from the exploding concussions. Then, uneven lulls crept into the firing. He heard the rat-a-tat sound of the gatling guns. Hesitant bursts of fire spit out their bullets from these older machine guns the Turks were using. George was looking for more targets. He was beginning to see the field of battle better. His exposure surviving hostile fire gave him a growing sense of confidence. But the feeling disappeared as quickly as it appeared. It was upsetting to hear the wounded cry out. A soldier to his right screamed out in pain:

"I'm hit! Damn it! I'm hit! Medic! Medic!"

Then he stopped yelling, because he fell across the back of George's legs with his eyes and mouth open, dead. Blood splotches welled up on his chest and George had to look away. There was nothing he could do. George thought he was going to get sick, but he gritted his teeth and resumed his shooting. He felt more in control if he was doing something. Their attack was stopped and became a battle of attrition. The rain lightened up and then stopped, mercifully. They had no rain gear. The Turks held the higher ground and had that advantage. George fired away at targets of opportunity. He looked at his ammunition belt. His ammunition would soon run out. He had to be more selective in his shooting. He spotted Halachis and shouted over to him.

"Halachis! How's your ammo!"

"I got plenty left! How's about you?"

"I'm running low. I'll have to go back!"

"No! Don't! I know where the ammo wagons are. Here, take some of my clips. I'll be back!"

With that, before George could say anything, Halachis threw him some clips and scrambled back. George just shrugged and turned forward to try to pick off Turks who occasionally stuck up their heads to return fire. Taking dead aim on one aggressive Turk, he squeezed the trigger and immediately heard a distant scream:

"Oh-h-h!" He heard, as the Turk stood up when hit and fell forward over the top of the barricade.

"All right! George! That's one for you! Nice shooting!" barked Pappy.

"Stay down, you big Greek!" motioned George, with a momentary feeling of pride and camaraderie.

George turned around and was pleased to see the medics dressing the wounds of the injured and seeing them taken safely back to the rear. He felt a quick admiration to these soldiers who carried no weapons and concerned themselves only with the well being of fellow soldiers. He just hoped he wouldn't need them. After a long while, George wondered aloud:

"Where the hell is Halachis? It's been two hours and no sign of him yet." And George was down to his last few clips. Then George spotted a tall blonde coming toward him. It was the Viking Captain Safiol!

"Captain! What's happening. We're been bogged down here for hours."

"I know. I know. We're stalled. Our supply lines are stretched and their defense has stiffened. We're digging in for now and consolidating. Keep your head down and harass the hell out of them. I've got food and more ammunition coming, so hang on. We're bringing reinforcements up."

"Say, have you seen Halachis? He went for more ammo and I've lost him."

"Well, he found the Quartermaster Supply area and was filling his stomach an hour ago. Said he needed some bandages for the front lines."

"When did he become a medic? He'll need some bandages when I finish with him!"

"A laggard, is he? Well, now you know. That's how he survives. And why he's still a private and always will be. Don't depend on him."

"Thanks, Captain. We all learn."

As the day wore on, the battle became desultory, with only occasional flurries of gunfire, interspersed with intermittent artillery and sniper fire. It was enough to keep one on their toes and their nerves on edge. Late in the day, exhaustion started to set in. You can only fight on emergency adrenalin for so long, they learned. The dark seemed to be welcomed by all. Halachis showed up just before dark. George couldn't resist taunting him:

"Hey Halachis, enjoy your meal back there? We missed you on the front lines!"

"Dilboy, what's your problem. I gave you all my ammunition. What do you want from me?"

"Any excuse to get off the line, huh? Your all heart, Halachis!"

"You shit head, Dilboy! Put down that rifle and we'll see what a big shot you are!"

Halachis lunged at George, who side stepped him and cut his legs from under him with a leg sweep. Halachis fell on his face and hit a rock on the ground, splitting his eyebrow. Halachis jumped up, felt his face and saw the blood on his opened palm, momentarily stunned.

George warned him: "Assaulting a superior officer is a serious offense, Halachis. This is the second time I'm letting it go. But don't push your luck!"

"Your not worth bleeding on, Dil*boy*. Now I have to go back to the medical tent for some food and rest."

"I always know where your back is, Halachis; to the enemy."

"Why don't you go back to Asia Minor, where you belong," sneered Halachis, as he scurried away.

"I may do just that, when this war is over." George didn't want to complicate his short career by busting Halachis. They needed every rifle, thought George. He then shook his head to himself and sat down to roll himself a cigarette. It has been a long day, he sighed.

"Why don't you ignore him, like Captain Safiol, said Pappy. "He's not worth your trouble."

"I know. I know. But he's still part of Company Karkis, and he has to carry his weight."

Shortly thereafter, Marvoulas threw a stone over to Pappy and motioned his thumb toward George. Dilboy was asleep.

THE OTTOMANS MOVE

The next morning dawned bright and sunny. Now that they were in close proximity to the enemy, there was no longer a bugle to call the soldiers to reveille. The Sargeants went around rousing the troops, those who hadn't awoke by themselves, or were shaken awake by others. Not surprisingly, George noticed that most soldiers in combat were light sleepers. Danger not being far away might have had something to do with it.

The supply line was having trouble with the newer horse transports, because the horses were being spooked by the shell fire. The problem was they were new and nervous. Some were so panicky, they had to be left behind. The other, older horses, mules and donkeys, more used to the sounds of war, were proving more reliable. The first three divisions were ordered into the line and awaited the command to advance. Mortor launchers popped out their lethal shells; the troops were too close for artillery fire. But instead of the usual hour, the shells stopped in half that time, puzzling the ground forces. But not for long.

There was no return fire. Having crested the defense fortifications, it became obvious that the Turks had withdrawn during the early morning hours. But this time their retreat wasn't so orderly. In their haste to withdraw, they had left behind many wheeled transports and, more importantly, a dozen artillery pieces. The Second Division was ordered to proceed double time to pursue the enemy. Word had reached the troops that the Greek Fourth Division, charged with circling around the Ottoman right, had caught up with the rear of the Turkish Eighth Corps and were exchanging fire. They had taken the high ground near the Porta Petra Gorge and there were able to intercept stragglers from the furiously retreating Turkish troops. However, the Turks apparently had some of their best sharpshooters in their rear contingent, because they were extracting fearful casualties on the pursuing Greeks. Some of this rear guard were fanatical, and stood their ground, fighting to the death.

The Greek Fifth Division, circling around from the opposite direction, to their left, was unsuccessful in its attempt to seize the Aliakhmon Bridge, because of a suicidal defense by a strong Turkish force. The crushing pincer movement hoped for by Crown Prince Constantine was broken. Most of the Ottoman Eighth Army escaped over the bridge spanning the Aliakhmon River and moved northwest to join up with the allied Ottoman forces fighting the cholera devastated Bulgarians, the Serbs, Greek Army of Epirus and the Montenegrins. It was a Greek victory, though not as complete as they wanted. The Battle of Sarandaporon was over and George and his Second Division were ordered to cut short their hot pursuit and to rejoin the other Divisions. They reluctantly did so. But later they were glad, because when they calmed down, exhaustion quickly overtook them. It was a time to rest and consolidate. While encamped, the tired Greek troops took stock of who was dead, injured, or unaccounted for. They were thankful of their own survival. Panos had survived, but his shoulder was shattered and he was sent back to Larissa.

"Too bad about Panos," said a subdued George, sipping on some coffee.

"His life isn't ended, but his fighting days are," summarized Pappy.

"Why do we lose good men like Panos, and guys like Halachis here come through?" cracked a critical Marvoulas.

"Hey, I contribute and I take care of myself. I was surviving '97 while you babes were kicking around a soccer ball. You guys haven't survived anything yet!"

"Kapos looked up and saw Sargeant Sardonis walking by:

"Hey, Sarge, what's happening out there?"

"How the hell do I know. Nobody tells me anything. The Viking's coming along. Ask him," spit out the dour Sargeant.

"Hey, Captain! Yo! What's going on?"

"I've just come from an Officers meeting. We're moving out as soon as the supply wagons catch up. We got them on the run."

"To where, though?" queried George.

"The Third Division overran Veria and cut off their rail line between Thessalonika and Monastir, an Ottoman outpost seventy five miles west in Macedonia. We're back tracking a bit to keep our supply line, which stretches all the way back to Larissa, from being intercepted and to watch our backs. It would be just like the Turks to sneak down and attack our northern flank."

"But we were told Thessalonika was our destination?" asked a perplexed Galitis.

"It is, ultimately. But the slippery General Hassan Taxim Pasha, has taken his Eighth Corps and annexed it to the western Turks. Together they are taking a stand at Yannitsa."

"So what's our plan?" Pumped George.

"I'm not supposed to brief Karkis Company until just before we pull out, but that could be soon, so here it is. First, Second and Third Divisions will move straight for Yannitsa, bypassing a number of villages, except for food detachments."

"Another frontal attack? What the hell! Are we the battering ram for this damn Army? Why can't our division do a flanking movement?" griped Halachis.

"Shut up, Halachis!" snapped Viking Captain Safiol. Continuing on, the Viking relayed the rest of the battle plan: "The Fourth and Fifth Divisions will follow along the Yannitsa Road, and secure it for our transports and supplies. Then they would fake a turning movement to spread out and weaken the right Turkish flank. Meanwhile our Sixth and Seventh Divisions were to cut over and dig in between the Axios River and the Ottomans to trap them and prevent another retreat across the bridge to Thessalonika."

"Didn't we just do this?" persisted Halachis.

"Similar, but with an extra division, now. Headquarters Command gives the orders; I just follow them. Like you will, Halachis. I've got to go for a final briefing. Stand by."

Once again, Karkis Company and the Second Division ate an uneasy lunch, breaking out their rations. It was November now, the winds were kicking up and colder weather was being felt. Men sat and stood around lost in their own thoughts, smoking and chewing tobacco. Conversation was sparse and hesitant. Some soldiers were irritable.

"Shut up! Just shut up, will ya? snapped a stressed out soldier as he leapt up and hurried off. The other soldier, who was trying to cover up his own nervousness by chatting, just shrugged, spit out his chewing tobacco and withdrew into himself.

By mid-day the orders to form up and move out came. It was a relief to get going, thought George. It gave a release to his pent up energy. This war business swung between sudden craziness and boredom. One seemed to accentuate the other. You needed internal shock absorbers. You got so stressed out, you had to go numb to survive. At times, you got so tired, you didn't care whether you lived or died. Everyone had a limit. You had to be lucky to survive. George found himself having these internal conversations to pass the time.

Suddenly, the peace was loudly broken by ear splitting explosions. Screams, fountains of body parts, dirt and loosened rocks blew in all directions. Shouts were heard:

Take cover! Take cover!

They were as unnecessary as they were late. Artillery flashes could be seen from the far hills ahead. They were approaching a local river and began to cross a bridge. The advance First Division scrambled back from the bridge and sought cover wherever they could. The Turks were aiming to trap the confined Greek troops crossing the bridge. The Ottoman guns were too far away for shorter range rifles to return fire. But some did anyway. They did, that is, until their automatic reaction was stopped by officer commands:

"Cease-fire! Cease-fire!

One Sargeant, red in the face, ran over to a still firing private and pulled the rifle right out of his hands.

"I said stop firing, you idiot! You can't hit anything from here! Use your head, don't lose it, you fool!"

The long-range guns had the first two divisions pinned down. It was frustrating for the helpless troops who could only curl up in a fetal position and hope the shells landed somewhere else. Finally, an order came to fall back to a position beyond the range of the Ottoman guns. As usual, it was confusing and chaotic, if only a little less so. The rest of the day became an extended barrage of artillery fire, as the Greeks rolled up their big guns and returned fire.

During the dark, the First and Second Divisions were ordered to cross the damaged, but still passable bridge, to position themselves to resume the attack the following morning. Besides, the Third Division was crawling up their backs. Taunts by some Third Division Commanders and the ranks to step aside and let real soldiers take charge, revived some inter-division rivalries and was a spur. As if to retaliate, the Third Division was held back in reserve and ordered to hunker down before crossing the river. The leading two divisions were now only a few miles from the bulk of the Ottomans main defensive line.

The Greeks renewed their artillery fire at daybreak, preparatory to the advance of the infantry. Now the Army of Epirus had arrived and was pressing the Third Division to forge ahead. They brought up their long range guns to add to the cumulative fire of the First, Second and Third Divisions in pulverizing the hillside defenses of the Turks. The cataclysmic and thunderous noise of the guns was ear splitting. George looked up in utter amazement and wondered how anyone could survive such a barrage. It was too much for Gregory Kapos, who suddenly stood up, holding his ears, went over the top and ran forward into no man's land screaming:

"Stop it! Stop it! Stop it!

George instinctively yelled out:

"Greg! Stop! Greg!"

Dropping his rifle, George jumped up and attempted to vault over the top, but was tackled by Sargeant Sardonis and pulled to the ground:

"No, George! NO! Greg lost it. Don't you!"

Together they watched in horror as Greg went berserk, charging ahead and flailing his arms wildly, oblivious to the shells exploding around him, until he disintergrated in front of their eyes. A shell blew him apart. George stared in shocked disbelief, then sank onto the ground, trying to absorb the reality of the horror!

"Why Greg? Why? For God's sake, Why?" Grunted a traumatized George.

Sargeant Sardonis, equally stunned, but more resigned to the craziness of war, uttered:

"Everyone has a limit, George. He just went over his. War can drive anybody insane."

CHAPTER FIFTEEN

BATTLE OF YANNITSA

By late morning, an all out attack was launched up the hills toward what was left of the Ottoman Turks. The Greek Infantry faced a rear guard of snipers who were relatively few, but deadly shots from a superior position. They exacted their toll, but yielded to superior force and numbers. Once again, the Turks abandoned their positions and retreated East. Although a Highlander Battalion in the Seventh Division had reached the Varda/Axios bridges, the rest of the Division split and lingered behind, as did the Sixth Division following behind the Seventh. The Highlanders couldn't hold the bridges without support and was forced back by the swarm of retreating Turks, who continued their frenzied withdrawal to the East. Strangely, some of the Turkish forces broke off and went the opposite way west.

The Seventh Divisional Commander petulantly answered his critics, that low lying fog kept him from supporting the Highlanders, and he couldn't shoot what he couldn't see. After all, he might end up shooting his own troops, he claimed.

"But the Turks could see well enough!" raged Crown Prince Constantine, who immediately sacked the Commander of the Seventh Division. The Crown Prince was tired of incompletely winning battles, having to chase the Ottoman Eighth Corps, and fighting them again another day.

Another opportunity for promotion provided by the sudden quirks and changes of war, thought George, when he later heard of the change of command. Change and chaos seem to be the constants of war. It's hard to keep a stable perspective when all around is unstable. He had to keep trying to make sense of it all.

The Greek Fifth Division and its 11,000 men, after securing the Yannitsa Road, thinking matters were well in hand, had found a target of opportunity and advanced toward Florina. To guard it's supplies, the Fifth Division Commander had left some troops behind because of renegade bands of Turks roaming about. This reduced his troop strength by a couple of thousand. He left additional soldiers behind at other outposts to protect his rear. He didn't want to be surprised from behind. The cumulative effect was to weaken the fire-power of his lead forces.

As if clairvoyant, but actually by chance, the Turk Commander in the area, Djavid Pasha, utilized the western section of the railroad trunk line coming down from the north, to merge 12,000 troops at Banica. This trunkline ran along the Monastir to Thessalonika route. His scouts had tipped him off about the movements of the Greek Fifth Division. Realizing the superior strength of his forces over the weakened Greek contingent, Djavid Pasha attacked and defeated this Greek Fifth Division in a lightning, surprise strike. The victorious Turk forces and a dozen artillery pieces captured from the Greeks were mounted on the railroad train and immediately routed to be used for the defense of Monastir against the approaching Serbs. The Serbs were not at all happy at this development and sarcastically invited the Greeks to come and face their own guns.

Meanwhile, back in the East, by the end of the first week in November, at the urging of the diplomats of the Great Powers of England, France, Germany, the Austro-Hungarian Empire and Russia, Hassam Taxim Pasha and Constantine started to negotiate the surrender of the besieged Ottoman Army at Thessalonika to prevent a slaughter. It took protracted and acrimonious bargaining sessions before terms acceptable to both sides could be arranged. The next day the Greek Seventh Division peacefully marched into the city, and the Ottoman forces surrendered their weapons. The Greeks took almost 30,000 Turk prisoners.

GEORGIE! MY GEORGIE! 175

George and his division entered Thessalonika the following day and they quartered in formerly Turk barracks. George and his cohorts were elated:

"Mission accomplished!" shouted George.

"When do we go home," asked Halachis.

"We don't," retorted an informed Sargeant Sardonis.

"Thanks to the Fifth Division's defeat at Banica, we are being ordered to assist the Serbs in their attack on Monastir, being defended by the Turks with some of our captured artillery guns. How do you like that; a chance to be blown up by our own guns!"

"Damn, this is an absurd up and down war," said a frustrated Niki Nakitis.

"What war isn't?" smirked Sargeant Sardonis.

"Oh, well," said a philosophical George. "That's the way it goes."

"Yeah, you can fluff it off, baby Dil*boy.* You've got a whole life in front of you. Some of us, who have been around for a while, want out!"

"I'll put you out, you misfit. I've had it up to here with you!" George leapt to his feet in a bound.

"Attention!"

In walked Captain Viking Safiol, announcing General Eraklis.

"Dilboy! Outside!" barked General Eraklis.

With that brief command, the three of them walked bristly outside, while the rest of the soldiers looked at each other in wonderment.

Outside, General Eraklis came right to the point.

"Dilboy, we're setting up an elite sniper group of Rangers. We're expecting a heavy defense of Monistir and we need specialists, sharpshooters who can take out special targets. Hopefully, it will shorten the siege and save Greek lives. Captain Safiol will take you to your briefing for further instruction. Carry on!"

The General snapped a sharp salute and left with his adjutant.

By the third week in November, the Army of Thessaly had moved into position around the besieged fortress-city of Monistir.

Preparations for an assault were made at the same time as attempts were made to get the surrounded Turks to come to terms, as was done at Thessalonika. This was being done in conjunction with the general collapse of Ottoman military resistance in Western Macedonia, to the knowledge and despair of the defending Turks. It worked. When the defending Turk Command saw that further resistance was hopeless, they sued for a peaceful and honorable surrender. So the siege ended. George never got a chance to actively engage in hostilities as a Ranger. The Ranger Company was disbanded and George returned to Karkis Company. Such are the fortunes of war, he thought. He was just as pleased.

The Macedonian towns and villages of Koritsa, Florina and Kastoria were overrun by Greek forces with token resistance by the end of the year. But in the meantime, the Crown Prince Constantine turned his attention to the undermanned Army of Epirus. He ordered General Eraklis to take a contingent of battle hardened troops of his Second Division, including George and his Karkis Company, and march them ahead to Epirus. This cut division of 4,000 veterans marched across the Pindus Mountains to join General Sapountzakis. While enroute, they were informed of their new mission at morning assemblies. General Eraklis orated:

"Soldiers of Greater Greece. This is the situation. The thin Army of Epirus we are reinforcing had originally contained not much more than a regular division of 11,000. It was supplemented by stout patriots that sailed from Crete to Missolonghi, and a loosely cobbled contingent of foreign Greek sympathizers, led by descendants of the great Italian patriot, Giuseppe Garibaldi, who united Italy in the prior century. This 2,000 man cobbled group of combatants joined 3,000 Epirote irregulars and by mid-December we all should meet at Ioannina."

"Hear me on Ioannina."

A large sheet was dropped between two trees.

"Ioannina is the only remaining Ottoman fortress in this part of the Balkans. We recently took Monastir. Ioannina is protected on its East by a large lake. From the North to the South it is overlooked by a string of hills that range around like a sickle. Forts were built on these hills. They dominate the passes leading to the plain where Ioannina is centered. In between the forts are mounted batteries. We know Ioannina has been reinforced by Ottoman forces and guns that escaped from Monastir before it surrendered. We are outnumbered and outgunned. But we will take the battle to them until the rest of the Army of Thessaly can catch up to us. Tomorrow we march on to our destiny. Dismissed."

Back at camp, the men of Karkis Company tried to unwind: "This is what we get for our successes, more battles." Remarked Niki Nikitis.

"Why doesn't Eraklis wait for Constantine?" Wondered Marvoulas.

"Glory! He wants to show off for the Crown Prince," ventured Halachis.

"Well, somebody has to start. Maybe we're to soften them up for the big push. Anyways, General Sapountzakis has had his own successes and he will have something to say about the Order of Battle." Said George.

"What do you think, Sarge?" Queried Pappy.

"I'm not paid to think. I just follow orders." Snorted the crusty veteran.

In a rare instance of arriving on time as scheduled, General Eraklis met the waiting General Sapountzakis. They huddled in Sapountzakis's headquarters tent. They were both anxious to start the assault. Sapountzakis wanted to launch his troops the following morning and inquired as to how far Constantine was behind. He seemed to Eraklis to want to earn his victories before Constantine arrived. In that sense both Generals had the same goals.

The following morning Karkis Company and the Second Division were called up and ordered to attack the main fort of Bezanie. Sapountzakis's soldiers attacked the two most southern forts. Both attacks were unsuccessful. Heavy rifle fire and mortar shells kept them pinned down. They were fighting up hill and being harassed by the gap batteries. The Turks were effective shooting down at their attackers. George aimed his rifle at a particularly pesky battery that had pounded them with mortar shells. One of these shells landed nearby and blew his hat off.

Jesus! That was close!" Sputtered an angry George.

He looked up and slowly took aim. He steadied his arm, held his breath and pulled the trigger. Bang! Got him! One of the battery loaders fell back with a yell! In the din, no one else noticed, but George did. It made him feel good and fed his confidence. Since, during the day, their casualties were mounting, Captain Viking Safiol finally called for them to fall back. At night, they withdrew out of range, staggered back to their base camp and counted their casualties. Six killed and twenty eight wounded; a costly battle for their company of less than 200, fully manned.

The following days turned into weeks. They weren't making much progress. Casualties continued to accumulate and they had very little to show for it. George led a couple of night patrols to probe their defenses. One night he stumbled onto a Turk patrol and an instant battle ensued. George shot first and killed the lead Turk soldier. But more important, he was also able to capture a prisoner who had lagged behind and was wounded by Halachis. Of all people, Halachis; this war has no end of surprises, thought George. He joked with Halachis that he was probably aiming at George and hit the Turk instead. George meant it as a joke, but Halachis wasn't laughing. Anyway, Intelligence was pleased with the capture and gladly took the prisoner off their hands, to grill him for information. Galitis had to be taken to the medical tent with a hand wound.

"That your shooting hand, Galitis?" Remarked George, kiddingly.

"No. It's my cigarette hand." Riposted Galitis.

"Thank God. Otherwise we would all be at risk with an impaired shooter," clowned Pappy.

"Heck, he's impaired on his best day," quipped Nikitis.

"Jesus, it's a wonder were winning this war with this motley group," said Galitis, in fake exasperation.

By years end, Sapountzakis and Eraklis agreed to suspend their attacks, and wait for the Crown Prince Constantine's full Army of Thessaly. In the meantime, a siege fire was maintained.

The Crown Prince Constantine arrived in mid-January with the Fourth, Fifth and Sixth Divisions from Macedonia, the Seventh Division being left behind for maintenance purposes. This meant 60,000 Allied Greek forces faced 50,000 fortified Turks. He immediately assumed command of all Greek Forces. With his Generals he studied the Ottoman defenses. He ordered the First and Third Divisions to re-assault the main Turk fort at Bezanie. It was started by a booming artillery bombardment. But this dual assault was only to focus the Ottoman Defenses on what was really a diversion. At the same time, he ordered the Second Division, including George's Karkis Company, to race around in a flanking movement to the south and southwest. The Lake would be to their left and would act as a natural protection for them. Accompanying them was the Fourth and Fifth Divisions. The Sixth Division was held in reserve.

The four-day frontal assault against Bezanie was unsuccessful. The Turks seemed to expect this attack and ferociously rained down withering fire on the upward attacking Greeks. They were fought to a standstill by the stubborn defense. Greek casualties were appalling. The Turks were using their dead as sandbags. When they couldn't stand the smell of rotting bodies, they catapulted them down at the Greeks to spread disease. This forced the Greeks to bury them eventually, and to expose themselves to Turk snipers. The Greeks countered this tactic by burying the bodies at night.

Having reached their assault lines, George's Second Division and the Fourth Division faced the last two fort-like redoubts. The Fifth Division stood at the ready in reserve, poised to exploit any opening broken through by the front line divisions. The Greek guns flashed their fire to open the flanking action.

The artillery barrage started at midnight. At 0300 hours, the infantry was ordered to move out. While the barrage continued they approached the hills in a half crouch. After half an hour, George heard a sudden yell. A man went down and disappeared from sight. Suddenly George's right foot slipped out from under him and he did a split. He had walked into a long trench; not a defensive trench, because it wasn't deep enough. It was meant to trip up a night attack, patrol or approach that couldn't see well ahead. The dark was thus a two-edged sword.

As they continued further up the hill, they must have been spotted because slit trenches up ahead suddenly lit up the night. Oil had been poured into the shallow trenches and it was set afire. Captain Viking Safiol ordered Karkis Company to charge! They were able to hurdle the oil-fired trenches, except for a careless few. Now the Greeks yelled their way forward. George found himself shouting: "C'mon, let's get those bastards!"

Mortor shells exploded amongst them. Nikitis fell over screaming.

George looked back and last saw Nikitis rolling down the hill. Everyone kept moving. George zig-zaged his way up, stopping every so often to fire his rifle. Yelling and screaming pierced the air, deafening artillery and gunfire rang his ears, dirt stung his face. Hell was here; mass confusion and chaos reigned. He was zig-zaging for his life! The closer they got the more hellish it became. He mounted the hill and came face to face with a screaming Turk with a raised sword slashing at him. George instinctively pulled the trigger and the Turk fell at his feet! Smoke was everywhere. He wounded another Turk that shot and missed him. George clubbed him with the barrel of his rifle. He kept clubbing him until he stopped moving. George was gasping with effort and looked around with blazing eyes! He felt like a wild animal! Hand to hand fights were all around him. The defending Turks were beaten back, but with heavy casualties.

The Turks were abandoning their guns and falling back. George got a grip on himself and dropped to one knee and fired with more accuracy. He got another Turk in the side as he tried to vault over the far end of the hill. He had an officer's insignia on his cap that flew in the air as he was hit and cried out some Turk curse. George ran over to him and he looked straight into George's eyes. Blood gushed from his mouth, as he raised his revolver and shot George point blank range! George was startled, shot back and hit the officer in the chest. He slumped over and died without a word.

"How the hell did he miss?" yelled George in amazement.

He didn't.

George now felt a burning sensation in his left leg. He looked down and saw blood coming from his leg. He felt the wound, but noticed that for all the bleeding, it appeared to be superficial. He quickly looked up as the fighting again raged hand to hand. Knives, swords and pistols were being used as much as rifles. The Turks that could get away were running. Others fought suicidedly. Some surrendered. After a while George heard Captain Viking Safiol shouting and racing along the top of the redoubt:

"Cease fire! Cease fire!"

The Viking was reprimanded before for delaying a cease fire order at Sarandaporon and two Greeks accidently shot and killed each other. George stood there as if frozen in place. He looked around at all the carnage and walked unsteadily in a daze. Smoke, groaning, and scattered fire greeted the bright orange rising of the sun. George found himself sitting on the side of a broken wagon next to a dead donkey. He was trying to take it all in. He was exhausted and his shoulders felt like they were weighed down by sandbags.

Later that morning when they brought up the water wagon, they were given food and told to settle down, until they could sort it all out. There was no pursuit. They were too drained.

Nikitis had returned still stunned, after being treated for shock injuries. Nothing serious, he was told. But he had a distant look in his eyes. George went to the medics and they put sulfur on George's wound to prevent an infection and bandaged his left leg. He considered himself lucky. So had the Greek troops. They had not only captured this redoubt, but Bezanie was finally overtaken, as well as four of the six forts surrounding Ioannina. Seeing this, the other two forts were abandoned and the Ottoman forces fell back into Fortress Ioannina.

IOANNINA

Now only the town of Ioannina stood. The Turk Commander was Essad Pasha, an experienced, career soldier. It took a month and a half to reach this point and it cost Karkis Company half its contingent. Other companies fared even worse. This was a battle of attrition. The Crown Prince was so stunned by the losses that he told his Generals to stand down and to rest the troops. They were too exhausted to fight on effectively and replacements had to be brought up. The Sixth Division was used to serve as replacements for troops in the line. After a week of regrouping, The Crown Prince readied his Army for a final all out attack on the town of Ioannina. He ordered the customary shelling of the Towns fortress walls. For two days the artillery shells thundered and tore at the walls of the fortress town, as well as its center.

Watching the growing destruction of the fortress-city, through long distance field glasses, the Crown Prince Constantine stopped the bombardment. He sent in a contingent under a white flag to ask Essad Pasha to surrender to avoid a senseless slaughter. Their supply of food was cut off and the Greeks controlled the roads, so it was unlikely any Ottoman troops could break through. The Crown Prince offered honorable terms. The artillery barrage would resume in twelve hours.

As the cease-fire was coming to an end, a Turk delegation emerged from the Town with a white flag, accepting Constantine's terms. George felt great relief. He watched as 35,000 surviving Turks marched out of the town into captivity, dropping their weapons along the side of the road. They were lined up into the open plain where they were searched for hidden weapons such as knives and pistols, and then herded into a guarded enclosure, for the time being. General Eraklis then led his newly reinforced Second Division, bolstered with replacements, into the subdued town and saw to the restoration of some kind of order. One surprise was the absense of Essad Pasha. He had shed his uniform, donned the apparel of a peasant and escaped to Albania.

Later that evening, George was resting in his assigned barracks. He was rewinding his putees, especially the one covering his healing leg. He was upset that blood was seeping through the cracked crust of a wound.

"Damn! Won't this thing stay clean? Every time a hard crust forms, it cracks and bleeds. Oh, I suppose I should count my blessings. It's just so irritating."

"It'll be more than that, if it gets infected, warned Pappy. "Blood poisoning and then leg amputation could happen. So keep it clean."

"And just how to you do that in this dustbowl?" asked a doubtful Marvoulas.

"Keep cleaning the wound and changing the dressing." Advised a medic passing by.

"Here, let me take a look."

Examining the wound, he lightly probed the area and announced:

"All flesh and no bone. That's a good wound. The blood itself can act as a clearant. Just try to keep it clean and watch for an infection."

He got up and bounded away, unconcerned. This was reassuring to George, who knew little about things medical, though he worked for a while in a laundry room at a Boston hospital in America.

Sargeant Sardonis mentioned the escape of Essad Pasha, and how maybe it was allowed to happen.

"What do you mean?" asked George.

"Sometimes they let a soldier escape to bring the news of their defeat to the enemy. The enemy is more likely to believe one of their soldiers, than any propaganda of ours. And once believed, it can serve to weaken their resolve in future battles."

George thought about that for a moment, then said:

"Mind games, huh?"

"Oh, it can be even more so. We sometimes deliberately don't surround an enemy, because we want to give them an out, an escape route. That way we'll have fewer enemies to fight, and fewer casualties when we do."

"But the problem with that is they not only take soldiers with them, they take cannon and live to fight us another day, like what happened at Monastir and here." Commented George.

"Hey, I'm just a Sargeant. They don't pay me to think. I leave grand strategy to the Generals."

George shrugged and said: "What do I know, I'm just sixteen . . . . Whoa! I turned seventeen three weeks ago, February

5, 1913! Christ, in all the turmoil, I forgot! Happy birthday to me! Happy birthday to me-e-e!" Sang a discordant, but delighted Dilboy.

"Now I'm not only alive, I'm legal."

"Big frigging deal! Only a lawyer cares about that, in this shooting war!" spit out Halachis.

"You know Halachis, with your stinking attitude, you should worry about Turkish *and* Greek bullets before you reach your next birthday." Retorted Pappy.

"Ha! With the way you guys shoot, I'm not worrying about any of your bullets. Except for the birthday boy, who shoots straight only because he freezes under fire!"

'That's enough, Halachis." Captain Viking Safiol had walked in unannounced. "Up and out. It's your turn for sentry duty at the west wall. Move!"

Cursing to himself, Halachis, grabbed his rifle and stormed out.

"Don't shoot any goats in the Lake, Halachis!" taunted Marvoulas.

Halachis looked back in contempt and thrust an obscene gesture at a howling Marvoulas. Others chuckled amongst themselves, one commenting:

"What's with him, anyway? Why does he love to cause trouble."

"Who the hell knows? He'd be a great study for that Freud guy that studies heads." flipped another.

GREATER GREECE

With the recent conquests, Greece was once again including Epirus in a new Greater Greece, along with Thessalonika and much of Macedonia. Their pre-war objectives were being met. Word later went around that Essad Pasha had turned up in the north in Scutari, Albania. There he succeeded the Turkish leader who was assassinated by a disgruntled Albanian irregular. He now led the defense of

Scutari against a siege from the Montenegrins and the Serbs. Montenegro was the smallest and poorest of the Balkan Allies and were fairly futile against the Turks. They asked for and got three Divisions of soldiers from the Serbs. Nevertheless, despite repeated joint attacks, the Serbs and Montenegrins were not able to conquer the stubborn Ottoman defense. So they pulled back and decided to wait and starve them out. Meanwhile, the attacking forces harassed them by long range artillery.

Surprisingly, they didn't have to wait long. By the end of April, Essad Pasha voluntary asked for terms. He was allowed to march his forces out of the fortress, fully armed and supplied. He was so allowed because a mail pouch brought by a horse courier disclosed that ten days before then, the Ottoman Forces and Bulgaria had agreed to an armistice, under pressure from the Great Powers. Bulgaria and the Ottoman Turks had the most soldiers in the field. The other belligerents just stopped their military operations, except for a few scattered skirmishes.

In this sputtering way, the First Balkan War ended.

CHAPTER SIXTEEN

SECOND BALKAN WAR

It was May, 1913 and George was enjoying the conveyed end of hostilities, after eight months at war. He was still quartered at Ioannina occupying the conquered fortress, thankful for his survival. He now had more time to write his family in Chios and America. And he did. He proudly wrote about his near death experiences, his uncanny luck, and his double promotion in the field. He felt so grown up and, being a survivor, his faith in himself increased.

But he knew his limitations. He couldn't see the big picture, he didn't know anything about politics and waited only for his next order. He had heard that Bulgaria claimed they took on the bulk of the Ottoman Armies and suffered most of the wars casualties, which the other Balkan Allies begrudgedly admitted. But the Allied Generals argued that was because of geography, inasmuch as Bulgaria is closer to the Ottoman Empire.

The disputes now moved from the battlefield to the diplomatic arena in London. It was a fight for the territorial spoils among the combatants. The Great Powers decreed that Albania would become an independent country and no longer a Turkish protectorate. This frustrated Serbia and its fellow Slav country, Russia, who wanted this territory for access to the Adriatic and Mediterranean Seas. The Austro-Hungarian Empire threatened to attack Serbia if it didn't surrender the just captured city of Scutari and withdraw its forces from Albania. Serbia withdrew, but with much anger and resentment. In retaliation, Serbia refused to pull its troops from the parts of Macedonia it conquered, but was allotted to Bulgaria by the Great Powers. Bulgaria was incensed with Serbia for this petulant stubbornness.

General Eraklis convened his surviving six divisions to bring them up to date on the war front, but it was really a political commentary as of the end of May.

"Soldiers of the Army of Thessaly" he thundered in righteous dignity. Greece has concluded a separate military treaty with our ally Serbia, with respect to Macedonia. Each country will keep the territory it has conquered."

On that announcement, a loud roar of acclamation rented the air! Chants followed:

"Greater Greece! Greater Greece!"

This referred to the long cherished urge of Greeks to collect the scattered race into one Greater Greek Nation, wherever their populations predominated, regardless of its location. This included Thessaly, Epirus, occupied Macedonia, Thrace, Asia Minor and the nearby Islands in the Aegian, Ionian and Mediterranean Seas.

"Hear me Soldiers of Greece! You are now situated in Ioannina, Greece. The Turks are gone! We have doubled the land area of Greece!"

With that, the assembled thousands leaped to their feet and cheered! They grabbed each other, hugged and kissed each other on both cheeks! They were heady with exhilaration! When the celebration and noise died down, General Eraklis told them they would have to continue their present duties until further developments reached a consensus. He congratulated them for their fighting spirit on the battlefield and thanked them for having done their country and future generations proud. He also thanked the Greek Navy for controlling the Aegean Sea, so the Greek Army didn't have to man the seacoast to prevent the Turks from landing an Army behind them. Finally, he released them to celebrate the rest of the night. Many took advantage of the occasion to engage in heroic drinking bouts and to partake mightily of the grape.

On the diplomatic front, Bulgaria controlled their fury at the secret Greco-Serbian Treaty and asked Russia to arbitrate the

Bulgar-Serbian dispute over Macedonia, completely disregarding Greek conquests and claims there. They thought that since both peoples were Slavic, Russia would hold sway over Serbia. Then they changed their mind, thinking that Russia would side with Serbia, for the same reason. Communications broke down between Russia and Bulgaria, despite their friendly past. Bulgaria, emboldened with their victories against the Ottoman Turkish Empire, and encouraged by an increasing militant civilian population, decided on their own to take up arms.

In the dark, moonless night of June 29th, 1913 the Bulgars launched a sneak attack against Serbian frontier posts and easily overwhelmed them. Now there was the spectacle of the largest Armies in the victorious First Balkan War, fighting each other. The Second Balkan War had begun.

The Bulgarians did not formally declare war against Serbia and Greece and postured the dispute as local and only within Macedonia. They did this to keep out the Great Powers. The three warring nations concentrated their troop movements in Macedonia, while leaving reserve forces to guard their borders. The Crown Prince, now designated *King* Constantine, moved the First five Divisions back to Thessalonika. Sargeant George Dilboy and his Karkis Company were part of the Second Division that were given these mobilization orders.

"Oh well, guys, at least we're familiar with the area, and it is now part of Greece. Let's finish the job and go home," remarked a philosophical George.

Others of his company comrades were not so accepting:

"I'm all for going on and I don't mind finishing the job; but I just don't want to finish me. Are we trading bodies, so the King can promote himself again?" said an irked Sargeant Sardonis.

"What can he promote himself to, God?" commented Nikitis.

"Why should we give up Thessalonika or any other territory we conquered for the greedy Bulgars?" said Pappy.

Since this seemed to make sense, further discussion melded into a resigned acceptance to fight for the gains they paid for with Greek blood and lives.

The Serbs and Bulgarians clashed along a seventy-mile front near the Macedonian-Bulgarian border. A Serbian counteroffensive began during the first week of July. Because of the mountainous terrain little progress was made. Bulgaria attempted to invade Serbia, but that offensive bogged down. The Greek Army of Thessaly moved successfully against light Bulgarian opposition at the towns of Dojran and Lahana. George's Second Division did not even need to use their artillery in overrunning Lahana. George jumped over a sandbag defense and captured two Bulgar soldiers. When he ordered them to drop their weapons, one of the weapons fired when it was thrown against an unhitched wagon. The bullet whizzed by George's head. He thereafter resolved to get surrendering soldiers to empty their rifle chambers first; then discard their weapons. In later relating this bizarre incident, George would complain that:

"Hell and damnation! There are countless ways to get hurt in war. It's ridiculous. You have to be lucky to survive."

"Amen, comrade." Said a nodding infantryman from Artos Company.

For political reasons of its own, and sensing a vulnerable rival, Romania declared war on Bulgaria on July 10. They marched toward the Bulgarian capital of Sofia. Not to be left out and trying to salvage some of its pride, the Turkish Army marched into Thrace and forced the Bulgarians out of Adrianople on July 23. The Bulgarian main forces were concentrated against Serbia and Greece. They could offer only token resistance against Romania and Turkey. The Greeks moved their Second, Third and Fourth Divisions to Western Macedonia to join their newly established Seventh Division. They attacked the Bulgarian positions at Kilkis. Before they could be enveloped, the Bulgars abandoned Kilkis under cover of darkness during the early morning hours, a favorite tactic of theirs. The Greeks gave chase harassing the Bulgarians as they fled north. The rugged mountains and the poor roads frustrated the pursuing Greek Divisions. The Bulgarian retreat stopped at the Kresna Pass where they set up a defense.

Constantine reached the Kresna Pass and immediately launched an attack. A huge concentrated Greek push broke through the center of the defense forcing the Bulgarians further north to avoid being overrun and encircled by Greek flanking forces. The Greek center had thinned its ranks as it moved further north. It inadvertantly separated itself from troops on its flanks. Now they were also in danger of being enveloped. Realizing this, the Greek troops were ordered to halt and consolidate their positions. Scouts had reported that the Bulgarians were reinforced by 20,000 fresh troops. Their plan was to engulf Constantine's Army in the Valley of the Strymon. They intended to enclose the strung out Greeks in a ring. The Greek forces moved up from the south and down from the north to bulk up for a concentrated protection. Then the Greeks counterattacked to keep the Bulgarians off balance.

At this point, a cease-fire was agreed to at Bucharest, Romania because the Great Powers were threatening to intervene, especially the Austro-Hungarian Empire, who felt that the war was expanding too close to its borders. The sudden silencing of the guns was as deafening as it was welcome, as only a combat soldier can appreciate. Though Bulgaria claimed it was not defeated in the field, it must have realized that their overall situation in the long run was bleak. On a map, a strong case could have been made that Bulgaria would have been overwhelmed by the numerically superior forces of the Serbian, Romanian, Turk and Greek Armies. Therefore, its agreement to cease all military operations on the first of August, and to withdraw completely from Macedonia, seemed prudent.

Thus, the Second Balkan War ended.

MUSTERED OUT

Though it involved only a year of his life, covering a two-year period, 1912-1913, George felt like the time flew by, on the one hand. On the other, he felt like he had aged quite a bit. War can do that to you, he was told. Now he was a blooded veteran who proudly did his bit for Greece. He hoped his family and, especially his father, felt as proud as he did. He couldn't wait to get into civilian clothes, and to be free to see his family.

However, as easy as it was to get into the Greek Army, it was not as easy to get out. A stand by Army was needed to assure their new territories security, on the one hand. On the other, the Greek government couldn't afford a war-time Army in peace time. Though there would be a mustering out process, at the same time, inducements would be given to get others to stay in and go regular Army for a longer enlistment period. The big question for most of the soldiers amongst themselves was:

"Are you staying in or going out?"

George saw enough injuries and deaths, so he opted out. He wanted to go home like most of the soldiers. But it took George two months to get mustered out. The Greek Command wanted to make sure the peace would hold. Restoring and maintaining order had them doing police work, which wasn't popular with the troops, but commanders believed it kept them busy. They also had to patrol the newly acquired territories. The Island of Crete in the Mediterranean Sea was occupied by Greek Military and Civilian Authorities and annexed.

George was taken back to Larissa and then to Athens, where he bought himself some civilian clothes. But he did take a little time to celebrate with other returning soldiers and enjoy the appreciation of the Greek population. After sleeping off an Ouzzo and wine-induced hangover, another first in his young life, George took the omnibus to the East Coast and sailed across the Aegean Sea back to Chios. This time he did not telegram ahead; he wanted to surprise his folks.

"I'll ambush them," said a delighted George, thinking ahead to his unannounced arrival. This time the crossing waters were very choppy, but after being on land marching his legs off for a year, he gladly bore the swaying of the rocking boat. When he got off the boat at Chios, a number of families were waiting for soldier sons or relatives. One of these soldiers that George talked to during the crossing, knowing he didn't have a ride, offered to drop George off at his family's place. He said they were going by the place anyway. George knew this wasn't true, but gratefully accepted the generous ride anyway.

Not only did George surprise his mother, she also surprised him. After schrieking on first sighting George, and smothering him in kisses and hugs, she gave him hell!

"Not a letter in months, we didn't know if you were dead or alive, and then we get four at once? And not one of them mentioning when you were coming home?"

"Ah, Mom, I tried to write every week. The war has messed up regular mail and travel routes because of refugees. You don't understand war. I wasn't sure myself when I'd get here."

"Your mother doesn't know war? I, who grew up with bodies at my front door, night raids, villagers being shot, knifed and killed and fighting all around me? I know it all too well, my son!"

"Yes, you have those terrible memories and I too have seen many killed in large attacks, sudden deaths. I don't want to talk about it, Mom. It messes up my head!"

"Oh, we all have seen too much. We fight for our country because we have too, not because we want to. I can't stay angry with you. I never could, even when you were full of the devil, my little Georgie."

"Believe me, Mom. Many times I was writing you, but I was so tired I fell asleep. I had to sleep when I could. Night attacks and all. I'm just glad to be home."

"And we are glad you're home. Come, sit here and talk to me of other things. No, first have something to eat and then you must rest. I'll keep everyone away until you're feeling rested. Sit down for some coffee and baklava."

"You look so thin, George. Didn't they feed you?"

"We ate when and where we could. Army food for thousands isn't home cooking. We also ate off the land. Fig Trees, grape-vines, olive trees. Foraging trips to villages and towns. The Greeks fed us, the Turks wouldn't, so we took the beans and wheat from what was our recaptured lands. Our food was enough, but we always could have used more."

The next morning, after a long night's sleep, George awoke to find much bustling, but muted talk and activity downstairs. When he wobbled down the stairs, shaking the sleep out of his eyes, he was following the floating smell of coffee and longed for its delicious taste. He was astounded at the size of the group of well wishers waiting for him to rise, and to welcome him home. Cheers and huzzahs rose from the throng. George was not only surprised, but a little embarrassed by the shouted greetings:

"Here's the General!"

"Attention!"

"Our hero is up!"

"I only made Sargeant, said George, in protest."

"George, my son, I tried to keep them away, but they were too excited," said his apologetic mother.

"It's all right, Mom. I'm just happy to see everyone."

Later in the day, when things had quieted down, George started to get into the routine of things, helping out with chores around the house. He also greeted local folks who stopped by to welcome him back. It was enjoyable renewing friendships, but also tiring. George delighted in sleeping as late as he needed and putting on a little weight. He was being spoiled and loved it. He felt that he was treated as a hero just because he survived a shooting war and was part of Greece's patriotic victories.

He wanted to visit Smynra to see some relatives of Angelika, but he was warned away by his family and neighbors.

"Not a good idea, George. The Turks in Smynra are unhappy with the loss of territories from the Balkan Wars and are harassing the Greek Quarter. Best to stay out. Why not write, telegraph or telephone?"

Having recently disengaged from hostilities, George was reluctant to chance a re-ignition. He tried to contact a few known relatives of Angelika, but was unable to reach any of them, and decided to leave well enough alone.

One evening, when all was quiet, George asked his mother what her plans were, before she could ask the same of him.

"Greece has just beaten the Turks in the Balkans, the Ottoman Empire is crumbling and Greater Greece is growing. Chios and Crete are to be annexed officially soon, if they haven't been already. For now, my future is here."

"This is what you want, Mom?"

"I want our lands back! I can reclaim them easier from nearby Chios, than America. The dollars you all send from America go far here, and help keep my dream alive. Think on that, my son."

"Mom, in your own way, you are as stubborn as Dad."

"And you, my Georgie! We are Greek; we are independent!"

Now knowing his mother's immediate plans, George thought about his. While doing his share of his domestic duties, George was turning over in his mind his own future. He found himself one early evening watching the sun going down. While lying on the shores of Chios, he listened to the hypnotic cadence of rolling waves; the fizzing bubbles washing ashore, bursting, and continuing on to disappear into the soaking sand. He spyed through his toes across the waters toward the horizon and Alatsata; the Turks had changed the name to Alacata.

"Well then, that's the answer," mumbled George to himself.

"Back to America. I've done my bit. I've got nearly a year's back pay from the Greek Government Army. Not much, by American standards, but it will pay my ship fare back to America. There, I can earn more dollars to send back to Mom, to feed her dreams, while fulfilling my own."

George's restlessness was starting to build again. Now rested and full of youthful energy, he felt reinvigorated by knowing his own mind. Yes, his mother was disappointed, but not surprised when George announced that he was going back to America. She didn't blame him, she said; he was young, adventuresome and his own man now. He had family, a future, job opportunities and someone named Angelika calling him back to America, and a proud father waiting there. If it made her son happy, she was happy.

STEAMING BACK TO AMERICA

Out of Pireaus, the steamship took a full seven weeks to sail the high seas back to Boston. To George, it felt like seven months. He had sent mail ahead by regular post. He thought about Angelika and sent her a separate letter. Her family was not especially enamored of George, thinking him an adventurer, who's only saving grace was that he was Greek. George admitted to Angelika that her parents were right; he was an adventurer. But what they thought was a criticism, George took as a compliment. George's enthusiasm became greater as he neared the American coast. He could only foresee good things ahead in his exciting life. And he beat the winter months, arriving in early November, 1913.

Antonios stood tall as a peacock, and the first thing he asked was:

"How is your Mama and the kids, George?"

"Fit as a fiddle. She and the kids are doing well and they send their love," reassured George to his father. He then brought him up to date on matters in Chios and Asia Minor. They talked non-stop for hours, when Antonios quietly asked:

"*Sargeant* Dilboy, is it?"

George could only smile. Then, as if to burst his son's bubble, Antonios continued:

"You may have thought you were alone. But I heard that up to 40,000 Greeks across America went back to Greece to fight. So there!"

"Yes." Replied George. "I served with many of them. They came from Chicago, San Francisco, New York City, New Orleans, Boston and Lowell, MA, and other areas."

Dropping his façade, Antonios beamed:

"You did us proud, Georgie. At your age, who would have thought it."

George couldn't hide his satisfaction. The gleam in his father's eyes was wonderful to behold. It made George glow inside, as he tried to control himself on the outside.

"Well, it's off to get a civilian job again. Who's hiring, Dad?"

"There's a new hotel opening up in Copley Square, Boston. Lots of jobs, I hear."

The men at the Sons of Ionia Club also mentioned local factory jobs. But George wanted to visit friends in the Greek Community around Kneeland and Washington Streets in Boston, so he would look into the Hotel job while he was in Boston. He also knew Angelika had relatives there. And speaking of Angelika, he should look her up.

When George called on Angelika, he was surprised that even her parents were welcoming to the returning hero, as they called him. They remarked on how much they thought he had grown, and how well he looked. George basked in the favorable attention from his former critics. Said her mother:

"Come Angelika. Look who has come calling, our returning veteran, Mr. George Dilboy. Angelica is a young lady, now."

Angelika self-consciously sauntered over and graciously welcomed George back to America. She seemed very pleased to see him. George was himself glad to see she was as pretty as ever, even prettier than he had remembered her. She appeared very much the young lady, thought George, even if she still wasn't quite five feet tall yet.

"Now, Mama, let them go for their walk. George didn't come here to talk to us," said Angelika's father.

Outside the house, Angelika suddenly turned on George and demanded to know why he didn't write to her more often!

"Oh, no. Angelika, I've gone over all this with my mother. I wrote when I could. Believe me, I would rather write than fight. War just screws up everybody's schedule. I'm lucky I'm alive and grateful to be home. Now I have to get a job."

"Ok, I forgive you. I know it must have been hard over there. I'm happy you're home too. Did you see your family."

"I sure did, and they are all doing fine. They will remain in Chios, for the time being."

"Where do you want to work?"

"Oh, my Dad tells me they're hiring at the new Copley Plaza Hotel in Boston. So I thought I would take a look over there."

"Can I go with you, George, I have relatives near there. Besides, I want to see the Greek Cathedral over on Ruggles Street."

"Sure, why not. Just get the ok from your parents. I don't want to get in trouble with them again."

George and Angelika went together to Boston by a series of trolley cars. Angelika's relatives were thrilled to welcome Angelika's friend, a returning Balkan War veteran who had fought for the homeland, and made him most welcome. When they went thereafter to the hotel, both George and Angekila were offered jobs, but Angelika declined. She already had a job as a dressmaker. George was sure that Angelika's attractiveness helped him get the job offer. George was to be a bellhop at a modest hourly rate of pay, but he would be allowed to keep the tips he earned from the high-class clientele the hotel catered to. He was also welcome to the leftover food from the hotel restaurant. But he would have to pay the cost of taking three trolleys to the hotel, even though the hotel wasn't two miles from his family's tenement flat.

Now he had a job and his girlfriend back. He would be exchanging the uniform of a Greek Army Officer for the uniform of a hotel bellhop. A comedown in status, but a new beginning, he thought to himself. And at least nobody here is shooting at a bellhop. He was, on balance, pleased and full of enthusiasm. He also went back to the Bennett School nights to learn more English. A year speaking only his native Greek didn't improve his English.

George also reconnected with Woz and the boys. The Woz welcomed him back from the *Baltic* Wars, though he didn't know much about them.

"Bal*kan* Wars," corrected George. "Bal*tic* Countries are Lithuania, Estonia and Latvia in Northeast Europe. The Balkan Countries include Serbia, Albania, Montenegro, Bosnia-Hercegovina, Bulgaria and the area that is part of the Balkan Peninsula in Southeast Europe."

"Ah, I know East Somerville from West Somerville. I know nothin 'bout those places."

"Many people mix them up, Woz. It's a common mistake because they sound so much alike, and they're both in Eastern Europe."

"We have gang wars over territory, so countries do, too, huh?"

"I never thought of it, that way. Maybe if we found a way to mend fences, we could mend borders."

"Oh, yeah, how we gonna do that?"

"Do what we're doing, talk."

CHAPTER SEVENTEEN

AMERICAN CIVILIAN LIFE

George was pleased to hear that the Massachusetts lawmakers passed a minimun wage law, requiring employers to pay workers like himself a minimum hourly wage. It was the first such law in this country. This wage was set last July. It made him glad that he came back to this country, because it would benefit not only himself, but his family back in Chios. However, the men at the Sons of Ionia Club also said that the Government now has an income tax each worker has to pay. George understood this idea, because of the "bread tax" the Greek community collected from its members to send back to the home country.

George did so much marching back in Greece and Macedonia that he longed to drive one of the new horseless carriage's that they called a motor car. The guys at the club told him that a man named Henry Ford had an improved assembly plant in Michigan that made them faster and cheaper. The new Model T motor car had dropped its price to $440. This businessman Ford claimed that every time he reduced the price of his car by $1, he got 1,000 new buyers. George wanted to be one of them. But to get an operators license to drive, one needed to get a license by taking a written English test and do a practice-driving test. So it was back to night school to enable him to learn better English so he could pass this test.

It was now the winter season and George had received a pair of double runner ice skates as a Christmas gift. Angelika asked him when he was going to use them.

"When I get a hockey stick, I'll play hockey," he answered.

"Oh, I don't mean that. I mean for you to just go ice skating. Let's go over to the Mystic River. It's not too deep there and the water freezes over quicker. It will be fun."

"Of course, I'm all for having fun."

"George, you're supposed to say: 'I'm for having fun with *you*'."

"Well, that's what I meant."

"But you've got to *say* it. You're older than me, but I have to teach you how to treat a Lady."

"Well, I'm learning, ain't I?"

"Yes. And it's about time. You're going to be eighteen next week and you're a world travelled, war veteran, and a man. So you have to start treating me like what I am, a woman. In case you haven't noticed."

"Oh, I have. I may be naïve in some things, but I'm not blind."

"See, there's hope for you yet."

"Say, that's funny. Are you playing with words? Blind and see."

"No, I'm playing with you. And you are proving to me that love is blind."

"Whoa there! You are only sixteen and I'm turning eighteen. Let's not get carried away."

"That's exactly what I hope you do with me, once you get established in the future. Am I in your future, George?"

"Are you in my present?"

"That's no answer, George Dilboy! You sound like those Irish kids, answering a question with a question."

"You always use my last name when you get angry at me. I like that. It's cute."

"And I'm cute enough to be sought after by Peter Boujoukos!"

"That little mealy mouthed, weasel worded muttonhead?"

"He's a good dancer! And he always asks me to dance at the Daughters of Ionia Socials."

"Big deal! Can he earn a living doing that?"

"Maybe not, but dancing is fun."

"So, I'll learn to dance."

Reluctantly, the rest of that winter, George would practice basic dance steps to the music of Angelika's new victrola record player. They used her front parlor until the kids in the neighborhood, hearing the music, poked their faces in the window and made fun of them. George would chase them away, but they made a game of it. Finally, Angelika's mother let them go upstairs to her room, but her door had to be open at all times. When the music stopped, her mother found reasons to frequently walk by her door.

In the late spring and early summer George, Woz and the guys liked to walk over to Charlestown to the bottom of Bunker Hill St. on the Somerville-Charlestown line. The attraction there was the "runners." In the past, horse drawn wagons raced down the hill and local wagers would be bet on them. Sometimes a local bar would sponsor a race against another bar's candidate. The police took a dim view of this. Occasionally, motor cars were matched at faster speeds and the stakes were raised. Initially, to stop this the City Government authorized the Police to deliberately put bumps in the road, but these were just ridden over. Then the city workers dug trenches across the street to stop the racing. This resulted in some spectacular races and crashes.

This cat and mouse game was a thrilling entertainment to the locals. George and the boys witnessed some dangerous races and saw a few serious injuries. Some of the participants were liquored up. When innocent bystanders, in addition to the drivers were hurt, as well as damage to properties, the Police widened and deepened the ditches and markedly reduced these incidents. While they lasted, they provided an oddly dangerous form of entertainment. After many false alarms, and early morning races, the crowds dwindled and they eventually died out. But there was always the odd late night or early morning drunk or daredevil who would try his luck. It didn't seem to matter to them if the street was empty of people, or some of their instigator, inebriated buddies were cheering them on at the bottom of the hill. Sometimes the Police would arrest them all and toss them into the patrol wagon.

Inciting Public Disorder, Disturbing the Peace and other charges were brought against them to discourage these incidents. Ultimately, it worked. George thought it foolish to save up and pay $440 for a motor car and then damage them so.

Angelika worked part-time in a dress shop on Massachusetts Ave, in Central Square, Cambridge. She was a seamstress, mostly sewing clothes in the back room. Many of their customers were the wives and daughters of professors or employees of MIT on one side and Harvard University on the other side of Central Square. Up the street at MIT, she could look across the bridge to the Back Bay side of Boston. As part of her job, she occasionally helped put corsets on the mannequins in the front store window. She was small enough to move around in the confined window area. And, at her age, she didn't mind bending and stooping to fit the female dummies. The only thing she minded was the boys who stopped in front of the windows to gawk, until a policeman moved them along. George, when he was able, would walk the mile to Central Square and meet her after work. They might go to a movie house or have an ice cream. Then they would take the bus home.

George liked the work at the Boston Hotel, especially the money tips he received. He thought it odd, however, that some of the wealthiest appearing guests, gave the smallest tips. Since he went out of his way to be helpful, he was generally pleased with the tip money he received. For example, sometimes he would be asked to get a newspaper for a gentleman, or cigars, even though they could have gotten them themselves in the downstairs hotel lobby. It also helped him to learn the local area, like where the theatre district, a certain restaurant or a sports hall was located, because hotel guests repeatedly asked these type questions. His quick, accurate answers ingratiated him to the hotel guests and they rewarded him with generous tips. He was learning from human nature; it paid to be polite.

However, during the summer, when many people abandoned the hot Hotels in Boston for the cooler summer vacation spots in Northern New England, the hotel staff was reduced and he was laid off for the summer. Back in Brickbottom, one of the fathers in the original twelve families was the shoemaker, John Petropoulos. John passed on the word that he heard through a fellow craft guild member that a new shoe factory was opening up in the city of Keene, New Hampshire. Keene was about thirty-five miles north of Boston. The Company used the local paper there, the Keene Sentinel, to advertise many job openings and promised to pay good wages. George discussed it in the family and he decided to give it a try. After traveling from Greece, a trip to the neighboring state of New Hampshire looked like a short hop.

KEENE, NEW HAMPSHIRE

By the end of June, 1914, George was stunned to read in newspaper headlines that a Serbian nationalist, who was still a student teenager near his age, named Gavrilo Princip, shot and killed Archduke Franz Ferdinand and his wife, of the Austro-Hungarian Empire in Sarajevo, Bosnia-Herzegovina. Trouble was boiling again in the Balkans. The newspapers reported in July that Russia was backing up its fellow Slavs in Serbia and Germany was supporting Austria-Hungary. Greece didn't seem to be involved, so George took little further notice.

George took the bus from Boston to Keene, New Hampshire on the first of July. On arrival he checked into a rooming house for a cheap place to stay. He walked over and applied for a job as a day laborer at the Ashuelot Shoe Company in Keene. He gave as references his prior jobs in a laundry room at a Boston hospital, a busboy at a restaurant and a bellboy at a Boston hotel. The Personnel woman told him that he would be notified if he got the job. In the meantime, Johnny Petropoulos had given him the name of a local Greek to look up. Through this contact George got a part-time job as a fruit packer with a Greek owned Bardis Fruit Company.

The town had an Independence Day celebration on July Fourth. This was highlighted by a parade featuring local veterans, politicians, high school bands, and fire department trucks. They were honoring the birth of the United States of America. George took in and enjoyed the festivities. He couldn't help noticing how young a country the US was compared to his country of origin, Greece. He also enjoyed the pastoral setting of Keene, with its rolling pastures and hills. It was a pretty countryside. He and Angelika agreed to visit each other when they could during the summer. Woz and the boys talked about traveling up to visit George in Keene, but it never came about.

George was notified to report to the Ashuelot Shoe company to work the day shift the following day, if he was still interested. He was. He was also able to keep the part-time hours at the Bardis Company by working through the early evening. He had the energy and ambition to go right from one job to the other, after swallowing a quick meal at a gulp and gallop coffee shop. He didn't doubt that the Bardis people liked having a fellow Greek as an employee and fit him in. He was saving to buy that motor car. And you could be sure that he wouldn't ruin the vehicle by racing it over trenches.

Angelika was not able to visit George on her own, even if she stayed at a friends house. Her parents did not think it would be properly chaperoned. Besides, George would be away only eight weeks; it would go by before she knew it, her mother pointed out. By summer's end, George was a little reluctant to leave Keene, because he had made some interesting friends in Keene. However, the fact remained that he could earn more money at his hotel job in Boston than he did at the two jobs in Keene. He got along well with the local people and he left such a good work record, that he was welcomed to come back anytime and a job would be waiting for him. This pleased George no end, because both companies made these offerings.

By the Labor Day Holiday, George had returned to Brickbotom and resumed his bellhop job at the Copley Square Hotel in Boston. With a distant interest, George followed the build up and the start of what would grow into the Great War in Europe and later called World War I. France, England and Italy and other countries would come in on the side of Serbia and Russia, while the Austrian-Hungarian Empire, Germany, Bulgaria and Turkey comprised the

Central Powers. Most of the major powers in Europe were pulled into the war. Greece was keeping its distance as long as it could, and trying to stay out of it, though it clearly had no sentiments in favor of Turkey. George was more immediately interested in saving for his dream motor car. Of course, his family got first call on George's earnings. That was his primary obligation and he was pleased to live up to it.

George and Angelika were frequently seen together walking. They would saunter in the cool fall early evening to a park area at the corner of Broadway and McGrath Highway, later to be known as Foss Park. It had a large, grassy area for picnics and had a centrally located water fountain. Angelika liked to lie back on the grass and stare up at the blue sky and watch the clouds move, if she followed them closely. George would watch the trolley cars clanging by, listening to the low roar of their wheels, and wonder where the passengers were going. Angelika and George were both in their own separate worlds. Angelika didn't mind because she thought it was romantic, even when they were silent; she enjoyed just being together.

"George, what are you going to be when you grow up?" Asked Angelika, as she gazed into the sky.

"What are you talking about? I'm already grown up!"

"I mean, what type career or job will you have? You won't be a bellhop all your life."

"I haven't figured that out yet. I'm trying out a lot of things."

"Well, I'm going to be a famous fashion designer. Maybe I'll get to own my very own shop in Boston or New York. Maybe even Paris or Milan!"

"Ha! You are a dreamer."

"What's wrong with that! I dream like anybody else. Don't you?"

"Oh, I dream too. But for things more practical, like owning my own motor car. If I ever can save $440, that is. Maybe Mr. Ford in Detroit-city will drop the price some more, and I'll get a better job and earn more money?"

"Huh! I'll bet you I'll open my own dress shop in Central Square before you own your own motor car. You wait and see, Mr. George Dilboy!"

"Well then, hold your horses. We'll just have to wait and see, won't we? Come on, let's walk back; I don't want to sit here and just fantasize."

———————————————

Angelika turned sixteen in November and was irked because George didn't get her a birthday present. George claimed the guys would scoff him unmercifully if they found out. Irked, Angelika loudly asked if he was going out with her or the guys. George hesitated and said: "Both, ain't I?"

"Well, I'm supposed to be *special.*"

"Ok, I'll treat you to a movie. I'm not doing that for them, so you're special."

George and Angelika's spirited natures clashed often, but they quickly made up and their relationship seemed all the better for it. For Christmas, Angelika gave George a flat scalley cap, what his Irish friends called a Tam O Shanter. He, in turn, got her a store bought hat. This was a treat for her, because she generally made her own clothes, including hats. She raved about the color and style of the gift hat; then went back to the store and exchanged it for a different one. It was too big for her petite body. The only reason he found out was because he never saw it again. When he asked her about it, she told him of the exchange, but she still purred George with appreciative kisses because it was the "thought" that counted. George was not overly demonstrative emotionally, but Angelika was. Rather than split them, their differences seemed to complement each other.

In the winter of 1915, George, Woz, Butchy, Nickie, Alex and Jim celebrated George's nineteenth birthday by taking him to a public dance at the State Ballroom on Massachusetts Ave in the Back Bay section of Boston. It was a Saturday night bash to cruise around and meet some non-Greek girls. Of course, being Polish, Woz's parents didn't care, but it would have bothered the closer knit parents of the others, had they known. Greek boys were to meet Greek girls. Greek tradition was more important to them than American mixing. This sanction made the dance more thrilling for the boys. They were striking a blow for their own independence; at least that's the way they saw it.

Afterwards, Angelika overheard the boys bragging and kidding each other about the dance. They freely tossed George's name around, relating how he fell during a polka and the girl he was dancing with ran off the floor unhurt, but embarrassed. George had just shrugged. When she confronted George about it, he readily admitted it and claimed he was practicing the dances she taught him. Besides, he said, the other girls only made her look better. Angelika replied that if he wanted to practice dancing, he could do it with her. Then she arranged for them to go to the Greek dance in Chinatown in downtown Boston, where the Boston Greek community mixed with the Greeks from surrounding cities like Somerville. A hall was rented for the occasion on the third floor of a building, in a gym over a union hall. It was located approximately half way between the Greek community around Kneeland and Washington Streets, Boston and Somerville. Many Greeks from the Lowell and Lynn areas also made the trip down and joined in merrily.

BACK TO KEENE

A couple of George's brothers were laid off from their factory and slaughter-house jobs. Since George expected to be let go for the summer again, and he had raved about Keene, NH, members of his family discussed moving there to get employment. A lower paying job was better than no job, was what they thought. Dimitri, the oldest brother of George, still had his job, but his company was laying off also, so he decided to leave before he too was laid off. Ultimately, George, his father, Antonios, Dimitri, Kostas, John and Marianthe went north to Keene. Marianthe went along to cook and clean house. Stamatia and Uncle Kostas remained behind to keep the flats.

The opportunities were there in Keene. All were able to obtain jobs. George went back to work at both the Ashuelot Shoe Company and the Bardis Fruit Company. They found an old farmhouse to rent. They were able to walk or take trolley cars or buses to their various jobs. Dimitri got a job shoeing horses at a stable. John and Kostas joined George at the shoe factory. They enjoyed the cooler weather north of Boston and the green countryside there was a pleasant change from the crowded conditions of three and four family tenements. They adjusted quickly and kept to themselves for the most part. Marianthe became a favorite of the downtown merchants because she was friendly, knew what she wanted and paid cash. She did not ask for any credit, as some local residents did.

Angelika was not thrilled with George's move to Keene, but she understood why. George needed to work and was too restless and energetic to stay unemployed long. They agreed to exchange visits when they could. Angelika lectured herself to make the best of it. George also missed Woz and the guys and the camaraderie of the Sons of Ionia social club.

Although the war in Europe was continuing now on two fronts, East and West, George took little notice. Greece was still consolidating its Balkan War accretions of land in Macedonia, Epirus and some offshore islands, especially Chios and the big island of Crete. He had heard from some Armenians in Watertown, MA about massacres of Armenians in Eastern Turkey by the Turks. Later, post World War I estimates went up as high as one million Armenians or more, massacred by the Ottoman Turks. He felt for their plight as the result of his families personal experience on the opposite, western end of the peninsula in Turkey. But it wasn't his fight.

CHAPTER EIGHTEEN

MEXICAN BORDER WAR

In the fall of 1916, George agreed to visit with Angelika in Lowell, MA, while she was visiting some relatives there. These relatives had heard about and wanted to meet Angelika's "man," and to talk with him firsthand about his Balkan War experiences. Some of their sons had made the patriotic voyage back and had their own stories. Since they had been in the Army of Epirus, and he was in the Army of Thessally, George had not had a chance to see them for anything but brief moments. He was looking forward to talking to them and comparing experiences.

Angelika reached Lowell first and visited with her kin. Later she met George at the bus station near downtown Lowell. She was dressed to the nines, in a frilly white dress, with one hand holding her hat on, and the other holding flowers. George liked the fact that Angelika favored flowers, though they held no special interest for him, because it reminded him of his mother's fondness for them. She gave him her sweetest smile and leaned toward him as he skipped down from the bus. George hugged her and kissed her on both cheeks. He didn't want to get too mushy in public.

"What are those for?" George said, pointing to the flowers.

"For you!" She beamed.

"Women don't give flowers to men, it's supposed to be the opposite."

"Hells bells, if I waited for you to give me flowers, I'd never get to enjoy them enough."

"It's a funny looking flower; what kind is it?"

"Honeysuckle. It's shaped like a trumpet, with long, purple and white flower petals. It has a distinct, sweet fragrance. Here, smell."

"That's ok, I'll take your word for it." Said George, with limited interest.

Angelika continued: "The long, wild stems wrap themselves around any object in its path. In Greek mythology, George, Choe and Daphnis were lovers who lived far apart and rarely saw each other. Daphnis prayed to the God of love to make the honeysuckle blossom last longer than a single season, so the lovers could spend more time together."

"Yeah, well that's very interesting."

"George, you're got to pay attention to the language of flowers. They send messages."

"I can listen to you for messages; I don't need flowers for that."

"George! You are impossible! You have to open up your mind to the natural beauty in life all around you."

"Yes. And for that, I don't have to go beyond you."

"Now, George. That's more like it. You can be so romantic, at times. It gives me hope."

George and Angelika spent a busy weekend visiting with her kinfolk and seeing the local sights. They were also able to get in a church service. While waiting to board a bus back to Keene, George treated Angelika to tea and pastry at a coffee shop near the transit station. During a pause in their conversation, Angelika noticed that George seemed to be lost in his own thoughts:

"Hello there, Georgie dearest. Anybody home?"

"Oh, I'm sorry. I was just thinking."

"About what?"

"I'm bored, that's all."

"Well, excuse me. I didn't know I was boring you!"

"No, it's not you, Angelika. You're wonderful. It's me. I'm going to be nineteen years old in February, and the world seems to be passing me by."

"You're too finicky, Mr. Dilboy. You have to be more patient, that's all."

"If I had a car, I could drive around and go places. See you more often, for instance."

"Maybe if we combined our savings, we could buy one," suggested Angelika.

"Angelika, I would like to do it on my own. But, thanks anyway."

ATTACK BEFORE DAWN

Two thousand miles away, they rode silently into town. Five hundred armed horsemen of Pancho Villa's irregular Army.

Only the riders could hear the muffled sounds. The horse's hoofs were covered with canvas cloth to smother their sound; the metal stirrups and leash couplings were covered in pig grease, and the muted, rhythmic strides of the horses disguised the trotting killers.

It was 0400 hours in the black ink of a quarter moon night. Only a bored American sentry stood between the approaching Mexican desperadoes and the sleeping town of Columbus, New Mexico. They saw each other at the same time. The sentry challenged the night-riders. The bandit deviltry answered by raising their rifles. They both fired at the same time. KA-Pow! KA-Pow! Went the rifles. The eerie silence of the night roared into deafening gunfire! Three of Villa's bandits fell from their horses, shot dead by a panicked, but accurately firing sentry. It was their mistake for being closely grouped. But the bored sentry, shocked alert by the suddenly appearing Mexican army, was killed himself by multiple bullet wounds. The horses galloped ahead, as the fired up raiders yelled:

"Viva Villa!

Viva the revolution!

Death to the Gringos!"

The only American soldiers up at that hour of the morning were the cooks, kitchen helpers and other scattered sentries. Hearing the shooting, they ran for their rifles. Others, springing out of their wooden canvas cots, sought to man the two machine guns in the camp. Fort Furlong was a US Army ring of shacks. It lay adjacent to a small, dust-covered pretense of a town named Columbus, New Mexico. It housed two old wooden hotels, a post office, a general store, a blacksmith barn, corrals, and a dozen other run down buildings.

An article in the Keene, NH Sentinel attracted George's attention and told the rest of the story:

"Just before dawn on March 9th, 1916, a band of Mexican revolutionaries under the leadership of General Francisco 'Pancho' Villa crossed the American border and attacked the town of Columbus, New Mexico. At the battle's end, three hours later, seventeen Americans and sixty-seven Mexicans lay dead."

It went on to relate that the US Calvary mounted their horses and pursued the retreating attackers for fifteen miles across the Mexican border. The Villa outlaws, also called Villasta's, split into many bands and scattered into the distant dark and mountains ahead.

Wow! Thought George. What was that all about? The article went on to state that the following day, President Woodrow Wilson requested the formation of a Punitive Expeditionary Force to pursue the murderers and bring them to justice. The force was to be placed under the command of a General John "Blackjack" Pershing. George thought that the nickname "Blackjack" was appropriate in this situation, because it conjured up an image of a club weapon to slug or bash another. A public call was put out for volunteers to complement the Regular Army in forming up this punitive expeditionary force. It excited George's interest.

George followed the matter avidly in subsequent editions of the newspaper. The followup articles reported America's indignation at this flagrant border violation, and cries for retaliation grew among the people and the Congress. The newspapers predicted that the call up would mobilize the largest troop deployment in the United States since the Civil War. The thrill of the anticipated chase fascinated George and was the subject of many animated conversations at work and at home. George could hardly contain himself; the adrenalin flowed and his pulse quickened. He wrote a letter to the Woz and told him he was going to sign up with the New Hampshire National Guard and join the volunteer force to chase after Pancho Villa. He told him that he wanted to be part of the Calvary, because he wanted to ride with mounted horse troops. That would be exciting, he said. Besides, he had walked all over Greece. Now he wanted to ride all over Mexico. Woz wrote back to wait for him; George wasn't going to be the only one to have an adventure.

But George wrote him right back welcoming him to sign up with him, but suggested he join the National Guard in Boston and ask to be assigned with George's unit. He lived in the Boston area, and the New Hampshire National Guard would only send him back there, anyway.

Shortly thereafter, George did sign up with the National Guard in Keene, NH. He asked to join the Calvary, but the recruiting Sergant said George could take that up with the Army brass when the National Guard volunteers were federalized and made part of the US Army, which was in the process of being requested at that moment. George didn't even tell his family he was going to sign up; he just did it. He turned twenty years old in February and he didn't have to add to his age or ask anyone's permission. His whole body was taut with tension and anticipation. When he telephoned Angelika through a friend, who had a telephone in her house, Angelika could tell something was up because of his lively voice. Instinctively she knew it was Mexico because it kept jumping into their conversations the past week. She already told George to stop calling her senorita. She didn't like his voluntering, but knowing George as she did, she accepted the inevitable.

Accompanying Woz into the Masachusetts National Guard was little Alex Constantine and the red headed Butchy Shaughnessy from the gang. Alex, however, was rejected immediately because of his poor eyesight, even with glasses. He was crestfallen with disappointment. But it heightened the excitement of the other two. Woz and Butchy were told that every New England unit in the Army was being sent to three sites in Texas, El Paso, Brownsville and San Antonio, and to Douglas, Arizona. There, they were to be assembled into the Expeditionary Force. When they got there, they could renew their request for a transfer. But it would be easier if their friend Dilboy asked for a transfer, because there was only him to move.

From their local and central armories, they took military buses to Boston and then were put on trains to go to Chicago and then south to Kansas City, and on to Fort Sam Houston in San Antonio. The officers of the New England National Guard contingent knew so little about the desolate and barren land of the US Southwest, that when the train slowed down and came to a lurching stop outside San Antonio, they immediately ordered the troops from the train, into a defensive perimeter, with rifles in a firing position, to fight back against the imminent Mexican attack!

When apprised that they were not in Mexico and they were not under attack by the laughing locals, the Commanding officer, trying to salvage his pride retorted:

"Well, isn't this where Americans were massacred by Mexicans at the Alamo?"

"Yes," he was told, "but that was seventy years ago, when San Antonio was part of Mexico."

Somewhat chagrined, to the further amusement of the Texans, the New Englanders reboarded the train and continued on their way to their ultimate destination, an assembly headquarters at Fort Bliss, near El Paso, in Texas. They were part of a mass migration of troop trains from all over the country radiating down and across to the US-Mexican Border. Because of an increasing number of cross border "pin-prick" raids by Mexican irregulars, General Pershing had been assigned to command the Southern Department of the Army in San Antonio two years ago, and a gradual troop build up had been going on there since.

This was the first time Woz and Butchy travelled outside of New England and they were enthralled crossing the country. They slept in their seats, played cards, some few read and there were a couple of fistfights. At train stops, they were allowed to get off the trains to stretch their legs, but were told not to leave the stations.

Some did, however, for different reasons, including desertions, some volunteers having changed their minds. They would be arrested and put in a military jail. Some of those were discharged from the Army as unsuitable, and some were allowed to catch up to and rejoin their units, at their own expense. Their pay was docked. George kept to the rules, learned how to play cards and enjoyed the joking and horseplay among the youthful soldiers. The Regular Army types, including officers, stayed together and, as a group, was older and much more serious than the volunteers. Though Woz and Butchy looked for George, they never saw him until they reached Fort Bliss. It was a brief sighting in which George saw them getting off the military bus at the camp, which they had taken after getting off the train. However, they didn't hear him, and George was told to move along by a barking Sargent. It was hot and muggy, with strong, hot winds blowing dust every which way.

"Get use to it, Boys!" yelled a full-throated Drill Sargeant. "This is Texas."

George didn't mind so much. After all, he was born and brought up in hot weather and dusty lands, characteristic of Asia Minor and Greece. What was missing here in the El Paso area was the cooling presence of mountains and the seas surrounding Greece. George also knew about border raids and killings by foreign forces. He couldn't wait to showcase his skill with a rifle. The recruiting Sargent in Keene, NH was impressed with George's experience in the Balkan Wars, though he had not heard too much about it:

"Balkan Wars? You mean there were two Wars?" He asked. "I thought it was only one. I stand corrected."

This war experience was duly noted on George's Personnel Record and the subject of comments by Regular army Officers. Some disparaged it with derisive comments, while others thought it explained the origins of the War now being fought in Europe, the Great War, so-called. Among the volunteers, however, the Balkan War experience gave George a special status. Many wanted to know what it was like. They were curious about its details and that part of the world. His stature was further boosted when he proved himself exceptionally skilled with a rifle on the shooting range. He was one of the few soldiers who earned the designation of "*Distinguished Marksman*," earned by fewer than five percent of the soldiers. This particularly impressed the previously unimpressed Officers, because many Texans were themselves experienced marksman. Among them, however, revolvers were more frequently used than rifles.

The Regular Army had full uniforms. The initial units of the suddenly raised Volunteer Force did not. Ultimately, however, after uniforms were made by rushed war contractors, full uniforms were distributed. The food wasn't bad to George, though others complained in high voice. Flapjacks, bacon and eggs, oatmeal cereal and coffee were typically eaten for breakfast. They were also gradually introduced to Mexican food, such as tortillas, frijoles and tamales. Tequilla was notably absent. But then again so wasn't American beer. Of course, that was on base. Off base, in El Paso, it was a far different matter, as the drunken revelries and brawls attested.

There was initial confusion at the time this camp was being set up, abetted by the fact that additional troops were coming in all the time. The guys asked a lot of questions, like who was Pancho Villa, what did he look like and why he attacked the United States. Some soldiers couldn't read, and some who could read, didn't bother to read the newspapers. Though George had a Greek accent, he could read and write passable English. The soldiers were given answers to these type questions in lectures and question and answer sessions. Additionally, some silent, English sub-titled films showed fluttering pictures of Pancho Villa taken the prior two years when he was on friendly terms with the United States. There was even one picture of General Pershing and Pancho Villa smiling and standing beside each other in a group photo. This would be the closest the famous duo would ever get. The films and lectures also stressed the political turmoil in Mexico. Crowning the political chaos was the fact of five Mexican Presidents in six years.

George absorbed it all like a sponge and understood most of it. Because of his non-threatening size and chatty nature, George fit in with the guys and made friends easily. George was generous by nature and displayed this side of himself by readily sharing his cigarettes and gum with others. He had a soft voice and smiled often. His energy was shown by the incessant tapping of his fingers and toes. If he wasn't talking, he was chewing gum or smoking a cigarette. He was a man who always seemed to be in motion. He would sometimes jump up spontaneously and dance, sing and entertain the boys, rescuing them from boredom. As a result of being so active and energetic, he slept well.

But not all went according to plan. George's request to be assigned to a Calvary unit was initially rejected because of his lack of horse skills. George could ride a horse, but not especially well. Riding slower mules and even slower donkeys in Asia Minor and Greece was not the same as the speedier use in the wide-open spaces in Texas and Mexico. This less than average skill was especially evident when he saw that most of the initial volunteers for this Expeditionary Force came from the West and Southwest, where the horse was still the principal mode of transportation. He was aced out by competition, George realized. So be it. He couldn't excel in everything, he told himself. But then he was advised by some veterans that when cavalry horses played out or had to be destroyed, the dismounted soldiers became instant-infantry and trailed along. When they obtained remounts, the grounded infantry would become cavalry again. Therefore, if he volunteered to deliver remount herds, he could work his way into the mix of advanced troops and get into the action. It made sense to George and he filed it in the back of his mind.

To his dismay, George heard that the National Guard troops were to be used for guard and back up duties on the US side of the border, because of their inexperience. There were to be some exceptions, depending on the developing needs of the Army. George thought he fit into the exception role. So he stubbornly asked an irritated Sargent to put his name in as a volunteer at anything that would get him into Mexico, where the real action was.

CHAPTER NINETEEN

DESERT COUNTRY

The hot, barren, dusty wide-open land of the Southwest was foreign to the troopers from the forested and treed parts of US. One can only imagine how it impacted on a New York City youth, who was accustomed only to crossing a busy paved street. Therefore, George thought that it was not to be wondered at when these weather hardened, tough, Southwesterners scoffed at and ridiculed the griping pansies of the Northeast and fueled many a fistfight between the hastily put up pup-tents and in the local saloons. It was a natural progression from these spontaneous flare-ups to set up officially sanctioned, recreational boxing matches. It fostered sport, unit pride and healthy release of energy for exuberant youth. Similarly, it aided competitive betting on results of the bouts. Not surprisingly, it naturally progressed into card games, foot and horse races, and clanging, horseshoe contests. As one doughboy put it:

"We weren't being paid much, but one of the ways to increase our pay was to gamble."

Though gambling was not officially condoned, it wasn't condemned either. It became a matter of benign neglect. For nights on the town during official leave, carousing, card playing, and visits with the local ladies, at bustling El Paso, Brownsville and San Antonio were available to the pent up spirit of the soldiers who chose those options. Subsequent sessions at religious services the following Sundays, were noticeably less well attended. Headaches, hangovers and time in the stockade were more the norm.

George didn't ask to be transferred to Woz and Butch's unit because he took pride in representing his current unit in rifle shooting competition against other units. Many in his unit bet on him and he received recognition and good-natured comments. In Greece, they called him "Hawk Eye"; here they Americanized it and called him "Eagle Eye." Besides, he liked the guys and bonded with those in his unit.

On the reverse end, when Woz and Butch asked to be transferred into George's unit, it was rejected as unnecessary, because most of the New Englanders were being kept together in the same infantry Brigade, if not the same Division, Company, Platoon or Squad, which was close enough, they were told. Besides, they would be moving out soon to their regularly assigned duties. A few would be ordered to special duties to cross over the Mexican border, and George hoped to be in this cadre. Aside from all that, "there wasn't time for these petty matters," said one Lieutenant, dismissively. An additional pressure to move out was the continuing influx of incoming troops. They had to make room for other troops to be trained.

In the meantime, red headed Butch was being harassed by other soldiers, who liked to refer to him as "shithead." However, this was curtailed by the Woz and his big presence. He made sure they didn't overdo it.

"After all, what are friends for?" spoke a protective Woz to an appreciative Butch.

"I hear you, Woz; you watch my back and I'll watch yours. Just like back in the old neighborhood, huh?"

"Something like that, kid," affirmed Woz.

When George heard about this, he chuckled. His way was different. He didn't try to intimidate. He wasn't big enough. But even if he was, he wasn't so inclined. He won friends, not arguments, he told himself.

Within three months of the Mexican raid in New Mexico, 150,000 National Guardsman and Army regulars had been mobilized and federalized, George would later hear. Wooden quarters and barracks housed the Regular Army and Non-

Commissioned Officers. Outside these buildings and the parade grounds for infantry drills and horse training areas, Fort Bliss became a tent city for the sprouting incoming soldiery. George shared a tent with three other Privates. Jeff Ashton was a twenty-five year old English farmer from Manchester, NH. He was a pipe smoking, dark, wavy haired man, pale complexioned, of average height and medium build. He was thoughtful and slow moving. He had a habit of shuffling his feet along, instead of walking. Because of his older age among the private soldiers, some called him, "Gramps," which he disliked. Others referred to him as "the Farmer," which he liked. He was married and had a son, three years old. He was the only one married in the squad, all housed in the same tent. Being a hunter, he was a good shot with a rifle. But he wasn't the superior marksman that Dilboy was, and this bothered him.

Abe Hershon was a Russian Jew who took a lot of kidding because of his marked physical features, like his hooked nose. Though he was only twenty-two years old, he also had a receding hairline. Bobby Kelleher kidded Abe that Abe wasn't getting taller, but his forehead was. He was irreverently called "baldy." It didn't bother him, or if it did, he didn't show it. He was thin and small. Quick and fidgety, he was a bank clerk from Nashua, NH.

Bobby Kelleher was a nineteen year old, Irish kid from Keene, NH. He was the youngest person in the squad. He was whimsical and quick to take offense. But he was also quick with a quip. He kept brushing back his black wavy hair. He was a handsome six footer, with an athletic body. He was a noted three-sport star in high school; basketball, baseball and football. He had worked as a stringer, reporting for a local newspaper, making little money. He was one of the few making more money in the Army, than in civilian life.

Because George Dilboy had previous military experience and had demonstrated unusual skill with a rifle, he was given an early promotion to Corporal. Though not the rank he had in the Greek Army, he thought it was his due. Others were skeptical, appearing to adopt a wait and see attitude.

"Hey, baldy. What's a Jew doing in the Army? Asked Jeff.

"Why can't a Jew be in the Army, just like an Englishman? Responded Abe. "Personally, I was bored and wanted to see Mexico." "Same here," said Bobby. "I want to see the rest of the country and some other part of the world. And Mexico is the closest action."

"Hey, Dilboy, what's your story. Haven't you already won your war?" Inquired Jeff.

"Maybe I want to help win another one. I like adventure as much as anyone else, I suppose," answered George.

"So what's this Pancho Villa like?" Asked Bobby.

"You saw the movie. He's got a drooping red mustache, so we were told. We can call him 'shitface'? He's broad shouldered and squat, with bowed legs from riding horses all his life. And he doesn't like Americans!" Said Jeff with authority.

"Why not?" Continued Bobby.

"Damn! Don't you see the newspapers? President Wilson recognized his rival, somebody named Carranza as President of Mexico. And Villa didn't like that. That was also told us at the lecture." Replied Abe, impatiently.

"Hey! Don't hook your banana nose into me, you refugee from Nauseous, I mean, Nashua."

"There's more to it, said Abe. The Mexicans have been fighting amongst themselves for six years. Anyway, I heard that twenty of Villa's revolutionaries fled over the US border from Government forces. As they were being deloused with gasoline, as was customary, someone threw a lighted match at them and they all burned to death."

"Also, during a battle between Villa's forces and Carranza's Government troops near the US border, we let Carranza's troops enter the US to get behind Villa. We also lit up the area with huge flood lights to expose the whereabouts of Villa's troops and they were slaughtered by Carranza's soldiers," added George.

"I was also told that Villa had prepaid a US merchant in Columbus for guns and supplies, but they were never delivered to him," intoned Abe.

"True, but President Wilson had issued an embargo forbidding any further sales or deliveries of weapons and aid to Mexicans over the border, in order to help stop the killing. Besides, how could you locate Villa? He's always on the run," remarked Jeff.

"He can't read or write, but he doesn't drink or smoke," commented Abe.

"Doesn't drink or smoke? Hell, he'd never make it in this Regiment!" advised Bobby.

"We're hearing it everywhere. Pancho Villa has ordered that any "Gringos" found in Mexico are to be killed on sight. Mexico has fallen into violent anarchy. The whole country is ravaged by outlaws, assassins, bandits, roving armed bands, and revolutionaries raping, robbing and running amok, holding up trains and burning and destroying towns and villages. The peasants are terrorized by these mindless and chaotic killings," added Abe.

"Hell, that sounds like a description of El Paso," cracked Bobby.

"While I was in the chow line today, I heard that El Paso, had to block its windows with mattresses to protect against bullets and artillery shells flying across the border," George informed the squad. And then he added:

"You guys know, I assume, that our training is being cut to rush us into the chase."

It soon developed that George was correct. His Company, because of the high number of skilled marksmen, were being ordered South of the Border. Later that evening their Company Commander was ordered to be ready to break camp at first light the next morning and to "turn out your troop!"

"And did you see who the Army is recruiting to act as guides and scouts?" Asked Jeff. "Old time trappers, prospectors, Apache's, Mexicans, muleteers, adventurers, gunfighters and anyone else who knows the area of uncharted Chihuahua, the largest State in Mexico."

"Well that's a motley crew, but we need them to help us when the trails disappear and the maps end," mentioned Jeff, philosophically.

For those in the infantry expected to go over the border, this expedition was expected to be a cavalry matter and the infantry were told that they would be used to maintain communications, supply lines and to provide camp security, for the most part. But the infantry hoped and believed that if the chase brought them into the mountains, where wheeled transports couldn't go, then the horse cavalry would have to make way for the infantry. They would bide their time, but was anxious for action. Camp drills and practice hikes were boring them and causing further reasons for brawls in the saloons of downtown El Paso. Better that they fight the enemy than each other, agreed the Commanders.

The hastily assembled American soldiers at Fort Bliss in El Paso were brought up to date on what had preceded them and what they could expect. The Expedition had first entered Mexico back on March 15 when the 13th Cavalry, led by Major Frank Tompkins, left Columbus and crossed the border through the little town of Palomas. They proceeded through the open plain and dusty town of Ascencion. Villa had a six-day head start. His horseprints showed that he avoided the hills and mountains to make a faster getaway. General Pershing, with his troops, led a second column from a ranch owned by a Culberson family about fifty miles west of Columbus. He left the following day at midnight, but he had a shorter distance to travel before both columns met at Dublan, where Pershing set up his first base camp. This town is situated about 200 miles south into Mexico. It's also where the Mexican Northwestern Railroad crossed the desert and intersected Dublan. Then it cut through and followed along the spine of the Sierra Madre Mountains that reached heights of up to 12,000 feet. Much of the first two hundred miles in the northern middle-state of Chihuahua, where the troops route would be, was a vast, open, flat desert area. Temperatures were extreme. The heat could reach temperatures of 115 degrees during the day, and drop to freezing temperatures during the night. They would be marching by thorny mesquite, prickly cactus, sagebrush, deadly tarantulas and scorpions, rattlesnakes, mosquitoes and tent flies.

George, Jeff, Abe and Bobby were initially re-assigned to join up with and to be part of F Company of the 16th Infantry Regiment. But then George's request to volunteer for remount duty was granted and he was selected. Boldly, he asked if the rest of his squad could accompany him. They also had earned their marksmen's medal, he argued, though they were not "Distinguished Marksman," as was George, which he didn't argue. Surprisingly, the harried Commander granted this group request, but they had to move out immediately. This meant the next morning. And they did.

As part of their training, they learned that a Regiment would be composed of 810 men, including 24 officers. As part of this instant briefing, they were advised that the first complement of this force had left with Pershing the prior month. They were reminded that Pershing had orders not to fire on Mexican government forces, which were also chasing Villa. They were also not to upset the Mexican civilians. With the European War raging and seeming to inevitably involve the US, President Wilson did not want a second war with Mexico. Toward this end, American troops would set up its tents outside the villages and towns, wherever feasible, in order not to be seen as foreign "occupiers." Many Mexicans were very uneasy at American soldiers coming into Mexican territory. The last time it happened, in 1846-48, Mexico lost half it's country to the US in what is now, Texas, Arizona, New Mexico, and part of Southern California. And they didn't care one whit about some old treaty agreement that allowed the US and Mexico to invade each other's country while in hot pursuit of border renegades, at the time, Apaches.

And so this cool April night they were told to get ready to move out at first light the next morning. Full equipment was drawn that evening as they geared up. George practiced getting ready by putting web belts across his chest and around his waist. The x shaped bandoleers held rifle ammo in five round clips. From his cartridge belt hung a bayonet, a small scabbard containing a knife, canteen, first aid kit and a machete and scabbard. As a corporal and squad leader, George was also given a Colt .45 automatic pistol. Besides a five-dented hat, he was given a nine-pound Springfield rifle. They were issued fresh, olive drab shirts and baggy breeches that flared out at the upper leg. Cloth wraps were strung around their lower legs and called putees, to keep the dust off their legs and to prevent pant bottoms from being caught in cactus, ground growths and sagebrush. They would live in pup-tents and sleep in rolled up blankets. No more wooden barracks, they were warned.

The soldiers from Texas spoke a mixed language called Tex-Mex. Outside of the Southwest's Mexicans and Native American Indians, there was a generous mix of Germans, Irish, Italians, Poles, Scandinavians and black Buffalo soldiers, so-called. George was the only Greek, as far as he knew. His background made him use to, if not comfortable with, the dust, heat and mountains, but not the lack of water. It would be a precious commodity.

A fleet of new trucks had gone out with General Pershing. Some of them were reportedly seized off the docks of New York City bound by sale for the Great War in Europe. Pershing supposedly had a Dodge Touring car as his portable headquarters, much of the time. There were also Ford cars and one Cadillac car with an eight-cylinder engine. Mostly, however, mule pulled wagons called "escort wagons" carried supplies, including food, and hay for the horses, until suitable foraging grounds could be found. Horses, mules or donkeys, whatever was available, pulled wheeled mortars and artillery pieces. Extra ammunition, shells and rifles were carted in horse drawn wagons. There was a medical wagon, which would be their field hospital. Primitive field radios were used by the Signal Corps. They were told they would have to shake out their boots every morning to make sure there were no dangerous creatures inside, like poisonous tarantulas or scorpions.

The troops had been told about a new Aeroplane Force that initially numbered eight planes. The model was the new Curtiss JN-2, nicknamed the "Jenny." But George and others saw that the pilots were having problems when they tried to turn the plane or encountered strong winds. Their underpowered 90 horsepower engines kept them low in the sky, only 20 feet above tree tops, when there were any trees at all. The underpowered machines made them unable to fly over mountains, and caused them to be vulnerable to ordinary pistol and rifle ground fire. For weapons, each pilot only carried a pistol. The planes were used mostly for observation, dispatches and mail delivery, moving seriously wounded soldiers, and for short trips. One aeroplane had equipment failure and crashed landed, bursting into flames and caused a forest fire through dry trees and growth for forty miles!

"The Mexican government was quite put out, while the fire wasn't," chortled Bobby Kelleher.

Ideally, Pershing wanted the planes to spot Villa's fleeing army with its wider range and view from the air. But to his dismay, they proved unstable and unreliable.

Nevertheless, the two great innovations in the Mexican Punitive Expedition were the Aeroplane and Motor powered vehicles. The latter included automobiles, trucks and motorcycles. The former included photograph reconnaissance that inaugurated an automatic camera that could develop a series of consecutive pictures. George, Woz, Butchy, Jeff, Abe, and Bobby were experiencing a novel, moving education and maturity like they had never had before in their short lives, even as they cursed the foul weather and survived their other aggravating living conditions. Progress and growth came at a price.

CHAPTER TWENTY

MOVE OUT!

Being roused from a deep sleep during the dark that brisk morning, the splintered detachment of the 16th Infantry moved out at dawn. They filed along in a column of two's, preceded and followed by horse and mule pulled "escort wagons" and carts. Those skilled sharpshooters too ill to march but not too sick to travel were loaded into horse drawn wagons, including the sick and injured who overindulged in secret caches of tequila, partying and brawling their last night in camp. Only the truly incapacitated elected to stay in the wagons for long, because of the punishing bouncing over rocks and ruts in the crude hard packed roads. Their jarring insides cried out for relief.

The longer an infantry soldier carried his backpack, the heavier it became. The infantryman couldn't fill his saddlebags for his horse to carry like a Cavalryman could. In the early marches into Mexico, many an infantryman was overcome by heat and exhaustion. He was left by the side of the road, while the others continued to march. He would have to catch up when he could. Until he did so, he was made to feel like an outcast or a slacker. It was not unusual to see an infantryman stagger into camp at night, hours behind the rest of his company. It was part of the toughening up process.

As the leader of a Remount Group, George and his squad sat uneasily on top of some second rate horse mounts. George was the point man leading the herd of replacement horses along the trail. Keeping the front horses on the path was critical because the others just followed along. However, because of the strong winds and whipping dust, George, and eventually the others, found they were buffeted less if they dismounted and walked. It gave relief to their saddle sore backsides; they not being born to the saddle. Though walking had its own curse because it eventually became tiring on the legs, it spared the rest of the body and promised a sound sleep. An open desert greeted them as far as they could see. So didn't 105 degree heat. Eyes stung by salted sweat made for a miserable trek and much cursing. Frequent water stops were required to refresh more the men, than the horses. Those soldiers with foresight, used the goggles they acquired, by purchase or pilferage, to protect their eyes from the swirling dust. The unwelcome hot wind and rolling wheels kicked the fine-grained dust into the stultifying air. The soldiers following behind gradually learned to cover their mouths with their bandanas, and the noses and mouths of the horses to keep those passages moist and to prevent choking and sneezing.

The first few nights inside enemy territory they camped out in the open desert; bivouacing they called it. They pitched their puptents or slept under the stars, rolled up in their blankets. Hot days and cold nights reminded some of the soldiers of how they felt when they suffered hot flashes and then shivering cold when stricken by the grippe or flu, as some called it. Food and water mixed with gritty dust made eating difficult in the open. But even when they retreated to any kind of cover, it was never completely avoided. Somehow the dust got into their blinking eyes, constricted nostrils and parched throats. Mouths puffed up and then split into blood caked and crusty sores. Throwing themselves into the Casas Grandes River during the hot day to cool off, and the rare watering hole stops helped, but the relief was temporary. The advanced Cavalry units strode ahead and covered twice the distance. Collapsing horses forced them to rein up, as did stretching their supply lines.

By the third day out, George's lips were swollen and bleeding. His face and hands were chapped and raw. The blowing dust was stinging his eyes and blinding him, as he leaned into the wind. When they switched places for Bobby to take the point, to block the wind, George walked behind the larger, six-foot tall body of Bobby

Kelleher, who cursed the air blue with Irish oaths. Gale winds were
so strong on one occasion that they knocked Abe Hershon completely
off his feet, like loose sagebrush. He got up and bent over into the
gusts of wind. Jeff Ashton tried to turn around to talk a few times,
but gave it up after swallowing sand. At other times, they would
turn and walk backwards or sideways to shield themselves from the
wind and protect their eyes, mouths and noses.

That night they reached a ravine in a chaparral, which they
quickly learned was a dense thicket of shrubs and small trees. This
partial protection from the swirling elements was appreciated.
Though it helped block the stinging dust, it was nearly impossible
to light fires for cooking. They huddled under their own blankets
to eat their corn, beans, hardtack and coffee, spilling as much as
they drank. When it wasn't so dusty or windy, they would dig a
slit trench to put their feet down into, and this allowed them to
use the ground as a table. To take the chill out of the cold night air
that went below freezing some nights, they used the previously
dug slit trenches and filled them with wood, brush and coal and
set them on fire. Then they would clean out the ashes and sleep on
the warm ground, partially sheltered from the overhead wind.
Finally, they collapsed on the open ground, wrapped in their own
blankets, and fell into blessed sleep.

The next morning they climbed out of mounds of dust and
sand, shaking themselves off like desert rats. Ironically, being buried
in the sand provided them with heat to fight the cold, night air of
the desert.

Dispatch riders kept the rear echelons informed of what they
ran into. The use of telegraph stations by Pershings US Signal
Corps was reluctantly allowed by Mexican authorities. But Pershing
was irate when the Mexican Carranza Government refused to allow
the Expeditionary Force to use their railroads to route troops and
supplies south into Mexico beyond Dublan. But he did it anyway,
when he could. Some military gringos, disguised as Mexicans, made
secret courier trips back to Columbus. This was thought necessary
because important, military telegraphed messages were being

intercepted by the Carranza Government operators and used against them. The detached element of the 16th Infantry finally arrived at the first base camp at Dublan. Actually, however, they decamped at Casas Grandes, four miles southwest of Dublan. Casas Grandes was a Mormon Missionary Colony where a few persecuted but enduring, religionists remained. They were pleased to see their fellow Americans.

George's D Company, under the command of Captain Gonsalvez, a tough federalized Texas Ranger, was ordered to stand down. They off loaded their equipment and pitched their puptents. Some collapsed to rest; others went over to the nearby Casas Grandes River and jumped in to cool off. They could see the beginning of the Sierra Madre Mountains in the distance.

The Mexican Northwestern Railroad also ran through Casas Grandes, following the river, but the soldiers were told that Casa Grandes was off limits because of traffic, storage houses, and the fact that poisonous rattle snakes were slithering throughout the area to get at the food and the cooler shade cast by the buildings.

"Do you think that's true? Asked Bobby. "Why would snakes go near all that scary noise? Or is it a ruse to keep us away from all that food and ammo?"

"I don't know whether it's true or not. Maybe the vipers are hungrier than scared. But if I'm fed enough, do I want to put my life on the line to find out? Not me." Responded Jeff.

"Speaking of putting ones life on the line, Jeff. Why does a married man with a son, volunteer to go to war? The rest of the squad is single," wondered Abe.

"Many reasons, if I wanted to tell."

"So what's the big secret," inquired Bobby.

"No secret. Maybe like you guys, I want adventure. Maybe, I'm bored being a farmer. Maybe I want a regular income. Maybe, my crops have failed, and my wife is hassling me to get a paying job. Besides, my son is only three years old; he needs a mother more than a father, at that age. Maybe I just want a change. Take your pick."

"All good reasons, Jeff." Said a conciliatory George, ever the peacemaker. "Don't let them bother you. They're just curious, that's all."

While waiting for Pershing's further orders for George's unit, Captain Gonsalvez informed them of the earlier fight with Carranza troops at Parral, five hundred miles deep into Mexico. It was the first US entry to a large Mexican town. A running battle ensued between the greatly outnumbered Frank Tomkin's 13th Cavalry and Carranza Forces. While the battle raged, Colonel Brown's 10th Cavalry of Black Buffalo soldiers heard the gunfire and rode into the fray. Together they joined forces and routed the Mexicans. Brown had traveled down from the Village of Santa Cruz, thirteen miles north. George's company cheered the news, and it fired their fervor to get into the fight!

Pushing his advance, Pershing had moved his headquarters two hundred miles further south to Namiquipa. He was chasing moving sightings of Villa at Galeana, El Valle and Las Cruces. His advanced scouts brought back numerous reports that Pancho Villa's retreating Army was most recently encamped at Namiquipa. Of course, he had moved on by the time Pershing's forces got there.

Pershing kept a camp base at Dublan to maintain his supplies and communication lines. To avoid the brawls and troubles he experienced at Fort Bliss and El Paso, and to keep US soldiers out of Mexican towns, Pershing had a Medical Doctor establish a house of entertainment, so-called, and had the Mexican women cleared and periodically checked to maintain health standards at the camp. These efforts to control the inevitable habits of some men their age succeeded in the soldiers having the lowest rate of venereal disease recorded in the military during the prior sixty years. It was remarkably lower than such incidences during the Spanish American War, the Philippine Insurrection and the Boxer Rebellion in China. It even surpassed such recorded incidents during the American Civil War. It was an awkward matter to be proud of politically, but a practical necessity for an Army General, especially one in the middle of a shooting war.

"It's not something I'm going to write home to my wife about, that's for sure," remarked Jeff, as he fed some of the horses their oats, in nosebags hung over the heads of the horses.

"And it's also ironic considering this is a religious Mormon Colony," said Bobby.

"Not really." Commented Abe. "Not if you consider the Mormon tradition of polygamy. They would not be in a position to be critical."

George was pitching some hay feeding the horses and stated further:

"The Signal Corps guys were telling me that General Pershing was surprised at the number of women who volunteered at camp. He knew that money would attract some, but then he was forewarned by Intelligence that some might be spies. So they were interviewed by the "Intel" types to pass muster."

"Ha! Can't you hear the warning to the soldiers, quipped a flippant Bobby:

"Button your mouth, while you unbutton your pants!"

"You should be the Company chaplain, Bobby," said a facetious George.

"Not this guy. Never!" snapped Bobby, who mistakenly took George seriously.

Though detached, George's Remount Group was considered part of the 16th Infantry Regiment. They made there way to Pershings advanced headquarters at Namiquipa. When the grizzled veterans quartered at Namiquipa saw George's ragged provisional reinforcements slogging by, one shouted out sarcastically:

"Well, Well! Look at what the wind blew in, Guys! Now Pancha Villa doesn't stand a chance! Hee, Hee, Hee!"

"Catch their faces, men. We'll discuss this further with them, later." Said a low growling Bobby.

"Save it for the Villastas, Bobby," muttered George.

After setting up their puptents in their bivouac area, the new arrivals were told of the wide sightings and skirmishes with Villa troops on the other side of the Sierra Madre Mountains. These reports were brought back to General Pershing by his dispersed scouts. Confirmations came back from towns named Rucjo, Cumbre Pass, San Miguel and Madera. At San Miguel, the main troops of the 16th Infantry, along with a young Lieutenant George Patton, trapped and killed the second in command to Pancho Villa, Julio Cardenas. Patton, however, didn't realize he had killed Cardenas, initially. Patton made a dramatic entry through towns and villages on his way back to his base camp at El Valle, by tying the bodies of the three Mexican guerrillas, including Cardenas, on to the front hood and grill of a Dodge touring car. Reportedly, he did it for the twin reasons to get others to identify the bodies and to have it be a warning to the Mexicans.

It was obvious to Pershing that Villa had broken up his forces and they disappeared into the high mountain passes and ravines that they knew so well. In addition, reports came back of many skirmishes in which every time US Patrols caught up to Villa Forces, they would fight for a time and then, before they could be overwhelmed during the day, or during the dark of night, they would scatter in all directions to break up the pursuing Americans, and disappear into the hills. Americans couldn't maintain continuous contact. They were only able to capture some wounded or slower stragglers.

To counter this dispersion, Pershing decided to decentralize his command. No longer would he send out Flying Columns to search and strike. Advanced patrols had penetrated as far south as they were going to go in the State of Chihuahua. Therefore, Pershing broke up the State of Chihuahua into five districts: Namiquipa, under the command of Major Elwood Evans of the 10th Cavalry; Guerrero, commanded by Colonel George Dodd of General Custers infamous 7th Cavalry fame; Bustillos, headed by Colonel Herbert Slocum (meaning "slow coming" according to rival cavalries) of the 13th (unlucky) cavalry, and San Francisco de Borja, commanded by Colonel James Lockett, including an infantry Regiment.

PART III

CHAPTER TWENTY ONE

LOCAL LOCO

"George, come over here," whispered a conspiritorial Bobby. "Look at this."

With that, Bobby took his machete, after looking around to see that he wasn't being observed, and slashed through a cactus, exposing the insides.

"Besides water, we can extract stuff from mesquite and cactus, and turn it into local fermented brew. Mescal is especially potent; it's a potent liquor fermented from the juice of cactus fibres. Who needs tequila? The Mexicans showed me this for $2 American. Now I'm set for the duration. What do you think of that?"

"Well, it can keep us warm in the cold and calm in the heat, I suppose."

"I'm just supplementing Army chow, that's all," rationalized Bobby.

"It's fine with me, but I don't think General Pershing would go along with it. Better keep it under cover," commented Abe.

"Well, Pershing chews lumps of sugar for quick energy, doesn't he? He does his thing; I do mine. Don't worry about me. I'm not going to ruin a good thing. You can bet on that!"

While encamped at Namiquipa, the 16th Infantry Regiment was joined by two Battalions of the 24th Infantry Regiment. These 1600 new foot soldiers were welcome because troops were about to be dispatched into the mountains where wheeled and mounted troops would be less maneuverable than infantry. Besides, the Cavalry would need the infantry sharpshooters to counter the snipers they expected to encounter.

The men of the 24th complained of wind driven sand, pestering their progress and stinging their faces; axles shearing over rutted dirt roads and oil pans cracking, flat tires causing motor cars to frequently break down, complaints well known to George and the boys of the 16th. They also ran into rain squalls that brought cool relief from the oppressive heat, but also left clay roads that sunk cars and marching feet in the muck. Often cars had to be hand pushed out of holes and mud. It was disconcerting to see the more reliable horses outdistancing the more modern motor cars.

At night, one soldier said that he had to sit on the back of a car with a flashlight, facing the following motor cars, warning them to slow down, or go around a sinkhole or chuckhole, or to watch out for a rut on the side of the road. Cars nevertheless bounced and jounced along and sometimes slid sideways into a rut. They were lucky if they could maintain a road speed of 15 miles per hour. Hills, valleys, rivers, canyons, ravines all provided an inhospitable terrain. George could only acknowledge these common complaints with a sympathetic smile. In this way, the 16th and the 24th were comforted in commiserating over their shared travails.

INTO THE MOUNTAINS

After the redistricting of the military command structure, George was assigned to take a dozen remounts and join the main troops of the 16th Regiment that were heading south on the other side of the Sierra Madre Mountains. They had advanced through Cumbre Pass, Madera and were to pass through Bachiniva, heading to Guerrero, where it was rumored that Pancho Villa was recovering from a serious gunshot wound to a knee. The 16th Infantry was to attach itself to Colonel Dodd's 7th Cavalry at some point before Guerrero. Major Howze and a detachment from the 11th Cavalry was to also catch up to Dodd and join him before Guerrero. Thus, three forces were to converge on Guerrero to trap Pancho Villa there.

As they were preparing to break camp, General Pershing's chief transport officer, Lieutenant George Patton, arrived as a sidecar passenger in a two seated motorcycle, at the head of a truck transport. He appeared to be very confident in himself as he strode purposefully to General Pershing's headquarters. Somewhat later, George was surprised to be taken by Captain Gonsalvez to meet Lieutenant Patton. Corporal Dilboy congratulated him on his killing of Julio Cardenas, Pancho Villa's second in command. "A lucky shot, that's all," said Patton. "I'm a crack shot with a pistol, but they tell me you're a sure shot with a rifle."

"I'd like to put it to real use, like yourself," replied George, modestly.

"Well, it looks like you're going to get your chance. You hope to trap that miserable killer Villa at Guerrero, I hear."

"That's the plan," replied George.

"I got the number 2 guerrilla; I'd love to get the number one guy. Wish I could be there. Good shooting."

The US troops were cheered by the news that the 17th Cavalry forces at Las Cruces killed a Candelario Cervantes, the actual leader of the attack at Columbus, and who was reputed to be the most able and ruthless of Villa's henchmen, next to Pancho Villa himself. These reports only served to spur George on, all the more, to get in on the action.

They moved out at dawn. The first town of any size was San Geronimo where they climbed quickly to 7500 feet up into the Sierra Madre Mountains. There they ran right into the teeth of a raging blizzard that drove the snow and sleet against their bent faces with wet stinging force. George was part of the *"spear point squadron"* that struggled up, around and down the mountains. The peaks in this area topped out at over 11,000 feet above sea level. The air was so thin at that high ground level, that unscheduled stops had to be made so the men could acclimate to the height and catch their breaths. The strung out column trudged up and down the lower gulleys and ravines when it could, but by avoiding the high ground, it made the trek longer. To keep from getting ambushed or shot in the back, the caves they uncovered were checked out carefully. They were also dangerous because they were the natural hiding places for dangerous, wild animals and outlaws, as well as enemy soldiers.

From a sweltering desert in the lowlands to the frosted puffs of cold air in the mountains, the soldiers endured. Men were falling asleep in the saddle, while still moving. Progress was slow and tortuous. The commanders were counting on the Mexican belief that nobody would travel in this weather. It was dark and bitterly cold. Because it had rained earlier, the rocks and stones glazed over in ice and made the ground very slippery. The footing was treacherous. Burros and donkeys refused to move fearing they would slip and fall on the ice. With forage buried beneath snow and ice, and hard to get at, the horses, donkeys, burros and mules chewed up their rope and leather halters. The animals were fed from the leftover grain, corn and oats the cavalry carried on their horse saddles. Wheeled transports were left behind. The dismounted cavalry soldiers pulled their reluctant horses along by the reins to make them move forward toward the leather reins they wanted to chew. The unhorsed soldiers themselves munched on rations they carried in their saddlebags.

One night George was sitting on the ground resting, during a stop. Suddenly a man came out of the dark. George looked up, startled to see General Pershing! George jumped to his feet and snapped a sharp salute.

"Corporal Dilboy, Sir"

"At ease, Soldier! Stated the General. "You're in the Spear Point Squadron," are you not? How far to Guerrero?"

"Twelve miles, by my reckoning, General," answered Corporal Dilboy.

"This troop movement could capture Villa and end the expedition. I want to be in on it. Patton's back at Namiquipa walking in circles because I said he couldn't take his motorcycles and trucks over the mountains. He can wish us luck. Carry on soldier!"

George whipped up a quick parting salute, as General Pershing disappeared into the dark. He stood there stunned, as Jeff and Abe rushed over and asked:

"Was that who I thought it was? The General himself?" Asked a startled Jeff?

"It certainly was!" responded George, getting back his composure. "Word is he likes to be near the front lines and the advanced troops."

"Damn!" Spoke out a flabbergasted, arriving Bobby. "I heard that he was a light sleeper and liked to prowl at night, but who would have expected that?"

"I surely didn't. But it positively keeps you on your toes, doesn't it?"

The next morning while breakfast of hardtack, which is candy for quick energy, bacon, beans and eggs were cooking, George smelled an odd odor.

"What's that smell?"

"That weird smell is goat brains, a local delicacy," responded Bobby.

"Goat brains!" Exclaimed George. "Who eats that?"

"Mexicans, and others who are hungry enough," offered Jeff.

"No thanks," said George, "I'm not that hungry."

They started to run into more Mexicans moving through the mountains, so they knew they were nearing Guerrero. But when they asked them questions about the whereabouts of Villa troops, they smiled and shrugged. Some insisted Pancho Villa was dead or assassinated. Nobody believed that because they had heard the same thing all the way down Chihuahua. It was obvious that the Mexicans wanted the Americans to leave Mexico and if they convinced them that Pancho Villa was dead, it would speed the American forces out of their country. Pershing would laugh now when he was told of the latest reported killing of Pancho Villa from different parts of Mexico. It became a running joke. George wondered why some cunning, Mexican bandito didn't shoot Pancho Villa, either to take over his job, or to produce his body to get the Americans to leave.

While trudging down a narrow canyon, George shivered and stamped his feet to get the blood circulating, and to keep warm.

His nose, toes and fingers would sting and then turn blue when numb. His extremities were losing all feeling, a dangerous thing. He would blow hot air onto his fingers next to his mouth to thaw out his nose and mouth. The horse he was leading by the reins kept turning his head away from the cold blasts of wind, as did George. Sometimes, to get relief from the piercing gusts of wind cutting into him like a knife, George would turn around and walk backwards leaning against the howling wind. To pass the time, he would try talking:

"This is the territory where the troops of Generals Crook and Miles, and their Apache scouts, hunted Geronimo, forty years ago," gasped George.

"How the hell do you know?" Asked Jeff, trudging behind.

"Lieutenant Patton mentioned it to me, back in Namiquipa. He's a nut on military history."

"We might as well be Apaches; we're riding with blankets around us, just like them. And if we don't get that devil from Durango soon, this foul weather will make us history," complained Abe, straining to hear.

"Durango? What devil is in Durango?" Jeff wanted to know.

"That's below Chihuahua, the State where Pancho Villa was born," answered George, knowingly.

"Who gives a sow's ass," blurted a trailing, faltering Bobby.

"That's the spirit Bobby! Glad you're still with us."

"Damn right! I'm here for the duration. There's no Mexican bullet with my name on it!"

George enjoyed the momentary comic relief. It was distracting and broke up the miserable march.

CHAPTER TWENTY TWO

GUERRERO

A messenger from behind rode up the narrow path at the gallop and hollered at George:

"Hold up! Hold up! Coporal Dilboy! Captain Gonsalvez says to hold up! We've lost out guides!"

"What do you mean?" Asked a puzzled George

"They bolted overnight. We must be coming up on Guerrero. They know what Villa does to Mexican guides who aid the Americans. They insisted on their silver and ran. Take a break until further orders."

The messenger reared back on his mount, turned around and sauntered back.

"Gonsalvez must have sent out a scouting party of Cavalry to look ahead," said George. "Pass the word. Stand down and rest."

George motioned for Jeff to accompany him to take a look over the next hill. They cantered over the crest of the hill and hadn't gone very far when they had to rein up.

"Whoa there!" George hollered, pulling back on his horse. "Wow! Look at that; Guerrero!"

George was staring straight down a steep cliff. He and Jeff quickly dismounted, so they wouldn't be seen as easily by any Villa outpost guards. They dropped to one knee and canvassed the approaches to the town. From this direction the town couldn't be seen until you were almost on top of it, looking down from this steep escarpment. George and Jeff stared down in wonderment as 500 to 600 armed Villa troops mingled throughout the town. Canyons and gulleys ran down both sides of the bluffs they were on. Trees covered the valley and the far off mesa. The Papigochic River ran right through the town. Since this was such an important vantage point, George was surprised Villa scouts hadn't spotted them yet. But he wasn't surprised long.

PING! A bullet ricochet off a boulder next to them! They were spotted! They jumped to their feet, but crouching down, ran back to their restless horses. They mounted them on the fly and wheeled around to gallop away, as follow up bullets kicked up the dirt near them and caromed off nearby trees and boulders. They galloped off the quarter mile back to their outfit. When they reached their lines Captain Gonsalez and Company D had already received mobilization orders to move down an old donkey trail found by the scouts toward Guerrero. As much as the Cavalry kicked and spurred their mounts onward, the horses, worn down from the climb, weather and exhaustion, wouldn't move faster than a slow trot.

Colonel Dodd had sent ahead a detachment under Major Winans to cross the river and to head off any Mexican retreat from the west. A Captain Dallem headed for the eastern end of town to cut off any Villistas fleeing into the gulleys and ravines and treed chaparral outside the adobe town. Some Villa's were scattering on their horses; the light rain that started to fall helped muffle the hooves of their horses. Other Villistas were taking up defensive positions behind walled haciendas' and adobe buildings. The Americans rushed their machine guns into positions and commenced firing as soon as they could be set up. Heavier rain helped cool off the muzzle of the machine gun.

The battle was on!

George and his Company rode to the east-end of the town, dismounted and took cover behind some fallen trees and nearby boulders. George commenced firing as soon as he unslung his rifle. At first he shot wild in his excitement, but calmed down in time. The rest of his squad came up behind him and hunkered down on either side of him. Bobby and Abe were to his right and Jeff to his left. They fired at the fleeing Villistas because they were more open as a target, and they would disappear unless the 7th Cavalry detachment could catch up to them. For all the Americans knew, the fleeing Villa troops were going for reinforcements.

The entrenched Villistas had a couple of machine guns and a mortor shelling them, attempting to cover for their amigos. It kept George and his squad ducking down, then peeking up and shooting one way and then the other. And they had to be sure they didn't hit their own cavalry, who were chasing the scattering Villistas. Then Jeff suddenly pointed and yelled out:

"Look! Over there! They're trying to carry Pancho Villa out on a stretcher!"

Jeff was pointing, then followed it up with quicktime shooting, at the far, eastern corner of the town. Out the back door of an adobe building were four Mexicans, two of whom were shuffling away with a stretcher, carrying a heavy set man, who was gesturing emphatically. Now all four in the squad were shooting at the fleeing desperados. George was taking careful aim at the man lying in the stretcher, but rain drops had gotten into his gun sight. Impatiently, he jammed his finger into the gun sight to dry it out. Dirt was kicking up all around the Mexicans, bouncing off the adobe house and the nearby boulders. The Mexicanos were not even trying to shoot back. George finally squeezed off a carefully aimed shot at the man in the stretcher. The man on the stretcher jerked up, simultaneously crying out, "Ow!" Suddenly, the stretched turned over and the man flipped to the ground.

Two of the Mexicans then unshouldered their rifles and fired back. The other two scrambled to carry the wounded man to a saddled horse, throwing his body across the front of the saddle. Then all four saddled up and galloped away. George had emptied his cartridge, and ducked down to reload. As he was doing this, he kept glancing at the fleeing horsemen, but had to keep his head down because one of the Mexican machine guns was sweeping their area. Bobby shouted out:

"He's hit! He's hit! Damn it, we got him!"

Bobby then yelled out and spun around:

"Ohhh! They got me! Shit! Damn!"

244   EDDIE BRADY

Bobby then fell to the ground, grabbing his shoulder and curling up into a fetal position, rocking back and forth.

"Stay down! Stay down, all of you!" George warned. He then dropped his rifle and lunged at Bobby:

"Easy Bobby, easy. Let me look at it." He then tore off Bobby's shirt around the wound and checked out the injury.

"There's a lot of blood, but it's a flesh wound. Let me tie it off, to stop the bleeding. You'll be ok, you Irish hothead. Just lie still behind this boulder."

"Bobby, here's your canteen. Take water, if you need it. We're still under fire," cautioned a helpful Abe.

"I'm all right. I'm ok. Watch out for yourself," said a calmer Bobby.

When George stuck his head up to aim again, his hat was shot off and he ducked down. He had to get that machine gun; it was devastating their efforts. He moved sideways to the corner of a boulder adjacent to the felled trees they were shooting over. He hollered at Abe and Jeff to relocate, as the Mexican machine gun had ferreted them out and was focusing on them. He picked up his hat and noticed the bullet hole in the top of the hat. He put his finger through it and whistled to himself:

"God! That was close!"

Then he tossed his hat on the ground. It made him a taller target under fire. He didn't now need protection from the sun; he needed protection from ground fire. They had to knock out that machine gun. From his new position lying on the ground, he looked and listened for the rat-tat-tat sound of that infernal machine gun. He saw it open up on a cavalry charge from its rear. As they turned the gun around on the roof of an adobe building, they exposed themselves, and George saw his chance. He steadied his rifle and slowly pulled the trigger. But before he could pull it off, the triggerman of the Mexican machine gun went down with a howl, and the gun feeder fled the roof. George startled himself to a stop and looked over at Jeff. Jeff had a grin a mile wide on his face and gave George a smug look as if to say, "You aren't the only sharpshooter in this squad!"

George slowly returned the smile and nodded his head in a congratulatory acknowledgement. He looked back at Bobby, and Bobby was tilting back his canteen drawing out some water; he looked ok, for the moment. Canvassing the battlefield, like a sniper looking for his next victim, George's attention, despite the scattered gunfire and occasional bursts of machine gun and mortor fire, was grabbed by Abe's yelling:

"Over there! Look! They're mounting up and breaking out!"

George glanced over and saw about twenty horsemen gallop off away from them, but then suddenly rein up and turn about, and then suddenly start up and race in a headlong gallop straight for them!

Jeff ran over to guard the injured Bobby, and threw him his own rifle to arm himself. They were galloping right at them, because there was less fire coming from their direction. Abe and George braced themselves and steadied their rifles. George growled a caution:

"Wait 'til they're close for the best shot!"

Before they reached their line, half a dozen Villistas were shot from the saddle by Dodd's chasing 7th Cavalry and Evan's 10th dismounted riflemen. The 16th Infantry continued their fire at the remaining dug in die-hards in the doomed town. George picked off the lead horseman, who corkscrewed to the ground, pulling his horse twisting with him, both disappearing into a circle of dust. The rest of the desperate runaways galloped and crashed head on and right over their thin defense line. They galloped helter skelter into the nearby mountains, scattering and disappearing. Jeff and Abe brought down another two of the enemy horsemen, who howled out as their horses bolted upright, and they fell, shot to the ground. As the Mexicans runaways hurtled and trampled over Jeff, he screamed out in pain:

"Aarrgghh!"

He went down holding his hip. He was taking short breaths, and gasping, with both hands now clutching his side.

"Oh! Damn! Oh-h-h!" He cursed.

Not noticing Jeff was hurt in all the commotion, George and Abe continued to shoot at the fleeing horsemen, as each had easy aim at the open backs of the fleeing enemy. Abe shot one out of the saddle and George hit another, who was able to bend over and hold on, as his horse staggered awkwardly on. The pursuing Cavalry followed and gave chase. George and Abe cheered them on.

Looking around, Bobby spotted the grimacing Jeff and yelled: "Jeff's down! Jeff's hurt!"

Abe and George ran over half-crouched, as shooting was continuing and mortor shells were exploding all around them.

"Jeff, where are you hit?" shouted George.

"My side, my side! God, it hurts!"

"Stay still, Bobby. Stay still! We have to see."

Jeff kept gritting his teeth, snapping his head up and trying to hold his side.

"There's no blood!" Exclaimed a surprised George. "Just torn clothing, with a bruised and swelling hip."

"It must be fractured or broken. One of the horses must have kicked him as it hurdled the logs," surmised George.

"Break open the medical kit! There's something for pain in there. We'll have to get both Bobby and Jeff to the Surgeon, who is accompanying us. Get medics from the 16th Infantry to take them in a litter."

"As soon as we can, Abe. There's still a battle going on. Heads up!"

"Guys, sit tight. We'll get you out of here as soon as it's safe," reassured George.

Evans 10th Cavalry made a final charge against the remaining defenders of the town. Once they had penetrated the length of the town, they charged back the other way; then the 16th Infantry was sent in to go house to house, in order to root out the snipers and those who insist on fighting to the death. Shooting was periodically stopped by orders of General Pershing, and a shouted message was called into the town to allow those who had enough of the fighting to surrender. Some did. Some tried to, but were gunned down by their own fanatical dead-enders. For every enemy that surrendered, it meant one less potential killer their troops had to fight. This was the idea behind the peace gesture to the surviving guerrillas.

Gradually, the firing started to simmer down to occasional sniper shots. The shooting had cracked the air from early morning to late afternoon. Estimates were given that there were 600 Villistas to 400 Americans at the battle, but surprise and American boldness of movement carried the day.

George and Abe got Bobby and Jeff taken by stretchers to the Medical Tent at the eastern rear of Guerrero for the medics to work on. Then the able-bodied George and Abe were assigned to round up and guard the prisoners, who were put up in a hastily set up corral beside the town. Grilling sessions were undertaken by the Intel Officers to gleam whatever information they could obtain from captured Villa prisoners. Some who talked most willingly said they were impressed and forced into Villa's forces, or they and their families would have been shot.

"Amigos! Hombres! Why you shoot us? We not Villa's!" They complained.

They also volunteered that Pancho Villa was indeed alive, although he was seriously wounded in the knee at the shoot out in Namiquipa the prior month. Rumors were circulating that he was shot by one of his own guerrilla's, who resented being forcibly impressed into his Army. Pancho Villa was also further wounded in the shoulder upon fleeing earlier that day, though not as seriously.

It turned out that Bobby was weak from loss of blood, but was not seriously injured, and would recover in time. Jeff, on the other hand, had a shattered hip in multible fractures, according to the Army surgeon. He had to stay immobilized until he was stabilized. He would be out of action for months. His recovery would depend on how well the fractures healed, and if he needed surgery. But both were expected to eventually recover, and this was good news to all in the squad.

"Hell, our first major battle, and we lose half our squad as casualties," moaned Abe.

"Yes, but only six fatalities, none in our Company," said an amazed George. "Surprise really is an advantage."

Before dark, a frustrated 7th Cavalry trotted back into Guerrero with less gusto than when they galloped out in hot pursuit. They lost the fleeing Villa troops in the hills, mountains, ravines and gulleys. The Villistas split into small groups and scattered in all directions, as they habitually did. When the pursuing Americans ran low on ammunition, they turned back. And "NO," they had no idea where Pancho Villa was! They were quite sensitive to the fact that he got away once again, despite being wounded by one of the sharpshooters in the "Spear Point Squadron." Their consternation would reach its height when they would hear later from a captured Villa how close they had come to capturing Pancho Villa. Villa and four of his personal bodyguards were hiding in a cave where the opening was camouflaged by heavy brush and branches. The American Cavalry was so close to the cave entrance, that Pancho Villa could hear their voices as they led their dismounted horses up the narrow path in the mountains above Guerrero.

By nightfall, after securing the town, and posting guards and sending out roving night patrols to protect against an unlikely counterattack, the battle weary Americans had no trouble falling asleep. In contrast to the wild noises and racquet of cannon and rifle fire throughout the day, the strange, eery quiet of the evening was deafening.

The next morning General Pershing, ever the optimist, masked his disappointment at the escape of the Durango Kid, as he derisively referred to Pancho Villa. Instead, he saluted his victorious troops by having Colonels Dodd and Evans let the exhausted men and horses rest at their ease until mid-day, an almost unheard of event in Pershing's strict schedule regimen. This allowed the wounded to be attended to, the dead to be buried, and a host of other supply concerns to be rebuilt. He also gathered his commanders to brief him on yesterday's encounters and the lessons to be learned from them.

One of the core events of the battle was the shooting of Pancho Villa.

"Who shot him?" Inquired General Pershing.

Captain Gonsalvez, who was responsible for the "Spear Point Squadron," was summoned to the post-battle session for his report.

The usual decisive and opiniated Captain seemed uncharacteristically flustered as he related the results of his own inquiry:

"Sir! Three members of the four-man point squad claim to have fired the bullet that wounded Pancho Villa. But the fourth man, Corporal Dilboy, is the only 'Distinguished Marksman' among them."

"And what did Corporal Dilboy say?" Asked General Pershing.

"Sir, he said that they all fired, and they all saw Pancho Villa immediately get knocked out of the stretcher. With all the shooting, a richochet could have gotten him."

"Maybe so, Captain Gonsalvez, but since there was nothing near the site of the hit, it's unlikely that a richochet bullet got him. For leading his men against an outnumbered and mounted foe, I want you to call *Sargent* Dilboy to headquarters at 0600 hours tonight. He will be awarded a combat medal and promotion. You will also produce the remainder of this special squad for the awarding of medals appropriate to their valorous conduct under fire."

Captain Gonsalvez exchanged a sharp salute with the assembled commanders and strode smartly back to his troops with a pleased smile on his face.

General Pershing's chief aide was amused and admiring of the General's sorting out of the Pancho shooting matter.

"By your leave, General, why did you select Corporal Dilboy?"

"It wasn't difficult, Colonel, when you consider his experience in the Balkan Wars, his demonstrated outstanding rifle skills in the US Army, and his promotion to Sargent in the Greek Army at age 16."

"With all due respect, General, the Balkan Wars weren't considered major wars here."

"They were over there. Besides, war is war. Battles may change; character doesn't."

CHAPTER TWENTY THREE

TOMOCHIC

General Pershing left the next morning with his contingent, and the after battle arriving 11th Cavalry, for San Antonios to meet up again with his Aide-de-camp Lieutenant George Patton. Pershing knew that he had a limited time to neutralize Pancho Villa and his bandit army, because the sinking of American ships and killing of American citizens in the Atlantic Ocean was inevitably drawing America into the war in Europe. Besides American Commanders in Mexico were increasingly reporting back to him about known German agents stirring up the Mexicans against American troops, offering them money and weapons. Pershing was under orders to avoid a complicating war with the Carranista Mexican Government. Further making him walk a tightrope was the local complications of Guerrilla bands fighting Mexican Government troops and other Guerrilla irregulars, and each other, at the same time these same Mexican Government troops were assisting Americans in some areas and fighting them in other areas. Shifting loyalties in which Mexican Government and Villa Forces were switching sides also added to the chaos. It made for a very confusing situation, to say the least.

Before moving out, General Pershing ordered Colonel Dodd and his 7th Cavalry to rest a day and to pursue Pancho Villa to at least keep him on the run, if they couldn't capture or kill him, the latter being preferable. Pershing fully expected to be told by the end of the year that President Wilson and his Cabinet would be satisfied if he merely scattered Villa's troops away from the US border, where he would no longer be a threat to US citizens.

Bobby and Jeff were left to convalesce under the care of the medical unit with the other wounded. They would join the 7th Cavalry when and if they could, once cleared for return to duty by the camp surgeon. George and Abe were assigned to the Cavalry. Their wish was finally granted in the field.

The next morning, Colonel Dodd broke camp and led his 200 horse soldiers on a fast trot southwest, following the flight of Pancho Villa and his scattered troops, who would frequently link up together again. Because this was their home turf, their message system was superior to the Americans, not surprisingly. The 7th Cavalry moved about 30 miles up and through the undulating Sierras to the small mountain village of Tomachic. It was an old village of only about a dozen adobe buildings occupied by a mix of Mexicans and highland Indians. It was a smaller version of Guerrero, sort of, because it was approached looking down into a valley, with a small river running through it, and surrounded by mountains 9000 feet high. Some troops got dizzy and others staggered as if they were drunk from the high altitude. Despite the conditions, acclimated advanced scouts excitedly reported back that 200 Villistas were quartered there!

To increase their chances of surprising the Villa troops and possibly Pancho himself, Colonel Dodd conducted a forced march throughout the cold night, taxing the strength of the horses. Some of the suffering cavalrymen cursed the frigid air blue with their colorful oaths.

"Damn this blasted weather! My legs are numb from the knees down!" Griped Abe.

"The thin air is making me dizzy. I need coffee to stay awake. Hell! If I fall asleep in the saddle, I could freeze to death!"

Heeding the chorus of complaints, Colonel Dodd reluctantly motioned a halt for one half hour only. Fires were immediately set and coffee heated up, as much to hold the hot cup, as drink it. Abe kept banging his legs and stamping his frozen feet, to get the circulation going. George breathed heavily into cupped hands around his blue nose. He could feel the crinkle of the icicles on his nose hairs. When they broke, his nose bled, before refreezing. They used their bandanas to cover their faces. Where they breathed, warm air turned the bandana to hard cloth.

When others complained of headaches, Colonel Dodd used this to restart the march ten minutes early, saying that the descent would lessen the air pressure and reduce the headaches. Because of the many turns and gulleys, the march downhill was slow and tortuous. Breaks had to be taken every hour. Fortunately, the winds died down as the sun came up. To avoid detection, they had to follow the treeline and cover, which extended their route. By mid-afternoon they started down a narrow, winding Indian foot trail, where they had to dismount and go single file. The village was at the 6000 foot level. Colonel Dodd had a machine gun crew emplaced on top of a ridge overlooking the village just hundreds of yards away from it. The remainder of the troops circled around another half-mile to emerge onto an open plain on a near approach to Tomochic. It was now late afternoon, but no matter; Dodd lined up his troops across the plain, rifles at the ready. Taking a last look at his troops straight across in the attack line, he confidently nodded, pointed his sabre, and gave the 7th Cavalry the command to:

"Cha-r-r-rge!!"

George kicked his heels into the side of his horse, lunged forward and urged his sorrel horse to leap out into a full gallop. But the haggard mount re-acted more like a stubborn mule, as it reluctantly broke into a tired trot, leaving George disconcertingly behind the rest of the attacking cavalry. Ahead of him, but also hanging back from the surging, yelling troops, despite bucking the horse onward, was little Abe, looking like a gnome. He was bouncing awkwardly in the saddle. Suddenly, Abe was knocked from the saddle and rolled on the ground, sprawling out in a swirl of dust. He had somersaulted and then sat there upright, as if stunned. Looking up and seeing George striding by, he earnestly waved him on. George didn't know if Abe was hit or not, but their orders were not to stop for anybody. They were to assume that the medics would get to the injured.

As George tried to catch up to the now firing cavalrymen, the Villas scattered for cover and returned fire. George could hear the American machine gun open up from its fire base, and it was music to his ears! Some of the startled Villas sprung for their mounts and galloped off in all directions. George wasn't used to shooting from a bouncing horse and he shot wildly. He noticed a Villista peel off from his posse and head toward the river to cross it and escape into the mountains. George instinctively gave chase. The lone Villista broke into the stream, which slowed him down, allowing George to close the distance, as he rode to the shore. The escaping Villista pulled his horse up onto an island in the middle of the river. But then the front legs of the horse sunk into the sand and the Villista fell forward onto the horse's neck, then snapped back. To George's astonishment, the back legs of the horse began to sink. As George reined his horse to a stop, he dismounted to get a steadier aim for his rifle. Raising his rifle to fire, he saw the horse start to disappear into the rising sand, with the Villista flailing frantically, which seemed to accelerate his sinking. The man sank up to his shoulders and neck in quick order, George realizing suddenly what was happening:

"Oh, my God! He's sinking in *quicksand*!"

Before George could go for his lasso tied to his saddle, he watched in helpless horror, as the man disappeared beneath the liquid sand, sucking him down, his screams muffled and whimpering, as he suffocated to death. Only his sombrero remained, sitting ominously on top of the sandy muck of a death trap! George stood there rigid in disbelief, his rifle fixed in a lowered firing pose, mouth frozen open. The shooting and shelling in the distance gradually intruded into his awareness and he snapped back to the raging battle. His adrenalin was once again surging, his heart wildly pumping, and his thoughts racing, as he whirled about, thrust his foot into the stirrup, mounted his horse and wheeled back into the fray!

He galloped ahead as fast as his slow steed would move. Mexican and American soldiers raced back and forth, bodies were being shot off their mounts, screams, dust, fountains of dirt rose into the air where shells exploded. The incessant short bursts of the rat-a-tat machine gun was spreading its death! The crack of rifle fire was everywhere! Ricocheting bullets and shell fragments randomly pierced doughboy bodies! Shouts, moans and curses rent the air! Some cavalry were so close to the Villistas that they holstered their rifles and drew their revolvers for close action fire, in which they shot faster and more accurately. Hand to hand fighting raged, sabres slashed wildly, knives cut and plunged into pierced bodies with a sickening thud, by wild eyed, flared nostrilled, grunting, desperate soldiers, in a kill or be killed, fight to the death!

George's roan horse reared up, as a knife wielding, screaming desperato pulled him off it to the ground. While the Villista lunged at his prone body, George quickly turned around, raised his Colt 45 revolver and blasted him into another world. George was splattered with the enemy's blood, blotching one of his eyes, and forcing him to blink and instinctively dig it out with the top knuckle of his non-shooting hand. He leapt to his feet to better defend himself in the middle of the raging carnage. He had to keep moving; still targets die!

As was the Villista way, some scattered groups escaped on their horses, others on foot, a few fought to the last bullet and died where they made their stand. The surrounding hills and gulleys swallowed up the fleeing Villistas, who broke away in all directions. Organized resistance literally died out and sporadic shooting continued despite the repeated orders to:

"Cease fire! Cease fire, God damn it!"

George stood there, in what passed for the middle of the main street, dazed and stunned into hesitant, jerky movements, as he looked around, breathing heavily and trying to calm down. He lowered his revolver to his side and looked for his horse. He spotted a familiar figure. He couldn't help smiling at the hatless, filthy face of Captain Gonsalvez, wiping the sweat from his forehead. George recognized him after a second look. Gonsalvez smiled back, but then caught himself and ordered George to forget his horse and search each adobe house for Villistas, so they could secure the village. George searched the nearer side of the street, going from window to window and door to door after calling out to anyone inside to come out with their hands up, using the few Mexican words he inevitably picked up. Flying Column training he called it.

He entered one house and noticed a doorway blocked by a beaded curtain. He brought his rifle up ready to fire because the curtain was moving and, as his eyes scanned down to its bottom, he saw a pair of feet! He called out:

"Out! Out! Pronto!"

Nobody came out.

He steathily moved forward and pointed the tip of the rifle through the beads and pushed it aside! There staring at him wide eyed, in silent terror, was a mother hugging to her side a little boy and girl. The girl was holding her mothers skirt tight with both hands; the smaller boy was nervously sucking his thumb. George exhaled audibly and relaxed, but then got angry. In a miffed tone of voice, he forgot himself and spoke English, then caught himself:

"Why didn't you come out? You could have been killed! Comprende?"

The mother was too scared to talk, shook her head from side to side, and gave George a puzzled look. The children kept looking up at their mother. George concluded she didn't understand English and motioned her to go outside. Colonel Dodd was riding by as they emerged from the house.

"Colonel, what do we do with civilians? Asked George.

"If they have weapons, disarm them. Otherwise, let them be. After all, it's their village. The Intel guys will want to question them."

George looked at the woman and waved them on, and he turned away to finish his house-to-house inspection. At the other end of town, he paused and was pleased to see Abe, who didn't appear injured and was walking with a shovel in his hand.

"Hey! Abe! **ABE!** You're on your feet! What are you up to?"

Abe halted, changed directions and walked toward George with a silly smile on his face.

"Me? I'm on burial duty. The medical guys were pressing Colonel Dodd to bury the dead to help stop any spread of disease. That's their job, after all."

"Well, I'm glad to see you're not at the other end of that shovel." Smiled George.

"Oh, that. I wasn't hit; I fell off my horse. But I'm telling others I was nicked. It's too embarrassing to say a cavalry man fell off his own horse by inexperience."

"That's ok, Abe. Think nothing of it. If my horse could have galloped, I might have ended up the same way. In the meantime, we're still alive and getting more experience."

"I certainly would like to think so, George."

"Did you see the pursuit troops straggle back in?" Asked George. "The Villistas, as usual, scattered in all directions and disappeared. No sign of that Mad Dog from Durango, Pancho Villa. I figure he'll head back to his home state, Durango, where he'll be safe. He's got friends there who'll hide him until he recovers from his wounds. He's probably figures that Pershing won't leave Chihuahua."

"That's probably true, but what do I know. Maybe the Intel guys can get some information from the two captured prisoners they brought back. One is badly wounded though, so they better question him right away, while they try to keep him alive. And who knows if the other is willing to talk?"

"Oh, he'll talk all right." Said George. "They all smile and talk. The real question is whether he'll say anything helpful. We've gotten enough false information, causing us to go off on useless chases."

George paused and continued:

"Hey! I just realized I had my first cavalry charge today! How about that!"

"Now that you mention it, so didn't I. But it's nothing to write home about, with me falling on my ass!"

"Damn!" spit out George. "Speaking of writing home, I meant to write my girl and family. But we got orders to move out so quickly I didn't get a chance. They'll wonder if I'm dead, so I'd better write while I can."

"But even if you did write, George, the mail delivery system we have is so erratic, it may not be delivered for weeks or months. That's the way of things in war."

"Besides, they give priority to military dispatches, and censor mail to civilians, which foster further delays," added George.

"True, but why don't you backdate letters and put the full blame on the military?" Asked Abe.

"Oh, they know from my letters back to them from the Balkan Wars. I told them how crazy communications get during war. Believe me, they know."

"Well then, we have come full circle. What you thought was a problem, isn't." Concluded Abe.

"I suppose, from a logical point of view. But people are not always logical."

"Don't I know that! Said a frustrated Abe. Just look at this crazy, illogical war. We don't know who the enemy is from day to day. We're just got to make the best of it, that's all."

While they were there, the US soldiers uncovered an unsettling incident at Tomochic. The local Indians, afraid of what they called the white mans typhoid, had to be stopped from further bunching the Mexican wounded and dead, pouring pitch over them and setting them on fire. Regrettably, for some of the Mexican wounded, the civilized American intervention was too late. George thought this Indian custom and culture is one he would never understand. Did it make life more precious or less? To him, the answer was simple; the wounded should be helped, not killed.

George and, at his request, Abe were again detached and ordered south to join the 11th Cavalry, which included an Infantry contingent, that could pursue mountain guerrillas through crevices, steep valleys and canyons. These were awkwardly traversed by hesitant cavalry horses, fearing falls and broken legs. The horses suffering broken legs had to be shot to mercifully put them out of their misery.

The 11th Cavalry was under the capable command of Colonel James Lockett, a stout, grizzled, veteran of the Spanish-American War, who had previously advanced down the eastern side of the Sierra Madre Mountains. He was losing men to bandit ambushers, who were harrassing their flanks and rear guard. They needed sharpshooters to pick off these guerrillas. Tired as they were, George and Abe rose to the occasion, and volunteered to go.

Before he did, however, he fired off letters to his parents and Angelika. He was embarrassed to remember that the last letter he wrote was to Woz and Butchy, who were doing border patrol duty up north at El Paso. He had his priorities backward. It didn't matter what he said, as long as he sent something, because it told them he was alive and well. George had to lecture himself to be mindful of their sensibilities, which was another casualty of war, he supposed.

> *Angelika, dearest,"* he wrote, *"every time I see or come near death, I think of you and how much I miss you. I dream of the carefree times we strolled over to the Charles and Mystic Rivers, hand in hand, swinging our arms, and not caring if anyone saw us. Remember how we would lie on our backs together on the green grass, facing the sky and counting the stars, guessing where they were going and wondering what our future together would be? How many children would we have? How many girls and boy children? Who would they look like? What they would become, before we knew what we would become? Isn't life backwards like that, at times?*
>
> *I long to hold your little hand again, squeeze you tight and feel your warm body next to mine. I yearn to smother you with kisses and to smell the fresh fragrance from your hair. I dream of nudging my nose behind your ear and pressing my lips against your soft ear lobes. I want to taste your delicious lips. Your perfume wafted into my nostrils and transported me into a heaven on earth. Every time I see a woman, I compare her to you and you always prevail, as you always will.*
>
> *Why is it I never appreciate what I have until I almost lose it? Why does it take death to appreciate life? As you know, I haven't been good at expressing emotions; I leave that to your better side. I feel awkward and silly; you don't. Sometimes I wonder why I do the things I do, or don't do. I'm still discovering things about myself. Sometimes it delights me, and sometimes I*

disappoint myself. Let's learn from each other. You lean on me and I'll lean on you. I'll rescue you and you can rescue me. We're a team for life.

I kiss this letter just below my signature. Smother it with your own lips. Splash some of your cologne on your next letter to me, and I'll pretend your letter is you and I will kiss you, dance with you and sleep with you next to my side. My own Angelika.

Truly, "absence makes the heart go fonder," in the short run, but watch out for the length of time that says, "out of sight, out of mind, in the long run." So keep my picture near you, just as I carry your picture with me at all times.

Remember, my dearest, though we are apart, we both look at the same moon, the same sun and the same stars. In that sense we are together. I don't mean to be silly or overly sentimental, but I want you to know what I am feeling, while I face death every day, and yearn to be once again in your arms.

Tired as I am, I had to get this letter off to you. I know that I don't write as often as you like, but please understand, it is not because I don't have you in my heart and on my mind every minute of my life. Our best years are ahead of us. Be there for me, my love.

Loving you always,
Your George
(kiss)

In time, after a seventy five mile trek, they reached San Francisco de Borja, where they caught up to a split column of the 11th Cavalry, led by the dashing and adventurous Colonel Howze, who spoke Spanish with surprising fluency. George was assigned as a flank scout to ride along the column's right side; Abe was given the left flank. Alive to his new duty, George was excited to be near the deepest penetration into hostile territory, because it was where the action was!

CHAPTER TWENTY FOUR

DIPLOMATS DANCE

President Wilson, trying to keep the lid on the Mexican powder keg, as he saw it, had the US State Department make a new overture to the Carranza de facto Constitutional Government. Despite being convinced that Carranza had no real control over the roving bands of Mexican irregulars that roamed helter-skelter over Northern Mexico, President Wilson, at the urging of his Military advisers, wanted the Carranza Forces and the American Expeditionary Force to co-operate. Specifically, he wanted General Hugh Scott, Chief of Staff of the US Army in Washington D.C. and Major General Frederick Funston, Chief of the Southern Department, to meet with Mexico's Secretary of War, the former General Alvaro Obregon. Wilson would like to see them agree to have the Carranza Forces drive Pancho Villa's maurauders north toward the waiting Pershing Expeditionary Forces into a trap, and to destroy the ruthless Pancho. This would then rid the US-Mexican border of its chief menace and allow the US Expeditionary Force to return home, in accordance with the wishes of all patriotic Mexicans, they were to explain to General Obregon and his Carranza advisers.

Though bold in concept, laudable and logical in its joint goal, as befitting an ex-President of Princeton University, Wilson knew that the chaotic conditions then prevailing throughout Mexico, as governments fell like bowling pins, would augur ill against his ideal solution. But he had to do something to prevent a two-front war in Europe, and at his Southern border. As an inducement to get Carranza to agree, at least to the meeting, Wilson suggested **they** select the meeting place. And they did; Obregon and his entourage selected Juarez, Mexico, the sister town across the narrow bridge separating El Paso and Juarez. They met inside a gritty, old concrete customs building. Obregon ignored the Pancho Villa problem postured by President Wilson, and kept asking Scott, ad nauseum, from the US point of view:

"Sir, when is General Pershing going to get out of Mexico?"

Obregon insisted Pancho Villa was dead or near death, but even if he wasn't, he was incapacitated, and his forces scattered, no longer a force, and he was now "innocuous." And since there was now no one to seek, he asked Scott once more to set a date to withdraw the US Expeditionary Force from Mexico.

Funston couldn't take it any longer. He blew up! He jumped up to his full bantam height of five feet, six inches; purple faced, veins bulging from his quivering neck, waving his hands wildly and slammed his fist on the table! In spit out, barely coherent words, Funston roared:

"**Villa is dead! Villa is dead! That's all we hear. Yet he goes on attacking! Villa's forces have been scattered again and again, yet he keeps on regrouping. Villa must be killed! What is Carranza doing about it! Never mind us getting out! You must get on!**" Thundered a sputtering Funston.

Everyone at the conference table was stunned silent, until Funston's fury spent itself out. Immediately thereafter a weird pause, a deafening silence, paralyzed everyone.

Scott was the first to speak:

"Gentlemen; and I insist you are gentlemen. Let's take a break."

The Americans, obviously embarrassed by the outburst, trailed General Scott out of the building. Once outside, Scott quickly fired up a cigarette and paused to exhale, a long streak of smoke exiting his nose and mouth. He was composing himself. The others did likewise or just turned and looked away, absently. Funston was visibly flustered and awkwardly attempted to apologize:

"Hugh, I'm sorry. I don't know what came over me. I lost it. I didn't want to listen to that crap! Villa is as dead as I am. Villa scattered? That's his standard fighting style! And that lying bastard knows it!"

"And don't you think I know that? The game is to know he's lying and work around it. The fool has to prove others wrong; the wise man is satisfied to be right, sayeth the wise man."

"Well, I just dealt myself out of this game. I'm withdrawing. I've lost whatever influence I had."

"You're right, Fred. What you said is true, but better left unsaid. Now you know why we have diplomats usually handling these type negotiations; it's a special skill. We're soldiers; we fight. Hell, you're been fighting for how many years, Fred?"

"Too many, apparently, when I can no longer keep a cool head under fire."

"This is a different kind of fire, Fred. Soft words are used rather than hard bullets. It's foreign to us soldiers. But we're here, and we have to make what we can of it. Our President and our country are depending on us. We have to remember that."

Wilson and his advisers had anticipated this single issue Mexican response, so redolent with its past repetitions, and instructed Scott to stall for time and say that he would have to consult with the diplomats and President Wilson for further instructions. The military contingent returned to the conference room, and resumed the conference, minus General Fred Funston. General Scott apologized for the over advocacy by one of their members, said he would consult with his Government about the American withdrawal issue, and in the meantime, asked General Obregon if he would confer on him the privilege of dining with him that evening, to discuss matters of common concern in a more informal setting.

"After all, we have to eat, don't we?" Asked a smiling General Hugh Scott.

To Scott's delight, Obregon accepted. They met in Scott's private railroad car diverted to a siding in the El Paso yards. Obregon was friendly, but stubborn. He hoped that General Scott understood that, like him, he had his own instructions and they called for him to insist on immediate American withdrawal. The dinner meeting, therefore, ended where it started, a stalemate. The meeting was adjoined on this inconclusive note.

President Wilson was pleased. Next to capturing or killing Pancho Villa, this was the best he could hope for, in his dire circumstances, he thought. He had a US Presidential election coming up in six months. His re-election slogan was, "He kept us out of war." Even though, with the Germans continuing to sink US ships at sea, he knew that the US entry into the European War appeared inevitable, he didn't want a sudden breakout of war in Mexico to sink his chances of re-election. Besides, the US needed time to prepare the American public and their meager Armed Forces for war. Meager, that is, compared to the massive millions fighting each other in Europe. Wilson was indeed walking a tightrope.

When General Scott got the opportunity to confer again with Washington D.C., he argued against any withdrawal, because it would embolden the Mexicans, be seen as an American capitulation and would encourage further cross border incursions and killing of Americans. Besides, American prestige on the world stage was on display. Their expeditionary effort cannot be so wasted, Scott counseled.

Just after the border parlay disengaged temporarily, the Commander of the garrison of Douglas, Arizona, a Colonel W.S. Scott (no relation to General Hugh Scott), captured orders sent by Carranza to Government Forces in the western state of neighboring Sonora. They were ordered to link up with fellow soldiers in Chihuahua. They were to cut off and destroy American Expeditionary forces, if they didn't agree to withdraw all their troops out of Mexico immediately after the Obregon-Scott meeting.

With this in mind, President Wilson compromised and told Scott that the next time he met with Obregon, that he was to tell him that American forces in Mexico would be withdrawn to a place where they could protect the border until the danger of further bandit raids had dissipated. This instruction was purposely vague to give Americans flexibility, yet still show a type of withdrawal, hoping it would cause Carranza forces to at least pause, seek clarifying instructions, or keep them at bay, for the time being.

Advised of these sentiments, General Funston of the Southern Department in San Antonio, Texas, publically spoke confidently that Pershing was equal to anything the Mexicans could throw at him. Privately, however, Funston worried about Pershings strung out and widely scattered troops. The Expedition was deployed as a strike force for offensive operations against guerrilla brigands. But Pershings isolated cavalry regiments could conceivably be cut off individually, and overrun by superior forces. Additionally, the supply line was overextended and thinly protected, and therefore vulnerable to attack from its flanks. It too, could be cut off. Funston's nightmare, that he kept to himself, was the disaster of five separate Little Big Horns at San Francisco de Borja, Satevo, Bustillos, Guerrero and Namiquipa.

Therefore, during the second week of May, he wired Pershing at Namiquipa to pull all his forces back to Dublan, his first headquarters. Relayed this order, General Pershing was not happy. It constricted his mission and constrained his movements to going north only; orders he had persistently defied when issued by Mexican Government Officers. But this order originated from the Commander in Chief of the US Armed Forces, the President of the United States. That was different. As much as he disagreed with the order, he felt compelled to follow it. And he did. As he ordered his troops to pull back to his second headquarters at Namiquipa, he received some further disturbing news from the south, near the village of San Jose del Sitio, about fifty miles north of Parral, just a few miles above the Durango State line.

Colonel Lockett had sent columns from his 11th Cavalry out in different directions to patrol his district and was to meet Major Howze at Santa Cruz de Villegas, and together they were to encircle Parral, searching for Villistas.

George and Abe had been summoned by Major Howze and assigned to a special advance guard of six troopers, a guidon, carrying the 11th Cavalry flag, and Major Howz, himself. They were casually approaching the village of San Jose del Sito on a trot, about fifty miles northwest of Parral. Suddenly they rounded a curve and came face to face with over two hundred galloping, well armed, angry looking, Carranza soldiers. Mutually startled, they both reined up their lurching horses. General Jose Cavazos introduced himself without ceremony and without saluting, an instant insult to a uniformed American Officer! Major Howze, honoring military protocol, returned the non-salute with a sharp, snappy salute. Cavazos expressively disdained the salute, as if he were confronting a non-military rabble leader.

Looking at the small scouting party, heavily outnumbered, and with scorn in his voice and hate on his face, General Cavazos nearly shouted:

"Captain! You will turn your little scouting party around. This is as far south as your "lost" squad is going!"

"General, I am a Major in the United States Army, not a Captain. And I assure you, I am not lost. I do not answer to orders from a foreign Military Officer."

"By whose authority do you dare enter Mexico?"

"By Treaty authority, signed by your Government and mine."

"We interpret this treaty different than you do and therefore, you are illegally in our country."

"With all due respect, Sir, that's not my problem."

"It will be, if you don't turn around!"

George and Abe sat up straight in their saddles, fearful and fascinated, while watching this confrontation. Their rifles were at the ready, ready for anything. George wondered if the Mexican General could see the two American machine guns being hurriedly set up on nearby hilltops, now also at the ready. He knew only too well that many lives were being held precariously in the balance, as the confrontation reached a crescendo!

While the two military leaders continued to exchange taut ultimatums, the General noticed with increasing alarm that the rest of the American troopers were catching up and closing behind the advanced guard. He scanned the mountain ridge along the ridgeline and saw the sickening sight of more and more US Cavalry soldiers coming into sight as far as he could see! The expression on his face changed. The scowl straightened out, and his horse backed away restlessly, as if to symbolize and signal a warning. Circumstances had changed.

The next one to talk was Major Howze:

"General, the only trouble I'm going to have is to meet up with my Commander on time, at Parral. So without wasting further time, we wish you adios, and we'll be on our way, **South**."

With that Major Howze raised his non-shooting hand and barked out to his long column of troops the command:

"Forward, Yo-o-o-o!"

The Americans did a march past the immobile command of General Cavazos, who was glaring in muted, cold fury! Once again, the masterful Mexican General was proving how he could act under the greatest pressure with consummate discretion, thought George facetiously.

In the meantime, up in El Paso, General Scott had met privately on yet another occasion with the one-armed General Obregon in El Paso and they tortuously worked out an agreement throughout an exhausting sixteen-hour negotiating session. American Intelligence had uncovered the assembling of a seventeen thousand man Carranza Force in the adjacent Province of Sonora, ready to hit Pershing from his west flank and to hook up with similar numbered forces in Chihuaha. This twin Force matched up against a fifteen thousand man American Expeditionary Force at its peak in Mexico. But Scott, in his polite, yet gruff and direct way assured Obregon that if the Sonora troops moved against Pershing, war would break out between the US and Mexico and the full armed might of the United States, the "Collosus of the North," as the Mexican Government irreverently, but fearfully referred to them, would descend on the Carranza Government Forces. The Carranza Government would then be fighting both the United States and Pancho Villa's Guerillas. The entire weight of the consequences thereof would be the responsibility of Obregon. Was he ready to accept the fault for the fall of the Carranza Government? Scott inquired.

General Alvaro Obregon, immaculately attired in his magnificent military gold and blue decorated uniform, with his empty sleeve neatly pinned to his lower uniform jacket, looked intensely at his roughly dressed, sandy brown uniformed adversary, and shifted slightly in his chair. General Obregon then asked for a recess. He returned shortly thereafter, and asked General Scott:

"General, what do we get for restraining our troops?"

"What you want," said General Scott. "Our withdrawal, provided you actively pursue and neutralize Pancho Villa, and our border is safe from further organized Mexican incursions, of course."

General Scott, unlike General Funston, exercised forbearance, and resisted the urge to state that if the Carranza Government forces were doing the job it should have been doing, the US Expeditionary Force wouldn't be in Mexico chasing Pancho and his Villistas in the first place. But he held his fire.

So didn't General Obregon.

They signed a document agreeing to those terms.

But Carranza himself wouldn't.

He read the Spanish copy and threw it and the English version aside. He refused to sign them, because the agreement wasn't immediately followed by the *unconditional* agreement by the US to get out of Mexico!

Although the Carranza Army in Sonora was held in place, the Carranza Forces in Chihuahua were moved north. And they weren't moved there to chase Pancho Villa because he was south, hiding in Durango, while recovering from his wounds. Reportedly, Pancho was becoming paranoid, not knowing whether he needed protection from his enemies or his friends, and unsure of who was who. When George heard this from a captured Villista who turned against Pancho, he found himself remarking to Abe that this, in a sense, was prototypical of the entire American Punitive Expeditionary mission, making sense out of nonsense.

"Or is it the opposite?" Queried Abe.

"Don't make it any more confusing that it is," cautioned George. And George continued :

"How cruely ironic for Pancho Villa to be surrounded by his own paranoia, a condition that he created and self-inflicted. He's come full circle."

The only thing that made any sense at all to the 11th Cavalry, as they discussed among themselves what was happening, was that Carranza wanted to encourage movement north and to oddly protect the withdrawing Americans from the complicating maraudings of roving renegades and irregulars on private lootings. That was all right with them, the Americans agreed; they would accept any assistance that would help them successfully complete their mission and bring them home to the US.

General Pershing reluctantly ordered Major Howze to return to his prior base at San Francisco de Borja and regroup with and return to serve under the command of Colonel Lockett. Major Howze was particularly pained by this order, because he felt he was on the heels of Pancho Villa. He bristled with frustration when he had heard how close he had come to the cave, in which the great Pancho Villa was trembling and hiding while Howze and his pursuit troops passed his camouflaged cave opening outside Guerrero. He had come closer than any other American Commander to capturing the elusive Pancho Villa. He was hot to the chase! But being career Army, back he went, grumbling all the way.

On the way back, as darkness fell, Major Howze attacked the small town of Santa Cruz de Herrera and routed a band of Villistas, who fled into the black night. There was a brief shootout, and George experienced a fleeting moment of terror as bullets whizzed by his head. Not only did they not hit him, they didn't hit anybody else, either. Any American, that is. Afterwards, a searching trooper uncovered a cache of abandoned small arms. But what irked Major Howze was the fact that they were arms manufactured in **Germany**!

He led his column out of town, but still within sight of it, before he motioned the column to a halt, because he didn't want to be ambushed by returning Villistas from behind. His tired troops swung off their mounts, and pulled their saddles to the ground. They would later use them as pillows on which to lay their heads while sleeping. For now, they grubbed down on delicious beans, hardtack and coffee, to quell their thirst and hunger. Not that the food was wonderful; it's just that when you are hungry, almost anything taste's like a Godsend. It also led to a brief, but spirited discussion about what hit you first, thirst or hunger. Some thought it was individual; others said it was thirst. While bivouacking there, they quickly rested and fell asleep, while the horses grazed. Just as George was resting comfortably, he was ordered to post guard at a perimeter for the early four-hour duty. Major Howze wasn't the only soldier who could grumble, groused George.

The next morning they decamped and made there way north to San Francisco de Borja and continued on to San Antonio de los Arenales and there joined up with General Pershing himself.

CUSIHUIRIACHIC

After lying low and resting his troops in San Antonio de los Arenales for a week, Major Howze got his chance to deal with his disposition; he was spoiling for a fight! In mid-May, Intel brought to General Pershing news from two fleeing villagers from Cusihuiriachic, called "Cusi" by Americans. Cusi was a small mining town fifteen miles south of San Antonio de los Arenales. The villagers reported that there was a daylong battle between Villistas and Carranza troops at the Ojos Azules Ranch, twenty miles south of Cusi. The Villistas were supposedly bragging that their thousand-man army would attack and wipe out the American force at San Antonio, after disposing of the Carranza troops at the Ojos Azules Ranch. The people of Cusi sent the villagers to warn the Americans and to ask them to come and save Cusi from the rampaging, ransacking and killing Villistas, led by three of Pancho Villa's veterans.

Pershing found their story credible and gave Major Howze mobilization orders to *"Move on Cusi and disperse the Villistas, if found."* Howze immediately assembled six troops of cavalry, a machine gun troop and a packtrain onloaded with three days rations of food and ammo. Howze also ordered the Apache Scouts to be the spear point, to be closely followed by his own scouts, including George and Abe.

Sargent Shoshone Killer, the Chief Apache Scout, was supposedly a legendary Chief of the White Mountain Apaches. He looked the part, with a wide face and body, covered with battle scars from old fights with Mexicans, white men and other Indians; but he was also tall, unusual for the typical squat apache. He was fierce looking and looked outsized sitting on an Apache pony. He prized the full sized horse recently assigned to him by the cavalry. He still favored his hip knife to a pistol, but liked his Springfield Rifle for mounted attacks.

By early evening, Howze assembled his officers and cavalry scouts, to brief them on their mission. The terrain in the area was level and east of hills that rose into the Sierra Madre mountains, so travel should be relatively unimpeded and swift, Major Howze told them. But this had to be balanced against the fact that this would be a moonless night, impairing their visability. However, this would also obscure their approach to enemy guards outposted. Whatever, they would have to make what they could of it.

"Any questions?" asked Major Howze.

"Yes." Said Lieutenant Shannon, the Apache Liason Officer. "How many hostiles will we be facing?"

"That's hard to say. The Villistas claim to have a thousand men in arms, but their history is unreliable. Either they can't count or their pretentious bragging makes them think they have more troops than they do. We'll see."

"Begging your pardon, Sir. But how many troops will **we** have?" Asked another officer.

"Adequate to our needs, rest assured," answered Major Howze confidently. "Don't forget, we have along a machine gun troop; the old equalizer. For those of you more comfortable with concrete numbers, we'll mount fourteen officers and three hundred and nineteen additional men. Besides, we'll have two other encampments within a days ride, should we need them, which I doubt."

Looking back and forth across the width of the assembly, he asked finally:

"Any other questions? Ok, let's get going. Lieutenant Shannon, scouts out!"

Late that evening, Lieutenant Williams and a small detachment were sent ahead to go straight into Cusi to scout out the town and report back, which they did. They found no Vallistas, but found quite a few Carranza troops drunk or passed out from drink. Those sober enough to talk spoke about an all day desperate battle, except for a stoppage of an hour for lunch, which the Americans found odd. They claimed to have killed many Villistas and suffered many casualties. But Lieutenant Williams could not see or find any bodies or graves, or injured or wounded, for that matter. Yet he saw many cartridge belts empty and bullet casings scattered along the path into town from the direction from the Ojos Azules Ranch. No doubt shooting took place, but no casualties from either side? Some shooting, he thought!

"Not surprising, Sir." Chortled the guideon carrier. "If you consider they were probably too drunk to shoot straight."

"Hopefully that's it," replied a wry Lieutenant Williams.

Lieutenant Williams so reported to Major Howze as he guided him to the Ojos Azules Ranch. From what he could find out, the ranch was a fenced-fortress in the center of an open plain, so an enemy approach could be seen. Adobe buildings within the fortress were arrayed around in the shape of an arc that covered an area of about three hundred yards.

An eager and anxious Howze urged the long column onward, refusing to halt during the early morning hours, and leaving exhausted pack animals behind, to catch up when they could; he was racing the coming sunrise. He wanted the Apaches, advance scouts, including George and Abe, and cavalry to split in two and circle around and surround the hacienda-fortress in a pincer movement. He also knew that many of the Villistas would not stand and fight, if they thought their escape route was being closed off. He would cut them down as they attempted to ride away. That was his attack plan.

When they got to within a mile of the fortified ranch, Major Howze broke the men out of their column formation, and spread them across the vista. He knew the moonless, dark night gave them additional protection, the better to sweep any fleeing Vallistas into their net. He unsheathed his sword and pointed it ahead toward the enemy, at the same time as he audibled his charge order, and led his cavalry into an attack gallop. The fenced fortress was breached by hurdling over fences and charging through busted gates. The thunder of the charging horses and the now yelling troopers startled the Villistas awake, with some Villistas struggling through the yard trying to run while putting on their trousers, and pulling at boots and belts. Some returned fire and some vigilant Villistas bounded onto their saddleless horses and galloped away.

One athletic Villista wheeled around his pinto pony and ran it straight toward the nearest fence and hurdled it to escape. George saw him and gave chase. His bigger horse caught up to the smaller pony. George, not wanting to chance hitting an American in the wild melee, leaned forward and shoved his pistol into the ribs of the Villista and pulled the trigger, blowing him off his mount and sprawling him in the dust. He bounced off the ground and rolled over and lay still. George reined up abruptly and whirled his horse about, to make sure he was dead.

He was.

The surprise dawn attack was so complete that it was over in twenty minutes, though it seemed longer. About forty dead-enders fought until they were killed or wounded. Outside the fortress, nineteen additional Villistas bodies were counted. Men wandered around in a daze, pistols raised and on guard, until Major Howze called out the cease-fire order, and other officers took up the call.

It was a complete rout. There was no other way to describe it. George breathed a sigh of relief. All scouts were immediately assigned to perimeter defense duty. The rest of the Americans were ordered to gather up the wounded in a central area for clean up and medical atttention. The apaches had to be watched to be sure they didn't mutilate or steal from the bodies. Once the doctor declared bodies dead, they were carried to a designated area outside the compound and buried. The US casualties were six wounded, one mortally, an apache scout. Additionally, one US cavalryman was killed instantly.

Abe.

George was shocked. He couldn't believe it! The doctor assured him it was true, a bullet through the middle of his right eye. George jumped on his horse and rode over to the burial area. He dismounted on the run and stumbled over to the laid out bodies. Sure enough, there was Abe, with his eyes open, staring straight up toward the sky, a purple bullet hole through his forehead and eye a sickening red blotch. The bank clerk from Nashua, New Hampshire, USA. George turned away and stared into space, oblivious to everything around him, unable to feel or think. He didn't know how long he stood there, uncomprehending and disbelieving. A voice broke through:

"They found him in back of the hacienda, where he was supposed to be. He was the only soldier killed. What a shame. He came from New England with you, didn't he?"

George looked toward the voice, hearing but not seeing. He just stared and said nothing. The burial soldier and his crew walked away. George was not only stunned, he was puzzled. There was so much death, why couldn't he accept Abe's? At first, George thought Abe's sudden death was hard to accept because they both joined the Army in Nashua, travelled together through the country and the war, and he was always there. Now he's gone, just like that!

But that wasn't it. The burial soldier was right. It dawned on George that Abe was killed doing what he was supposed to be doing, closing the pincer to prevent escapes from the rear. That could have been me just as easily, thought George. But he had broken off his gallop to the rear, to chase the front escaping fence jumper. That saved him. By such a small difference was his life spared. But why? Why did he survive and Abe not? Wondered George. God only knows. And I am not here to question God's judgment. With these thoughts, George tried to comfort himself. It would have to do. George finally decided that he didn't want to think about it too much, because if he did, it would drive him crazy. God has his reasons, and there are some questions that George will never be able to figure out on this earth. He would have to make his peace with that and trust in God's judgment. He had to have Faith. He would have to live with that, because he couldn't live without it. But God, it hurt!

George sank to the ground, bent over, buried his head in his hands, and wept. The burial crew, sensitive to George's grief, walked further away, to break for a smoke, and to leave George to work through his private feelings.

CHAPTER TWENTY FIVE

CARRIZAL SETBACK

While things had quieted down for the moment in Chihuahua, George had heard about some northern border skirmishes in the southern Texas sister-settlements of Glenn Springs and Boquillas. They were only a few miles apart, and too small to be called towns or villages. So he wrote Boz at Fort Bliss to see if he or Butch had got in on the action.

"What's happening with you guys up north? Falling asleep on guard duty?" Joked George.

"Damn it, George," Answered Woz. "I'm not chasing bullets like you glory boys with Pershing; I'm chasing bodies of Mexicans playing tag with our border, seeking booze and broads!"

He reported that Butch was busted from Corporal to Private for starting a brawl at an off limits bar in El Paso. Seems he was propositioned by a woman of the night, and he laughed at her. She felt insulted, started tearing her blouse off and screaming "Help! Help! Rape! Rape!" Some of her regular customers came-a-running to her rescue and a riot broke out between them and Butch's outfit. Butch, fingered as the "instigator," spent the rest of his leave in the stockade, facing charges.

And to top it off, Woz was bitten by a dangerous Gila Monster while on temporary duty in Douglas, Arizona! He was bitten on his right boot, but his foot was fractured when he crushed the critter to death, pounding on it with the heel of his rifle and mistakenly striking his foot during his fury.

"The damn rifle did more damage than the Hela Monster! Don't that beat it all?" Complained Woz. "I was plastered with a foot cast for six, miserably hot weeks. I could think of better ways of getting 'plastered,'" chuckled Woz.

"It cut short my Douglas assignment too, and I was re-assigned to desk duty back in Fort Bliss, shuffling paper. The only lead I used was in pushing a pencil!" Moaned Woz.

George was pleased to get mail from anybody and amused by the travails of his buddies from Brickbottom. It reminded him of his father's oft spoken comment that:

"A person without problems is dead; so it's nice to know we're very much alive."

With respect to problems, Captain Gonsalvez was telling George that he heard a fantastic tale uncovered by US agents in Mexico that filtered down into the field through the U.S. State and War Departments. It was known as the *San Diego Plan*. The San Diego in Mexico, not California. Supposedly, it was originally plotted the prior year. Its plan was for the wholesale takeover of a large number of the U.S. States by revolutionaries in both the U.S. and Mexico. It was drawn up by prisoners arrested by the military for planning political coups in Monterrey, State of Nuevo Leon, southeast of Chihuahua, Mexico.

This incredible plan was a scheme to start a revolution in Texas, Arizona, California, Nevada, Oklahoma, Colorado and New Mexico. Its purpose was to establish an independent republic, spawned by Mexicans, Indians and Negroes. The new republic would then help the Negroes to select six more of the now disunited states to form a Negro republic.

Newspapers in Matamoros, Monterrey and Tampico in Northeastern Mexico printed the manifesto of this startling new movement. Additionally, the print press of Northern Mexico ran sensational articles for days to give glittering versions of victories won by revolutionaries. With their wishful thinking and runaway imagination, the Mexican reporters described the capture of towns, the looting of banks, the killing of American soldiers, the headlong retreat of other American soldiers running for their lives, the abandonment of Washington by President Wilson, and the fleeing of the American Congress.

This grand plan was reputedly funded by $40,000,000 furnished by Germany, and traced back through a New York Bank by experts in US Intelligence. German mine and other industrial investments in Mexico were to be protected and oil was to be shipped to Germany through the Mexican port of Tampico, for the European war Germany was then in the midst of.

The new republic was either to remain independent or become annexed to Mexico. It would reverse the results of the U.S. war against Mexico in 1846-48, with additional allied territories added for reasons thought appropriate by the conspirators. They believed this would be historic justice against the U.S. for it robbing Mexico of most of these territories.

"This *Plan of San Diego* was given new currency," claimed Captain Gonsalvez, "after the American incursion into Mexico by General Pershing, and, more recently, by the recent threats of Carranza soldiers to attack the American Expeditionarry Force in Mexico."

George at first listened in silent disbelief to this remarkable conspiracy. But as Captain Gonsalvez related more and more, George burst out laughing; he couldn't help it. It was that incredible.

"Good God! I don't know anything about history or politics, but this grand plan is the product of some imagination that's as tall as the the tallest Sierra Madre Mountains."

"Maybe so, but we know the Germans are here stirring up the Mexicans. And didn't the British chase the President and the government out of Washington D.C. during the War of 1812? In fact, didn't they burn down the capital?"

"I know some Germans are here, because I've seen them. But ask me about Greek, not American history. I'm a Greek immigrant. My knowledge of U.S. History is limited to what I had to learn to become a U.S. Citizen. So you tell me."

"As unbelieveable as it seems, that's the talk that's going around now," confirmed Captain Gonsalvez.

"Oh, I believe you, but I'm more interested in what's going on here, not in Europe or in international intrigue or politics, because all I've got is here and now."

Getting back to the local scene, Pershing moved his headquarters further north back to Casa Grandes, three miles from Dublan, his first headquarters, because supply lines would be shorter and communications would be better.

George was warned at a Battalion meeting to be wary of "friendly" Mexicans. From his own experience, he was well aware of their smiling ignorance of any knowledge of the whereabouts of Pancho Villa or his bandit hordes. It was understandable that they would be fearful of retaliation by Villistas for any perceived co-operation with the invading, foreign Americans. After all, life was worth little in Pancho Villa's Mexico and many Mexicans who fingered Pancho, forfeited their lives pronto, and their bullet ridden or hung bodies were put on public display as a warning. To Villa's terrorists, shooting was preferable to hanging, because it was faster, unless they were low on ammunition. What was more upsetting to Americans was "friendly" Mexicans deliberately going out of their way to give false or misleading information merely to frustrate them, usually with a smile.

Besides the problem of "friendly" Mexicans, matters took an ominous turn the next month at Carrizal, in northeastern Chihuahua. Pershing was concerned after one of his patrols reported that a fifteen thousand man Carranza Army had moved to the Ahumada area, within seventy five miles of his new headquarters at Casa Grandes-Dublan. It put them to his East, and made Pershing an easy target within striking distance. To deal with this danger, Pershing sent on June 18th Captain Boyd and his 10th Cavalry detachment of forty three experienced black soldiers and forty six other soldiers from K troop of that Cavalry to reconnoiter the Ahumada area to check it out.

On his way through Carrizal, Boyd ran into a hostile 400 Carranza Force armed with machine guns. Ambitious and aggressive, Boyd disregarded Pershing's order not to start a fight with the Mexicans, and ordered his outgunned and vastly outnumbered cavalry to attack the town. The result was the worst battle disaster suffered by any unit of the American Expeditionary Force; twenty-four captured, twelve wounded and ten killed. The fifty per cent killed/captured casualty rate was unprecedented. The only consolation was that the Carranza troops suffered a much worse number of casualties, forty wounded and thirty killed.

Was this the trigger to start a war with Mexico? George and many others wondered. President Wilson, once apprised of the matter, demanded an immediate release of the Americans taken prisoner at Carrizal. At the same time, he was preparing a message to address Congress to prepare them for war with Mexico. Carranza became alarmed when the Germans pointed out that the American forces were undermanned, but not for long. Facing a very real possibility of war with the "Collosus of the North," Carranza had noted that on June 16th, Wilson had federalized the National Guard across the entire United States. On mature consideration , therefore, Carranza ordered that the American prisoners from Carrizal be freed immediately. They were forthwith taken by train and returned safely to the border.

George found himself scratching his head at the swift speed of developments:

"Hard to figure, ain't it? Just as things get worse, they get better," said George to his equally bewildered squad.

After this bit of brinkmanship, things quieted down for the rest of the hot summer. The heat may have had something to do with it. Or maybe Carranza wanted to cease active hostilities with their success at Carrizal. Whatever, the summer passed with George back at Casa Grandes-Dublan and going out on probing patrols with little or no contact with Villistas or Carranza troops. It almost seemed like an undeclared cease-fire, though a few border skirmishes occurred as they always did up North.

Word came down to George and the rank and file that Carranza made a decision not to go to war with the U.S. Additionally, he reasonably proposed that three commissioners from each country be named to form a Joint High Commission to discuss and reach an agreement that would satisfy both countries. Wilson was delighted and immediately agreed. The diplomats were called in and cordial notes were exchanged to implement this process.

In the meantime, back at base camp, Bobby had written George a letter. He wrote that Jeff's hip injury was so bad, even after a series of surgeries, that he was scheduled to be invalided home after he was stabilized. Bobby was able to visit him, but didn't learn too much because Jeff was sleepy from sedation. An attending nurse, however, told him that the Doctors wouldn't give a prognosis. They would only say that his was a complicated injury and would require extended rehabilitation.

As far as his own injury was concerned, his wounded shoulder was indeed only a flesh wound. However, the injury site got infected and caused him unexpected misery. He had had trouble breathing as he turned awayed from the suffocating smell of sulfur that was applied to kill the infection. However, once the infection was killed, the wound healed quickly. He was grateful when he recovered and was medically cleared to return to duty. He was reassigned to border patrol duty out of Fort Bliss. So how was George doing, he asked?

"Aside from dying of boredom, I'm pretty lucky, I guess." George wrote. "Many close calls, but just a couple of superficial crease wounds. We'll have to discuss our experiences over a few beers some time. Meanwhile, I'm happy that Jeff will be going home. After all, he has a wife and kid waiting for him in New Hampshire. Maybe farming will look better to him now. Everything's relative, isn't it?" Wrote George.

Normal for the area, but not anticipated by the Americans, was the summer rains of July and August. They gave some relief from the scorching sun, but turned the dusty ground into a clay morass that sucked at your boots. Sand holes from slippery, spinning wheels dotted the camp roads. George stepped into a puddle and suddenly sunk down over his ankle. Angry at the sudden soaking, he kicked his foot into the puddle and inadvertently dug out a dead snake, apparently drowned and crushed by a passing wagon wheel. George shuddered and moved quickly on.

The mailed arrived one September day and George was thrilled to receive another letter from Angelika. And another. And another. Three letters at once! Each letter was dated approximately a week apart. The Army mail service must be bunching the mail and then sending them on. George ripped open the most recently dated letter, in order to get the latest news first. George liked to smell her letters, even before opening them. He loved the feminine aroma that wafted off the envelope and pages, or from his imagination, or both, it didn't matter which. Just the fact of receiving a letter from home was a thrill. It was a reminder that he was loved and remembered. The letters represented a bridge for his dreams to carry him back to his home, his loved ones and family. They gave him an instant psychological boost and spiritual high. It was euphoric, a feel good lift. Others noticed and benefited by it, because, metaphorically speaking, a rising tide lifts all boats.

Angelika had a habit of numbering her pages on the bottom. When George asked her why she did that, when most people wrote the page number on the top of each page, she replied that she was so anxious to write to George that she was at the bottom of a page before she realized she was rushing into the next page, and should number it. Reasonable enough, thought George. It wasn't that important, but George wanted to know everything about Angelika, including the little things.

> Dear George,
>
> I smother you with a thousand kisses! Now turn the other cheek!
>
> There! Doesn't that make you feel better? That's just a sample of what's in store for you when you come home! I will attack you with smooches, against which there are no known defenses. So don't even try, my wandering adventurer.
>
> Now I want you to start packing your bags. I have it on good authority that President Wilson is now negotiating to bring you boys home. And for that he will certainly get my vote. And why shouldn't he? 'He kept us out of war,' is his re-

election slogan, even though he didn't keep you out of war. But that is your mistake, not his. I will love you so much that you will only want me in your future, not war. So there, Mr. George Dilboy, make your peace with that!

Other than that, I want to open my own dress shop. And I will, too, once I can overcome my parent's objection. I'm too young, they say. Actually, it's Mom. She worries about me too much. Dad will do what Mom says, at least as it regards my dream of owning my own shop. You, of course, will be my first model. I will dress you in the finest cloth and you will be the grandest groom in Hellenic history, don't you worry.

Have you grown taller? After all, it's been over six months since I've seen you last. I have grown almost a full inch! I'm talking about my height, not my measurements, you naughty man! Look how you have got me writing! My parents would die if they saw this letter! It's your fault, because you've driving me crazy. But that's ok; I'm crazy for you, too. As if you didn't know!

But don't be too smug. There are plenty of young men tipping their hats, holding doors open for me and looking at me longingly, so don't you get smug or take me for granted, my intended. I know what it must be like asking a girl to marry you, knowing she's going to say "yes."

*I'm sending you your favorite brownies with plenty of nuts in them, just the way you like them. They are for you, and you are not to pass them all out to your buddies, like you are want to do. So pay heed to **my** orders, Sargent Dilboy!*

Your Angel,
(kiss)
Angelika

Woz wrote that the squeeking wheel does indeed get the grease, and he wasn't referring to George's country of origin. He complained so much about pushing paper at a dull desk job, that his desk

Sargent had him removed and transferred from Fort Bliss to Columbus, New Mexico, where he became a guard watching an Ordnance warehouse. If he doesn't get blown up from all the stored weaponry, he'll get plenty of exercise. Because he had no seniority in this new job, he drew the night shift. But that was all right with him. There was nobody around to bother him, save a few drunken civilians trying to stagger their way home. Some drunken soldiers too, if the truth be told. OOPS! Who said that! Seriously, however, his chief concern was watching out for burglars, who wanted to break into the stores of ammo in the warehouses, and sell them to whoever has enough money. A sort of black market.

He also wrote that he dreamed that Pancho Villa came back in the early morning hours again to the scene of the original crime, Woz killed him in a shootout, was given a triple promotion, topping George's double promotion in the Balkan War, and he was awarded the Congressional Medal of Honor! So what did George think of that dream? Woz asked.

"I wish it were true. Then we could all go home and get on with our lives." George wrote back. *"And it would be more fantastic than the San Diego Plan of disuniting the United States."*

George thought that Woz's dream of capturing and killing Pancho Villa was an example of a quirk of human nature when we spin off and personalize a private war against Pancho, even as we fought a public one. And George chuckled to himself that it would be the height of irony if fifteen thousand armed men chasing Pancho Villa couldn't catch him, but Pancho exposed himself to one man who did catch him. It was an intriguing thought, made more so by the possibility that it could happen. As could anything in this crazy war, concluded George.

George was also interested in the reported changes in Columbus, New Mexico. The previously unheard of little desert settlement became a boomtown, of sorts, after the Pancho led raid. All kinds of construction was going up. Buildings were being erected, railroad tracks were being repaired and ditches were being dug all around and through the bustling town to thwart any repeat of the now infamous Pancho Villa night raid. Columbus was also a major supply depot for the Mexican Expeditionary Force, with trains moving in and out every day carrying horses, supplies and ordnance to General Pershings forces.

Both Woz and Bobby, who hadn't met each other, had mentioned that a 2000 man troop contingent from the Massachusetts 2nd Infantry had come to Columbus and what a great sound it was to hear those Boston accents! The "Texicans," as some soldiers from up north called the Mexicans, and Texans from Texas, kept saying "What?" to the Boston accent. To Woz and Bobby it was like a message from home. Of course, they found every excuse to mix and mingle with the men from Massachusetts.

TARANTULA TAUNT

October brought a refreshing coolness that took the sting out of the sun, but made the nights crisp. The negotiations waxed and waned, heated up and cooled off, as rumors of their developments proliferated. But that was supposedly fine with President Wilson, who was three weeks from being re-elected, he hoped. As long as the American and Mexican diplomatic principals were talking and only desultory border and interior incidents rippled the sand, Wilson was content. George and his fellow soldiers were under strict orders not to start any fight with Mexicans, and to shoot only to protect their lives and limbs. Paradoxically, as the Mexican Expedition wound down, the European War wound up, as far as potential U.S. involvement was concerned. By November, after U.S. and other countries complained about German attacks on ships in the Atlantic, Germany had twice stopped these unrestricted attacks. But Germany's determination to starve Britain into submission, promised future attacks on U.S. shipping to England, that might bring them into the war. The only question was, would it be sooner or later, despite hopes that it would not happen.

George now bunked with a tentmate named Tito Martinez, a former Texas Ranger, born in San Antonio, Texas. He was tall and taciturn, and liked to chew and spit out his tobacco. He was also an expert with a knife. George had to leave the tent flap open because Tito was always throwing that knife around at his various targets, and needed the light. This habit was a nuisance to George and when he cautioned Tito to be careful with it, Tito claimed that he was just practicing. When George suggested that he practice by whittling, he replied:

"That would sharpen the blade, but not my throwing. And didn't this skill make me a better soldier, all the more to protect your back?"

"As long as it didn't land in my back," riposted George.

George liked the logic of it all, but not this continued irksome habit. But George had learned to live and let live, and dropped the matter. He decided it just wasn't that important to make a bigger deal of it.

On November morning, as George was getting dressed, Tito came into the tent and asked George if he had heard the news that President Wilson was re-elected. George hadn't, but was glad to hear it. He had voted for Wilson, thinking he was doing a fine job, as far as he could tell. Tito volunteered that Wilson didn't get his vote, not because he didn't deserve it, but because Tito didn't get around to vote. But it was nice to see him re-elected, because if he had voted, he would have cast his vote for Wilson. It wasn't that he liked Wilson so much, as he didn't like Charles Evans Hughes, or anyone else that had to use three names. George just laughed, as he thought of the range of reasons that motivated people to vote for a particular candidate.

While so engaged in talking to Tito, George reached for his second boot that he had stuffed with paper to keep out scorpions and tarantulas seeking warmth. As he pulled out the paper, tipped the shoe upside down and shook it loose, out fell a dark, large tarantula! George yelled, jumped up and stomped the furry spider with his booted foot! He found himself taking short, bated breaths, as he calmed down from this startling, sudden shock. He knew from other soldiers having been bitten, that the dangerous scorpion was capable of inflicting a painful sting, though seldom lethal.

"Why the hell would a hairy tarantula climb into a boot?" George wondered aloud. "I can see a naked scorpion seeking warmth, but not a furry tarantula!"

"You forget how cold it gets at night, George, especially as we near winter. Fire and food can also attract coyotes. We're bivouacking out in the wild, after all. And that's more their natural habitat, than ours."

"Your right, Tito. But that doesn't make me feel more comfortable. It will, however, make me more careful. You're not safe anywhere, in this country."

"You did as you were instructed, George. Every morning bottom-up your shoe and bang on the sole to shake out whatever may be in there. That's all you can do. There's no guarantee of safety here, that's for sure."

George went through the Thanksgiving holiday with no big celebration, other than to recognize its occurrence with a special eat-time, roasting local pigs and animals. Since it was an American holiday, the Mexicans gave it scarce notice. George also told Tito that he would just as soon not make too big a deal of it, because it only highlighted his absence from his family. He did, however, take advantage of the downtime to write more letters and to mail Mexican blankets back to his family as Christmas gifts. He hoped they would arrive in time to be put under the Christmas tree before the twin holyday-holiday. The well made blankets were heavy and warm and much appreciated during the many cold nights, especially up in the windy, weather-hostile Sierra Madre Mountains. He was sure they would be equally welcome in chilly New England.

He also took whatever leave he could to visit other camps and once went back to Fort Bliss to see the guys. He didn't notify Woz or Bobby specifically when he would be coming, because he didn't know for sure when he could get a leave, and because he wanted to sneak up on them and surprise them with an ambush visit, as he called it. George was bored and tired of this war and yearned for a little change and excitement. A surprise visit wasn't exactly a thrilling experience, but was the best he could do in his winding down and limited situation. He had to be practical.

They met and had a great time catching up on the past year with their war stories, appropriately embellished by exaggeration and spiritous liquors. Their talk was ultimately consumed by questions like, "What do you hear?" and conversation replete with references to peace prospects and going home. They even bet a case of Mexican beer on who would be the first to cross over the New England border. At leaves end, George, normally a non-drinker, dragged his happy, but hungover body back to the troop train to Dublan. His late return was generously interpreted by Captain Gonsalvez as the train being late, but not George, in the spirit of the times. The Army was all one, big happy family during their drive to get the troops to sign up for another tour of duty or go Regular Army. Only an idiot didn't realize this meant leave, followed by the U.S. likely joining the European War.

FORT BLISS?

Why it was named Fort Bliss, was something George could never figure out. Of all the words he could use to describe this God forsaken, desert, dust bowl of an Army camp, "bliss" would be the last one. It was a sprawling encampment run through with a giant railroad yard adding to its ugliness. But it was an important site because of its location and because it also served as the main supply base for the Mexican Expedition. It was also adjacent to the largest U.S. City closest to the Mexican border in the Southwest, El Paso. The city's importance well overshadowed its unattractive physical attributes. This significance was about the only shadow you would get in this treeless flatland, where the only shade you got when the sun was straight above, was from whatever you put on your head, and it better be something. When the sun was rising or falling, you would quick step from building shadow to shadow, slowing down when you entered the dark, to prolong its comforting, cool feeling.

The closest thing he got to bliss was George uncharacteristically getting blitzed from an overdose of spiritous liquors celebrating the New Years holiday ushering in 1917. H Company was excited at the near prospect of the Expedition being recalled back over the border and home, except for the Regular Army guys, that is. "Regs," they were called. George sensed the end of the Expedition was near, not just because of all the rumors, or the vastly reduced fighting; in fact there was more fighting among bored Americans than between Americans and Mexicans. But what tipped George off about the end of the Expedition was the "Regs" trying to get the rest of them to sign on as Regular Army, with glowing promises of a promotion filled future, and all-of-a-sudden new base privileges making the Army experience almost enjoyable. George laughed at the transparency of it all. The big question in camp was:

"When are we going home?"

CHAPTER TWENTY SIX

IT'S OVER

Every day they expected to be ordered home. Many of the soldiers became feisty and angry when they began to believe that the U.S. Government was delaying their recall, because they wanted them still to be in the Army when they declared war on Germany in the European War that seemed to be slowly sucking America into it. That would save the Government from having to draft them back in. As the Villa Expedition wound down, many American soldiers watched the happenings in the European War with growing apprehension. But they needn't have. At least, as it turned out.

The U.S. Army Mexican Punitive Expeditionary Force was ordered to pack its bags and be back across the border by February 1, 1917. That gave them less than two weeks to break camp. The whole camp was ready well before then. The march-back was organized in daily Officer Meetings. The Officers then reported to their units in individual Company briefings. Attendence and attention at these gatherings was at an all time high, as was the morale of the ebullient troops.

George fired off excited, quick letters to Angelika and his family. But he later learned that the public newspapers announced the good news before his letters could be delivered. Officially, despite the target date of February 1, the last U.S. Soldier crossed over the border back into the United States on February 5, 1917. But the important date to George and his H Company was the date **they** crossed over, January 30th, 1917. George had entered Mexico as an infantryman and came back as a mounted scout in the Cavalry. He ended up where he wanted to be, though initially thwarted. He was pleased.

George was back in Fort Bliss along with thousands of other U.S. troops not moved along to Fort San Houston and other outposts to wait for their mustering out. It was a happy, somewhat chaotic situation. Anxious as he was to get back home to Angelika and his family in New England, George congenially put up with the ritual drills and mundane keep-'em-busy dog duties because he knew he could put up with anything knowing it was temporary. Besides, he knew the Army wanted to reduce its budget by getting rid of these serving short-timers who wanted nothing more than to shed their military uniforms and put on their "civies." The Army wanted them out and they wanted out. To this everyone agreed and they were all walking on the same side of the street, so to speak. It made for friendlier times and conversations that included comments like:

"What are you going to do when you get out?"

That was easy for George. He was going to collect his accumulated pay, turn in his cavalry mount, and buy himself a basic, model T Ford motor car. Then he would drive his beloved Angelika around the countryside, running that vehicle as fast as the engine would allow! No two ways about that! Just you wait! If there was a happier horizon, George didn't know it. He was in paradise.

Finally released, troop trains radiated out from various points in the Southwest, particularly Texas. George and his unit entrained from Fort Bliss in full uniform to and through San Antonio. The train took them north to the snow and cold through Kansas City stockyards and across to St. Louis, the gateway to the West, except that they were going North and East. During the long train ride, George refused to succumb to the blandishments and entreaties of his army brethren to join the hot card games broken out by card sharks hoping to win big, and thus relieve their less skilled brothers of their accumulated back pay before reaching their destination. Some enterprising bootleggers even offered free booze to cardplayers. George good naturedly endured the caustic comments from excited or slurring fellow soldiers about how an "Angel" had a prior claim on George's money and virtue. George indulged their indiscretions with sparring remarks of his own, knowing some would wake up the next morning with empty pockets and heavy heads trying to remember what happened.

After reaching the great cow, railroad and old Indian City of Chicago, the trained troops quieted down from their earlier enthusiasms, tired from a variety of questionable activities affecting their health and wallets. The winners and soberites were conspicuous by their normal behavior. Those not so favored sulked in sullen silence, staring out the dirty windows, as the train chugged noisily across the upper Middle-West toward the giant motor car city of Detroit and onwards to the incomparably colossal New York City, arguably the worlds most exciting metropolis. Others couldn't have cared less, but George noted to himself, with a silent pride, that metropolis was a Greek word, meaning the mother-city of a state or colony in ancient Greece. In the Greek religion, the word also refers to the Chief See of the Metropolitan Bishop, especially the main Diocese of a specific Ecclesiastical Province.

From New York City, the train emerged from beneath the depths of the great underground subway to Connecticut and on to Boston. Angelika, in her gushing zeal to see George, wanted to meet the train in Boston's South Station. George tried to dissuade her, because he still had to report to his post in Keene by the next day, in order to officially be mustered out. It involved something he didn't fully understand, about President Wilson federalizing the National Guard and George having to report back to his New Hampshire National Guard to which he reverted, once his unit was defederalized. Angelika didn't care about that; he could take a later train to Keene and still report the next day to be given his final release papers, she argued. Persuasively, as it turned out.

HOMECOMING

Soldiers streamed out of the smoking train, squeals of delight rang into the air and rushing bodies collided all over the platform, as exuberent loved ones and family members welcomed home their heroes. Hugging, kissing and wheeled wrestling matches whirled everywhere in uninhibited scenes of joy. Smiles were smitten on all faces. People bounced more than they walked their way out of the station. Angelika strained her neck repeatedly, as she searched frantically for her Georgie. The bunched soldiers bursting out of the train exit doors thinned out into a lengthening line. Then the stragglers lagging behind emerged. And there, smoking a cigarette, and carrying a brown duffle bag, was George!

"George! George! Screamed Angelika. "Here! Over here!" She ran as she yelled:

"Oh, my God! It is you!" She squealed.

George looked up and saw Angelika racing towards him, her arms thrown up. He instinctively dropped his bag and waited for the flying hug. She flung herself at him, knocking her hat off and his cigarette away. She was crying, she was so happy. George could only mutter:

"Angelika. Angelika. My senorita."

They hugged each other tight and George lifted her off the ground and kissed her fully on the lips. They clung to each other, locked together in a long embrace, savoring the moment. They alternated between hugging and kissing.

"Senorita. Senorita? I'm your fiance, not some Mexican hussy, Mr. George Dilboy!" Fumed a mock serious Angelika.

"You look great! Just great!" Gasped George, ignoring her feigned fury.

"I'm greatly relieved to have my amore back. Let me see you! Stand back! Stand back! I want to see all of you. You gorgeous creature."

Angelika preened herself with shy modesty. Then George pulled her toward him again, and they embraced and kissed once more. It was then that George noticed his Uncle Kostas waiting patiently in the background. He momentarily straightened up, kissed Angelika yet again and lunged toward his Uncle, hands outstretched.

"Kostas! How nice of you to come!"

George spontaneously engulfed Kostas in an avuncular hug, then slapped him vigorously on his back. Angelika magnaminously shared her loved one with his Uncle, beaming joyfully in their heartfelt greetings.

"You're looking grand! You needn't have bothered to come. But I'm glad you did," spouted a pleasantly surprised George.

"Oh, I just wanted to count the bullet holes in your body; maybe I'm a Doubting Thomas from our Christian Bible."

"As you see, I am not Jesus Christ, though he surely was looking over me. And unlike Swiss cheese, I am quite whole."

"Ha, ha, hee, hee, cackled and heehawed Angelika and Uncle Kostas at George's frivolity and Uncle Kostas's facetiousness.

Ever the hostess, Angelika interrupted their buffoonery by suggesting that since George mentioned food, maybe they could all grab a bite to eat. After all, they had three hours to wait until George's train would leave for Nashua and he could meet the rest of his family there.

"Of course, but let me first buy my ticket for the Nashua train before it fills up." Cautioned George.

"That's not likely, George. Not too many people take the train from Boston for Nashua at 10:00 o'clock at night in the middle of the week. But you might as well ease your mind by buying your ticket first. Then we can enjoy our dinner without rushing to buy your fare at the last minute."

For the next three hours, they regaled each other with local happenings during the past ten months, with George and Angelika bubbling over and interrupting each other with reckless abandon. Uncle Kostas didn't even attempt to intervene, as he thoroughly enjoyed their fervered conversations, which included him by an occasional nod, glance or light tap of Angelika's hand.

Finally, Angelika looked fully at Uncle Kostas and remarked, while giggling:

"Oh, Uncle Kostas, you must thinks us foolish clowns!" Bubbled Angelika.

"Not at all. You look like two young adults in love. What's not to admire in that?"

The time flew by too fast and when they heard the "all aboard" announcement for the Nashua train, they saw George off. This send off was pleasantly subdued, not only because of the late hour, and their three hour non-stop ebullent talking, but because of the knowledge that George was to come back to Boston as soon as he met his family and mustered out. He would stay with Uncle Kostas in Somerville while he got resettled. George's future looked bright and promising, and Angelika basked in the certainty that she was central to it. They would talk and plan their futures together. Angelika looked forward to their conjoined future with unabashed joy and excitement. Her man was home. She couldn't be happier.

The train to Nashua, after local stops, got into the station there before midnight. There to meet him was Marianthe and John, George's older sister and brother. Smiling faces, hugs and kisses were exchanged between them. Marianthe could see that George was tired from the long train ride and late hour.

"And how was Angelika?" teased Marianthe.

George marvelled at her perspicacity:

"And just how in the world did you know that? Did she tell or write you she was going to meet me in Boston?"

"No, silly. Her perfume is all through your clothes and face. Women pick up on those things, you should know."

"Well, we could have used your kind of intelligence in our Intel Unit in Mexico. We wouldn't have been so easily mislead by the Mexicans. It would have saved us a lot of wild, useless chases."

"You're home now George. That war is over, and Pancho Villa and his bandits are on the run and away from the border. Mission accomplished," congratulated John.

"I'd like to think so, John. In any event, it was an interesting experience. And I'm glad to be home. How are things going here?"

"Swell. We're all fine. We'll discuss it in the morning. You must be exhausted. Other than being obviously tired, you look good," volunteered Marianthe.

"That I am. But it's nothing a good night's sleep won't take care of."

With that they took a taxi home, sharing some stretched small talk. The others stayed up to see George home, and he was warmly greeted, but quickly shooed to bed. They all agreed he needed sleep more than anything else. They could talk in the morning. They only wanted to glance at him to assure themselves that he was indeed all right. Satisfied, they showed him to his room and blessed sleep.

COMES THE MORNING

Antonios almost pushed George out the door the next morning after an animated, lively breakfast. He seemed more anxious than George to report in, so he could be officially mustered out before the European War pulled in the United States. Since George was of the same mind, he all but flew out the door. But he needn't have rushed. The Army bureaucracy reasserted its legacy and required the returning soldiers to wait while their discharge papers were typed up. And because of the number of returnees, there would be an unspecified delay. The returned veterans were up in arms, in a manner of speaking, they punned. They had wives, families, jobs and careers in jeopardy, to hear them tell it. Resentment turned into anger, into near physical confrontations, and some absences without official leaves.

The local Commanding Officer, assessing the current disorder, decided to give a more liberal interpretation to the Standing Orders Governing Discharge. Upon review, it now allowed for the soldiers, who had duly reported in, to go home on leave. Their Discharge Papers would be mailed to them, effective as of the day they signed in. Great, thought George; they would mail him his Honorable Discharge. On hearing this, and the order, "Dismissed!" the soldiers assembled in the Armory snapped to a smart salute and charged out of the entrance to the armory, shouting all the way. They were now civilians.

George stayed in Nashua just long enough to talk with his family about his future plans. He would go back to Somerville and Boston, and stay with Uncle Kostas and get a job. Of course, he had most of his family and two job offers waiting for him in Nashua. But they realized his heart was with Angelika and his future in

Boston, where he believed there were better job opportunities for him. George and Angelika had all but announced their engagement. Angelika's family and current job were in the Boston area, also pulling him there. He was twenty-one years of age and had to blaze his own trail. George knew his family would support any reasonable decision he made. They would back him up; they always have; they would always be there; they were family.

So he packed his bags, waved his goodbyes and boarded the next bus to Boston, because it was earlier and cheaper than a train, though it arrived in Boston later, because of more stops. He was saving his money to buy Angelika and him his long desired motor car! But it also occasioned a later argument with Angelika. However, that came later. First things first.

Angelika was telephoned and advised by Marianthe of the time of George's scheduled Boston arrival at the Park Square Bus Station. Actually, George wanted to surprise Angelika, but Marianthe decided it wasn't proper and telephoned ahead. Angelika promised to keep Marianthe's telephone alert a secret. It was time someone turned the tables on George and his ambush games, Marianthe determined.

"We women must stick together!" Implored George's older sister.

Angelika was in total agreement with her future sister-in-law. She was at the Greyhound Bus Terminal early, not wanting to run into any accident or delay on the trolley car or subway system, as sometimes happened. She was going to thoroughly enjoy jumping George's smug expectations. Just the thought thrilled her. George was indeed surprised and, at the same time, miffed at his oldest sister.

"So Marianthe prattled on me, did she?"

"No. You tattled on yourself. You told me you would report in the next day and ship out the day after. I spoke with your family and was told you left. I was just confirming what I already knew. So put that in your pipe, Mr. George Dilboy know-it-all!" Riposted a petulent Angelika.

"I don't smoke. But if I did, I'd still think it was Marianthe, because she told me, in so many words."

"Why do you complain when people do to you, what you do to them?" Asked Angelika.

"That's a fair question. Maybe I like being a doer more than I like being a receiver."

"Why can't you be both?"

"I take your point, without necessarily agreeing with it, because of personal preferences." Answered George with what he hoped was a final comment.

Sometimes he thought Angelika went out of her way to argue with him as her way of telling him that he couldn't push her around. He'd rather move her around on a dance floor, anyway. And he loved her, in part, because of her spirit. They were still feeling out each other's boundaries, in the getting-to-know-you stage, George surmised.

FLOWER SEEDS?

They took public transportation to his Uncle Kostas's apartment house, that he now owned. In helping George to unpack, Angelika took out an odd item from his duffle bag, flower seeds! His mother had sent them to him in Mexico all the way from Chios, George explained.

"Only a mother could believe a soldier would plant flower seeds during a war. And in a dusty, windy, desert land like Mexico, too. Can you believe it?" Marveled George.

"Well, isn't Greece and Alatsata dusty, windy and desert like? And they have flowers, don't they?"

"Angelika, stop killing me with common sense. Men just don't plant flowers during war."

"Did you plant them?"

"I thought about it. But I didn't have time and nobody else volunteered. We were on the go. Besides, who would water them?"

"You wouldn't have to. Nature would provide rain, as it always did. If it didn't rain, it would be God's way of waiting."

"Was I a soldier or a gardener?" replied an irked George.

"That didn't matter. It wouldn't have hurt to plant some beauty in all that ugliness. Besides, it would have taken your mind off your war obsession."

"When my life is at stake, Angelika dearest, I'd better be obsessed with preserving it, or I wouldn't live long. Besides, God takes care of flowers, remember? And I'm not God."

"But you can help. And doesn't God help those who help themselves? Don't we put flowers before God on our church altars?"

"Angelika, as my father said to me, 'Enough already.' You can be as stubborn as my father!"

"Yes! And I think God and your father are good company."

George just threw up his hands, and walked away muttering: "God help me; God help us all!"

Holy lightning, thought George to himself. I'm getting shot at more here, than in Mexico. Where's the nearest shelter? He wondered, as he strode purposely away to take a walk.

CHAPTER TWENTY SEVEN

WHEELS

One bright, sunny, Monday morning George asked Angelika if she wanted to go with him to a motor car dealership in Cambridge to help him buy one of those new motor cars. She was a little concerned at this seemingly whimiscal purchase, on the one hand; on the other, she knew he long coveted its purchase. So she agreed to accompany him on this expensive, exciting trip to buy. She called her work and told them she would be in to re-dress the window mannequins in the afternoon, because something sudden had come up at home.

Her being miffed at the short notice was somewhat mollified when she did recall and confirm her memory of George's frequent longing during recent years to purchase a motor car, knowing that he didn't then have the money. Thus, she confined her irritation to the short notice, rather than the intended purchase. But then again, it was something that endeared him to her, but also exasperated her, at times. She didn't want to exaggerate the matter, because George was just being himself. And if she loved him, how could she fault him? She accepted him, warts and all, as they say. She had her quirks too, like her argumentative nature. She smiled at reminiscing how George would call her, *"my little meteorite"* and say she should have been a lawyer; then she could argue herself to the grave.

They took a trolley car to Union Square, and changed cars to go along Washington St. to Harvard Square. Full of excited anticipation, George advised Angelika that Washington St. was named after the American Revolutionary War General, George

Washington, and that Harvard University started as a religious school to educate the native wild Indians. Underwhelmed with this unsolicitated information, a clearly bored Angelika replied that:

"I am interested in George Dilboy, not any other George, and there are more Indians with turbans on their heads at Harvard today than Huron Indians."

"And speaking of Huron Indians, Angelika, Huron Ave in Cambridge is named in their honor. So you know more history than you realize."

"I am more interested in today, than yesterday. In bygone yesterday, you couldn't afford to buy a motor car. Today you plan to spend a lot of money, even before you have a job. So it's in your interest to pay more attention to today and your motor car, than to history."

"Is that my history lesson for today?" jabbed an amused George.

"If you like," said a much unamused and serious Angelika.

"Besides, I already have a job. I was told on leaving almost every job, that it would be there for me if I wanted to come back. But even if they weren't, I have years of savings to pay for the motor car. So I'll owe nothing on the car and can get to jobs farther away with a car. And we can motor to Nashua to see my family."

"That was then; this is now. Those offers often disappear with time and bosses long gone. You have no current offer. Be realistic."

"Maybe it comes down to attitude. I'm more of a risk taker; you're more conservative," thought George aloud.

"You're also a dreamer, Mr. George Dilboy."

"Guilty! I plead guilty. And I feel sorry for all those who don't follow their dreams. They must lead a dull life. You dream of owning your own dress shop, don't you?"

"Yes, I surely do. So maybe you're right. Maybe it comes down to attitude."

"And timing. I'm just ready earlier to follow my dreams than you are, because of my riskier nature."

"So how's your 'tude' today?" Punned Angelika.

"I'm in a buy 'tude' today," riposted George.

They laughed together, enjoying their paring and thrusting. George had primed for his operators driving license by accompanying some precocious friends, members at the Sons of Ionia, and Uncle Kostas in their driving. And they let him practice-drive enough under their tutelage, being quick on the uptake, to pass his official Massachusetts driving test. This fueled his desire to own his own motor vehicle.

They got off the trolley car at Harvard Square and boarded a third one rolling up Massachusetts Avenue, with the loud roar of its iron wheels accompanying its wooden, box shaped chassis. George endured half a dozen jarring stops with his arms hanging down from a looped, worn leather strap. Angelika had to make do, hanging on to George's jacket with both hands, tightening her grip with each jolting stop and each lurching start of the trolley car. George much enjoyed being in Angelika's grasp, as opposed to Angelika's acute embarrassment. It was particularly difficult for her, because she frequently had to let go with one hand, to rescue her bonnet, tilted perilously on the side of her head. Her hairpins had to be hurriedly readjusted during trolley stops.

During periodic crossing of bridges which lessened the noise of traffic, Angelika asked George why he didn't visit the motor car dealership on a Saturday, when she wouldn't have missed a morning of work. He replied that the guys at the Sons of Ionia Club counseled that a Monday visit to the car dealership would find fewer customers, because it was a work day for most people, and he would be treated better and less rushed. This was recommended by a relative of a member, who knew someone who worked with the salesmen on the sales floor. And besides, George said, Angelika told him that she worked so much she had excess vacation time. And thus, he buying a motor car would help them enjoy their future vacations so much the better.

The trolley car went through Porter Square and roared on toward North Cambridge. They got off the trolley car right in front of the motor car dealership. They were greeted with open arms by an alert, waiting salesman. When the salesman saw that George was a serious buyer, ready to buy, he lavished attention on them. He recommended that George take the car of his choice out for a test drive with him, and he invited Angelika along. Angelika hesitated, at first, asking if she could stand on the running board beside the car. But the salesman dissusaded her by claiming that she would be safer inside the car, away from the sometimes dangerous passing traffic. With George's urging, she agreed, but only if she could ride in the back seat. The salesman readily agreed, saying he could more easily point out the driving features of the car to George if he sat in the front seat with him.

So they were off. George carefully drove out of the side entrance of the dealership building into a side street. He then turned right onto the wide Massachusetts Avenue. He drove drove north toward the Arlington town line, as faster cars passed him by. But he passed with some satisfaction the slower horse drawn wagons. He turned around at the Arlington-Cambridge line and headed back to the dealership with a little more confidence and driving more up to speed. Angelika appeared cowed by the ride and remained silent. George made his decision to buy when he completed this turn, depressed the gas pedal, and confidently drove forward.

Back at the dealership, George delighted the salesman and his boss by agreeing to the purchase and pleased them further by paying cash. Three hundred and ninety five dollars. The cost of a model T Ford had dropped forty-five dollars in one year! George's long saving habit saved the day. George and Angelika drove back to Brickbottom as if on a cloud, even though the car bounced noisily over the cobblestones. He was told to be careful on rainy days when the cobble-stones could become slippery, especially when covered with horse droppings that turned to brown mud. And George was particularly advised to be careful when driving along trolley car tracks, which could cause his car to skid for a bit. The loss of control might only be momentary, they warned. But nevertheless, it could be long enough to cause an accident. And while thinking of street conditions for his new driving exposure, George told himself that one just had to get use to the smell of horse manure, before it dried and turned to dust. He realized he would have to co-operate with the inevitable; Angelika, less so.

WHERE TO PARK?

When they got back to Uncle Kostas's house, George tried to park his brand new model T in the pathway beside the house. But he couldn't fully open the door to get out. So he backed out, while Angelika and Uncle Kostas watched. His Uncle helped direct him to back up, but George pushed the gas pedal down too low, and it bolted backwards on an angle, striking the side of the house.

"Damn!" He cursed.

The jerking of the car caused him to involuntarily turn the steering wheel. Quickly pulling the car forward off the house, George braked and stopped the vehicle. Through a tight squeeze, he slid sideways out of the drivers side door. He looked to survey the damage. Both the Ford and the house were damaged, but not seriously. George was more embarrassed than angry. But he could only blame himself. He had owned the car less than two hours and he had his first accident. He swallowed his self-consciousness and parked it on the street in front of Uncle Kostas's house. Then he eagerly got out before he caused any more damage. He would review his driving behavior to see what he did right and wrong. Angelika smiled and took his arm to show her support. She was with him right or not right.

He kissed her impulsively, which was his want. And did so in public, which was not his want, because of Greek cultural frowning against open displays of affection, at least among the men. Men were to be stoic and strong. Not that this was verbally expressed directly, but was indirectly conveyed with disapproving gestures and obliquely condemming comments. Without being able to explain why, the man got the negative message. It was little consolation to the sons of Hellene that this cultural custom was not limited to Greek-Americans. So George's amorous, spontaneous gesture in publically kissing Angelika was all the more remarkable because it was counter-ingrained. Love does indeed conquer all, if this little example means anything, thought Angelika, as he thanked her and shushed her off to work. Heading off, Angelika couldn't be more thrilled for what it portended.

BELLS ARE RINGING

Having invested in this treasured transport of a motor car, George heeded Angelika's admonition to get a job, so that he could afford the petrol to run it, and maintain its cost to keep it road worthy, and fulfill its promise.

George's exemplary service was indeed remembered at the Copley Square Hotel and his service in the U.S. Mexican Expedition stood him in good stead, and he was eagerly given employment and handed the civilian uniform of a veteran bellboy. Not only was he given a raise from his old earnings rate, he was promoted to Supervising Bellboy. George was very pleased with both intimations of his value as an enhanced member of the hotel family. The heavens were smiling on him and his own family, in America and in their ancestral home in Asia Minor. George credited his good life to divine intervention. He was following his Masters plan. He raised his thoughts to the celestial heavens and silently praised God.

"Thank you God. Thank you God," he repeated.

He took nothing for granted and this was his way of expressing his appreciation to his heavenly father in his own informal, private style of prayer.

The men in the Sons of Ionia welcomed George and his new motor car, but frowned on his bringing Angelika into the club. This was a *mens* club, he was reminded by various comments in different ways.

"After all, they had their own Daughters of Ionia Club, didn't they?" This was the gist of their complaint.

They did. But why couldn't the two clubs be inclusive, rather than exclusive? Wondered George. By himself, he couldn't change Greek custom, which some of the old guard thought America's more liberal ways were challenging. The culture clash would have to be reconciled in some mutually acceptable way, if not totally agreeable, to both traditions. But that was in the future. And as Angelika reminded George, he had to live in the now. Greek insularity could be irksome, even among its own people. But George asked himself, if he couldn't be patient with his own people, who could he be patient with?

ON THE ROAD

The thrill of owning his own motor car turned George into a road gypsy, not only taking Sunday drives out into the country, but on many other days when he could get Angelika to ride with him. If Angelika wasn't available, almost anyone would be welcome. Solo drives would do, if no one else had been available. It got so that George would drive over to the Sons of Ionia Club around the corner, when walking could have been done just as easily. But what's the use of having a motor vehicle if he didn't use it, he reasoned. The novelty of the car would wear off and its overuse would rectify itself in time. And it did.

In the meantime, other modifying factors were the cost of petrol and frequent tire blowouts. George also determined it was easier and safer to have a companion along on his country drives. Sharing enhanced the fun. And two shorten the road, goes a Chinese saying. Not only were dirt roads prevalent, but they were rougher. Bouncing kidneys, he discovered, were something less than healthy over time. And headaches were not strangers to troubled trips, either. Nonetheless, George looked for the first opportunity to visit his folks up north in Nashua. It was an all day round trip, so George would stay over and make a weekend of it, often as not. Angelika lobbied for and got side trips to the mills of Lawrence and Lowell to shop for her precious cloths for herself and sometimes for her dressing shop, though the mills had their own manufacturers representatives to bring sample clothing bolts, swatches and their order forms to the retail shops.

It was when the dress Shop ran short between supplies that the owners frequently asked Angelika if she was planning a trip "up north" and would she mind picking up an extra bolt of cloth or two. Angelika tried to be accomodating, as was her helpful nature, even when it was an imposition for George, if not for her.

Generally, George didn't mind, except on a couple of occasions when he thought they were taking advantage of her. For the most part, however, it worked out. Compromise often smoothed the way, George believed. George and Angelika seemed to bond together and work well as a team. They were perceived as an intended couple. When you saw one, you expected to see the other.

One hobby Angelika didn't particularly care for was George's fondness for rifles. However, she also realized that it was a weapon that he grew up with as a necessity in those times in that dangerous area of the world that she also grew up in and knew all too well. But a rifle was a lethal weapon, and had to be both respected and feared. A necessary evil, if you will, that like fire, could warm a cold body, but also kill you. But Angelika asked herself, why would George need a rifle in America? He was not a hunter who liked to go into the mountains to shoot wild animals. He was not and didn't want to become a Policeman, who had to deal with weapons. And she was not going to try to become an Annie Oakley, who Sitting Bull admiringly called "Little Sure Shot," because Annie already proved that you can't get a man with a gun. Besides, she didn't have to; she already had him. She just didn't want to lose him to a stray bullet. When she tried to talk to George about it, he became angry. He didn't want to discuss it, other than to say that it was a skill he liked to practice.

"Practice for what?" Asked a puzzled Angelika.

"When you're good at something, you just like to do it, that's all," explained George, a little impatiently.

And he did do it. Though he was not a member of a Sportsman Club, or a Hunters Group, who were licensed hunters with weapons credentials. He was licensed to use firearms in designated areas, where he practice-shot with off duty policeman and military veterans and wanna be military types. George did not enter shooting contests because his skill was established and proven under hostile fire in real shooting wars. He was confident in his skill and felt he had nothing to prove, and resisted all challenges from macho types who wanted to gain a quick reputation by beating who they thought was the best.

America's Wild West mythology was legendary in reporting challenges and gunfights to determine the fastest gun in the West. The next top gun wanna-be was always just coming over the horizon waiting to quick draw himself into history, and sometimes succeeded all the way to the grave. George distained this American tradition that lingered from its frontier days, when taken to extremes, and beyond the law and ethics. Today, it was generally subsumed into more civil manifestations through sports and business competition. But it still could take a dangerous turn when dealing with the various forms of modern weaponry. George liked to compete against himself at his skill level, whatever it was. That was enough.

Angelika and George were coming at it from different angles. To Angelika, shooting was inherently dangerous and should only be done when necessary. To George it was a fun skill, with a lethal side that only should be used as a last resort. But how do you maintain a skill if you don't practice? Asked George. So, on balance, and in a sense, they agreed in part and disagreed in part. Maybe it was a guy thing. And her attitude was a girl thing. George let it go at that, but kept shooting. Angelika would have to make peace with it, if that's the right word. And she did.

Though not overly fond of drink, George would sometimes be invited and go out to a local country bar or pub, with some of the shooting range guys, and an occasional woman, to exchange ideas on types of firearms and marksmenship techniques to better hone their shills. The police, more than the military types, with a little prodding, would tell tales of their exploits and close brushes with danger and guns. George was particularly interested in educating others about the little heard of, Balkan Wars. It was difficult for them to grasp who was against who and why. After all, they cited, America was a melting pot and different nationalities seemed to get along reasonably well, for the most part.

Questions were hurled at George like:

"There are Turks and Greeks in America, and they aren't shooting each other, are they?"

"Though America is mostly a Christian country, there are Muslims here in peace, are there not?"

"There are criminals and ne'er do wells in all countries, aren't there?"

"Yes, I suppose. But sometimes you have to be there to appreciate different viewpoints. Besides, didn't history tell us about Christian Crusaders invading the Land of Islam?" George suggested.

"But hell, the Crusades was centuries ago. Why not bury the past before the past buries you?" Asked Captain Fennessy of the Somerville Police Department.

"Of course the the Crusades were long ago, but some customs and cultures linger into modern times. America is a country of ideals and quick changes. Much of the world is not. We may have similar desires, but different belief systems. They have to be accommodated. Hey! I don't have all the answers. I'm looking for a peaceful solution myself."

FASHION SHOW

"But I don't want to go to a fashion Show!" Pleaded George.

"Why not? Don't I go to your Sons of Ionia Club, even though I'm not welcome there; don't I go to your Gun Club practices, though there's little for me to do there? Don't I travel to Nashua, even when it's not convenient for me? Shall I go on?"

"All right, Angelika. OK. You've made your point. I'll go."

Not only did George go, but he was recruited to do some of the physical work in moving racks of clothes to and around the back rooms, where Angelika did her cutting, stitching and practice dressing of some of her favorite work companions, the mannequins.

"They are ideal models because they stand still, and don't talk back. Something you could learn from, my gypsy adventurer," remonstrated Angelika.

"Circle the wagons, I'm under attack!" Said a mocking George, faking alarm. "It's not bad enough I have to do this demeaning womens work, but I'm compared unfavorably to a dummy, am I?" Protested a martyred George.

"Jesus the Christ. Come down off that cross. Nobody's crucifying you. I'm merely trying to get you to slow down and enjoy the finer aesthetics of life."

"Well, I have you. That's enough for me. I'll leave the rest to you. You and my mother can do the flowers and the fashion stuff. I know my limitations."

"Keep an open mind, my intended. You'll learn more."

"As an intended, my mind is closed. You are it. Get use to it."

"That's what I like to hear, George. You're getting more eloquent by the moment. And so smart. Your judgment is so exquisite."

"Well, I'm glad we agree on something."

"We agree on the important things. And that's what counts, that's what's important. Did I just repeat myself? See what you do to me, George. You've got me talking to myself."

"Good. That'll give me a break. I really love this work, when can I leave."

"When we're finished."

"And when's that?"

"I'll tell you when. This is my show, remember?"

"How can I forget?"

George suffered before and during, particularly during the Fashion Show. He was very conscious of the fact that he was one of the few men there. Joining him were a few uncomfortable, but intrepid males obviously dragged there by their wives, mothers, aunts or girlfriends. At least George was distracted by some work, and could occasionally disappear into the back rooms for part-time relief. But even there, he could be embarrassed by some shameless hussy exhibitionists deliberately flaunting their half-dressed bodies, as they changed into the next dresses they were modeling. At the same time others were glaring at him to hurry by so they could protect their modesty and finish dressing, making him feel like he was a peephole pervert, oogling them.

Angelika was breezily oblivious to George's awkward situation. Then, after it was all over, she had the nerve, George thought, to ask him if he got his jollies leering at the young women diving in and out of different dresses. George noticed mostly that they frantically readied themselves to walk across the stage, strutting their stuff, while pretending to be high fashion models. They seemed to love the glamour and glory of adorning themselves in the perceived beauty of their finery and raiment. It was a feminine spectacle that escaped George's understanding. His relief after the show was palpable. He marvelled at the things he did to maintain a relationship.

The payoff for George was that it put Angelika in an ebullient mood that inured to his benefit in many ways and made him happy. Positive payback is what it was. But whatever it was, it certainly lightened the atmosphere. What you sew, you shall reap, he believed the Bible said. The pressure that built up bringing everything together, burst into the evening's activities, and gave forth with after-show merrymaking and congratulations. It fortunately carried over and impacted favorably on Angelika's business, social and personal life. The bottom line was that the Fashion Show was important to Angelika, and therefore, important to George.

As Angelika's Dress Shop flourished, and George's Boston Hotel catered to the well healed, George got quickly bored once he settled in to the general routine of his bellhop job. Even as a supervisor, with its irksome management problems, the biggest attraction, financially, was the potential tips from the guests. His base salary was barely a living wage, and the management bonus's and incentives were few and largely unreachable. And though some guests tipped generously, usually the less well healed, the majority tipped less than the amount he had hoped. He was looking for something better. Maybe he would apply to the Police Academy. Maybe he would go back to school or learn a higher paying skilled trade, like being an electrician or plumber. He would talk it over with Angelika, his family and friends.

Woz didn't get mustered out until a month after George. Discharge priority had been given to those who saw active service in Mexico, like George. When they caught up to each other in Brickbottom, Woz's fractured foot had healed nicely, especially with the arrival of the warmer weather. In fact, his foot healed so well, he was given a zero percent disability. Now he could joke along with his friends about being his own worst enemy because he had bashed himself in the foot. They scoffed that he needed a bodyguard to protect himself against himself, and that his fellow soldiers had to turn their backs to the enemy and watch out for Woz. All in good fun, thought George.

Shortly after Woz was discharged in Boston, the Germans attacked and sunk three American ships in the Atlantic Ocean without warning. For President Wilson, this was the trigger that caused him to face reality and the probable pulling of the reluctant US into a European War. After conferring with his confidants and Cabinet, President Wilson, on March 20th, 1917 issued a proclamation calling all National Guardsmen into Federal Service. This proclamation was considered to be an emergency, and the National Guardsmen were ordered to report to their local armories on that very day and the days immediately following. They were called into service to act as guards for railroad bridges, shipyards, arsenals and factories. In addition, they were to be in emergency readiness for any overt act of war against the United States. The nation was preparing to go to war. When the Kaiser once again scoffed at and dismissed the protests of the United States as conveyed by our Ambassador in Berlin, President Wilson went to Congress and asked them to declare war on Germany.

Congress did so when Wilson's war resolution passed both houses on April 6, 1917. Thus America's neutrality ended and Wilson went from a Peace President to a War President. Wilson had taken much public criticism for his stand against getting involved in a European War by super-patriots like former President and still popular, Thedore Roosevelt. The former President Roosevelt had excorciated the current President Wilson when the English ocean liner, Lusitiana, the largest passenger ship in the world, was sunk by a German U-Boat in 1915, drowning 1200 of 1800 passengers, including 128 Americans, and Wilson limited his response to a strongly worded official diplomatic protest. Roosevelt questioned Wilson's soft response, as he saw it and, ignoring his own advanced age, sought to set up his own volunteer fighting force to get ready for the European War certain to involve America, in his view.

Now being committed to war, Wilson changed his stance dramatically. Striving to stir up public patriotism and fervor for the war, he inaugurated immediate measures to send our boys over there. Wilson's public relations chief was a man named George Creel. Creel had been a Wilson loyal supporter and former newspaper journalist of some note. He sold Wilson on the idea of establishing a Committee on Public Information to explain to the nation why the USA was in the war and how it could help. To aid the war effort, he was instrumental in getting Wilson to push and get passed the Trading with the Enemy Act to confine, corral and jail, if necessary, war opponents who interferred with the war effort.

Creel was later quoted as saying that his goal for the Committee on Public Information was to instill *"a passionate belief in the justice of America's cause that would weld the American people into one white hot mass instinct, with fraternity, devotion, courage and deathless determination."*

To attain this lofty status, the ever ebullient Creel recruited 75,000 "Four Minute Men," so-called, to give four-minute public, patriotic speeches to encourage enlistment in the US Armed Forces. These roving patriots were instructed in public speaking skills and told to add a local personal touch, while the reel of a movie was changed, which not so coincidentally took about four minutes. They developed memorable catchphrases like *"If you don't come across, the Kaiser will."* One of the movies shown was a propaganda film entitled "Under Four Flags," referring to the now common war effort among England, France, Russia and the USA. It would culminate in France's Marshall Foch leading eleven million Allied men in arms against the German led Central Powers of an equal number of Germans, Austrian-Hungarians and Turks in the first world war.

These on-the-go four-minute men spread their message across the country in every available club, theatre, hall or street corner. One of these hot patriots commandeered a flatbed wagon and had the draught horses pull it in front of the recently opened Union Square Recruiting Office. This was the same office used to recruit soldiers for the Union cause in the Civil War between the States over half a century before and gave Union Square, Somerville, its current name. One of the more than interested observers was a veteran named George Dilboy. It stirred him deeply. He was being called to the colors again. But he wouldn't do anything on impulse. He wanted to think about it. And there was Angelika to consider. He was very conflicted. What to do?

He would talk to his father. His father listened silently. George told him of this strong feeling, a pull he had to go back into the Army, yet he wanted to marry Angelika and raise a family, too. They had made plans to do just that, as soon as George got settled in a job again. What's was he to do?

"Nothing. That is, nothing until you have talked it out with Angelika and others you trust. If you don't volunteer, you'll still have to register for the draft. Sooner or later, you'll be called into service. Do you want sooner or later? Follow your heart. Your heart tells you what the head doesn't know. In the end, it's your decision. The right decision will come to you. That's all I can say."

George left his father pleased with the feeling that his father would back him up no matter what he decided. But George was still conflicted. Would he be happier staying home or joining the Army? But how long could he stay home? Sooner or later he would have to go. What happens if he wants sooner, but Angelika wants later. And what's the difference? A few months? Are there advantages to one or the other? He would sit on it for now. He had to talk to Angelika.

The nationwide United States military recruiting efforts met an enthusiastic reception. Not surprisingly, many volunteers came forward. To provide for a continuing need, legislative plans were in the works for the conscription of a draft Army.

Both George and Woz had been stunned by the quick declaration of war, but not really surprised, given the deaths of so many Americans on ships sunk by the Germans over the past couple of years, and their interference and instigations in Mexico against America. It was just that they had been living with a foreign war since the summer of 1914 and most followed it with remote interest and gratitude that they weren't in it. Now they were. Suddenly. It took some getting used to.

A month later, on May 18, Congress passed a conscription bill enacting a war time draft. On June 5, George, Woz, Bobby and 9,000,000 other men between the ages of 21 and 30, in accordance with the new law, registered for service with its local draft board. Having just come back from the Mexican Border War, George, Woz and Bobby must have thought they were only out on temporary leave. George left Nashua so quickly, he never got a chance to see Jeff, who invalided out earlier, or Bobby, who was discharged later than George.

Angelika was beside herself with consternation. She and George had talked about getting married as soon as George got set in a career.

"Now what!" Shouted an exasperated Angelika.

At first, she was so upset she couldn't talk to George. She just cried.

"This wasn't fair!" She wailed. "He just served his country! He did his bit!"

And, although non-Greeks in this country didn't care, George had just risked death by fighting in two Balkan Wars for Greece, she thought.

"Enough is enough! We have our lives to live, not to lose." She sputtered in frustration.

She sought consolation with her parents and anyone else who knew her plans and empathized with her. It helped little.

"Is there no justice?" She railed.

George, though still a civilian, knew he wouldn't be one for long. Long enough to get married? This turned out to be the big issue.

WEDDING BELLS

A crisis ensued. Should George and Angelika marry now before he is called into service or should they wait until he returns from the European War?

"Now!" Was Angelika's decision. We're together now. And now is all we have. Our love has waited long enough."

"Angelika, you're thinking with your heart; not your head."

"What do you mean? If we don't marry now, we may never get the chance."

"I'll come back from this war the same way I always have. If I was going to get killed, it was more likely when I was younger and more foolish. I know how to protect myself. I'm a veteran."

"A live veteran. I can't marry a dead one."

"Nor can I. Angelika, if we marry and I don't come back, your future will be marred by a whimsical, whirlwind marriage, especially if you are left with a child."

"But I'll have your love, and a child to carry on the Dilboy lineage."

"Angelika, it's no fun being a single mother, bringing up a child on your own. You've got most of your life ahead of you, don't cripple it now. Other women your age will be socializing; you can't be saddled with staying home, just because you rushed into a marriage."

"We've been planning this for years. I'm not rushing into anything!" "Angelika, if you really love me, you'll wait for me. I'll feel better if you're not locked into an absentee marriage and feeling forced to stay home, stopping your life and fretting about me. I don't want to burden your life with my death."

"But if I don't mind, why should you? We're a team."

"Yes. And we'll be a better team with a longer future if we wait. I'll do what I did in Macedonia and Mexico, step between the bullets."

"Oh, George, this is no time to be funny."

"I'm just trying to lighten you up. Look, Angelika, let's think on it. You discuss it with your folks, and I'll discuss it with mine.

After all, you're only nineteen years old. Let's see what they have to say."

"I'm old enough to make up my own mind. But, of course, I'll talk to my folks. I value what they have to say. You should discuss it with your family, too."

"Naturally, I will. And I have, at least with my father. He'll back our decision whatever it is. Both our parents will, I'm sure. No final decision has to be made at this very moment. You're right, Angelika, no matter what, we're a team."

With that, and Angelika's face looking mottled and strained, as if she was going to burst into tears, George impulsively hugged her tight, then kissed her lovingly and long on the lips. After a passionate moment, they burst apart, gasping for breath.

Angelika reached for her pocketbook, looking for a hankerchief, to dry her watery eyes. George pulled out a hankerchief he had and offered it to her. Gulping down a sob, Angelika quickly took it. She was grateful that her mother hadn't come into the room to find them arguing. Her mother would hear of it soon enough. Angelika needed time to regain her composure and organize her thoughts. Of course, she knew her parents would agree with her and back her up, as they invariably did.

But they didn't. What a shock!

Angelika was especially nice that day and went out of her way to help her parents and increase her chances of catching them in a good mood. But it was as if they could see right through her and knew what she was going to say. They read the papers too. But what particularly upset Angelika was that they didn't hesitate; they thought it best to wait. It wasn't that they were taking George's side over hers, they said. It was the best thing to do, in their opinion. Angelika couldn't help it. She burst into tears and ran from the room, too distraught to talk.

CHAPTER TWENTY EIGHT

WORLD WAR

They had walked back from church together this beautiful Sunday, July morning. They were in Angelika's kitchen being served Greek coffee and their favorite baklava pastry by Angelika's mother, Christina. Her mother and father, Lambros, who resisted the American version of his name, Louie, were concerned and extra solicitous toward Angelika these days. As much as they now liked George and accepted the fact that Angelika chose him as her man, they made it quite clear to Angelika that they could not bless their wedding until he came back from the war. Most other relatives and friends, though not all, who were asked their opinion, agreed with her parents. Angelika felt helpless against this solid majority. Besides, she couldn't force a man to marry her.

Occasionally, Angelika's steeled stoicism gave way to bouts of crying, but for the most part, she got a grip on herself, and accepted the fact that she would have to wait to marry George. As an emotional teenager with an assertive nature, it was difficult for Angelika to deal with a war over which she had no control. She kept repeating her mother's words:

"Make the best of it, dear. Wars don't last forever."

What choice did she have? She asked herself, sighing in resignation.

After they engaged in some desultory small talk and they finished eating, George reached into his pocket and pulled out a letter. He pulled out a single sheet of paper and handed it to Angelika. Christina and Lambros looked on knowingly. George looked uncharacteristically serious as he gave Angelika the letter. At the same time, he said:

"I've received my draft notice. So hasn't Woz and others in the neighborhood. I have no real choice now."

"You already made your choice. The government just confirmed it. But I suppose I wouldn't love you as much, if you weren't you. So that's that. When do you have to report?" Angelika asked, as she gave the letter a cursory look.

"July 25th."

"Who else has been called up." queried Angelika, with a blank look in her eyes, like she was just making conversation, her mind elsewhere.

"Who hasn't been would be a better question. It seems like everyone our age, healthy enough, is going." Said George.

"It seems unfair, in a way, that we have to send our best." Said Christina.

"This country deserves our best. That's why we prevail," commented Lambros.

Angelika had three weeks to have George to herself. She talked with her mother about having a going away party for George. Christina heartily agreed. She thought it would help Angelika channel her churning emotions and occupy her racing mind into something constructive. It worked, because Angelika became a whirlwind. George, on the other hand, calmly went about settling his affairs in a measured fashion. For example, he signed over and sold his new 1917 Ford Motor car to Angelika for one dollar. She protested that she didn't even have a license to drive.

"Then this is as good a reason as any to get one," suggested George.

Angelika wanted to have him sign it over to one of his brothers. But George thought they would run it into the ground over the rough New Hampshire roads and he would come back to a used, busted up, worn down motor car.

"It would be like a taxicab up there; driven all the time by half a dozen people. And I want a roadworthy car, not a run down hulk, when I return."

"And you *will* come back to me."

"Of course I will. What am I going to do, take up with a French girl who can't speak my language that I'll never see again, in a foreign country?"

"Love is a universal language. Isn't that what they say?"

"That's lust. I only love you, Angelika, and I always will. Keep that sentiment in your head, to warm your heart while I'm away."

"What choice do I have?"

"You always have a choice, Angelika. You're my choice, and I'm yours. We're together as a team, remember? Any separation is temporary. Just keep that in your lovely bonnet. Promise me you will."

"I will, of course."

"There, you see. We've already exchanged vows. We will yet exchange "I do" for "I will." We are already married in our hearts. We'll take care of the civil arrangements when I come back. Rest assured. Angelika, you must have faith."

"I do."

"There. You said the magic words, 'I do.' Now I might become a bigamist."

"George, you are exasperating! You're driving me crazy with your joking!"

"That's because I'm serious."

"Oh, I give up! You're hopeless. But seriously, my mother and I are planning a going away party for you, at the Daughters of Ionia Hall the Saturday evening before you leave. Now, I know you won't like it, George, but do it for my benefit. It's the only joy I'm going to get out of all of this."

"All right, Angelika. You've got it. I'll be there pretending to enjoy it, for your sake."

"I would have preferred to hold it at your Sons of Ionia Club, George, but as you know, they don't allow women in their precious club! And even among the men, even Greek men, you have to be a member! It's so ridiculous!" "It's just another example of Greek insularity. We don't join Unions, we have our own organizations. It's either our biggest strength or our biggest weakness."

"Whatever, please invite Woz and the other's *'going over'* in the neighborhood. We can share our celebration; we are all Americans."

"Indeed we are. I'll spread the word about the party. It'll be a grand time."

At the gala evening, the festivities were heightened by George's family coming down from Nashua and by Antonios surprising the gathered group by speaking, though he spoke Greek. Non-Greeks may have been puzzled by Antonios's typically short, curt comment that implored George with an old Spartan saying to:

"Go to war. Come back with your shield, or on it; I care not which."

Immediate applause erupted. Woz, not understanding Greek, looked puzzled and asked George what he said. George repeated the comment in English and Woz looked even more bewildered. Noticing this, George explained.

"What he said, in his own abbreviated way, was, 'Go to war. Come back with your shield or on it; I care not which. *I'll love you anyway.*" But he couldn't say the words, 'I'll love you anyway.'"

"I know a lot of men who have the same problem."

"Whatever it is or isn't. There's a lot of it going on since we declared war on Germany and the draft is calling men to arms. Young, adventureous, age eligible teenagers are asking each other as they meet in the streets, if they are *'going over.'* Similar parties and parades are going on all over this country. It's patriotic fervor at its peak. If they only knew what war really means, nobody would ever rush headlong into that inferno; they would enter it only as a last resort. Ugly death, destruction, deplorable injuries, emotional and mental scars for life, devastated families, instant widows, unbearable loss and excruciating grief. That's wars legacy." So went George's lament, he still being young, but already a seasoned veteran.

"We should know, George. We've been there. You, certainly more than me."

"And yet, Woz, war has its appeal, crazy as it sounds. The threat of death brings an intensity, an alertness to life, because it can end with the next breath. To many buried veterans, it had. Surviving veterans know it's gut wrenching terrors. They have witnessed eternity in a second. Life is suddenly treasured, because it no longer is taken for granted. Life becomes spontaneous; you live for today, because that's all you have. Nobody is guaranteed another second of time. Your time may be up. Now is all you have."

As if in a trance, George continued talking, as if to himself, in this uncharacteristic serious manner, showing another side of himself that few people saw. "War brings along with it a boring routine that erupts into explosive suddeness, and then shocked silence when the firing and the fighting ends. You battle alongside your fellow soldiers protecting each other, comrades in arms. Some die; some survive. But you're never the same. Feelings get buried into the deepest recesses of your being. They have to, for you to survive. You grieve for killed comrades, until there are no more tears. Then there are no more feelings. Then you don't want to get too close to anyone, because it hurts too much when they die, or suffer horrible injuries. Crazy fetishes, superstitions and good luck charms are clung to. You feel suffocated by feelings of guilt for surviving the death of better men, anger for the futility of it all, frustration from failures, and taut-tensioned, tight-muscled, stomach flipping fear. Death and oblivion may be a bullet away."

George then startled Woz. George came out of his trance and burst out laughing. He couldn't help it. It was spontaneous.

"Clue me in, George. What's so funny?"

"This." He pointed toward the crowd partying. "They're enjoying life to the hilt, while some of us are facing certain death, and even worse, uncertain death. Our lives are on hold. It all seems so absurd, so ridiculous, it's funny. Angelica gets miffed at me for joking. But it's just my way of coping. I can either laugh or cry, but it's more fun laughing. Angelika will do the crying for both of us, I'm sure."

"Oh, I suppose," said Woz, "before we're all done with this war, there will be a lot of laughing and crying. It's the human condition. And the reason doesn't have to be war. Hell, I could be run over by a trolley car going home from here tonight and there would be tears and laughter at my life's escapades during my funeral. So what's our choice?"

"That's the answer, Woz. It's a choice. How we look at it, how we deal with it, is individual. That defines our character. We cope with life's dilemmas in our own way, one that makes sense to us. And that is a tribute to our own individuality. It styles our unique personality. Would you have it any other way?"

"No, I guess not. Anyway George, I need to lighten up. Let's party. I'll cry tomorrow."

DOUGHBOYS

George drove back to Nashua with Angelika a few days before he was to be inducted back into the U. S. Army to give a final good bye to his family. Though George had just seen most of his family at the going away party, Dimitri was sick and hadn't been able to make it down. Dimitri didn't want to infect George with his sickness. His summer cold was as severe, as it was odd, for that time of year. Besides, George was restless and wanted to channel his nervous energy into the trip to Nashua. George noted that his own moods lately fluctuated from calmness to restlessness. This probably reflected his conflicted feelings. He wanted to get married and start his own family with Angelika; but he was also "itching" to get back into the action. He wanted to get the experience or education for a better job in which he could better support a family. Being a supervising bellhop at a swanky Boston hotel was not his idea of a dream job. Boring as it was, he considered it a bridge job to a new start and, in the meantime, it paid his bills.

He also had to make a new start in the U.S. Army. His former rank of Sargent earned in the Mexican Expedition ended with that service, he was told when he inquired about it. His prior service record would be taken into consideration, along with current circumstances, to determine his present rank, he was assured. Meanwhile he re-entered the U.S. Army as a Private, First Class.

In some ways, George felt like he was just coming back from leave. It had been only five months since he was honorably discharged and mustered out. Though he had originally registered to join the National Guard in Nashua, New Hampshire, he no longer resided there, and changed his mailing address back to Somerville when he went back to work in Boston at the Copley Plaza Hotel. And though he lived with Uncle Kostas, he had his mail delivered to the local Greek kafeneion (coffeehouse, that is, at the Sons of Ionia Club) for privacy reasons, and so as not to clutter up his Uncle's mail box, he said. So Somerville was where he was instructed to report back on his draft notice.

After George bought the Model T Ford, Angelika had taken driving lessons and obtained her license to operate a motor vehicle. She was a quick study, was one of the few women to drive a car in Somerville then, and was in a hurry to do a lot of things. She decided to co-operate with the inevitable and not to further fret, at least in public, figuring the faster George and the Army went to war, the faster he would return.

George packed his stuff and Angelika drove them, and members of his family who insisted on coming down to see him off, to the armory. She led a two motor car convoy to the Highland Ave fortress. It was an imposing castle towered, stone building and the site of the Somerville Armory. Not surprisingly, it was crowded with family, relatives, and friends of the inductees. Because of his many trips, George was not a stranger to this type of Godspeed farewell. Nonetheless, he still got choked up. Try as she might to control her emotions, Angelika burst into tears even before her final hugs and kisses.

"Oh, God," she sniffled. "I promised myself I wouldn't."

George smiled and pulled her towards him and kissed her flush on her lips. Angelika sunk down on top of her under five feet height and hugged George tight. When she couldn't let go, George reached out and shook his brothers hands, while still clinging to

Angelika. She finally let go and buried her face into her hankerchief. George then hugged and kissed his father, and the rest of his gathered family.

An Army Officer emerged from the building, and looking at his watch, blew a whistle and ordered all inductees into the building. George grabbed Angelika for a quick last kiss and waved goodbye as he grabbed his duffle bag and moved toward the front door of the Armory. As he did so, he spotted Woz leaving his family.

"Yo! Woz!" He yelled. Looking over, Woz saw George and smiled. They threw an arm around each other and marched together into the armory:

"Comrades in arms again!" Said a smiling George.

"What would this Army do without us, George!" replied a proud Woz.

Their families looked on in various stages of mixed emotions. For the Dilboys and many others, World War I had now intimately reached in and involved their families. Some families stayed to chat with friends and neighbors, and to talk about the war. Some left because it was too painful to stay, and others stayed to see the buses leave, to Camp Devens in Ayer, MA, thirty miles northwest of Boston for their training base. The Dilboys opted to stay and talked with Woz's parents, brother and sisters. Within the hour, children came running from the driveway leading out from behind the armory and yelling:

"The buses are coming! The buses are coming!"

While their parents were calming them down, the buses started coming out. They streamed out one behind the other like a military convoy. People strained for a last look at their loved ones off to war, wondering if they would ever see them alive again. Some were smiling, some crying, but all waving, whether they saw who they were looking for or not. The men were leaning out the windows, though they were instructed not to, shouting and waving wildly at the similarly waving crowd. Army discipline would have to be drilled into them. The happy warriors were either forgetful or oblivious to the Army warning that carelessly waving arms and heads leaning out of bus windows in crowded cities had, in the past, led to broken arms and fractured skulls from poles and trees whizzing past.

When the buses sped out of sight, an ominous silence enveloped the armory and the crowd dissipated gradually, with a low murmur. The Dilboy two-car caravan returned to Uncle Kostas, where a backyard cookout was had to make a family day of it. Angelika sat in a corner disconsolate, losing her battle with tears, and refusing all food. After a while, she went home, too distraught to stay. John Dilboy accompanied her to see her safely home.

CAMP DEVENS

The Army buses clattered through the local roads of Cambridge, Arlington, and Lexington, and headed west and north through Concord. The latter two towns were famous battle towns well known to American schoolboys as the places where the American War of Independence began in 1776. George, sitting next to Woz, listened to him with new interest, wondering if France would look like the passing green fields of Lexington and Concord. The chatter on the bus was animated and lively, as would be expected of men on either side of age twenty. Since George had experienced this scenario twice before and knew what came afterwards, he remained quiet, wondering how this war would be different. And they were all different, even if their horrors were the same George was told and indeed had learned.

As soon as the buses entered the campgrounds, it was as if the Drill Instructors, DI's so called, were waiting to ambush them. They were shouted out of each bus and told to line up in five columns of eight. They were told to stand at attention, while the DI moved quickly up and down the columns, shouting at them:

"Attention! The object of this war is twofold: to win and survive. All those manners your mother taught you—forget them! Shoot first or be shot. Kill or be killed. Do or die. It's not nice, but that's the way it is. It's the only way you will come back vertical. Now let's get to work."

"Pull in that stomach! Straighten that back! Lift that chin!"

George stood erectly at attention, stiff as a board, and bored, having gone through this standard procedure before. He knew enough to go along with the system, as the easiest way. Others, however, not use to being yelled at by strangers, were clearly bewildered and uncomfortable. Even if told what to expect, the reality was unsettling, especially after being told what heroes they were. Now they are told they are scum, dirtbags and fit for the garbage heap! Mama's boys will be rooted out and sent home to suck on their baby bottles! George and Woz had been exposed to it all before, and were unfazed.

After being welcomed into the United States Army by the foulest language some of them had ever heard, they were told to pick up their bags, and then quick-step marched over to the laundry building to get their gear, before most of them knew what a quick-step was. They had to imitate the DI.

"Watch me! Watch me, you idiots!" He roared.

Because there was a shortage of uniforms, some doughboys were given overalls to train in. Now loaded down with Army gear and boots up to their chins, they were barked to attention until all in their group were outside. The gear got heavy. The Drill Instructor suggested, sarcastically, that the others were taking their time, knowing that the more time they took to join them, the less time they would have to stand in line holding their gear that kept getting heavier and heavier for them.

"Are you going to let them get away with that?" He growled.

"No!" Shouted the early group, in chorus.

"What are you going to do about it?" Inquired the DI at the top of his lungs!

A few of the men turned to go after the others to hurry them up, but were stopped with:

"You're at attention, you slime balls! Nobody leaves the ranks!"

"Why don't you tell them to get their asses out here! You're got voices, don't you? Won't you tell them what you're going to do to them, if they don't get out here, right now?" With that encouragement, the men started yelling invectives and threats of their own!

"Get out here, you bastards! Hurry up, you assholes! Move it, you fuckers!"

Hearing the threats of the mob outside, the men inside attempted to hurry up, but the supply clerks seemed to have gone into a slowdown, now working in slow motion. Now the inside men were threatening the innocent and shocked looking supply clerks. This standardized harrassment continued as the inside men ran helter-skelter out the front door of the laundry building to rejoin their screaming cohorts.

Once all together and slowly inspected, the DI then called the forty men individually on a name count, while they answered:

"Present!"

"Here!"

"Yo!"

"Here! Sargent Dear!"

"Presently present!"

"Up yours!"

"Fuck you!"

After a run of civil answers, as the Drill Instructor went down the list, the responses got increasingly daring and vituperative. The DI, seemingly amused, noticed names of the more abusive replies, and plotted retaliation. He then pocketed his pen, snappped the clipboard to his side and ordered the troops to:

"Right Face!

Do it again, dipshits! I said, Right Face! Watch me! Watch me!"

Looking at his clipboard, his face turning red, he screamed:

"McHale! Are you deaf or are you blind? I said Right Face! What's your problem!"

"Sir, Your right is my left, because we're facing each other."

Not believing what he was hearing, the DI, purple faced, and apoplectic with rage, screamed with a high pitched voice:

"McHale, fall out! Company! Right face! Quickstep march!"

McHale was left behind, confused. He wandered around not knowing what to do, but soon drew scornful remarks and ridicule from passing soldiers who thereby exposed his inability to keep up. Humiliated, he ran after his company.

With that command, the remainder of the company short-stepped it over their assigned barracks. They selected their own bunk beds. Generally, the smaller guys went on top, for safety reasons. Harangued to get their civies off and get into their military skivies, they weren't in the barracks five minutes it seemed, when the DI pulled out a whistle and ordered them to fall in outside!

"Now! Move it! Let's go!"

Frantically scattering to line up, the men rushed to finish dressing, some tripping over themselves as they struggled to dress on the run. George noticed with amusement that the DI was already noting the slaggards for later special attention. The men were told that they would now run in place to get the lead out. Then they were ordered to forward march over to the camp barbers to get their hair shorn. This not only included their top hair, but beards and mustaches. Those who didn't inquire and realize before hand that beards and mustaches were not allowed in the American Army, were given special assignments to clean out the outhouses and did garbage details to work off the extra time it took the barbers to shave them clean.

"Why?" Asked an intrepid soul? "Why do I have to shave my beard? I take care of it, nobody else does?"

The barber started laughing hysterically. When he came up for air, he said:

"Because the Army says so, and you're in the Army now, Mr. Van Dyke! Do you think the war is going to stop while you trim your beard?"

The next barber overheard and answered more seriously:

"Hell! I'm glad he's not in my Company. Can you imagine my life depending on someone with that attitude?"

The inexperienced soldier realized the stupidity of his remark and thereafter kept his mouth shut, hoping only that the incident would be forgotten.

Then they were taken to the drill field and instructed in marching drills. They were given wooden sticks for guns because they were being manufactured as they trained. They then went to lunch in a giant, noisy cafeteria, with barely enough time to eat before being taken on an announced-as-you-go five mile hike into the woods, of alternating walking, quicksteping, spot drills and running. That's when those who ate too much upchucked their lunch, unwittingly fertilizing the forest. The lesson to be learned by them was not to eat too much, a discipline for some of the weightier boys. Back at camp, they were allowed fifteen minutes to use the latrine and rest. One man even fell asleep. But not for long.

Bootcamp to Woz and George was the same exhausting, but dull routine known to both of them. But George didn't realize how quickly he was spoiled by civilian life, and how somewhat out of shape he was. This regimen was rough on him, and rougher on Woz, with his big bulk and size. George was lucky; he had little weight to lose. It's just that George had less to do to get back into top condition, since he was almost there to begin with.

Many ate that night in a trance, they were so tired. George walked back with a wiped out Woz. Luckily, Woz reached his barracks before George, with Woz wondering if he would fall asleep in his khakis. There is no other way to explain it; the first day in boot camp is a physical nightmare. And it didn't seem to get easier with experience. Mentally, however, it was a different story. Now he knew that the reason they shave you and rough you up is to toughen you up, by stripping you of your old, comfortable habits, to train you to respond immediately to command, to become killers to protect yourself and your fellow soldier from being killed. And most dearly of all, to be able to come home alive and hopefully healthy to your loved ones. This had to be explained to some of the clueless, young hotheads. Given the law of large numbers, however, there were always a few who couldn't adapt to the necessities of Army life, would be a danger to themselves and others depending on them, and were discharged from the Army. They didn't know it, but thereafter they would incur the stares and scorn of the home front civilians demanding to know why they weren't "over there" with their fighting countrymen. It chased some back to later volunteer for at least an administrative or support post. The others frequently had to endure the contempt of the citizens doing their bit stateside.

Back at camp, the trainee doughboys only chance to recover and recreate was on weekends, when those given leave, hit the bars. Anything to get out of camp. Many of the outlying towns had bars. The town of Ayer had only one Main Street, but two bars. The Camp Devens soldiers may have been their most thirsty customers, but not their best behaved. Alcohol does different things to different people. To many, it lowers inhibitions and dulls pain. It causes many, especially young men testing their limits, to occasionally make fools of themselves. And that assumes they didn't drink themselves into oblivion, so that they remember little of anything. This can sometimes test friendships or solidify them.

It happened to George and Woz, one forgettable Saturday evening. A drunken soldier in a near-camp bar tripped over George's leg and fell on his face, spilling his beer. As George tried to help him up, asking if he was all right, the guy got up and threw a punch at an astonished George, yelling he tripped him intentionally. The glancing punch caught George on the side of his face and knocked him off balance and to the floor. Woz instinctively grabbed the drunken soldier, and threw the drunk's limp body across the floor, knocking over another table and a brawl was on. From prior experience, the Military Police were just outside the bar and ran inside to restore order. They also arrested people, including George and Woz, who were fingered as instigators or participants. Participants they were, indeed. It landed them in the camp lock-up.

On Monday morning, they were taken by an MP wagon to Concord District Court to face an assortment of criminal charges. When the Assistant County District Attorney and Army Counsel convened at the pre-trial conference, they worked out a plea bargain. Though George claimed not to have thrown a punch, others in the melee claimed otherwise. George pleaded No Contest to

Disturbing the Peace and Woz to simple assault. Their sentence was time already served in the Camp Lock Up that weekend, and the incident, not uncommon in Army Camps, was forgotten. Everybody knew they were to ship overseas within the month to defend their country at war, so allowances and accomodations were common.

George was a tested, blooded, combat soldier, but he wasn't a combative person. Although it wasn't his nature to look for fistfights, he, like most people, if cornered, would come out swinging. The same was true of the big oaf of a Pole, Woz. He was intentionally avoided in a scrap because of his size, but, if truth be known, he was easy going, placid and generally of a peaceful disposition. You can't judge a book by its cover, it is said. That would be true in both their cases.

CHAPTER TWENTY NINE

OVERSEAS

Their basic training completed, the camp recruits were assembled and George and Woz's units were detached and told that they would be assigned as replacements for guardsmen who were rejected by the Massachusetts National Guard for various deficiencies and would be combined with other National Guard units from the Maine and New Hampshire. They had themselves joined together at a Westfield, MA camp to all form the 26th Division, the so-called Yankee Division of New England States. The Eastern Department of the US Army had released New England and that region was to be included into the new Northeastern Department. A Major General Clarence R. Edwards, a Regular Army, West Point career man, was assigned to the command of this new Department.

Like many Regular Army Officers of the time he loved horses. He arrived, along with the rain, on April 28, 1917 at the Copley Plaza Hotel in Copley Square, Boston. This was noticed by a wide-eyed bellboy captain by the name of George Dilboy. George was fascinated at the swirl of activity around this military star, and found every excuse to be near the General.

He saw first hand that the General was tall, and smartly dressed. He had shortcut, white hair and was a man of regal bearing, who strode purposefully wherever he went. He appeared very decisive. Despite his intimidating presence, the assistants around him seemed to genuinely like him. In his West Point days, he was reputed to be quite a boxer, George learned. Later, General Edwards would assume command of the newly formed Yankee Division.

"Yankee Division? Why that name?" Asked George.

Woz answered: "A Captain Hawkins told me that an old timer of a newspaper reporter from the Boston Globe, a Frank Sibley, suggested it to General Edwards. He was forming the Division at his Huntington Ave office at the time. Sibley recommended that name because the Division would be replete with old line, rich, Boston Bramins and Yankees. General Edwards told Sibley that though he had pretty much determined on that name already, Sibley was the first one to his knowledge to speak it aloud. It was so named."

"Sibley? Don't you remember him in Mexico, Woz? For an oldtimer, he gets around!"

"No, I don't. But you fought in Mexico, I didn't. I guarded the border. So you should know."

"But rich Bramins? I didn't see any rich Bramins in Brickbottom! Far from it," spouted an amused George.

"Neither did I, but that's supposedly the origin of the name. And agree with it or not, that's the name of our division."

The newly formed 26th Division, henceforth to be known as the Yankee Division, was an *infantry* Division of doughboys. The origin of the term "doughboy" has many claimants, one going as far back as the U.S Civil War. But the more recent claim attributes it to the dough that was used to make bread at our training camps, or more cynically, to the claim that they joined the Army to earn dough, or money.

It was here that George and Woz met up with and befriended a Sargent Alfred "Al" Klick of Company H, Second Maine Infantry. It began when he laughed so hard at one of George's pranks against Woz, giving the big lug a hotfoot, that all three of them ended up laughing hysterically and became instant buddies. Thereafter, they gravitated together whenever they could, which wasn't too often, given that Sargent Klick was a non-commissioned *officer* and George and Woz were buck privates.

"Hey, Sarge, said Woz. "Do I have this correct? The Army chain of command goes from Army to Corps to Division to Brigade to Regiment to Battalion to Company to Platoon to Squad to Soldier."

"Wozlowski," said Sargent Klick, barely paying attention and with mock seriousness, "you're absolutely brilliant. I can see you're destined to become a full braided Field Marshall of the Army."

"The American Army doesn't have Field Marshalls," retorted Woz.

"Oh, I'm sorry. The Greek Army then."

"Hey! Leave the Greeks alone," snapped a fake-furious George.

"Ok, the Turk Army then. Now leave me alone. Go get drunk and toast each others promotions to Field Marshall of any Army you like. I'm busy."

They got ready to be shipped overseas. They were encouraged to write home, but not to mention where they were going. Their mail would be censored for security reasons. Signs around the camp cautioned them that,

"Loose lips sink ships!"

Caution was certainly appropriate to their situation, as they were going to take troop ships three thousand miles across the dangerous Atlantic Ocean, infested with German submarines prowling beneath the waters. The doughboys were sternly warned that one-hour out into the Atlantic Ocean they would enter an early war zone, a wilderness of water, well before they reached the newly developed barbed wire entanglements of the Germans on the battlefields of France. The Germans knew that if they could sink the American troopships while vulnerable on the high seas, their Armies wouldn't have to fight them on land.

Therefore, German U-boats were using the dangers of the deep against the perils of the sitting duck troopships to sink any enemy vessel in sight. They believe they'll have few excitements to match the thrill of sighting an enemy troopship across their bow, especially one bursting with soldiers. So while on deck, keep a keen eye on the water's surface for signs or sightings of the enemy below, the Yank ground troops were warned. That early, dire alert got their attention and motivated them to aid in their own defense.

The end of September arrived and they were all bused to Boston and then entrained to Hoboken, New Jersey, their port of departure for Europe. Since German spies had been caught near port cities before and after suspected sabotages, the military authorities went to great pains to keep the time of embarkation a secret. German submarines were known to be lurking off the Eastern seaboard. Such news was kept from the American public to prevent panic. In furtherance of their safety precautions, all troop movements were made at night. Inland units broke camp on an hours notice, after dark.

On September 25, they boarded the English liner, *Saxonia*, and shipped out serenaded by local bands playing patriotic tunes and inadvertently adding to the confusion and organized chaos. Because of the large number of soldiers boarding the troop ships, only military personnel was allowed near the departing ships. Restraining fences were erected around the port to restrict access to the area. The doughboys were encouraged to advise relatives to say their farewells by telephone or by mail, and to remain home to assure their loved ones a safe departure.

Nevertheless, thousands came anyway. They strained to try and get a last glimpse of their doughboys going off to war. This was a forlorn hope and unlikely, given the distance from the boarding ramps they had to stand. Regardless, the civilians cheered the passing busses crowded with doughboys leaning out windows and waving their hands. The whole atmosphere was like a giant New Years celebration. Among the waving and raised hankerchefs there was as much crying as cheering, as some wondered if they would ever see their loved ones again.

But since the French ports of disembarkation were backed up with waiting ships, they would be diverted first to England. They sailed across the Atlantic crowded into every nook and cranny on their ships. Bunkbeds were four tiers high, and three sleeping shifts of eight hours each used the same canvas bunks. Poor air circulation, the sour smell of many doughboys vomiting, made air down below stifling and living conditions appalling. High waves and rough seas brought many a seasick soldier to the rail to involuntarily disgorge the contents of his stomach. The seasick soldier was not given wide berth, because there was no room to give him on the jammed packed troop ships.

They traveled in zig zaging convoys to better defend themselves against the predatory submarines of the Germans, silently moving beneath the ocean waves, searching to launch their lethal torpedoes. This proved surprisingly effective.

The ships crew practiced shooting at phony pericsopes sticking out of the water, simulating German U-boats. Because of the overcrowded ships, they also had to practice a shortened version of lifeboat drills anticipating a possible "abandon ship" command. At night, all the lights were put out and the ship eerily and silently slipped through the open, ocean waters. The brooding darkness of the threatening night hung over the swishing ship in its inexorable push through unknown space ahead. Escorting destroyers discouraged U-Boat attacks for the most part, but did engage against a few intrepid attacks that damaged, but didn't sink, any troopship in George's convoy. Hurried shots from harried U-Boats caused a number of torpedoes to miss their mark. But some of the near misses were heart stopping. George actually held his breath on one dangerous occasion when a soldier on deck, peering through binoculors, shouted a warning of fired and approaching torpedoes. Dramatically, he pointed his extended arm and finger at two torpedoes that were plying through the dark waters and heading straight toward their bow:

"Torpedoes! Torpedoes! Off the starboard bow!"

With hundreds staring helplessly, the ship reversed all engines to slow down, causing them to lurch sideways, as they watched in awed silence the two torpedoes plough through the water, just missing the front of the ship's bow. After a few seconds of stony silence, the soldier-passengers burst into instantaneous applause. Whistles, hoots and backslapping busted out from the released tension of grateful soldiers for surviving a near catastrophe.

To distract the soldiers from the dangers of the open sea, to give all a chance at fresh air from below decks, and to relieve the monotony, rotations of time on deck from below were scheduled. In addition, singers, dancers, and other entertainers were recruited from the ship's passengers to supplement the inevitable card and crap games. In-place exercises were conducted every morning and encouraged thereafter. Unit meetings were held to keep the troops informed of their situation, progress and destination.

They received a lecture about the English people, their customs and culture.

All of you remember. And remember it well. You are invited guests on foreign soil. You represent the United States of America. Most of you will be meeting in person an English individual for the first time, and they you. You'll never get a second chance to make a first impression. Though we both speak English, some of their customs and their culture may seem strange to you. Because of differences in speaking styles, you may have difficulty in understanding them, at times. Be patient. They are different, to be sure. That doesn't make it wrong; it's just different. For example, they drive their motor cars on the opposite side of the street. That's opposite side, not wrong side. Get it?

If you don't, it could cost you a serious injury or death. Be careful stepping off the sidewalk. You must train yourself to first look the opposite way, or you could easily get run over by a horse and buggy, trolley or a motor car. Do not make any disparaging remarks about the King of England, their Royalty or its tradition of titles. Titles are forbidden by the U.S. Constitution, but are an important part of English history. If you happen to see any, do not make fun of Scottish kilts the men wear, or skirts as we call them. The Scots can be tough, and will prove it, if you provoke them.

We will be in England. It's their country, not ours. We must honor and adjust to their customs and culture. They have their own history and traditions that have served them well for over two thousand years. The United States is only 141 years young. England's history, customs and culture are as important to them as our Declaration of Independence, Uncle Sam and Statute of Liberty is to us. Respect and courtesy is the order of the day. If this advice is not honored, then if English justice doesn't get you, America's will.

Always keep in mind that theirs is a war torn country and has been for three long years. They are war weary and savy. We are new to the fray and inexperienced in this European War. They are our allies against the Boche. We are marching shoulder to shoulder against the common foe. Befriend that British soldier next to you. He may save your life. Keep that in mind.

Questions? There being none, that's it. Dismissed.

———————————

While crossing on the ship, despite the crowded conditions, they were required to disassemble, oil and clean their weapons. It would be their best friend in combat, along with their training, they were constantly warned. They were also told that their rifle was their guardian angel that could save their lives, and get them to a healthy old age. Most of the soldiers didn't need much convincing. Some did.

"Hey, Woz, you clean your rifle today?" Asked George.

"Ya, I checked it."

"No, *cleaned* it, not just checked it," retorted a serious George.

"Lend me some of your oil, will you, George."

"I don't mean to bark at you, Woz, but it's for your own protection. And mine, too. If you are protecting my back, I'll feel better knowing your rifle is in firing condition."

"I know, George. I know. You're just quicker than I am."

The convoy arrived at the large English port of Liverpool. There, they quickly disembarked and entrained inland to a Camp Borden or Oxney at Aldershot in the interior. They spent fourteen days at this camp drilling, exercising and practicing their shooting skills. They viewed films, listened to lectures, and were updated on the war situation on the continent. The doughboys were allowed to go off post on weekend leaves with a stiff warning to behave themselves. Most paid heed; others paid the price for not doing so.

WEEKEND LEAVE

A British Society of Women hosted a dance social for the visiting Americans at a local, large dance hall. These women, without their boyfriends or husbands, and some widows being eased into a social life once again by their well meaning friends, longed for some semblance of normality during this crazy war, and looked eagerly to socialize with the Yanks come to help them win the war. The blackout and shortages in England made the British eager to party and celebrate almost anything. The American doughboys, young as they were, were almost as enthusiastic, less inhibited, and they had some money to spend. The eagerness to celebrate the moment was attributable, in large measure, to the exigencies of the perilous and ever threatening war. The mindset of the moment eminated from a governing philosophy that declared today we live, tomorrow, who knows? As a result, good times were had by many.

But not by George.

Like the other doughboys, George knew that he would only be in England a couple of weeks before he and his U.S. Army buddies would be shipped to the fighting fields of France, where the harsh realities of the European continental war raged and waited to change their lives forever. One, therefore, learned to enjoy the moment. For some, it would be all they would have on this earth. George, however, being committed, didn't feel so great a need. But he still enjoyed a fun time as well as anyone else. The music, the partying, the conversations he looked forward to. Most coped by hope. They always hoped they would survive and thought bad things would happen to the other guys. They had to block out any other reality in order to function well and go on.

With the reality of the moment on him, George was all smiles as he and Woz entered the large fortress like, oblong red brick armory of a building, converted to a dance hall. The converted hall was alive and abuzz with the low roar of a thousand chattering, voices conversing happily. The smoke from lighted fags, as cigarettes were then and there widely called, and the socializing affects of beer and ales charmed the festive evening. George drew back on his fag and blew a stream of smoke toward the air above his head, as he scanned the huge hall.

The variously adorned, flower and print, colorful dresses of the mostly shoulder length haired women pleased his eye. The band played graceful dance music and popular tunes of the time.

Couples, who only moments ago were strangers to each other, swung their moving hips and bodies in rhythm with the tuneful beat of the band. Many partners swayed to the music and others more actively convulsed and jolted their forms, moving to their own internal bands. They swung, swayed and swirled around the dance floor in euphoric splendor. Scenes of unfettered joy and merriment circled round and across the floor.

Woz and George commented in asides as they purviewed the huge hall and directed each others attention to any interesting woman that caught their eye. Pretty features, trim bodies, wow figures or warming and winning smiles were enough to elicit a comment. Woz pulled his drink quickly from his mouth when he spotted what he thought was the girl of his dreams, leaving George amused as he watched Woz make his move in her direction. George smile turned wan as he realized he was now alone in a room of men and women mostly paired off, with his best friend about to be coupled. George felt the urge to do something. Outside of Angelika, and his sisters, he felt more at home among men than women. Social occasions like dances highlighted this insecurity. To hide it, George smiled, while wondering, at times, what he was smiling at.

While so paralyzed, George himself did a double take when he spotted a straight faced, raven haired beauty, standing alone in a darkened corner of the armory. It was as if she was trying to hide in plain sight. She was standing straight across the dance floor beside and behind the band, watching the dancing couples twirl and swirl around the polished wooden dance floor. George felt a sudden urge to move toward her. He did, but first he moved in the opposite direction to disguise his ultimate destination. As he walked casually away, he circled around to her flank, while keeping her in his peripheral vision. He suddenly realized that he was circling around to the wrong side of the band, because he wasn't going to advertise his approach by crossing in front of the band and mount a frontal, direct attack on her. That might scare her away. Besides, that was the style of a Marine; he was an army doughboy. He used more finesse.

Once out of her sight for a moment, George turned around and circled back in a wider circle, and did it in a more purposeful glide around the far perimeter of the dance floor. This time, after a furtive glance at her to fix her position, he intentionly looked away from her and focused his attention straight ahead as he crossed her field of view. He completed his reverse circle beyond her sight and turned to slowly ease her back into his sight. Yup! She was still there, staring around as if she was looking for someone. Now George moved sideways toward her left flank. George chuckled to himself as he became acutely aware that he was secretly stalking her as he would an enemy soldier. He thought it funny that he would attend a social affair among his friends and allies and end up sneaking around as if he was on a battlefield stalking an enemy. It amused him immensely. He couldn't escape his military training from four wars on three continents before he finished his twenty-first birthday.

George paused each time as he gradually closed the gap between them. He noticed that she held a drink in her hand and never once took a sip. What does that mean? He wondered. She also never smiled. This made him smile, the more to encourage her to do the same. But he was cranking himself up to move on her, his target. He thought how ridiculous it seemed that he could face a faceless enemy in war, with less trepidation than facing a strange woman at a social dance. However, he was encouraged by remembering his mother's sage comment that a stranger is a friend you haven't met yet. If she didn't feel that, she would never have met his father, she reminded George. That made all the sense in the world to George. It energized him.

George threw caution to the wind and finally made his move. "Hello, smily."

She turned sideways toward George and her big brown eyes looked up and she replied:

"My name is Joan, and I'm not smiling."

"Well, I am, and my name is George. You can have some of my smile."

"What's there to smile about. We're at war."

"Yes. But you and I aren't at war. Are we?"

"No. I suppose not. You Yanks are here as allies. I hope you survive."

"Woo there! Don't go heavy on me. This is a dance and we're supposed to be having fun."

"I'm not dancing and I'm not having fun."

"Are you not having fun, because you're not dancing?"

"No. I'm here because some of my friends are silly and all but dragged me here. It's for the war effort, they said. And I want to help."

"So don't I. Can't we both help the war effort by dancing together?"

Joan seemed startled by the suggestion, and hesitated. George seeing this and to cut off a growing awkwardness, pointed to the dance floor and added:

"After you, Joan, if you please. One dance won't kill you and we'll both be helping the war effort."

"Well, Ok, but only because it's a slow dance and I like this song." She said, as she placed her drink on an unused piano.

"Good reasons. I've danced for less."

They found a space on the dance floor and segued into a fox trot. George was not an especially smooth dancer, but she held his hand stiffly and her body was rigid. She looked to be George's age, petite, with smooth white skin, and gorgeous brown eyes. She was drop dead beautiful, and she had what Woz would describe as a blockbuster figure. There was a faint hint of cologne or perfume, George could never tell the difference, though he was told perfume was more expensive. Whatever it was, it enchanted George's sense of smell.

She was taller than Angelika, but otherwise reminded him of her. Though he had Joan in his arms, he was yearning for his Angelika. God he missed her so. His longing gave him chest pains, if he thought about her long. Joan danced as if she was doing her duty, her bit for the war. She remained silent. When he asked her if she was from this area of England, she looked at him coldly, like he had dared to interrupt her silence.

"I'm on the dance floor to dance, not talk."

"Well, I admire your ability to focus and to concentrate on your dancing."

They finished the dance in an awkward silence, with her holding George at arms-length. Clearly, she was telling George to keep his distance. George was becoming less impressed with her stunning beauty and more influenced with her dour mood, converting his to match hers, against his wish. When the music stopped, she quickly dropped her arms and walked quickly off the dance floor, back to the extra piano where she put down her drink. George followed her hoping that she would now want to talk.

She did, did she ever.

She reclaimed her drink and abruptly turned on George:

You said one dance wouldn't kill me. You were right, because I'm already dead. I died when my husband was killed in the second battle of the Somme. Where the hell were you Americans when we needed you. We've been fighting to save the world's democracies for three and a half years, while you spineless Americans were chasing apache Indians and small time Mexican bandits. You overpaid cowboys think you can come over here and expect women to throw themselves at you just because you want to play soldier and become instant heroes! Well, you and all the Yanks can fuck off!

Tears of rage ran down her face as she threw her drink in George's face and then hurled it to the floor, smashing it to pieces and scattering shards and slivers across the floor. George was so shocked he stood stone-still, speechless. Others turned toward the sound of the shattered glass wondering what the commotion was all about. Then they moved away. Joan's female friends ran after her. A British Navy Officer came up to the still-stunned and motionless George and patted his shoulder, sympathetically, saying:

"Sorry about that, mate. A distraught woman troubled by the war. Her husband killed on the Somme. They were only married a month before he shipped out. Her friends meant well, but she isn't ready for this scene. She's still grieving."

"Thanks," said a still stunned George. "I understand."

"My God," thought George to himself. "That could be Angelika, if he didn't survive the war." He didn't want to think about it. Some American and British Military Police arrived and were quickly apprised of the incident by the same British Officer and just as quickly dispersed, as a maintenance man swepped up the shattered pieces of glass.

Woz appeared and asked George:

"Was that you George? What the hell happened?"

"Let's get out of here, Woz. I've had enough excitement for one evening. I'll tell you later."

"Ok, George. I'll meet you at the bus. I have to say goodbye to Gladis."

"Gladis? Woz, we'll be gone in another week."

"I know. But we came through England to go to war; we may come back the same way. One never knows. You're spoken for, George. I'm not."

"All right, Woz. We'll exchange stories back at camp."

The fallout from the British Welcoming Dance to the American doughboys was the talk of the camp for the rest of the week. Despite George's regrettable run-in, the doughboys enjoyed the English hospitality and their morale soared. So didn't George's, but for a different reason. He couldn't help comparing his limited and distorted experience with English womanhood with his Angelika, and she came out tops, as she always did. There was only one Angelika and she was his, he reminded himself, thankfully.

All week the doughboys split their remarks between raving about the swell time they had at the prior weekend's dance and anticipating the next and final one this coming Saturday evening. They were to ship out the following Monday. Many soldiers planned to look for a special someone they met and liked at the first dance. The camp was electric and morale soared, having been high to begin with.

Come Friday night, the buses were jammed with boisterious doughboys raring to go paint the town one last time before they shipped out to the continent. Woz was one of the first to board his bus. But George was not among them. He would hitch a ride into town the following morning. He would spend Friday evening writing sober letters to Angelika and his family. This raised a few eyebrows among the Officers, and many barracks-quality derisive comments from his partying compatriots:

"Is he sick?"

"What's he crazy?"

"Hey, George! Let's have your black book names and telephone numbers. I'll take care of the girls for you!"

"Did he get VD already?"

"That angry widow must have loosened a few screws!"

After the noisy departure of the hootin and hollerin doughboys, the Borden camp at Aldershot looked and sounded like a ghost town. When George actually sat down to write his passionate letter and tell her about the grieving widow incident, he suddenly stopped like he was clubbed on the head by a military baton.

"What am I doing!" He lectured himself.

If I tell her about the grieving woman, she'll think I'll be next and she will be the next grieving woman. I'd better put a lid on that incident. Instead, George wrote her about the mostly uneventful crossing of the Atlantic. The letter represented an arm across the ocean enbracing her in his heart and imagination. She and America were his future and he clung to it with a pining passion.

> Dear Angelika, my passion flower!
>
> That's what my mother called you before I fell in love with you. She knew before I did. Is that mother's intuition, my dearest? I'm fine and in good shape. Not as good as yours, but you know what I mean. Though they talk in a clipped, abrupt way, the English women here are very polite and attractive. Not as attractive as you, of course, but nice. No matter how pretty they are, they only make you look better. That's because there's only one Angelika, my Angelika.
>
> Every time I hear the romantic, bouncy tune: 'It's a Long Way to Tipperary,' it reminds me that it's also a long way to my girl in the USA. And it bothers me that Woz has found the

girl of his dreams at a local dance sponsored by a Brit Woman's Auxilliary, to welcome us doughboys. At least that's what he claims. But you have to take what Woz says with a grain of salt. Woz's mother told me he falls in love with every girl he goes out with. That certainly agrees with my observation. You can't fool a mother.

Eventually, we will leave for the continent. I can't tell you anything more. But everyone knows we came over here to go on to the continent, even the Boche. I'm a little tired now, so I think I'll close. I want to follow you into my dreams. I could go to jail with what I'm thinking of doing with you in the privacy of my imagination. Let's just say that I think you are ravishing!

All my Love,
Your Georgie Pogie

Ps: Don't show this letter to your mother.

George thumbed a ride on an Army lorry into town the next morning. He didn't eat on base, even though other soldiers told him he would find British breakfasts bland and sparse, compared to the typical American's. He wanted to experience England on its own terms. Despite dire warnings, he enjoyed the tea and crumpets. The rare and costly eggs and Canadian bacon, fish and chips were delicious, too. When you are hungry, food tastes better, George reasoned. He then took himself to a picture show and saw a blinking movie. He had trouble following the fast clipped British pronunciation. Despite clear enunciation, they seemed to cut off and swallow some words. George's comprehension suffered. Some meanings he missed completely, while others were delayed in his understanding them. It made for a frustrating listening experience. It made him feel stupid. But it would probably be worse in France and the worst in Germany.

After the movie, George made his way to a local pub, where he met other doughboys and some Tommy's from the Gordon

Highlander's Division, if he understood them correctly. One Sargent in the British Army had a little too much to drink and confronted George:

"Hey, Yank. Wot's 'is aye 'ear 'bout yer General Pers-shing callin our Prime Minister, Lloyd George, 'a son of a bitch,' eh?"

George, attempting to defuse a hostile ally, shrugged and said, "Damned if I know. I'm just a private. Generals and politicians don't talk to me."

But the British Sargent pressed on, "See here, for a large country, you Yanks have a small army, almost no air force, not enough rifles, hardly any tanks, no artillery and no ready reservests. How 'n 'ell ye going to fight a war, eh? And what worthy foe have ye's fought, anyway. Indians? Spanish? Mexicans?"

"The British," replied George.

The British Sargent seemed stunned for a moment, then smiled and had to agree. "Blimey, ye got me there, Yank. Bartender! Give this bloke a frosty ale on me. 'e's ok for a colonist."

When the toasts and celebrations got too noisy, the bartender cautioned the group to:

"Mind your P's and Q's!"

Pints and quarts of ale were what he was referring to. And what he meant was for the soldiers to quiet down, because they were making too much noise. The British pubs were more family oriented, jolly and less morose than American bars. While George was making the rounds to different pubs with some other doughboys, he heard about a disturbance that occurred at the armory dance hall. American Military Police entered the current pub he was in, whistled and ordered all the American personnel back to their camp units, on the double! All weekend passes were summarily cancelled.

Jumping on to one of the nearest army buses hurried into town, the rounded up doughboys were abuzz with news about a big brawl that broke out at the dance hall in the armory. It seemed that white American soldiers objected to some black American soldiers dancing with white women. This especially appeared to bother Southern white American soldiers. The white women didn't object and just wanted to dance with soldiers, white or black. But heated comments lead to angry words, which accelerated into flying fists, overturned tables and screams of frightened and hysterical women. The hall lights were shut off from the main switch, pitching the huge hall into blackness.

A wild chaotic scene ensued and a mad rush for the exit doors followed. British and American Military Police flooded the area and gradually restored order. Some of the more drunken and belligerent combatants were arrested and thrown into police lorries and wagons and thrown in the nearest brig or jail. Police clubs had to be used and a few shots were heard. The British Military Police were only armed with batons.

"Damn it all," complained one doughboy. "It only takes one hothead to spoil it all for the rest of us."

"That's why we have a segregated Army," offered another soldier. "American blacks and whites can't seem to get along for long."

"But we are in England and they do. I wonder how they do it?" Commented another American.

George piped in: "England is an Empire. They have colonies all over the world. They allow or bring colored colonials back from South Africa, West Africa, India, Australian aborigines and others from all parts of the world. Maybe that has something to do with it?"

"There's something ironic here, interjected an Army Officer, because America is supposed to be a classless society, where merit and hard work count more than inherited status. Yet a class conscious society like England handles race better than America."

Adding his thought to the conversation, a lawyer in civilian life, now an Army Captain said:

"The US Constitution declares that "All men are created equal,' but we have our contradictions with our historic treatment of North American Native Indians, blacks, and women."

A Chaplin proffered the biblical command: "We are all God's children and entitled to respect. If that precept had been honored tonight, there would have been no problem."

That last thought quieted the passengers and the bus drove back to the base in reflective silence, escorting a morose mood because a weekend was suddenly cut short by soldierly indiscipline, to put it mildly, mused George. At this time on Saturday night when their gala weekend should have been at it's merriest, doughboys were streaming back to base to their barracks if they were lucky, or to the medical tent or camp jail, if they weren't so lucky.

The Camp Commander called for a meeting of all officers early the next morning. The prior night's fiasco was summarily reviewed and generally attributed to the soldiers being jittery and edgy before "going over" to the fighting fields of France. Race was subsumed into the greater war effort. Besides, the American Expeditionary Force was being led by John "Blackjack" Pershing, a staunch supporter of black troops, the Camp Commander informed the assembled group of Army Officers.

The end result was that all pending charges relating to the prior evenings punch up, as the Brits called it, would be dropped and the soldiers patched up and ordered to immediately report to their units. Further, they were to be ready-packed for shipping out to the continent, at once.

Almost as an aside, the Camp Commander mentioned a sobering report from the British Military Police Adjutant, "You doughboys may have your internal frictions, but on the whole, they were involved in fewer crimes than other nationalities on this island. That says something."

Speaking off the record, and emboldened by the imminent sailing to the war on the continent, the Camp Commander further related that General Pershing was born in a small Missouri town that quartered black "Buffalo" cavalry soldiers and their horses. He grew up daily interacting with black troops and came to understand and trust them. As a result, he later volunteered to lead the elite 10th Cavalry of black troops in the field. This, at the time, put him in the minority, with all the puns, permutations and combinations of meanings that entailed. From this legacy, he was crowned with the nickname, "Blackjack."

"Now this may surprise some of you," he continued, "but it is true. The other soldiers outside Pershing's command, and some inside, but secretly, actually called him, 'Niggerjack' Pershing. But the press journalists, thinking that too crude, changed that to 'Blackjack' Pershing. And history has forever after known him as such."

With that explanation, the Camp Commander released the Officers back to their units to prepare them to ship out.

CHAPTER THIRTY

PORT OF LEHAVRE

September 25, 1917. Sargent Klick, George, Woz and the 26th Yankee Division of the U.S. Army woke to the harsh bugle call of reveille. They were ordered to the continent! The boys were excited. They were finally going to get into it, shoulder to shoulder with the Brits and the Frogs, as the French were called. Someone volunteered an answer to the unasked but frequently pondered question as to why the French were called frogs.

"It's simple. One of the favorite food delicacies of the French is frog's legs. They love to dine on frog's legs, though they don't like to be called frogs. So be forewarned."

This they didn't have to worry about for another few days because of bureaucratic snafu's and maneuverings among competing interests, conniving to get troop transports through the backed up ports along the coast of France. German U-boats waited in underwater silence salivating to torpedo any troop transport at anchor in the open sea, lallygating dead in the water, and yearning to go ashore to charge into "the show." Most doughboys stepped ashore at Brest or St. Nazaire. But most of the 26th Division sailed to the port of LeHavre. Because of shipping limitations, some sections had to be detached, but would catch up to the Division inland.

"Who cares where we land?" said a disinterested Woz. "The French are on our side, so what difference does it make where we step ashore?"

"The Brits were swell to us, weren't they? They sure went out of their way to welcome us," enthused an appreciative George, looking back to the safety of the English shores.

"Well, why wouldn't they be? As that Churchill guy said, we're both English-speaking people. But though the English live on an island, they are closer to the war than we are. Of course, we have a lot of immigrants who emigrated to the US from Europe, so there's a connection. And we have a common interest in putting down a bully-country, under a Kaiser who threatens the whole world."

The troops were formed up right after breakfast and marched to a local train station, met by smiling British women auxlliaries offering tea and biscuits. Amid a more subdued atmosphere than their stateside sendoff, yet still enthusiastic in a typical British understated way, they boarded their military commandeered trains and chugged away to the port of Southampton. From there they piled off the train and immediately were hustled up a gangplank and boarded a waiting steamer to cross the English Channel for LeHavre, France.

Again they were crowded like sardines for the relatively short trip to France; short compared to the long crossing over the Atlantic Ocean.

"What do you suppose LeHavre is like, George?"

"To quote you, Woz. Who cares? We're going to go through LeHavre like Sherman went through Georgia in the American Civil War. The fighting is inland."

"Hell, George, it's embarrassing to have an immigrant tell a native born American about U.S. history."

"Woz! Knock it off! I'm a naturalized citizen now. I may be Greek born, but I'm American by choice. I was born in the middle of a civil war in Asia Minor that wasn't so civil, remember."

"Sargent Klick says LeHavre is in the Normandy region of France and is the main port for importing coffee. Just as I'm getting use to English tea, I'm about to be fed French coffee," chortled Woz.

"If that's your biggest problem, you big Pollack, you're got it made. You'd better remember to keep your head down. Guys your size make easier targets," riposted George.

"I'll worry about that when we go into the line. And I won't need a boost to go over the top, you shrimp. Hee, hee," said an amused Woz.

"You're a real comedian, Woz. Your jokes go right over my head. Ha! Ha! Ha! Gotcha! Hee! Hee! Ah, I love it!"

While anchored off the coast of France awaiting clearance and landing orders, as they did when crossing the Atlantic Ocean initially, the restless troops exercised in place, cleaned their weapons until they were sick of it, played cards, and watched silent movies. For further diversion, they were entertained by soldier-singers and dancers, good and bad. They told each other stories of home, listened to lectures about the enemy, and learned key French and German words. Spontaneously, the soldiers, on their own initiative, set up boxing matches among rival outfits that made for the inevitable bragging and bets. Sometimes the fights in the crowd were more entertaining than the official ones in the hastily set up boxing rings on the ships. For two days they weighed anchor dead in the water, awaiting clearance to land. They had to hold back while they landed emergency supplies ahead of them. The doughboys cursed in frustration:

"When the hell we getting off this worthless tub?"

"Sarge, how long will this can float?"

"Getting up the courage to land, Sarge?"

The suffering Sargent endured the taunts with a martyred grimace and ignored them with utter disdain.

"Patience was never a virtue of the young and restless," remarked a wry Sargent Klick, as he heroically fended off endless complaints from impatient Sourdoughboys, as he now called them. "Gripers all!" he fumed.

Finally. Finally! They disembarked and landed on Sunday, September 30, 1917.

The cliffs overlooking Normandy had been viewed with a mixture of surmise and excitement, as they wondered what awaited them in the great beyond. The majestic cliffs diverted most of the northwesterly winds over and beyond the port and made it more aproachable. It also made their docking easier. The merchant port was now taken over as a military landing base. The harbour was flooded with ships and transports of all kinds and sizes. The steamers had to go slowly to avoid hitting other vessels. Some hair-raising near misses were gulped down by intrepid ship captains. But, ultimately, they made it to port with only one heartrending incident.

One of the doughboys who was a German-American was walking down the gangplank when he spotted one of the German prisoners of war loading boxes onto a wagon. It was his brother who stayed behind in Germany and joined the German Army! The German-American doughboy broke ranks and ran over to hug his brother, shouting all the way, "Gunter! Gunter!" He had to leave him, but at least he knew his brother was alive and well fed. It had to be one of the poignant ironies of the war.

Once they were on shore, it felt good to be on solid ground, thought George. He stamped his feet, as if to convince himself that he actually landed. Though something of a world traveler, this is the first time he stepped on land in Western Europe. Harsh operatic shouts of U.S. Army Sargents commanded them to hustle up and move along inland. The apoplectic purple-faced Sargents had to compete with the organized chaos of the noisy disembarkation and port clamor.

Once ashore and away from the steamship, they mingled around food wagons and were fed sandwiches and coffee. The ravenously hungry, youthful doughboys chewed and swallowed energetically, even as they complained about the army food. Chronically hurried, they were called to attention, while shoving down the remainder of their sandwiches and cold coffee, licking their fingers, wiping their mouths, hurling oaths to the heavens and cursing the air blue! Too soon, they were shouted down by red faced and bulging-eyed Sargents, and quick-marched to trains that were already running, though stopped. With ships backed up in the clogged port, the doughboys had to be moved out, on the double!

George and Woz were part of Company H, 2nd Battalion, 103rd Infantry Regiment, 52nd Brigade, 5th Corps, 26th "Yankee"

Division, 1st Army, American Expeditionary Force (AEF). The Division was still commanded by Major General Clarence Edwards. Though a fellow West Point graduate, rumor had it that he was not a favorite of General Pershing and might be replaced. The reason was somewhat obscure, but had something to do with Pershing not overly fond of National Guard units and personally disliking Edwards going back to their West Point days. In any event, they hiked out to the train station and, on orders, boarded the train. Shortly thereafter, the engine chugged and smoked out of the station and headed across the French countryside with a destination to a place called Liffol-le-Grand, a former French combination work, rest and training camp.

"Liffol-le-Grand?" Questioned a laughing Woz. Someone roughly translated it as sounding like "The grand life."

"It probably is, compared to the front lines," remarked a somber George.

An enlisted College student named John Malvey volunteered that,

"It's just a few kilometers south from Domremy, the birthplace of Jeanne d'Arc, France's heroine from the Middle Ages. Also, about an American mile from her home lies a Julian plateau where Ceasar's troops camped on one of his campaigns. How's that for predecessor tenants?"

"Hey, Johnny, I give a good fart, really," quiped a flip Frankie Flannery.

"Hey, George," said an excited Woz, "Sargent Al," as Woz privately called Sargent Klick, "tells me we are to be billeted there for further training."

"Pershing wants to make sure we give a good account of ourselves in combat. It will make it easier to keep the American soldiers under American command," opined George.

"But I heard we were going to go right to the front to fill in as replacements for French and British casualties," replied Woz.

"That's what you get for listening to the Allies, Woz. Marshall Foch and General Haig want that, but our General Pershing will have none of it! America is an independent country. Therefore, we should fight alongside the French as an independent American Army per his orders, not just plugging holes for the Allies under the command of foreign French or British Officers. That's what I hear, anyway," said George.

"That makes sense to me," said a concurring Woz. "That's our General Pershing; Americans for Americans. He didn't bring us over here to be carved up and skeletonized among three countries."

"Did you hear what happened when General Pershing first arrived and marched through Paris with a special advanced contingent of American soldiers?"

"No. What happened?" Queried George.

"While having a beer with Lieutenant Winooski, he told me that after America declared war on Germany, the British and the French sent delegations over to Washington D.C. to brief our big-wigs on the war. What they wanted most was American troops in France to show the flag around. This would buck up the Allied troops and buoy their battered morale. So Gereral Pershing and 190 other American soldiers secretly sailed across the Atlantic to England on May 28. But word got out and everyone knew they were coming. On June 13 they landed in France."

"General Joffre, Major General Foch and other French big wheels, accompanied General Pershing and his staff off the train and from the station in Paris for the two mile car convoy to the Hotel Crillon. Pershings chauffeur said he could hardly describe the nearly hysterical mob scene. Anyone who witnessed the incredible scenario will never forget it, claimed the chauffeur, still in awe."

"Get on with it, Woz. What did he see?"

"Thousands of war weary Parisians were weeping openly and screaming:

"Vive l'Amerique! Viva Pers-shing! The Americans have come!"

"No streets could be seen, just a mass of people yelling their heads off, waving flags, handkerchiefs and banners, hugging and kissing the marching soldiers, throwing flowers and tearing at the soldiers uniforms. They were at a fevered pitch, in tears, gone half-mad and shouting their gratitude until they were red in the face!"

"The chauffeur said he was stunned and overwhelmed by it all. He reportedly said that if he lived a hundred lifetimes, he would never forget the hope that our soldiers gave them. The Americans had come to help the French protect them against the charging horde of Huns threatening their beloved Paris."

"Wow! That must have been something to see," said an impressed George.

Woz continued enthusiastically: "And when he finally arrived at the Hotel Crillon, Pershing was called by the surging crowds until he appeared on the balcony overlooking the Place de la Concorde time and again. And when he grabbed the French tricolored flag and kissed it, the French cheering, rising wildly beneath the balcony, reached a thunderous roar!"

"The poor Parisians probably remembered horror tales told them by their grandparents when Bismark's Prussian Army marched through Paris after they defeated the French in the Franco-Prussian War of 1870-1871." Remarked an understanding George. "And that's when they made Alsace-Lorraine part of Germany. It's a bitterness the French feel even today."

"And to think that all we got when we landed at Le Havre was coffee and sandwiches," said Woz.

"The privilege of rank. When he was our age, I heard Pershing ate dust chasing Apaches into Mexico," responded George.

"Let us hope we can fulfill the trust the Allies are putting in us and feed their hopes to ultimate victory. We'll give them our full measure and the best that's in us, that's for sure," said Woz

"That's the spirit, Woz! I'm glad you're on our side!"

As the troop train chugged its smoky way inland across the French countryside, heading to the agreed Lorraine sector, the doughboys stared through the dirty glass at the supply line of bouncing Army trucks strung out along the rutted roads. The doughboys were getting their first impressions of France and complained about the weather. It was cold, rainy and muddy. However, the French seemed to accept this type weather as natural. The French people were hospitable, kind and friendly enough, frequently smiling and welcomed them as invited guests. Although they were refreshingly direct and frank, they also openly performed personal hygeine functions that most Americans would do in private. Indoor plumbing was not always available. This amused some doughboys and embarrassed others. The French were a hardy people that hoarded and sparingly used expensive fuel, frequently going without heat. They unabashedly and openly discussed sexual matters that confounded the Americans.

On the other hand, the Americans did endear themselves to the French merchants by spending their money freely. Not surprisingly, given their youth and ebullience, anything alcohol-based was fair game for the high spirited doughboys. Popular with their purchases was the local wine and cognac. The proprietors, emulating American entrepreneurs, pushed the local stuff. This fact the doughboys could understand. However, misunderstandings caused by cultural differences and customs were inevitable and would bewilder, anger and amuse both the French and Americans throughout the war.

The crammed train continued past the towns of Rouen and Beauvais, north of Paris. As the long train moved inland the cool breezes turned cold with the arrival of an early winter that hit at the same time as the approaching November. George and his troop huddled together hugging themselves and stamping their feet to warm up their toes, fingers and nose. Much of their winter wear and equipment was being sepatately transported by supply ships and trains. Priority was given to troop movements. Thereafter, oblivious to the discomfort of the cursing doughboys, the troop train roared east without stopping through the towns of Compiegne, Soissons and into the major city of Reims, the capital of the Champagne region, as the sun went down and the blue-black night engulfed them.

At Reims the train stopped to the derisive cheers of the doughboys to permit them to use the outhouses and for hot coffee and cold sandwiches. Men with impatient natural urges, urinating and defecating out of the opened train doors, did not endear themselves to the gaping French farmers, watching their farms being sprayed and fertilized by the pride of American boyhood. The American Diplomatic Corps and Public Relations types were not amused when so apprised by their French compatriots, who gesticulated with admirable enthusiasm. To stop this unauthorized shooting war that was watering and fertilizing French soil, old milk cans were later supplied the troop trains. When Divisional Commanders were bulletined by higher ups to keep their troops in line, this type incident being cited, they were less than impressed. Said one, wryly:

While we're trying to stay alive, controlling an explosive war, it's nice to know that our Diplomatic Corps is in on the ground floor helping us to win this war by confining the personal aims of the private parts of our soldiers. Praise all.

In any event, they were allowed a half-hour to eat and rest. Because of lines, it took an additional fifteen minutes to onload the boys, who entrained again while gulping on the go, and cursing the bull Sargents rushing them.

"Damn it all, Sarge. I got to eat, don't I?"

"Never mind you're guff, McDuffy. Move!"

While stopped, the train had kept its engine running. White smoke puffed out of the black engine-funnel, bent sideways with the passing wind, and thereby obscuring sight lines and hissing and belching strange, discordant noises throughout the semi-disciplined chaotic scene of the train station. To the accompanyment of station shouts from hoarse Army officers,

"Let's go! Lets Go! On board! Get on board, soldier!"

As the train released its brakes and jumped ahead with a jolt, preparing to leave the station, George and Woz spotted dark smoke coming out of the roof of the main station house. It ran down a chimney to a hot stove heating the station. George and Woz looked at each other.

"You thinking what I'm thinking, Woz?"

"I am now!"

George turned to two other members of their squad, Phil Dodger and Davy Cochrane, who hung together, and asked them:

"You guys tired of being cold and miserable?"

"Yeah," they both answered frostily.

"Then follow us!" spouted George.

With that, George and Woz, followed by Phil and Davy, jumped off the train and ran back into the train station. They ran by the startled Station Master and civilian employees and pulled the stove off its moorings, grabbed two loose planks of wood and squeezed them against the sides of the stove and carried it out of the station and loaded it onto their train car, to the boisterous cheers of the occupying doughboys. As the train noisily pulled away they waved back at the Station Master, still frozen in disbelief at what he had just seen. The appreciative doughboys rubbed their hands and gravitated toward the heated stove. Automatically, in a spirit of fairness, they warmed themselves, then drifted away to make room for their fellow soldiers to do the same. They filled the newly warmed air with ribald jokes and loudly seconded a spontaneous motion to make George the Company Chief Morale Officer.

Though the astonished Stationmaster wrote the loss off as an incident of war, later claiming that the thieving Americans would probably come back for the smoke, other less audacious pranks were not ignored and the US Government had to set up a Claims Department to review and pay damage claims for alleged acts of misconduct by US soldiers. In the spirit of even handed justice, the US Government, sheepishly, set up their own counterclaim section that was considerably less busy.

After Reims, the train turned southeast to Chalons, Vitry-le-Francois, St. Dizier and finally stopped to disembark at Chaumont, headquarters for Pershings Allied Expeditionary Force. It was a beehive of activity, to put it mildly.

Chaumont looked like a city swallowed by the swirl of war. It was dwarfed by a tent city of soldiers. It was a patchwork, frantic scene of muddy, board strewn, dirt roads of military supply dumps, horses, lorries, trucks, ordnance, drilling troops, troop maneuvers, grenade, mortor and artillery firing ranges, dugouts, and winding miles of dug trenches. At this American encampment, with French advisers, the French spoke their broken English to teach the fresh faced, inexperienced, naïve American doughboys survival skills in trench warfare.

This caused some tension with Pershing because he wanted the soldiers to get out of the stagnant trenches, bogged down by three years of atrittious immobility, featuring thrown grenades and artillery. That fighting style proved to be ineffective, Pershing fumed. He wanted the Allies to go after the enemy, to get the soldiers moving into an open, mobile war of strike and maneuver. He wanted to use the finest rifle in the world, in his opinion, the 1903 American Springfield rifle, as the weapon of victory. But he allowed the French trench-training as a necessary beginning. Nobody ever won a war ducking their heads, he bristled with righteous indignation, or so went the word around the doughboy headquarters. Pershing's point of view swept through the ranks, as it was so intended.

Most of the American soldiers were initially and intentionally billeted in quiet sectors. There they were trained by the French against the peculiar dangers of trench warfare, based on three years of deadly experience by the battle hardened French. In a token compromise, Pershing detached some specialty troops, like Engineering contingents, to repair bridges and roads; Artillery elements, to augment decimated artillery teams, and Signal contingents, to lay wire and to repair cut telephone lines destroyed by enemy artillery shells, rifle grenades and trench mortors. And since the American soldier was not sent immediately into the line as combatants, their casualty rate was initially low. Therefore, Pershing authorized American Field Hospitals to help their British and French Allies. The British Tommies greeted the doughboys with waves and shouts of welcome. The Brits looked on them as replacements or re-inforcements. Either way the British Tommies were happy to see them. Some of the doughboys returned their greetings with their own friendly gestures of greeting, while others just smiled and looked on in interested, respectful silence.

"After all," said one doughboy, though speaking for many, "they have been in it for three long years."

"Grizzled survivors of battling the fearsome Boche," said George, as he surveyed the exhausted, worn looking veterans. "They fought the greatest land army in the world to a standstill," said an admiring Woz. "You have to tip your cap to the French and British, don't you?"

"Yes. And you can be sure they are taking our measure," replied George. "It almost feels like they are saying to us: "'We've done our bit, bub. We've held them, until you could get over here. Now let's see what you can do?'"

"And I hope we can measure up," said a beseeching Woz. "That English guy that has an American mother, Winston Churchill, claims the survival of the English speaking peoples depends on us closing ranks to rout the Huns, the scourge of Europe and the world."

"Let's hope that he's right in saying that right makes might and we prevail," responded a wistful George.

At the busy Chaumont train station, they detrained and immediately uploaded onto a limited number of trucks and lorries, with the rest ordered to march. It was Company H's luck to be left behind to march. And to make it more miserable, it was raining again. The troop transport motor trucks took off. The drumming pitter pater of the rain hit the passing metal roofs of the truck cabs. The tires hissed against the wet pavement. The truck engines groaned and shrieked, with one truck slithering sideways on the slippery, muddy road, as the canvas covered vehicles sped by. This was rain country, Lieutenant Malone told them.

Slogging behind, George, Woz and the Company H doughboys trudged through Chaumont, water drops smashing on the hard surfaced streets. Rain pooled on the front of his high campaign hat and dripped over the brim. The now heavy water fell down from the roofs overflowing gutters, making waterfall like sounds. Then a bolt of lightning slashed across the sky, which shimmered in light, the flash turning the falling rain silver and the grass white.

Once the military convoy dumped its human freight at Liffolle-Grand, Company H's destination and Neufchateau, the headquarters for the 26th Yankee Division, the trucks and lorries turned around and returned to pick up the rest of the troops in mid-march. This troop transit was a continuous, effortful mobilization. The last troops didn't arrive at their base camp until near midnight. The hazards of marching long distances made themselves painfully known in time. Feet become sore from the constant pounding of walking, especially on a hard surfaced road. Legs ache from the never ending tramping of hobnailed boots on hard macadam road surfaces, hard packed dirt roads, muddied by the remorseless rain. Seventy five pound packs weighed down on bobbing backs, causing back straps to cut and burn into shoulder blades, and create an assortment of back problems, upper, lower and mid back, depending on the peculiar way one twists and turns when walking. They were expected to endure, because it was part of being in the Army and they were at war, after all. It wasn't supposed to be a picnic, they were chided, with non-commissioned officer gusto.

George, Woz and Sargent Kick and Company H were among the last to arrive and they were exhausted from traveling all day and night. Even then they had to set up their own tent which was given to them as part of their carrying gear. The rain had mercifully stopped. The tent came in two pieces that had to be buttoned together to make a tent. Even if your tent kit was complete, and not all were because of the American hurry-up to war, some doughboys had to improvise and use their rifle for the front pole and their bayonet for the rear pole, to hold the canvas tent up. The dead-on-their-feet doughboys then collapsed to their blankets on the wet, cold ground into a sudden sleep.

The next morning the latecomers were awoken at reveille, same as the early arrivers. To their gripes, the drill Sargents gave no ear, merely saying that war is unfair, get use to it. However, they were given another hour to eat breakfast, unofficially. At the breakfast table George and Woz groggily sat across from each other.

George was the first to speak, "Griping seems to be the soldiers lot. I hear the French criticizing the Brits, and vice versa. Everyone's criticizing Americans, including ourselves. We're all fighting the German led Central Powers, so we need each other. But we're fighting two wars, external and internal."

"There's one exception," said Woz. "The Canadians and the Brits get on. Generally have. And it didn't hurt their relationship with that great victory the Canadians had when they drove the Boche from Vimy Ridge a year ago against incredible odds. They'll be talking about that one for years, I hear."

"Well then, that's the answer. Gripes are forgiven by victories," concluded George.

"Parlez-vous, Francais?" said Woz.

"Do I speak French, you're asking me? As much French as I have to," answered George. "In fact, I'm learning as much from French gestures as I am from their words. Back in the good old USA, I'd probably be accused of making obscene gestures."

"They say the Italians are even worse about mixing their speaking with emphatic gestures," offered Woz.

"And the English, with their stiff upper lip, speak with almost no gestures," George noted.

"So don't the Germans. Can you imagine the French and Italians with their emphatic gesturing, speaking with the brunt force of the German accent?"

"That's called a brawl!" Interjected George. "No wonder we're all fighting!"

"We're fighting because of some hotheaded, Serbian teenager in Savajevo, who shot to death an Austrian Archduke and his wife. That started it," lamented Woz.

"Hopefully, we're here to end it."

"Before it ends us, God willing," said Woz with finality.

Before reporting to an assembly post, Sargent Al Klick, 2nd Battalion, Headquarters Intelligence section, non-commissioned officer, came to their mess and told them instead to get ready to move out again. Because of overcrowding, their 2nd Battalion of the 26th Division was detached and sent on to a newly opened French Training post at a place called Ver Luxeuil, about 45 miles southeast of Liffol-le-Grand. French wagons were assigned to transport them. Some were motor driven and some horse drawn. The officers were driven in the motor transports because they had to attend a special, early meeting. The non-commissioned officers and doughboys traveled by horse and wagon.

———————————

PART IV

CHAPTER THIRTY ONE

BLUE DEVILS

George and Woz were in the same Company, but different squads. After mess, Captain Hawkins assembled them and told them their Company H was assigned to be trained in trench warfare by an elite group of French troops called Chasseurs, more popularly known as the Blue Devils. Many considered them and the legendary French Foreign Legion troops to be the toughest in the French Army. To get the Blue Devils to train Americans, a job they felt was beneath their abilities, a French Commander mistold them they would be training the toughest American soldiers, the Marines. George learned this inadvertently when he was approached by a Blue Devil Squad leader, who said:

"You Marines are zee special best, qui? We Chasseurs are so. We be best fighteurs und drinkeurs in Europe."

Besides being the best *braggeurs*, they also had a diplomatic way of correcting the Americans. "Tres bon, tres bon, mais," meaning "Very good, very good, but . . .". Then they would patiently, and paternally show the doughboys *their* way. Eventually, however, this was interpreted as condescending and resented by some of the doughboys. And the resentments started to build up.

Since they predictably spoke mostly French, a lot of "watch me" demonstrations, including hand and body motions were done. As they interacted, the Americans and the French were sizing each other up.

The French liked the American energy and enthusiasm and eagerness to get into the fray. On the other hand, they told their Commander, General Jacque LeMaire, that the Yanks were too brash and overconfident. The rugged veteran Commander assured their Chasseurs that the Yanks would lose their carelessness and foolhardiness in the crucible of battle, and not to worry about it.

The first thing the French told the Americans was to get rid of those envelope caps and cowboy hats and put on a steel helmet. Flying and falling shrapnel will shred those cloth hats and hatchet their heads, they warned. They also told them that in trench warfare the pistol, grenade, trench knife, and bayonet were more useful for close combat than the rifle.

"Monsieurs, you are not chasing Mexicans across desert plains or Indians across zee open prairies here," they warned. "We will supply you with these canvas pouches to sling over your neck. They are to carry hand grenades in. Learn to move steathily with them so you don't blow yourselves up, si vous plais (if you please)."

Some Americans were offended by the downplaying of the rifle as a fighting weapon by the French, because the American Springfield rifle was considered the world's best firearm and it seemed to diminish the already demonstrated superior sharpshooting skills of the American infantryman. They griped to Captain Hawkins. He listened and then answered:

"Look guys, don't take it personal. Analysis of recent wars has taught us that ineffective fire in battle was the exception more than the rule. For example, only one-third of the individual rifleman fired at the enemy in any direct way that might hit an enemy. Panicked firing could go anywhere, even against your fellow soldiers. Firing at shadows and ghosts from nervous, trigger happy soldiers was not uncommon, nevermind the poor marksmanship that fired straight ahead, aiming at sounds, and hoping to hit something."

"But we've received rifle training," complained a Doughboy.

"Yes, but the Allies are skeptical. We have to show them in the field. The French and the British have been fighting a stalemated trench war for over three years. But it's three more years of fighting experience than we have. They have earned their superior attitude, especially the Blue Devils. In trench battles, what they are saying makes sense. We have to start somewhere. So we defend in the trenches before we attack. And attack we will. General Pershing wants a war of movement. But he wants to train us to be prepared so that as many of you as possible will survive this war to go home, safe and sane to your families. In short, listen and learn. Now get out of here!"

The men broke up and walked away buzzing with mollified conversations, though some weren't entirely satisfied, and fewer others would ever be, given the eternal malcontents that every army has. The majority, however, left with a better perspective and understanding for more tolerance.

Despite warnings to accept the French ways, George and Woz heard about a minority incident involving Company K up in Liffol-le-Grand, that caused a concerned General Pershing to personally involve himself, once he heard of it. Some doughboys on weekend leave had hitched a ride to Bar-Le Duc that had an early reputation for providing local delights, including cognac and "good time women" for virile Yanks willing to spend money. At one such bar, a near inebriated American soldier overheard two Blue Devils talking about the Yanks:

"Qui, they are here. But will they fight?"

Without any warning, the American soldier slugged the Blue Devil, saying simultaneously

"You mean, like this!"

All hell broke loose. The brawl was on! Chairs scraped backwards, tables turned over, glasses broke and loud yells filled the bar room. Fists were flying everywhere and bodies tumbled in every direction. The Military Police, both French and American charged in, blowing their whistles and joining the fray, clubbing freely and adding to the chaos. Eventually, more from the wild swinging soldiers punching themselves out than from anything else, the melee settled down and wholesale arrests were made after the injured were treated at a nearby medical hospital.

Pershing was livid. "They want to fight, do they? We can arrange that," he roared. He cut short the training of the units involved, by a few days, and assigned them to a defensive position near the front. His final comment to the incident was to merely say, "They are obviously ready." To assuage the bruised feelings of the French,

Pershing sent a personal emissary to the local French Commander apologizing for any misconduct by American soldiers under his command. He then ordered that henceforth for all American personnel, Bar-Le-Duc was off limits until further notice. The French Commander was very understanding and offered his own apology for his fiery French fighters.

"When soldiers drink, these things happen, mon General."

On Sunday morning, October 21, 1917, the leading elements of the 26th Division, including George's Company H and four others, were the first units of doughboys to enter the front lines, ten kilometers northeast of Nancy, in the Somerville sector. This entailed about a sixty mile trip north for them. The trip was made without any unusual incident, mostly at night.

The general fighting between the Germans and the French and British seemed to slow down with the approaching holidays. The Americans started first with their Thanksgiving holiday. Almost all of the warring countries were heavily Christian and celebrated Christmas in accordance with their respective festive customs and cultures. It brought some sanity to the madness of war. It not only brought a relative quiet, but it also brought sadness, a longing for their families and a nostalgia for their former peaceful lives. The doughboys became somber and reflective, especially after receiving mail or packages from home. Many were teenagers who, being human, became homesick, yearning to reunite with their loved ones and families. A few brooded and became very apprehensive.

"If I ever get out of this death trap, I'll never leave the United States again," vowed a young doughboy, tight with tension and fear. He was the sensitive type who noticed all the sad looking French women wearing black, who were mourning their dead husbands, boyfriends and brothers. He also noted with particular anguish that the only young men his age he saw in the passing villagers and towns seemed to have missing arms or legs or were talking to themselves as mental casualties. Some of his fellow soldiers were more cynical, claiming that he sensed more than he saw, and that he would never survive the war unless he changed his attitude.

Unfortunately, they were right because he was destined to be killed during the first week in the line. He was on a night wire patrol, checking for cut wires, when a high explosive shell attack commenced, and he panicked. Confused, he ran into no man's land toward the Boche lines, instead of his own, despite frantic cries from his squad leader calling him back. Being one of the Company's first deaths, it brought home to the rest of the Company the sudden, lethal whims of war that could take you "**west**," to use a doughboy word, meaning death.

Just before Christmas, Captain Tom Hawkins, the commander of H Company, called an assembly to update the troops and told an amazing story.

"Yes. It's true, guys. The rumors you heard and were asking me about were true. German, French and American soldiers from our First Division stopped the war for a while to join as Christians and sing Christmas songs. Near the furthest trench line along the Nancy-Metz line of defense, some German soldiers were heard singing Christmas songs earlier this week, near on midnight. The words were German but the sentiments were universal. The Americans joined in and were soon accompanied by the French. It was a strange, surreal, but uplifting experience. For an unforgettable time, the killing war stopped and kindness prevailed."

The assembled soldiers were silent, not knowing how to interpret this amazing news. A buoyant moment of faith and sanity in an insane war. It gave everyone hope. Strangely, it was a repeat of a similar incident earlier in the war that was condemned by the Allies and thereafter forbidden as fraternization.

"That having been said," continued Captain Hawkins. "The next morning at 6:00am, the Boche shelled the Allied trenches, injuring and killing our soldiers. Now we, as well as our French and British Allies, have standing orders against such fratenization. So stay away, stay alert and keep your guard up."

The Division was kept occupied with learning about trench mortors and machine guns as a sort of cross training to at least familiarize them with these specialized weapons, that had special units to handle them. They hiked the hills, practiced on the rifle range, threw grenades and practiced their bayonet thrusts. They were shown to drive the blade into the groin and throat areas as the most disabling. It was the French belief that injuries inflicted on the enemy in these parts were most likely to save their own lives in close combat. With three years of survival experience to rely on, the doughboys listened with avid interest.

George's experiences in the little heard of First and Second Balkan Wars was considered by some of his fellow Yanks to be a young boy-scout adventure. George was given little serious credit for it. He endured the taunts good naturedly. This sporting response to their sometimes vicious humor endeared George all the more to his fellow soldiers in the Company.

George and Woz were also known as "*Border guys*" for having served on the Mexican border in 1916 and 1917. The US Regular Army guys saluted this service, but the National Guard and the National Army guys, the draftees, mimicked the British and the French in belittling that border service. For example, when George removed his boots to empty them of nothing that the others could see, since France did not have have the tarantula or scorpion problem that Mexico did, the guys would start in:

"Hey George. Is that what you cowboys did south of the border in that Bow and Arrow War?"

Another doughboy added: "Yeah. Didn't 15,000 US Cavalry chase '*Punchy*' Villa in circles until they lost him?" The ridicule included deliberately miscalling Pancho Villa as "Punchy."

"What? We fought desperadoes who had been killing each other for near ten years," retorted George. He continued, "When Pershing chased after Geronimo and his Apaches thirty years earlier, *that* was a Bow and Arrow War. But Pershing did all-right for himself didn't he?"

Woz chuckled to himself, admiring George's parrying. But then he added:

"George, never mind them. Stretch your vocal chords and practice your singing to celebrate, because Captain Hawkins has called a Company assembly for 2pm this afternoon. And rumor has it that we will be moving into the line, up north somewhere."

"Well that will be good news, but I'm not going to worry about my singing, because I can't sing a lick. But even if I could, we are no longer allowed to 'fraternize' with the enemy, as it is called. Violate this order and you face a Court Martial or could be shot as a spy, as I heard it."

At the assembly that afternoon, Captain Hawkins got right to the heart of the matter as soon as he finished with some housekeeping matters and announced,

"Oh, by the way, another rumor that is also true, is that the rest of Company H and the 26th Division is scheduled to move out and go into the line next month."

With that announcement, a spontaneous "Huzzah! Yeah! All right!" roar went up from the leaping up, charged up, champing at the bit doughboys, eager for action.

"About time! Yes! Let's have at "em!" And further oaths and cries rendered the disturbed air!

Captain Hawkins continued, "So Happy New Year, Yankee Division. As we move into 1918, we will join our advanced elements and also be assigned to a sector, to hold a defensive position, about six miles northeast of Nancy, along the Somerville section. The French also spell it Somerviller or Sommerviller. Don't ask me why. We're replacement troops for a French Division that'll be pulled back for rest and recreation. You'll know more when I do. Any questions?"

"Captain!" Waved Dilboy. Did you say the Somerville sector?"

"Yes. Why?"

"I come from Somerville, in Masachusetts. Now I don't know whether I'm coming or going!"

"When have you?" Shouted a fellow jokster.

When the Company tittering, snickering and snide remarks receded, Captain Hawkins interjected:

"That's not the only thing that might confuse you in France, Dilboy. If you haven't already noticed, they have towns with the same name, only in different *provinces*. But then again so don't we, only in different *states*. So let's not be too critical."

George took an instant liking to Captain Tom Hawkins. Hawkins was a chestnut haired, brown eyed, roman nosed, sturdy six-foot, athletic, almost handsome, former football star and recent graduate of West Point. But he was different. Unlike many West Pointers, he didn't seem to look down on National Guard troops as amateurs, even though that's what they were, at least compared to the Regular Army guys. He didn't take himself too seriously, had an easy sense of humor, and knew his own mind. But he would listen to the rank and file, not just give orders. Though he was with Captain Hawkins since Camp Devins, George had little direct contact with him, because Hawkins had to stay on top of the screw-ups. George knew enough about survival skills from his Army experiences in wartime to follow the rules and his training. Those who didn't were the first to die.

George, on the other hand, earned Hawkins's notice because George had a veteran's presence and quiet poise about him, despite his youth. He knew George was a Mexican *Border man*, and thought that was a positive credential to George's credit. There was nothing outstanding about George's size, being smaller to average in height, and having a trim build. But with the features of a Greek God, women must have noticed him, more so than George noticed them, by all accounts, thought Hawkins. The Captain also noted that George mixed well with his fellow soldiers, had a willing nature and a happy-go-lucky personality. The troops enjoyed his fun loving ways, spontaneous dance steps and positive nature. It was easily evident to Captain Hawkins that George won over his fellow soldiers by his humorous and cheery qualities of mind and heart. George's sharpshooting skills were well known and the target of some resentful remarks from less skilled wanna-be's. Thus, although Dilboy was not universally appreciated, Hawkins was well acquainted with the truism that:

He who is spoken well of by all, would be false to his father.

Captain Hawkins had penciled George in for promotion potential, as he had been trained to do at the "Point." Part of the education of leaders was the spotting of other natural leaders for field promotions that would be needed as the battles took their inevitable casualties. But, of course, Private Dilboy, like everyone else, would have to earn any promotion during *this* war, at *this* time, and in *this* Company H, cautioned Captain Hawkins to himself.

Barred from Bar-Le-Duc, George and Woz took a weekend pass to Grandrecourt, about ten miles north of Liffol-le-Grand. It got them away from AEF headquarters in Chaumont and the 26th Yankee Division headquarters in Neufchateau, where they would be less likely to be recognized if they got caught in any mischief, not that they were looking for any. While enjoying the free time away, they had a funny incident occur. As they were passing a store, an elderly woman stopped them and asked:

"Are you Apache's?"

Woz was amused into silence, but George started whooping and dancing up and down like an American Indian doing a war dance and said:

"You mean like this? No. See, we don't have any war paint on, and we use rifles, not tomahawks."

The old woman looked uncertain, then said, "Mais qui," meaning "But yes," and walked on.

"What kind of people do they think Americans are? Do they think we are backward and crude?" Wondered Woz.

"I don't think it's that so much. It may be the American movies they saw and they remembered American Cavalry chasing Indians."

"Or it could be they remembered that American Wild West Show that was touring Central Europe when the World War broke out in July, 1914. They were stopped, confined and roughed up in Berlin, until the American Embassy obtained their release. Once freed the Iraquois Indians drummed out an official declaration of war against Germany," commented a passing doughboy, who overheard the exchange.

"Whoa! That must have had the German High Command shaking in their boots," punned a sarcastic Woz.

Smiling and chuckling to themselves, George and Woz nodded a grateful acknowledgement to the passing doughboy, waved and smiled at him as he walked on. "Oh, well, maybe they're just curious and wondering what an American Indian looks like," finalized George.

"Speaking of wondering," said Woz, "we better get back to camp before it's too late and they wonder where we are and mark us A-W-O-L, absent without official leave. Then it's the stockade for us. Stockade? Hell, now I'm even talking like an Indian."

Camp duties kept them busy for the rest of January. While resting on his cot one night, George mentioned casually to his tentmates at the end of the month, that he had one more week to enjoy before he left age twenty one and became an old man of twenty two.

"You're not there yet, Georgie boy. But since we are in a so-called quiet sector, there's a good chance you'll make it. Other than that, buddy, I couldn't care less."

"Frankie Flannery, my Maine patriot, you warm my heart. You're obviously a man of great compassion for your fellow man."

"George, George, me boyo, my best friend is me. It's called enlightened self-interest. If I go down, who is going to take care of my family?"

"What family? You're not married."

"But I plan to be. And I also plan to live well beyond the age twenty two, you seem to be dreading. My body is over here fighting the bad guys. I'm doing my bit. I will have earned my hereafter on this earth. So I am selfless, not selfish, as you suggest."

"I'm not suggesting that at all. I just think that in looking after your buddy, you are also looking after yourself, because he covers your back. That's all."

"Are you a Preacher, George? Then cease with the Preacher crap, will ya? This is war. It's kill or be killed. It's as basic as that. Now leave me alone. I've got to get my rest so I can lead the charge into Germany to save my fellow man. Now are you happy?"

"Will both of yousa shutta da uppa? Howsa Pasquale gonna getta my sleepa with yous flappin with the mouth, alla time? Then I is'a happy, you is'a happy. Alla rightta? Jesu Christa!"

CHAPTER THIRTY TWO

TO AND FROM SOMERVILLE

Before George reached his next birthday, orders came down to move out. The 26th, Yankee Division was going into the line and relieving two French Divisions. George remembered a French Combat Division contained half the number of soldiers as an American Division, typically. The double sized American Division was necessary because of the lack of mid-level American Officers.

They marched out of camp and treked to a waiting train to take them to Nancy, to a northeast corner in the Somerville sector. It was approximately a thirty mile move. There, they were to man the trenches as of January 21st for defense purposes, sharing the defensive line with the French on their flanks. This was the first occasion that a full American Division went into the line. Despite the short distance, the train was stopped twice to check out possible sabotages. Each proved uneventful. When the train finally arrived at its destination, they detrained immediately and were called to attention for a roll call and march off. While marching along the soldiers broke out into scattered and then spontaneous song, singing,

We're going to hang our laundry on the Sigfriedg Line, do you have any washing, mother dear?

It helped to lighten up the dreary sights seen, while looking over the area.

"Where in God's name are we? Is this hell, because it sure isn't heaven," remarked a dour doughboy.

"Quiet down. Quiet down. Knock it off! Do you want to wake up the whole Boche horde announcing our arrival? They'll send back some "archies," which artillery shells are called over here. You tweety birds, save the singing for daytime."

The 26th Division doughboys were markedly unimpressed by this new sector assignment, to say the least, thought George. Craters, mudholes, damaged stone buildings and tilted wooden shacks were scattered about. They were told to expect bone-chilling cold, ceaseless rain, sleep disturbing, harrassing shelling and gunfire, poison gas, muddy, waterfilled trenches, and squishy, wet boots, trenchfoot, lice, rodents, dysentry and cutting winds. The place looked God forsaken.

The French were dirty and looked tired, but pleased to see the American doughboys, muttered welcomes, and well wishes in French and scattered English, and made friendly gestures. The trenches were filthy, and full of mud and debris that froze at night. The eery night also brought out large rats scurrying around looking for warmth and food scraps. They were told that wooden planks were placed at the bottom of the trenches, called duckboards, but were buried beneath caked and now frozen mud. The trench walls were buttressed by long wooden planks and tree posts mostly horizontal, with vertical postings where the Engineers planted them. Elevated walkways made of wide planks could be stepped up on to get closer to the top of the trench line. They were called *fire steps*, because you stepped up on them to fire your rifle over the top at the enemy. Ladders were also placed between the plank platforms for going over the top to launch an attack.

Upside down J, I, and other odd shaped and angled periscopes were mounted against the upper half of the trenches to peek over the top. They could not be left exposed for any length of time because of German snipers and sharpshooters looking through their telescopes for a raised head or periscope. They were especially alert to the arrival of fresh replacement troops who were more likely to be careless in failing to keep their heads down. Often, German artillery would give a loud welcome "party" to the new replacement troops. Sometimes, German tunnels or patrols were close enough to either listen in to Allied outposts or trenches, or they threw in missiles, dud grenades, stones or rocks with written messages welcoming new troops to their graves, and even naming their outfit and commanding Officers. It was a real coup to pick off or capture an isolated officer or other enemy prisoner to be questioned and tortured for intelligence purposes.

"Jesus the Christ almighty! These trenches are going to get some getting use to," said a shocked Woz.

George was equally stunned, but merely commented, as he surveyed the breadth and width of their new quarters,

"How did they endure this filth and these squalid living conditions for three and a half years?"

"If you raised pigs on a farm like I did, dirt and mud can become right friendly, let me tell you. You can get use to anything in time," remarked an already settled Frankie Flannery.

Flannery's bulky body was well padded with natural insulation from his own body fat. His red hair went with his fiery disposition, though he got along well with his fellow soldiers, because he seldom took offense and was as quick to laugh, as scowl. Even when he got angry, he never held onto it very long. He was a rare tough-guy that was adaptable. He would select when to take a stand. And when he did, he was difficult to get around. As a result, he seldom had any serious clashes.

George was to notice that troop movements were understandably made mostly at night, to more readily hide them from enemy observation balloons and aeroplanes, whose pilots wouldn't hesitate to call in artillery on the enemy below. Therefore, except for emergencies, replacements were sent into the lines also at night to keep the casualties down. But there were no guarantees, because flares could be used to light up an area, as well as the glare and light from high explosive shells falling in an area. Moonlight could also light them up for the enemy to target.

However, this area, though fairly close to the current German front lines, was a quiet zone, that was not generally the focus of much fighting or shelling. Both sides seemed to use it to break in fresh or new troops, or as an area for rest and recuperation from a hot zone of furious fighting. Of course, these quiet zone designations could change with a new General in the area or a change in plans by the High Command of the General Staffs. War is predicably unpredictable, as is well known.

Actually, the 51st Field Artillery Brigade of the 26th (Yankee) Division was deployed to this area the day before to practice their own team drills under actual line conditions that wouldn't be overwhelming in a selected quiet zone.

One of the problems with this Lorraine section of the Alsace-Lorraine region of France that was assigned to the Americans, is its history. It was part of France until the 1870-71 Franco-Prussian War, won by Prussia. As part of the spoils of war, Prussia annexed the Alsace-Lorraine region and made it part of a new unified Germany. This made France bristle with indignation, especially since Lorraine was the province that was home to its famous heroine, Jeanne de Arc. But France, being defeated, had not the military power to stop the annexation. This sore in the side of France festered for nearly half a century. Therefore, today the region was full of both German and French civilian spies, and there were few secrets between them. Given such a civilian citizenry with divided loyalties, it was not surprising that the Germans and the French were well informed about each other's movements in this area of the war.

That night they slept in the trenches for the first time in cut out caves in the side of the trench walls, buttressed by lumber and posts. Cold as it was, at least it blocked the wind and provided shelter from any snow or rain. Poor Woz, thought George. He pulled sentry duty the first night, and was the worst for it. That's the price he had to pay for looking big and strong, which he was. George's teeth chattered beneath the extra coats and blankets provided. He thinks he fell asleep as much from shaking to get warm, as from exhaustion. He fell asleep shaking and woke up the same way, when the Sargent shook him awake at first light the next morning.

"Dilboy, you, Flannery, myself and DeGregorio are assigned to a squad to go out on patrol with a frog scout."

"Huh. On patrol for what?"

"We're probing the wire to check to see if we have any cut wires, to look for signs of tunnels, to see if we had any visitors last night, and to to try to spot any new machine gun or mortor emplacements."

"What do you mean visitors last night? There was no incoming and I didn't hear any shooting."

"There wasn't any. But that doesn't mean we didn't have any visitors. The Frenchies tell us sometimes the Boche crawl through the wires to get close enough to hear our conversations. We have our listening posts out too."

Flannery snapped himself awake from their talking and joined the conversation:

"Hey Sarge, what about the German snipers?

"What about them? You have a rifle don't you? We're at war, Flannery, in case you haven't heard."

"Yeah. And I'm such a lousy shot, Sarge, I just might shoot **you** by mistake, so don't get me disoriented."

"Let's go to mess. I'm hungry. Where is it, by the way?" Interrupted a now alert George, as he was pulling aside the hung blanket that was their front door to the dugout.

"To the rear, across the field," pointed the Sargent. "You'll see the rolling kitchen wagons at the entrance to the woods. Just follow your nose, Dilboy." "I'll be right behind you."

"Ha. With my luck, the wind will be blowing the other way and the Germans will know it before I do."

"If they do, you'll know about it because they will send over some archies to go with your morning coffee," said a following Flannery.

"Hey! Yousa paisans. Waita for me. I'm a lighta my cigarette," pleaded a trailing Pasquale.

At the kitchen wagon, they were told to eat light because they were going into no man's land on patrol and didn't want anyone getting sick from overeating. They assembled back in the trench line near their quarters where they met Sargent Fouchet, a small, but tough looking Blue Devil, and a veteran of many of these wire patrols. He led them out. In his broken English, he told them not to bunch up, but to move out in single file, at least five meters apart, to avoid a cluster of injuries if they were hit with machine gun fire, hand grenades, trench mortors or distant artillery shells.

They were to keep their heads down at all times, talk only when necessary and to keep their voices low, because the wind can carry voices. When moving, they were to alternately leap frog ahead, covering each other at all times, when they jumped from shell hole to shell hole. They were given canvas pouches to hang from their necks and in which they would carry hand grenades. They were to keep their rifle in front of them with their trigger hand on the rifle neck, ready for three potential uses, to pull the rifle trigger, go for a hand grenade or their trench knife.

They were all to head back in two hours, in case they got separated, unless circumstances dictated otherwise. As they moved out into no man's land, George's nose involuntarily wrinkled up in disgust at a suffocating smell that reminded him of an overloaded latrine. It was an excrement dump site thrown in front of their trenches to discourage Boche spy approaches. Right now, he heeded the frog Sargent's caution to maintain silence and to use hand signals as much as possible, and speaking only as a last resort. Flannery and DeGregorio had to be motioned twice to keep their heads down. After about an hour of zig zaging across the open cratered field and getting closer and closer to the Boche wires, the rat-atat-tat drum beat of a machine gun broke the silence and whining bullets kicked up the dirt in front of and around the squad. This was immediately followed by another machine gun raking across their positions. The machine gun bullets hit the barbed wire with a whiz-zing sound or a loud ping if they hit the iron pole holding the wire upright. They dropped down and hugged the ground, with Sargent Foughet now shouting:

"Down! Down! Le bastards have spotted us!"

The squad was pinned down. They couldn't move because they were enfiladed by two maxim machine guns that criss crossed their position like the letter V. Sargent Foughet pulled out and slowly raised up a portable periscope and tried to locate the machine gun emplacements. He alternately raised up and lowered the periscope in his frantic search. He cleverly did this along some clumps of grass blades and thistles that grew around the top of the shell hole he was in. That growth, sparse as it was, helped camouflage the periscope.

But not well enough, because one of the scattered bullets shattered the top of the periscope and rendered it useless. When George raised himself up to see if he could spot where the machine guns were, he was yelled at to stay down.

"Hell, we can't just sit here!" George yelled back, but was again waved down.

Instead, Sargent Fouget shouted that if their own artillery didn't cover them by shelling back, they would have to make a run for it. They couldn't stay there long, because German artillery shells would be incoming soon, and a Boche assassination squad would follow after that.

Not long thereafter, the American artillery opened up and returned fire. Now the Boche had to duck, or at least had their attention diverted.

"Now! Monsieurs. Out! Out! Zig zag back from hole to hole. Disperse! Disperse! How ze say, spread out, spread out! Go! Go!"

With that, the doughboys took off and Sargent Fouchet stayed behind to cover the squad's withdrawal. He then withdrew himself, as the predicted Boche shells arrived to blanket the area. The squad ran back through no man's land trying desperately to reach their own wire line. George went over to help Sargent Foughet's rear guard action and to offer his rifle expertise. But Sargent Fouchet seemed irked and cut George off in mid-sentence:

"Courir! Courir! Run! Run! Monsieur!"

He frantically waved George away, threw himself against the top of the shell hole and started firing his rifle. A shell landed nearby, the shock of the blast knocking George off his feet and flinging his helmet onto the frozen ground. The showering dirt spray cut into George's face, and hands, while stinging his eyes. George cleared his eyes, and when he saw Sargent Foughet was allright, still waving him off, he quickly grabbed back his helmet and took off.

Stumbling, falling and jumping up again, George ran unevenly across the open field, pocked marked with old shell and mortor holes, chasing after the rest of the wire patrol. Bullets kicked up dirt all around him and the shell explosions got closer and closer. They spread out, every man for himself, and dashed headlong across no man's land, until they had reached their own wire lines. They threw themselves under and over the wire entanglements into their own lines, with covering fire now coming from the riflemen from their own trenches. All but Sargent Fouchet and DeGregorio flung themselves over the American trench tops and fell into the dugout holes. Flannery came out of nowhere from behind George, almost came down on top of him, and smashed one his ankles on a broken trench board. He cried out in pain:

"Ow! Ahh! Damn! I make it all the way back unscathed and I get hurt in my own trench. Don't that beat it all?"

"Hey. You're alive aren't you, Frank. Count your blesings," reprimanded an out of breath, but grateful George.

While Frank was being helped to the nearest aid station, George wondered aloud where DeGregorio was. Just then some nearby doughboys in the Company asked what the hell happened? Where was the frog Sargent? Did you see any Germans?

"Hey guys, give me a break, will ya? I'm just trying to catch my breath," pleaded George.

But Captain Hawkins interceded and ordered the men to get back to their posts. He then asked George if he was all right. George looked himself over looking for blood and felt around his own body. He knew that a strong surge of adrenalin after a strenuous exertion sometimes numbed and masked an injury, temporarily. Although he saw nothing to show he was injured, he kept grabbing his body and feeling his clothing, as if to reassure himself that he was really ok. Still doubtful, but increasingly reassured, he smiled through his sweating and filthy face and jokingly remarked to Captain Hawkins,

"Do you see any bullet holes in me? Did I miss anything?"

"It looks like they did the missing. Congratulations, Border-man, you're now a combat veteran of *this* war."

With that George heard a commotion in an adjacent trench. When they looked toward the sound of the happy agitation, word came down the line that DeGregorio had staggered over the top, with some barbed wire cuts and torn clothing, but otherwise unhurt. But to listen to him, you would think he was dying with his Italian curses railing up into the sky, even as he damned the Germans to an eternal hell for trying to kill him. The doughboys calmed him down and fed him some bracing hot coffee and backslaps of congratulations. As one wag put it:

"Now he thinks he's faster than the Boche bullets! He should count his Catholic blessings, never mind the Bavarian Boche bullets."

"Dilboy, after you have finished your coffee, I want you to go back to the medical tent, not the aid station. Let the docs check you out to see if they count the same number of non-bullet holes in your body as you do. Then come into my tent and give me a report. I'll need one from all of you for my own report to Battalion headquarters. Good to see you back safe and sound."

Having said that, the Captain turned and went on his way to see about DeGregorio and Flannery. But after walking briskly away a few strides, he suddenly stopped and whirled around and faced George and said:

"Oh, by the way, Dilboy. Sargent Foughet is none the less for wear. He reported that you guys stood up well. He was the first one back."

"First one back? How the hell did that happen? He remained behind to cover us! He should get a medal!"

"I'm not surprised. He's a Blue devil, isn't he? They're supposed to be their best."

With that, Captain Hawkins disappeared around the far corner of the trench and George was left to contemplate what had just happened to them. Having been under fire many times before in his other wars, however, he recovered his equilibrium quickly.

"Look at Him! Sitting there smugly, like he doesn't have a care in the world."

So spoke Woz. He ran over to the still sipping George and inadvertently caused him to partially spill his coffee, as he slapped his back and congratulated him on his exciting morning and safe return.

"As I live and breathe, George, like a cat, you must have nine lives. The Turks couldn't shoot you, the Mexicans couldn't hit you and now the Boche bullets miss you. You're a good luck charm. I'm glad we're in the same Company."

"Oh, I've been hit before. It's just that they haven't hit any bone yet. There are advantages to being small, Woz. But that's something you wouldn't know about."

"Well now, there are advantages to being big too. It's just that in a war, I can't think of any."

"Hey, Woz, don't go getting intellectual on me now. But you're right. Every status has its advantages." "I know what you are doing, George. You're staying healthy so you can go home and marry that fiery fiance of yours, who claims she's an angel."

"She doesn't claim to be an angel, I claim she is. She told me in a letter that she loves me so much, she hates me. But she can't divorce me yet, because we aren't married yet. So I have to marry her so she can hate me and divorce me. Does that make any sense?"

"No. But it's not supposed to. You're in love. And when you're in love, nothing makes any sense. So you are right where you are supposed to be."

"Tell that to the Germans and Angelika. They both wish I were somewhere else. Come to think of it, so don't I. And speaking of Angelika, I better write to her soon, or I'll be getting another scolding letter from her."

"Well, you can tell her that the boys of Company H think you are leading a charmed life and are bringing good luck to the whole outfit. That should make her feel good."

"Thanks Woz, I'll do just that. Now get back to your own post, in your own trench, before my luck runs out and you end up in the brig. I have to be debriefed by Captain Hawkins, so he can make his daily report."

The following day George was out at a listening post with Private Frank Flannery. The sector was quiet and they were just chatting to help pass the time, until this duty posting was over. It was safer and less boring, and with more activity back in the main trench line. During the day they were allowed to smoke, so Frank was rolling a cigarette while asking George a question:

"Say George, did you hear the latest story the Frenchies are passing around about our President Wilson?"

"No, I didn't."

"After war was declared, he called together the heads of the Army, Navy and Air Corps. He told them that he was concerned that the German U-boats might sink the ships transporting our troops to Europe. But he thought of a solution. Just heat up the Atlantic Ocean. It will force the the U-boats to the surface, where our fleet can sink them."

"Pershing supposedly asked him, 'But Mr. President, how do we heat up the Atlantic Ocean?'"

"Wilson answers, 'Don't ask me, I just establish policy.'"

George smiled and said: "The beauty of Wilson's lack of war experience is that he'll let Pershing run the war."

Two days later George's first squad and Woz's second squad were detailed to shore up the trench walls that had become unstable because of loose, broken and falling posts and cracked duckboards used as floors in the trenches.

"Hell, Sarge, don't we have an Engineering battalion that does repairs to roads and bridges?" Complained Flannery.

"Yes, but our trenches are not roads and bridges. Shut up and help me pull this post out," directed Woz.

"Hey Pasquale, roll me a cigarette, will you?" Asked Flannery.

"No. I no roll-a cigarette for any paisan. Betta I giva you thisa and you roll-a your own."

"You tell him, Pasquale. Don't take his guff."

"Pasquale, me a good American. Lasta year I go see the Federal Judge. He aska me questions and I answer. But I tolda the Judga, who hada white hair, black robe and much tall. I saya, 'Excusa me, Mr. Judga, Pasquale, me no speaka Englisha too good.'"

Gesturing grandly with his hands, and speaking slowly, but emphatically, Pasquale went on to say:

"The Judga, a mucha handsome paisan. He looka down at me and saya:

"'Thatsa allright Pasquale.'"

"He's a paisana too! America A-ok. Is a gooda country. You roll-a your own cigarette. Qui?"

"Pasquale, we're both U.S. citizens who share, Qui?" Flannery placated a proud Pasquale and handed back his tobacco pouch.

CHAPTER THIRTY THREE

CHEMIN DES DAMES RIDGE

After only two weeks in the Somerville sector northeast of Nancy, the Yankee Division was ordered into the line in a defensive position at Chemin des Dames, replacing the French. Interestingly enough Chemin des Dames means home of the dames and refers to the fact that Louis XIV kept his lovers there. More recently, it had been part of the Sigfried line, later called the Hindenburg Line when extended, before the Boche pulled back. The transfer of the Division required a hundred-mile move northwest from the Nancy-Somerville area by train and marching. Chemin des Dames is a high ridge on a plateau that runs fifteen miles long, running northwest to southeast. Gullies and quaries run down from the ridge. It is an excellent observation post for viewing the countryside for miles around. It has a narrow top ridge that slopes down slightly allowing defending troops to hide from the view of any attacking enemy. The narrow top ridge also helps block the wind when it's blowing in from the direction of the enemy. Its elevation and sharp slopes facing the Boche make it an ideal location to defend the sector.

Much fighting had occurred there earlier in the war. The Germans and the French took turns, back and forth, pushing each other off the ridge. The terrain was a winter wasteland of shell holes, dugouts, and sheared off trees. Winter has a way of freezing time, thought George. He and Woz surveyed the area and shook their heads in dismay:

"Is this mud flat worth fighting for?" Asked Woz rhetorically.

"It must be; they keep fighting over it," replied George.

"It's got to be the sightline. You can see for miles around from up here. It certainly favors the defender in a battle. Whoever controls this ridgeline controls the whole sector," concluded Woz. "Maybe so, but we still must be careful," said George. "For example, when the sun comes up from behind our back, we can be exposed to enemy fire by our dark silhouette."

Company H, commanded by Captain Hawkins, the pipe smoker, took them through the main trench line. Squad by squad they were taken into their dugouts, which were mere crude cutouts, cave like, dug into the side of the trench lines. Army blankets, hung from the top doorframe, served as a door and gave some protection from shell blasts and a hint of privacy. When the Americans came into the line there weren't enough bunks initially, and the ground was frozen, so drafty sandbag houses were built, covered with corrugated tin roofs. They provided protection from the rain, snow and wind, but not the cold. Crude coal and wooden stoves heated water and cook pans, as well as throwing off some, but never enough heat. Unprotected fires of wood, paper and coal were lit, though officially not allowed. They warmed the hands if you got close enough, but not too close, because clothes could catch fire.

It was a constant irritant among the doughboys that the French overcharged them for coal and wood and other necessities, yet they were in France to help save their country. It fueled many an argument or brawl in the rear, protected cities, when on leave. It also may have contributed to some Doughboys feeling free to "liberate" goods from French merchant, stores and shops. The French, for their part, claimed that coal, wood and other goods were scarce and therefore higher priced during wartime.

"Oh, yeah." Spit out an irritated Frank Flannery. "Then how come we get supercharged for the wine that is so plentiful in this country? And they call us thieves!"

This sector was live with shell fire from the rear echelons of the nearby German trenches on the other side of no man's land. From the enemy lead front lines, they were told to expect trench mortar fire and to be ready for grenade raids by the Boche to capture prisoners. Being new into the line, they should expect such "welcoming" attacks from the sneering Boche.

To quell German citizenry fears that millions of Americans were coming into the fray to overwhelm them, the German public relations types denigrated the American soldier as inferior, overmatched against the proud Prussian progeny, unworthy of opposing the professional German soldier, and fit only for fighting a bow and arrow war against naked prairie Indians riding little ponies or Mexican bandits riding donkeys. Hee, hee, they laughed. They enjoyed ridiculing and heaping scorn on the greenhorn hillbillies, plowboys and soft city slickers who would have no stomach for a European War. Ironically, the British and French professional soldiers thought the same way, and this must be one of the reasons Pershing wants us to fight well, thought George.

"And for God's sake, keep your heads down, there are snipers out there," barked Sargent Klick.

In their dugout, George and Woz discussed the reasons for the contempt the Boche had for Americans, and the doubts by the French and the British about American fighting abilities.

"George. It bugs me. They have this superior attitude because they have been getting killed for over three years and we are too foolish and eager to get into the fray, they say. Our inexperience and carelessness endangers them also. Yet they are the ones stuck in the trenches all this time, trying to figure a way out."

"Ease up, Woz. Take it slow. No angry speeches, please. They have a point, up to a point. Let's learn what they have learned before we criticize them. After all, they have lived through three years of war, we haven't."

"Their idea of a war is to dig a hole and use each other for target practice."

"Keep your knickers on, Woz, Pershing has promised a war of movement as soon as the American armed forces are ready."

"How about this, George. Did you hear about the guy in Paris who darted into the street and was hit and killed by a passing US Army truck?"

"No. What about it?"

The French joked that the Americans have killed more French than German's."

"Hee hee. Well, that's funny, not for the victim and his family, of course. And maybe it was true in that city, at that time. Besides, we've killed more French rats, lice and flees than Germans, too."

"Don't give me that crap, George. Are you now a French Advocate, or whatever the French call their Lawyers?"

"No. I'm a US soldier, just like you, my buddy. Let's shoot at the enemy, not ourselves. Fair enough?"

"What the hell does it take to get you angry, George? You're too good natured for your own good. We are at war, you know."

Yes, but not with each other."

"Fair enough, George. Your point."

INCOMING! INCOMING! Someone yelled.

The whistle and whine of incoming high explosive shells suddenly split the air. Explosions shook the ground, throwing dust, bending sideways some candle flames, and blowing out some others, while causing the lone bulb to blink. The soldiers instinctively threw themselves flat on the ground as they were trained to do. They automaticaly ducked their heads and covered their faces to protect their eyes and mouths. Curses and epithets from the downed doughboys swirled in the air. George's arm's and hands began to pain him from the tightness of his self-gripping, so he had learned to let go and loosen up between shell explosions.

George yelled:

"Woz! You ok?"

"Yeah. But where the hell is our own artillery? We've got to give them back some of their own, or we're in for it."

"They have to fix on them first."

"Then where the hell are our lookouts, scouts, observer balloons or aeroplanes?"

A shell landed right next to their trench dugout, the ground trembled, their blanket door was blown out swaying away with the wind, the sole light bulb shattered and they were sprayed with sharp pieces of flying dirt and glass. George jumped up, grabbed his cot and slammed it against the now open door to block further blasts. He then tripped and fell over an ever-cursing Flannery, whose bark was worse than his bite.

"Bastards! We never have enough artillery or aeroplanes! How are we supposed to win this war?"

"Wait a minute! Hold on. Listen. There's our return artillery! Go get 'em boys! Yeah!" Yelled Sargeant Klick.

"It's about God damn time!" Exclaimed a furious Flannery.

"Wait up! What's that smell?" Sniffed George.

From outside the dugout, they could hear the voice of Captain Hawkins:

"Gas! Gas! Masks on! Masks on! Spread the word! Gas masks on!"

"Hell, where is my mask?" Asked George of noone in particular, as he fumbled around his waist. He groped his own body feeling for the mask pouch attached to his belt.

"We're supposed to have them on within six seconds to avoid damage," barked Woz, fumbling and putting on his mask. His voice tailed off, as it was smothered by the mask.

"What smell is he talking about? I don't smell anything," groused a bothered Flannery. "This nose guard irritates my nostrils."

"Just put it on," snapped George. "The Captains been through a gas attack with an advanced detachment, we haven't."

Because the covered faces made talking difficult, or at least hearing difficult, the men, after a few futile attempts to talk, switched to hand signals and motioning. And they had to squeeze whatever talk they did between shell explosions. The incoming shells were intermittent and irregular. The noises of the exploding shells accentuated the silence and the opposite was true also. Most of the talk was unnecessary, and more of a nervous release of fear and tension.

"Damn!" Yelled a frustrated Woz. "My strap broke. It's too small for my head. In adjusting the strap, it broke."

"Here, take mine," volunteered George. "My mask is too big for me, but it'll probably fit you."

They switched and Woz put it on right away and it fit! He gave George the thumbs up sign and tried to help George fix the broken strap. George had been without a mask on for a while now, but it didn't seem to bother him. When he saw that he couldn't fix the broken strap, he pushed Woz's helping hands away and simply tied the loose strap in a knot. Though not airtight, it would do, thought George.

During the next lull in the shelling, Captain Hawkins was again making the rounds, but now he was calling out for the Company to fall back to the second line of trenches: "Fall back! Fall back to the second line. Now! Now!" He was motioning impatiently for all to get out of the front trench line and withdraw. He waved off any questions and pulled up his mask slightly to yell, "Go! Just go!"

The men of Company H, along with the other Companies in the Battalion, clambered out of the trench lines and scrambled back three hundred yards to the back up trench line. The men ran in haphazard order, a contradictory term, back toward this next line of defense. They entered the second line in all sorts of manner. Some climbed down ladders with a semblance of athletic grace and dignity, but most staggered and stumbled like a drunken sailor across uneven, hard ground and leapt and slid into their sudden new home, breathing heavily, safe and excited.

"What the hell was that all about?" Asked a still bothered Flannery, rubbing his ankle up and down from a bone bruise he picked up jumping down into his new trench line. He had banged it against a ladder.

"We can ask Captain Hawkins, when we see him. Where the hell is he, anyway?" Asked Woz.

"Hey, Sargent! What's up?" Yelled George.

"Gas Shells. They followed the high explosives with gas shells. With no breeze to blow the clouds away, we had to get out of there," replied the Sargent Klick.

"What gas? What clouds? I didn't smell anything or see any clouds," complained Flannery.

"Flannery, shut up! You don't know diddly about gas. You don't smell mustard gas; it's almost odorless. It sometimes takes a couple of hours to get into your system. It's individual. Besides we had to get out of that trench line, because mustard gas remains potent in the soil for weeks after the gas shells burst."

Captain Hawkins had come up behind Sargent Klick and added:

"And, in addition, we didn't know if there was an infantry attack behind that high explosive and mustard gas shelling. That's often the case. We'll gladly let them have a trench line chemically infected with mustard gas, their own, no less."

"Hey, Flannery. Over here." The Captain waved him into a nearby dugout through a blanket-door. Once both were inside, the Captain looked serious and through a tight mouth said, "Listen up Flannery, because I'm only going to say this to you once. When I give an order, you jump. You give me any more backtalk and I'll have your ass in a sling all the way back to a rear echelon court-martial. You should know better. Do I make myself clear, Private Flannery?"

"Yes, Sir," replied a chastened Flannery.

"Good. Now get out of here." With that he saluted the Captain and briskly exited the doorway.

Outside, George, Woz and the Sarge looked as if they knew he was reprimanded, but they busied themselves with their own personal doings and said nothing. George pulled out his cigarette pouch, offered Flannery one and they both rolled themselves cigarettes to smoke. They had to get their smoking done during the day; it wasn't allowed at night. No sense lighting up their faces for the enemy snipers to target or trench mortars to zero in on. Woz locked his rifle latch, put it down and joined them.

"Don't mind if I do, thank you George, said Woz as he also took an offered cigarette.

The Sarge lit and raised his pipe to indicate he was all set. They were settling down, after the excitement of the day, reviewing its highlights. It always helped to slowly wind down, if it was quiet, before hitting the sack for the night. First squad was off any duties that night. Through it all the first squad was a team, mused George. They backed each other up, trusted each other and their lives depended on each other. A bonding could result that was

stronger than family, at times. It was comforting and a community
of sorts.

When George bent down to take off his boots to turn in, he
suddenly felt funny and noticed that blisters started forming on
his arms and face. They itched and he instinctively scratched them,
but that seemed to inflame matters and make it worse. Then he
started to cough, choke and feel sick. At this point, Woz noticed
George's discomfort and asked:

"George, what's the matter? You all right"

"No." George gasped. Then he gaged and fell to his knees.

"George! George! Shouted Woz. Frank and Sargent Klick looked
up at the commotion and jumped up and hurried over. The Sarge
ran outside and got a slop bucket and charged in to help George
who was vomiting.

At the same time Frank ran outside yelling, "Medic! Medic!"

Captain Hawkins ran in, looked at George and sized up the
situation immediately:

"Get him to the medical tent! Gas poisoning. He's the second
one, and they'll be others."

"All the docs are tied up with similar cases," said Frank Flannery,
as he ran in.

Woz and the Sarge grabbed a still wretching George and half
carried and half dragged him out of the dugout and back to the
rear medical tent.

"Keep him standing. Don't lie him down. He could choke on
his own vomit," shouted Captain Hawkins. "I've got to see to others.
We've got a slew of these!"

The next day it was relatively quiet, as it usually seems after
an attack, so Woz and the Sargent Gonsalvez from his squad,
were allowed to visit George. However, he was sleeping when
they got there. The nurse told them that after he disgorged
whatever food he had in his system, he was showered to clean
him up and the blisters were treated. They were told it would

take a while for his system to get rid of the inhaled and ingested poisonous mustard gas. He would have difficulty talking for the time being because the mustard gas got into his lungs and dulled his voice.

However, George was expected to recover in time, though somewhat weaker and with some loss of appetite and weight. Long term, they thought he would be all right, as long as he didn't have repeated exposures that could cause some respiratory, breathing or skin problems in the long run. But, as a counterweight, there was some tolerence developed with additional exposure. They would just have to watch and see, hoping for the best. George was young and strong, which was a favorable condition in and of itself, she said.

"Thanks, Doc." Said Woz.

As an aside to Sargent Gonzalez, Woz spoke in a low, confidential voice:

"The Nurses always smile when you call them Doc. It's a compliment when you call a nurse a doctor, because some of them believe they are the ones who really do the hands on healing."

"Oh, ok Dr. Woz Freud, I don't see you as a real lady killer," said a sarcastic and skeptical Sargent Klick.

"I have my hopes. Maybe after I win the French medal Croix de Guerre and become a Brigidier General in this here American Army, the French girls will come after me instead of just the officers."

"Ha! With that mug, it wouldn't do you any good. You'd be better off walking around with a wad of money in your hands. That's your best bet, Mon General."

"Sarge, just because you're ugly, don't try to put the kabosh on my social life. I'm young yet. I just have to develop my personality more."

"Dream on, soldier. Even with the most alluring personality, you'd still be ugly."

"Then we're twins, except you're little ugly and I'm big ugly. _____ Wait a minute, I don't like the way that sounds."

"Ha. You stepped into it there, you big Pole."

"When next we go on leave, let's see who gets the girl. I'll show you."

"You'll have to spend all your money on flowers and candy."

"No I won't. Liquor is quicker."

"Oh, by the way, Sarge, why didn't the Boche take over our front line. They had to know we pulled back," asked Flannery.

"Because they are smart. Having shelled the trench line with poisonous mustard gas, they aren't going to take over the trenches and poison themselves with their own mustard gas."

"That probably means it'll be a race to the front trench-line in two weeks, when the trenches are cleared."

"Or sooner, Woz. Because we've got chemical experts periodically testing and checking the trench lines for poison gas levels. And we are already on the ridge and can look down on them. And we can more easily hide under the lip of the ridge. So we can spy on them better than they spy on us. After all, they must come up the slope, we don't. The age old advantage of higher ground."

"Well, we'll see soon enough."

Just before two weeks had expired, and to cut off any takeover of the front trenches, they were ordered back to the trench lines they had temporarily abandoned. Aerial surveilance, balloon observations and scouting patrols did not reveal any Boche movement to take over the ridge. This surprised the Intelligence people, given the tactical advantage of the heights and the battle history of this sector. But it also suggested that something was going to happen somewhere else, because the German High Command was planning a big push all along the Western Front with a million new, but battle hardened troops. These, they knew, were being rushed from the Eastern Front, now that Russia had capitulated to the terror-twin German Generals, Hindenburg and Ludendorf.

The German's wanted to capture Paris before the Americans could arrive in strength and the Yanks were already landing 40,000 troops every month and more in the French ports. The Allies were getting stronger, while the Central Powers, primarily Germany, were getting weaker. The Germans wanted to either win the war or force an Armistice while they still had an intact Army and were not backed up fighting on German soil. They wanted to negotiate from strength. Time was against them, so it was of the essence. Though the Chemin des Dames Ridge was a hot spot earlier in the war, it was supposed to be a quiet zone now, and was one of the reasons the Americans got this sector to take over from the Frenchies to continue the defense, the guys in the Yankee Division were told.

George was welcomed back into the line by the guys in Company H with their typical brand of affectionate humor, characterized by a generous supply of insults and caustic remarks.

"Dilboy, were you grabbing those French nurses?"

"Hey, George, you're the only guy I know who got a vacation in a hospital for breathing."

"Say, Mr. Border-man, did they give you a purple-heart for inhaling Flannery's fart-gas?"

"You know, if you guys used your trigger fingers as well as your mouths, we could win this war sooner," George shot back, smiling and thrusting back with his own barbs.

"Does anybody know why we were put beside the French instead of the British, when both the Brits and us speak English?" Asked Roddy O'Byrne, a beefy six footer, and handsome ladies man in Woz's second squad.

"Lets ask Dewey Akers, he's English," said Private Phil Dodger, a rascal in George's first squad, who had a permanent smirk on his face, as if he knew something you didn't.

"Whadda ya asking me for? Phil's English too," protested Dewey.

"I'm only half-English. You're a full-blooded limey," answered Phil back.

"Hey, Phil, don't call me a limey. That's what they use to call British sailors because they gave them limes to go with their daily portions of rum while at sea. I'm in the Army, the United States Army, in case you hadn't notice, you donkey's ass."

"Oh, for heavens sake, does anybody know?" Queried Dave Cochrane, a red haired Celtic descendant who claimed his ancestors originally came from Germany.

Captain Hawkins entered the conversation and offered an interesting opinion:

"Possibly because we would be too quick to argue with the British, both speaking English, whereas we have to stop and understand the French first. Besides, the British still think of us as a runaway colony of theirs."

"Well the Irish are part of the British Army and they don't get along," commented Woz.

"Yes, but they are a British colony or something like that, aren't they?" asked George.

"They must be, because they keep talking about Home Rule for Ireland, whatever that means. Some type of self-government," said Roddy O'Bryne.

"But that's a British-Irish thing. The British don't get along with the French either. They also have a feuding history that goes back centuries," said Captain Hawkins. "And I'm English by my ancestry."

"This French Blue Devil was telling me that the British are ok once you understand their peculiarites, chimed in Sargent Gonsalvez. "They appear remote and standoffish, but they do care. For example, they have a stiff upper lip style of sizing up a situation. They talk about the time forty years ago when a small British unit was defending an outpost in the Transvaal in South Africa, wherever that is. The British soldiers were surrounded by ten thousand Zulu warriors. There are only two Brits left alive, a thousand spears are in mid-air and they're seconds from death, when one turns to the other and says,

"Bit of a sticky wicket, Sir."

"No wonder they think we Americans are so excitable, crude and undisciplined," said George.

"And we think they are rigid, inflexible and pompous know-it-alls with their understated ways," exclaimed Davy Cochrane.

"I wonder if the Germans have this problem with the Austrians and Turks?" Wondered Woz.

"No, because they just give them orders. It's the Prussian military way, given their history," said George.

"Looks like we all have our differences. We've got to learn to get along," reasoned Captain Hawkins.

"That's the most sensible thing I've heard tonight. Captain, if we could, we would make you the chief diplomat and you could stop the war all by yourself, and we could all go home," stated a confident Sargent Klick.

"And I'm German, that is, German-American now."

They all laughed at the absurdity of the comment, and broke away to turn in for a good night's sleep.

———————

For the time being the Chemin des Dames Ridge lived up to it's recent label as a quiet sector for both sides. Artillery battles occasionally broke out from long range, but for the most part it was certainly not a hot spot of attacks and counter-attacks. Though the lull was appreciated, it gave both sides the opportunity to build up their forces so they would be ready to enter the warmer attack and battle season fast approaching. French, British and fewer American aeroplanes were seen headed to and over the front lines to observe and occasionally, but more frequently, to bomb and strafe the ground forces with machine gun fire.

The Allies knew from the huge build up of German troops that attacks were coming, but just when and where? They only knew they wouldn't have to wait long, because the weather was improving, and this favored movement. They were right.

CHAPTER THIRTY FOUR

QUIET ZONE, THEN . . . .

George was walking jauntilly back to his dugout with a big smile on his face, as he excitedly opened a letter. Roddy O'Byrne was walking the other way with that trademark silly grin on his face, when he spotted George.

"Hey, George, did you get another letter today at mail call, me boyo? Jayus, you must have more than one girlfriend."

"Two letters today, as a matter of fact, you smirking boyeen, you. And I have only one intended. She's as loyal and her letters are as frequent as the mail service here allows. And you'd trade all your temporaries for one permanent, like my sweatheart. So eat your heart out."

They each laughed and waved at each other, as they continued on their separate ways. George couldn't wait until he reached his bunk, so he just squated down where he was and read the letter, absorbed in its contents.

> *Dear Georgie-Porgie,*
>
> *I am fine. And so are my folks. That's why we need to hear from you, because it means you're alive. I get sick with anxiety reading the casualty lists published in the newspapers or posted at church and at the Post Office.*
>
> *I am having trouble getting bolts of cloth for the shop. Much is being diverted to the war effort for military uniforms, sheets, bandages and the like, for our fighting doughboys. I am enclosing handkerchefs and mittens so you can clear your nose and keep your hands warm. I don't operate the motor car much*

because petrol is rationed and instead, I take the trolley car up
Webster Avenue to Central Square to the shop.

I try to write as often as I can. I know you can't always,
but do try. I so worry. And don't tell me not to. I can't help it. My
mother wants me to go to the Army socials and dances to help
entertain the soldiers and keep their morale up. I go, but I see
those uniforms and I pine for you. I just close my eyes and pretend
that I'm dancing with you. That helps my morale.

You are in my prayers always. I have made a deal with
God that if he brings you home safely into my arms, I'll control
my temper and be nicer to you. And I'll help out at the church
more, too.

All for now. I love you truly. Here's your kiss.

Love,
Your Angelika

George looked up and said to nobody in particular,
"Ha, can you believe it? She sends me handkerchefs and mittens.
Mittens! How can I pull a trigger with mittens on? Who uses
handkerchefs on the front lines? What next, china and silverware?
Oh, well. She means well, that's the important thing. I don't care
what she sends or says, as long as she writes. She's my lifeline."

"Hey, George," yelled Woz, you talking to yourself again?"

"Yes! You bet," said George, smiling back. "And when I stop
talking, that's when you can take me to the crack-up squad."

"Oh, Georgee honeybee, may I see that lovely, laced
handkerchief?" Teased an innocent looking Private Dodger.

"Yes, George, could I borrow your mittens for a sleigh ride?"
asked a female poseur, Dewey Akers, while twittering his fingers.

"All right, Guys, knock it off. You've had your fun," commented
a chastened George.

"Don't mind them," piped in Woz, "they're just jealous."

George got up, while folding his precious letter, and announced
he was going to see the posted duty roster to see what his next
scheduled assignment was, because "somebody in this God forsaken
company has to stay on the ball."

"You do that George, and don't forget to put your mittens on. You don't want to get frostbite, the missus will never forgive you," chided a parting Sargent Gonzalvez.

As George walked over to the duty post in the rear, he wondered to himself,

"What is it this time? Skywatch, messenger duty, sentry post, wire patrol, scouts out, radio post, sniper squad, stretcher aid or stand by, as he ran over the list of possibilities in his mind. He looked at the list for his name and tomorrow's assignment, as other soldiers backed up behind him.

"Argonne Forest?" George found himself speaking out spontaneously. He looked at the others and all they did was shrug and walk away with their own assignment. George hurried away looking for Captain Hawkins for clarification.

"Hey, Sargent Sardonis, what's my assignment to the Argonne Forest mean?"

"Damn if I know, George. See the Captain."

"I'm looking for him already."

"He's by the mess tent," said a passing doughboy.

George hurried ahead and caught up to him. "Captain! Captain! What's happening in the Argonne Forest?"

"Oh, Dilboy. Yeah, I had yet to get a hold of you. You and a few others in the 26th are being sent as temporary sniper squad special detachments. The Boche have infiltrated back into the Argonne Forest and are digging in with machine gun nests. Corps Headquarters wants them driven out pronto. They think it may be a breakout point for their expected spring offensive."

"But that's sixty miles northwest of here?"

"I know. Check in at daybreak at Battalion Headquarters. They are trafficking the special detachments. Your travel plans are on a need to know basis, and I don't need to know. Pick up your orders first at Company Headquarters. Good luck."

George went straight to Company Headquarters where a Lieutenant Farrugut gave him his special orders and told him something about the Argonne Forest. "It's a dense forest, with many close growing trees with heavy leaves, ideal for defense. It's on a ridge that rises about 300 feet above the ground around it. It rains a lot in the area, which is about fifteen miles long by five miles wide, north to south. Best of luck."

George went straight back to his tent, his home when not in the front trenches. He was two days away from a ten-day relief from his support role. Barring emergencies, his rotation cycle was ten days in the front trenches, then a ten day stint as support in a secondary defense line and then ten days back in the rear in reserve. At the end of that cycle, his Company was supposed to stand down on leave for rest and recreation from twenty four hours to three days, depending on the situation as determined by the Commanding Officer, usually a General. His special assignment trumped his line status.

"Too bad, George" said Woz. But we're lucky to be in a quiet zone, so that's some consolation."

"And I might get to meet some of our British brothers. They are up in that direction somewhere. In the line, we never get to see the big picture. Maybe they can add to my limited knowledge. We have to look ahead and survive. Which reminds me. I'd better write. Nobody knows if I'll have a return trip from a special assignment."

George sat down and wrote to his parents and then to Angelika.

My precious Angelika,

Here we are somewhere in France surviving on Army grub made edible by my constant thoughts of you. It is nourishment that will get me from here to your warm side. I think of you constantly. Your beautiful face takes me from these pockedmarked, barren fields, the lice, the always hungry rats, the cold, rain and mud, and lifts me to a dream world where I hug you to my heart and it warms my soul.

Oh, how I long to fall into your loving arms, to whiff the alurring aroma of your perfume, to hear your sighs and feel your fresh breath against my face, and to sink into your full lips. I even miss your sharp voice that narrows to an anguished point when you are miffed at me, push me away and formally call me

"Mr. George Dilboy," like a stern teacher. And you are my teacher, and I hope I am your favorite student.

We talk tough in the trenches, but we are really scared boys, yearning to go home to hold our loved ones. We all think the other guy will get hit, not us. But only God knows. I cannot change my destiny. It is heartbreaking and pathetic to see our soldiers suddenly shot down wounded and crying out for their wives, sweathearts, mothers and their God. If I think about it too much, I'll go crazy.

I don't know how the medics do it. They are the real hero's of this war, going out into no man's land unarmd, to drag back injured doughboys, while ignoring explosions, rifle fire and machine guns. The Salvation Army is a Godsend. They give us food, clothing, cheerful encouragement and want nothing in return. They complement the fine efforts of the Red Cross and Special Service People, who try to entertain us and help according to their limited means.

Keep your letters coming, my angel. They keep me going. I don't feel as brave as I try to look. When you sign your name, kiss it and I will also. That way our lips will meet across the miles. My dearest, I long for your touch.

Your dugout dandy,
George

ARGONNE FOREST

Because of George's keen marksmanship, he was considered a specialist and had been told that he might be pulled out of sector and specially assigned as part of a rolling group as an attachment to special unit duty. War being predictably unpredictable, he was told he could be called at any time and to be ready to leave on a moment's notice. He could not even tell other members of his unit. They would be told only that he was on special assignment.

A chess game and a war of nerves was being waged to unsettle each other, as each side maneuvered to be in the better position to start the spring offensive that everyone knew was coming. Meanwhile, local skirmishes and harrassment raids continued. George had been looking forward to the scheduled rotation of moving out of the line to a support and then a reserve position, and then leave. Sometime during this backup position he was looking forward to getting deloused. His itching and scratching lice all over his body was driving him to fits of distemper. The "cootie" or lice parasites caused many of the trench fevers that would force many doughboys into the medical tents for several days with high temperatures, fevers and would drain their energy, and weaken them considerably.

The vermin, individually, was the size of a small grain of uncooked rice, until they gorged themselves on the blood of their victims and became like blood sucking leeches. To control this menace, the Army had a delousing program. However, this program consisted of visits to the troops that were all too infrequent. The delousing machine was a crude, awkward device, consisting of a large tank-truck connected to a steam generator. It looked like a cement mixer. The soldiers had to strip naked, even in the cold of winter, wrap their clothes into a bundle and throw them into the tank. Once the lice infested clothes were inside the tank portion of the truck, hot steam scalded the critters and killed them. Meanwhile, the doughboys covered their shivering, naked bodies with overcoats, jumping up and down to generate some body heat and stood as close to the tank as possible, to absorb the heat.

In addition, any heat generating alcohol was gratefully welcomed, though officially forbidden. Either the officers overseeing this operation got dust in their eyes, or they winked at this rule. An officer who was an Attorney in civilian life helped the cause by saying the rule was directory, not mandatory. This made a lot of sense to the shivering doughboys. Some lawyers were all right, they agreed.

This cleansing process made them temporarily louse-free, until they went back down into the trenches, crawled into their dugout hay-beds, and again became infected. It couldn't be helped; this was war.

George formed up with his special detachment that was given the specially assigned name of Quick Company, which they certainly were, and herded to a truck convoy to the nearest train. The French controlled the train system. They traversed the countryside, while discussing their briefing above the rythmic clattering of the noisy train wheels. They had to almost shout to hear each other.

"They're sending us against machine gun nests?" Asked George, seeking confirmation.

"That's right. Machine guns are most effective against a mass attack, because they can kill more soldiers. But if they are only fighting against our sharpshooters, they have less to shoot at, and waste a lot of ammo. We have hit their ammo dumps to drain their supply. Besides, General Pershing wants to demonstrate the value of the best rifle in the world, our Springfield '03, and our best sharpshooters. That's the theory, anyway," said Captain Hawkins, also detached and assigned to lead Quick Company.

"Maybe, but we can be enfiladed easier, too. Are we being experimented with or sacrificed?" Continued George, as the others listened.

"No. And you won't be unsupported. Air cover and surveillance is promised. You'll also have some hotchkiss machine gun support, artillery call-up, trench mortors and some French tanks. We aren't expected to drive them out of the forest, just back. We want to test their strength and to keep them off balance. If it's a major thrust, we'll be pulled back into a waiting defensive line."

The train stopped in the middle of a ravine and they marched off to their assigned positions. What they saw when they first looked at the Argonne Forest surprised them. It was quiet. No enemy activity could be detected. Patrols were sent into the forest, while George and his were held in reserve. When the patrols reached their assigned penetration point and reported no enemy contact, they were tasked to go deeper into the forest to a second penetration point. Captain Hawkins and Quick Company were ordered into the forest to verify there were no signs of Germans. George and his Company bent into a crouch and spread out fifteen to twenty yards apart, always staying in sight of the man to their right and left. Hand signals told them when to stop. Radio contact kept the extreme points informed of each other's situation.

The silence was eerie, thought George. In this deathly quiet forest, listening to the moaning of the spirits in the murmur of the pines, George heard his own uneasy breathing struggling to stay calm, and fighting the urge to scream to break the building tension. But he caught himself, by thinking of his mother's earthly wisdom calling him to remember that God is the friend of silence. Look at nature, she urged, and see how trees, flowers and grass grow in silence; see how the moon, the stars and the sun move in silence; and see how the falling snow waltzes down from heaven, in silence.

The only noise in the sound-muted forest was an occasional wind, whispering through the high trees and knocking an occasional leaf off its limb. George watched as one leaf snapped off its branch and floated and swayed its way to the ground. It was calming to watch its descent, but George had to shake his head to snap out of a mesmeric trance and to stay alert. There were no enemy planes to look out for in a tall, full leafed forest, and the enemy would be on the ground. He blinked his eyes to stay focused and to stare ahead at the long, straight avenues of towering trees whose foilage roofed the forest floor. George knew he was approaching the trees, but in an odd instance of optical allusion, it seemed that the trees were approaching him. George attritributed this reversed phenomenon to the factor of fear that can distort your perceptions, and make your mind play tricks on you. George comforted himself with the thought that this is when faith in God's will makes you persevere and to trust and follow your instincts. Acknowledging this, he nevertheless maintained a sharp look out ahead for any sudden movement that might mean danger. This also honored his belief that God helps those that help themselves. Though George never thought of himself as overly religious, it was amazing how such a quiescent belief takes center stage when death may be a bullet away.

After a couple of hours through the forest, they stopped to rest and ate some rations. The advance patrols had reached the outer, other side of the forest and reported all was clear. The troops walked back out of the forest relieved, but also wanting to know what intelligence there was to merit this special detachment chasing ghosts. Apparently, the Germans weren't the only ones that were nervous. George and his Quick Company cohorts relaxed their guard, but also felt foolish. They were recalled to their starting point and brought back to the train siding where they had to wait. Because a train couldn't be comandeered immediately, due to other priorities, they had to bivouac in the ravine overnight. The train arrived late the next morning and they rolled back on the rails to the Chemin des Dames Ridge again.

Back at camp within two days of leaving, Woz accused George of going on a 48 hour leave and living it up.

"Well, if I did have a 48 hour leave, how come these damn lice didn't?" Complained George, as he freely scratched away at his body.

"OK, George, I believe you, don't scrape yourself raw on my account. I have my own cooties."

"Just don't ask me why we went on a wild goose chase. But at least it broke up the monotony."

"Well, Flannery won't be bored for long. Private Flannery, have you seen the duty board?" Asked Sargent Klick.

"Not yet. What's up?"

"Your nose, for one thing." Captain Hawkins added.

"Oh, no. Not the crap squad!" Groaned Flannery.

"Waste bucket duty, is the appropriate term," said Private Dodger, trying hard to smother a chuckle. "If we weren't trapped so much in the trenches by enemy artillery, and were able to get back of the lines to the latrines, we wouldn't need waste buckets for our body wastes."

"Why am I not let out of this offal duty, I'm allergic to it."

"You're allergic to your own crap?" Asked Corporal Cochran, incredulous.

"No, to someone else's."

"Too bad, Flannery, you're both in the same war," responded Cochran.

"The French don't complain, they just do it," commented Roddy O'Byrne.

"Oh, yeah, well I'm not French, which makes me wonder why I'm even here? Queried Flannery.

"You're here to save Democracy. That's what Wilson says," remarked Dewey Akers.

"No, we're not. We're here because the Germans kept sinking our ships and killing Americans," protested Flannery.

"We went to war when the diplomats failed to maintain the peace," claimed Sargent Gonzalez.

"Peace? We'll have peace when one side runs out of soldiers, ammo, or food. Simple as that," claimed Flannery.

"Well, if that's true, then the million new German troops released from the Eastern Front with Russia's collapse will be met by three million American soldiers coming. So we'll win," asserted Sargent Sardonis.

"That's why the Germans will attack now, before our Army gets too big," said Cochrane.

"And that's why the Brits and the Frenchies are doing cartwheels to get Pershing to put the American soldiers into the line, ready or not. Otherwise, it may be too late," opined Sargent Gonzalez.

"The French are always catastrophizing and Lloyd George is deliberately holding back additional British troops from his own General Haig and the front, because of the huge injuries and deaths of British soldiers," added Sargent Sardonis. "He's catching hell from the widows back home. He's afraid his government will come down."

"I'm glad all I have to do is pull the trigger," said Flannery, as he slowly staggered toward the front trench line to do his duty.

"Poor Flannery, he doesn't know the half of it. When I left the trenches last night, the engineers were trying to work the pumps

EDDIE BRADY

to empty the trenches of two feet of water," confided Captain Hawkins.

The following day Company H and the rest of the 26th Yankee Division were pulled on schedule from their support rotation and were to stand down early on leave for a ten-day period, skipping a reserve status. They were told that they were pulled out of the regular rotation because they would be reassigned to a new "hot" sector when they returned from leave. For security reasons, they were not told where they were going until they returned from leave. What they weren't told, but could surmise, was that the Army command did not want to jeopardize their mission by an overdrinking doughboy spilling the beans while on leave. German spies and agents were about. They understood the need of the troops to unwind, but did not want to burden them with mission details that might compromise the safety of their fellow soldiers.

George, Woz, Frank Flannery and Pasquale DeGregorio went on leave together. Flannery referred to Pasquale as Pas. Since they were forbidden to go to Paris without special orders, they went to nearby Soissons, the important railroad crosroads town to do their partying. They were accorded a warm welcome, that is, their money was. While at a local bar, and as the night wore on, a British Journalist got into an argument with an American Intelligence Officer. Both had been drinking freely. With his inhibitions thereby reduced, the Brit writer lit into the American officer:

"It has been ten months since your Congress declared war on Germany. By now we expected to see two million cowboys throw themselves on the Huns and we see only a few thousand damn workers building warehouses. When are you going to fight?"

The American Intelligence officer replied that:

"Britain didn't have to transport combat troops 3, 000 to 6,000 miles, as well as all the support units required to put a full Army in the field. We are also more a land nation, not an Island nation like Britain, and don't have a ready fleet to transport two million troops in a matter of months, never mind the required time to properly train raw recruits."

While this spirited discussion was going on besides George's group, George was urging his guys to stay out of the argument, the American Intelligence Officer was handling it and keeping the lid on. Trying to mind his own business, George was amused as Flannery went after a local damsel who let him buy her a drink. They paired off and moved to a separate table. Woz had a weakness for blondes, brunettes and redheads and waved at George as he signaled to him that he was going to work the floor, and walk around. Pasquale got involved with a friendly discussion with a couple of French soldiers.

George was holding his drink and looking around the bar, when he was approached by a dark haired French woman with a short, pixie haircut, who was trying not to fall out of her low cut dress.

"The handsome Yankee soldier would like a good time, qui?"

"I am having a good time, thank you, Mademoiselle."

"I charge you only fifty francs, you say yes, Monsieur?"

"Why has the price doubled since yesterday? What gives?"

"Me Francine, I give you cognac, food, service, qui? Why not you give me money? You have money, qui?

"You mean you are charging American soldiers these high prices just because we've got the money?"

Francine just shrugged and said: "That is the way, c'est ne pas, is it not so in Amerika?"

"Charging a fair price, yes. An unfair price, no."

"What else can you spend on? I give good time, convenient. You pay for both, so is higher. We are at war, are we not?"

"Oh, I see. Blame the war. Your French soldiers are in the war, but you charge them less."

"I make love, not war."

"Oh, you don't want to get together with me. I have one of those transferable disease's," warned George.

"Qui, Monsieur. It is, how you say, ok. So have I."

George was so stunned by this answer, that, at first, he couldn't say anything. Then he got a hold of himself and, pulling his empty pockets inside out, he said:

"See, I don't have any money."

"Oh, Monsieur, you joke with me. I go!"

She then bolted away in a huff, throwing her hands up in the air, and muttering a common French curse. Woz had returned and heard the latter part of the conversation and asked George:

"Why did you tick her off, George? You have no disease and you do have money."

"Yes, up here in my shirt pocket. I'm wary of pickpockets. As to her, I just wanted her to go, and she did. Mission accomplished."

Back at the local, available room where they were able to get a double room, the guys discussed last night's happenings, since they were now in the early morning. Flannery talked about meeting a Marine who disembarked at Cherbourg, and who overheard two Boche prisoners working the docks. While watching seeming endless streams of doughboys walking down the ramps, one says to the other:

"Schmidt, there's no end to them. The Kaiser is kaput!"

But now Flannery was already passed out asleep, having drunk himself into oblivion, muttering inaudibly to himself, something about sleeping in a real bed. The rest of the foursome was sitting at their beds smoking and regaling each other with their experiences of the prior evening.

Woz talked about running into a soldier from the Irish Guards. He introduced himself as a Jimmy McBride. He asked the Irisher if he was drafted or enlisted.

"I enlisted, I did. It's me head. I must have been daft,' said Jimmy.

"I asked him why he enlisted."

He said to me, "I'm daft, I tell yer. I believed the Brits and their posted ads and lorries carrying signs all about Dublin. The signs said, 'Better the trenches in France than the slums of Dublin.' Serve the Crown and make history. Make history? Be history is more likely."

"So the trenches aren't better?"

"Are you after being daft, yourself, laddie? Of course t'isn't! I was eighteen and without work. What did I know about this here war?"

"I suppose a lot of us could say that," I said.

"I was snookered, was I not?" He countered. "I gets me a clean uniform, a roof over me head and adventure. For what, I asks yer? To be blasted to hell, flooded, rat infested trenches, lice until I'm always lousy, poison gas, mortor and artillery shells, putrid food, buddies blown to bits and me mind all scrambled. Three fecking years of it! I don't know how much more I can take. It's the man upstairs who will decide when my time has come. Me Da says I'm to do the best I can and me Ma says ta keep praying. So that's what I do. Let's lift our drinks, me boyo. To your health, Yank. Let's hope yer can help us end it."

"I'll drink to that," I told him.

"George, the poor enlister was all but worn out. Let's hope he's right and we can both help end it all."

"That's why we're over here, Woz. Let's get some shut eye, while we're on leave and not being shelled."

When their leave expired, all too quickly, George and Woz reported back to the Chemin des Dame Ridge for re-assignment.

CHAUMONT

The signing of the Treaty of Brest-Litovsk took the defeated Russians out of the war. Thus, what the Allies most dreaded, happened. As forecast, this released a million battle hardened German troops from the Eastern Front. These troops were cocky after crushing the Czar's Armies. On March 21, 1918 the Germans began their long expected spring offensive. They took aim at the British across the River Lys in Northeastern France and against the French further south driving toward Soissons and Chateau Thierry. The British and especially the French were panicky.

A few days later, Pershing received an unannounced personal visit at his American headquarters at Chaumont from a clearly shaken General Henre Petain, the savior of Verdun. The Commander in Chief of all French Forces on the Western Front was a desperate man when he walked in on a surprised General Pershing.

"The Germans had broken through both the British and French Forces in a massive offensive attack all along our lines," he announced dramatically. "If Pershing didn't release American troops to help now, it might be too late and the Americans could conceivably be fighting the Germans alone."

A stunned and clearly impressed Pershing realized that he had to do something. To reassure a pleading Petain, Pershing stated with equal drama that he would put all American Expeditionary Forces at the service of Marshall Foch, as Supreme Commander. Pershing authorized release of American combat troops to critical defense points along the Allied Front. Specifically, he rushed American infantry norhwest to join the British Army in the defense of Amiens on the Somme River and later to Cantigny. He also issued orders for American doughboys to immediately entrain further north to Ypres and Kemmel, thirty miles inland from the important coastal port of Calais.

He would also shortly issue mobilization orders to get US Marines up to the enlarging Chatieu Thierry bulge into Allied lines to block the anticipated German drive toward Paris. This would also, even more critically, involve the Marines and US Army's 26th Yankee New England Division in the desperate defense and then offense at Belleau Wood. The Germans, stopped cold at Chateau Thierry, would try to go around the dug in Marines by rushing west to Belleau Wood, only to be stopped again and again after seven separate counterattacks against US Marine and Army units, before being driven back in the American counter-offensive. The Americans were now being thrown into the war all along the Western Front, ready or not.

CHAPTER THIRTY FIVE

TOUL-BOUCQ SECTOR

Meanwhile back at base camp, Captain Hawkins called Company H to gather round, while he stood on top of a lorry. This time the horses were detached and taken away. No chance that still-attached horses would suddenly bolt and throw off the officer speaking to the assembled troops, like happened to Captain Warrenton of Company C, back at Liffol-le Grand. The troops learned something every day, more on-the-go training.

"All right, listen up. Can you hear me in the back?"

"No. You gotta speak up!" Yelled a chorus from distant small group.

"Wrong! **You** gotta move up, retorted the Captain. Otherwise, ask those who can hear."

"Ok, you've been bugging me for days, so here it is. The 26th is moving out to Apremont-Seicheprey line in the Toul-Boucq Sector. Seicheprey is pronounced Sea-pray. That's a ten-mile line of defense. This is a **hot zone**, so you better stay alert. And that's twenty four hours on alert. Even asleep, you may have to leap up."

"What sleep?" Came a voice from the ranks. Captain Hawkins ignored it.

"You're coming from a quiet zone into a hot one. Pershing designed your training on a step up basis, from a quiet zone to an active defense to a hot zone. Everything is subject to change in this war. You may be given no notice, so be ready for anything. This is mean and nasty territory. Questions? Just yell out."

"Where is this place?"

"Toul is about ninety miles southeast of here. It's fifteen miles from Nancy, which is right on the frontier of no man's land. Nancy is a larger town than Toul, but Toul is one of the most critical railroad links on the Allied side of the front. The town is important enough to merit almost daily aeroplane bombing attacks by the Boche. In this sector, Apremont and Seicheprey are small villages on opposite ends of our defense line. Next question."

"When do we move out?"

"Now."

"No other questions? Ok, form up in columns of four. Sargents, take over and move them out quick-step to the 40 and 8 trains."

With that dismissal order, a loud groan and shrieks of complaints rented the air. The French 40 and 8's were cold, drafty and rickety cattle cars used to transport soldiers. They were very uncomfortable and dreaded by the troops. Since the doughboys favorite activity was to gripe, their complaints were deflected:

"Save it for the Heinies, you bellyachers! Move it out!" Scowled Sargent Sardonis.

They treked a short distance to the waiting train cars. They moved rapidly up a pair of wobbly planks, with one doughboy losing his balance and falling off. The doughboys roared in laughter and heaped on the embarrassed doughboy gratuitous insults:

"Hell of a swan dive, Conroy!"

"Take ballet lessons, you idiot!"

"Was it a strong wind?"

"Who farted and knocked him off?"

"Jayus, how far will a bullet knock him?"

As on their train trip across France from LeHavre, they seemed to spend more time stopped or on a siding than in motion. They hadn't gone forty miles when, after one long stop, they were ordered off the train. They plunged into deep mud, made worse when it started to rain. While track repairs were being made to shell damaged rails they were marched along the undulating counrtyside. To quell the angry outbursts from the dismounted soldiers, Sargent Gonzalez broke out in song, leading a garbled rendition of the popular song, *"Pack all your troubles in your old kit bag and smile,*

smile, smile." It put some rhythm into their steps, distracted them from their misery, and helped pass the time.

Led by a Marine Sargent guide, they marched for seven hours. The exhausting march led them through a number of small villages, by roofless houses, shattered windows that left glass spread across the ground like glistening snow, crumbling concrete walls and machine gun bullets marks stitched across stone cemented buildings.

One village was large enough to have streetcar tracks and a church spire that had been cut in half by shellfire. Some villagers had fled west, but most stayed home tolerating, with a martyr's patience, the German incursions into France from close-by Lorraine. These poor villagers had endured the rumble and explosions of gunfire for three long years and appeared tired and resigned. But when they saw the soldiers marching past were Americans, who had come across the ocean to help the Allies throw back the hated Hun, smiles cracked their faces. Men doffed their caps, women waved their aprons from street corners and shop doorways, while uttering weary, but hearty hurrahs. "Viva Yanks, Viva Wilson," and "God bless you's," rang out, while the glint of the sun flashed against the tears of those who dared to hope for deliverence. Some Children jaunting along tried to march in step with the doughboys, while others innocently waved their hands, copying their mothers and fathers. It was not the wild scene as happened in Paris, but a battered, local village version hoping its wishes would come true.

Out on the roadways, trucks carrying infantry drove by and taunted the crews ferrying artillery guns being pulled by draft horses. The doughboys bantered back,

"Hey, you artillery gunners move outta the way. We'll be lunching in Berlin before you reach Metz."

"Without artillery to bail you footsloggers out, you'll be in Berlin allright, as prisoners of war."

Marching along nearby, Woz remarked to George that, "We ought to appreciate the artillery accompanying us, or we would be getting the guff they're getting."

"Artillery just takes up more of the road and draws attention," said George.

As soon as George said that, they heard, "Move over for a real Army, you National Guard play soldiers, the Big Red One of the First Division is passing! Eat our dust!"

Woz couldn't help himself as he yelled back, "Yeah, you start the fight and we'll finish it, as usual!"

Other transports passed by, including old double decker omnibuses that previously had plowed the streets of Paris. They had the bottom windows blocked by wooden boards, so the windows wouldn't shatter and injure the doughboy passengers. "But didn't omnibusses make bigger targets?" Wondered Woz.

George noticed Captain Hawkins and Lieutenant Malone checking their watches periodically. He assumed they were anxious to reach their designated points on schedule. They knew that Pershing and his command staff wouldn't hesitate to relieve an officer who they thought lagged behind and couldn't cut it.

Though the rain had finally stopped after thoroughly soaking the marching doughboys, it still threatened, so they pulled off to the side of the road and camped under trees on the edge of dense woods for some leaf cover. They had rested for fifteen minutes, more or less, every two hours or so. Then having travelled an additional thirty miles since detraining, they rested for an overnight bivouac. The next morning they were awakened by the noisy, but welcome, sound of a troop transport train.

"Hell, I never thought I would be glad to see one of those damn French 40 and 8's," remarked a smiling George.

"It sure beats walking and it's got a roof, of sorts, to block the rain," commented Woz.

The train, this time, took them the rest of the way to their destination, which was only about twenty miles. They detrained the last day of March, "just in time for the spring winds and rain," remarked Private Flannery.

"That's better that January and February's cold, frost and snow," rebutted George.

"Dilboy, you're such an optimist. You must be in love, with all those letters you get."

"Ha! He's on to you, George," chuckled Woz.

"What if I am? You're all just jealous. Eat your hearts out."

Once the American 26th Division arrived in the Toul sector, the French 1st Division was withdrawn. When relieving the French comrades, they greeted the doughboys effusively in broken English and fluent French, shook their hands, hugged and even kissed them on both cheeks, as was their custom. They wished the Americans luck, answered questions enthusiastically, like how to detect the difference in the sound of the shells, which were friendly and departing and which were arriving and German. They told how the German's were trained to group sing patriotic songs, which the Allied forces could hear if the evening was quiet, or the wind was blowing towards Allied lines. They told their replacements to be careful of picking up German souvenirs, because they are frequently bobby-trapped with grenades. They warned about the Boche raid parties to capture prisoners to interrogate them to find out who their new in-the-line adversaries were and other intelligence information.

They further warned that this was a particularly difficult sector because it was on the Lorraine border, where many Germans and French lived mixed and conflicted lives with divided loyalties, because the Germans had stolen the French Alsace-Lorraine Province after the Franco-Prussian War of 1870-71 and spies abounded. They warned the doughboys to be on the lookout for German Shepard dogs, because the Boche used them to carry messages. They also related how French pilots spotted a farmer plowing his field in the shape of an arrow pointing to French artillery hidden in a wooded area for Boche Observation balloons that the French called sausages. They were told to only use the telephone when necessary, because the Heinies tap the underground telephone wires to detect any unusual or high volume traffic to signal them that something is up in the Allied lines. Finally the French troops were ordered out, and they went on their jubilant way.

This time the 26th Division would be entirely on its own, for the first time. Now there wouldn't be any Frenchies telling them how to do it their way, although the French still had trench lines to man in adjacent sectors. Enough doughboys had been hit or killed to bring some caution into their actions, but not much. They were still full of pent up energy, anxious to get into the fray. So far they had heard and felt many artillery shells, trench mortars, machine guns, rifle-grenades, but had seen few Boche. That would change in a major way.

George, Woz and Company H had entered the trenches during the night at the Seicheprey end of the ten-mile front and were sickened by the sight. A mean, stinging, drizzle of rain was falling. They couldn't even see the duckboards at the bottom of the trenches because it was covered with water and mud above their ankles. The men sloshed back and forth through the watery mud along the narrow confines of the trench. Wet slickers rustle against one another in the narrow walkway, and the French and English gas masks that were issued the Americans, and were hanging from their hips, caught on broken timbers and each other as they passed in the debris strewn and rat infested trenches.

Woz had stepped up onto the fire step to look over the top of the trench line through no man's land toward the Boche lines. The fire step plank was itself a danger when it cracked and broke, dumping those standing on it on their duffs. So Woz gave it a careful look before placing his big and heavy body weight on it. Up he went and over he peeked.

"Hey! Wozlowski! Get that head down. Are you looking to get it blown off? They have snipers out there. Most injuries in trenches are to the head, so keep it down," warned an irked Lieutenant Malone.

Since Lieutenant Malone was the type who seldom raised his voice, Woz paid heed. He was chagrined because he knew better, but he had allowed his curiosity to get the better of his judgment for a careless moment.

"Damn you Woz, I can't keep an eye on you all the time. At your height, you always have to be careful, cautioned George.

"I know George. Don't rub it in. I just wanted to get a look around. I guess I lost my head."

"You did mentally; it could have been actually. We can get a better look around in daylight," admonished George."

"Give me your cigarette pouch, will ya, George? I need a cigarette. My nerves are up."

"You sure? The rain and moisture will make the cigarette damp, and you'll have to draw more."

"That's allright. I need to keep moving or puffing on something, and the tobacco will calm my nerves."

While they were cleaning up their trenches, the artillery gunners could be seen back of the main trench lines struggling in the mud of the dark gun pits to get their gunpieces into position in the quickest possible time. The French Hotchkiss machine gun was almost as heavy as the German Maxim gun, which was 125 pounds. The set up couldn't be soon enough because of what happened next.

Suspecting a change in the line, the Boche sent up huge flares that lit up the area as they hung from parachutes above the American trench lines. Night turned instantly into day. The doughboys looked up in surprise at the aerial display. Those that reacted by commenting spurned the night show with sarcasm:

"Whoa! Look at the gorgeous fireworks."

"Ah, wouldn't my girl like to see this."

"O-h-h, is this a welcome party?"

"At least the Boche aren't color blind."

"Aww, don't try to soften us up, Kaiser baby. We're going to kaput you anyway."

Ever serious, Lieutenant Malone remarked, "You guys won't be so cavalier if this turns out to be a prelude to an artillery bombardment."

The Division had been briefed that if a green rocket was launched by Allied artillery, it was the signal, warning of an impending gas attack and to put on the assigned gas masks. As it turned out, that night's flare show was merely a curiosity look-see by the Boche to attempt observing the changes being made in the Allied front trench lines.

Lieutenant Malone was overheard by George commenting to Captain Hawkins that, "the Boche knew we were coming long before last night, what with their village and farmer spies embedded throughout this area. But not wanting to be too predictable the Boche held their fire. Otherwise, we would have received a welcoming barrage to ruin our first night in the line, when we would be most vulnerable."

"Not only that," replied Captain Hawkins, "but we must be on the alert for the 'double-agents' who work both sides of the line to maximize their greed. Their reward, however, may be a double threat to being exposed and the firing squad. It's a dangerous game they're playing. Few have the nerve for it, and fewer are those who succeed."

"That said," continued Lieutenant Malone, "it makes me wonder when we **will** get our 'welcoming party.'"

"Before that happens, I want you to sternly warn our observation and listening outpost units to be especially alert to Boche raiding parties sneaking up to capture prisoners. Their Intel officers will want to know our strength to determine what's facing them. And I don't have to tell you, they have their ways to make prisoners talk," warned Captain Hawkins.

"Yes. You heard of the 'Alamo Seven' saga last October, where five doughboys came to the rescue of two observation post doughboys who were besieged by a Boche raiding party. They weren't in-sector two days when attacked. The Hun wanted to test the fighting spirit of the newly arrived Americans. A fierce fight ensued, including bayonet and hand to hand fighting. Since the Boce outnumbered the doughboys by a ten to one margin, the doughboys were eventually overwhelmed. Two were killed, four injured and one suffered a bayonet wound and was taken prisoner. His own bloody bayonet was left broken on the debris ridden ground. The Boche abandoned the post as soon as they took it," said Lieutenant Malone.

"Yeah, who hasn't heard about that tragic incident," replied the Captain. "Though it was a relatively minor battle, we certainly don't want it repeated here on any scale."

Now that they were within 18 miles of the German front lines, the first thing they noticed was enemy aeroplanes flying over their front lines for observation, mapping troop movements, and directing German shell fire. The Allies at this time did not have a very strong contingent of their own aeroplanes to contest the German Air Fleet, so the Boche had pretty much the run of the skies. But this was to change shortly, because 20 pilots of Squadron 95 of the newly formed American Air Service, led by American ace, Eddie Rickenbacker, was tasked to leave Epiez Aerodrome and move east and north to Toul. The American pilots flew their French Nieuports to Gengoult Aerodrome recently abandoned by the French for their exclusive use.

Besides temporary aerial supremacy in the Toul area, the Boche Army also had distinct geographical advantages in the area. They had held nearby St. Mihiel since the start of the war and had beaten back repeated attempts by the French to take it.

Therefore, this area was also considered part of the St. Mihiel salient, a large protuberance into the French lines. Mont Sec was a 460 foot high plateau, located about a mile inside the German front line. The Boche had masterful sightlines with which to observe the surrounding countryside for miles around. Inside the mountain was a network of reinforced tunnels, gun emplacements and sight outposts keeping track of Allied positions and movements. It provided the centerpiece for an ideal defensive position and accounted in no small measure for the repeated defeat of every French attempt to overrun them and flatten out the salient. The Germans believed it to be their strongest defensive position in all of France. Their battle successes seem to bear them out. In this area also was the Vosges Mountains, which was thought to have too rough terrain to be invaded by both the Boche and the French. The country was covered by rolling hills and heavily treed forests. This area was also within easy flying distance of the major German City of Metz. And circling Metz, a number of German aeroplane squadrons of bombers and fighters had their airfield on a hilltop plateau. Though a rainy area of France, it was a hotbed of air activity when weather permitted.

By this time, in April, 1918, America's Air Service, which began as an Aviation Section in the Army Signal Corps, was still woefully inadequate, though growing fast. Most of the planes flown by American pilots in the war were made in France or Great Britain. One day, George and Woz looked up to see a lone German Albatross, two seater, observation plane crossing their lines heading back to the German side. It had most probably been directing German artillery fire against some American positions in the St. Mihiel—Toul-Nancy triangle. What surprised them was the black smoke of German Anti-aircraft shells exploding in front of their own bomber. The German shells emit a black smoke when they burst, whereas Allies' shells show a white smoke. Though momentarily surprised, George startled himself with recognition of what was happening.

"Those shells are warning the German pilots that Allied pursuit planes are approaching them from their rear and to take evasive action. They are close enough to get their attention, but not close enough to damage their own plane. The three bomb bursts tell the German pilot the number of Allied planes coming. And the height of the shell bursts tell him the height of the Allied planes closing in. That's a pretty ingenious signalling system, isn't it?"

"George, how in hell did you know that?" Asked an amazed Woz.

"Oh, there's no secret to it. While you were chasing the ladies onto the dance floor on our last leave in Soissons, I was talking to some French and American pilots. Simple as that. Otherwise, I'd be as puzzled as you."

"But aren't they wasting a lot of shells?'

"What's the cost of a few shells compared to the cost of an expensive aeroplane and valuable pilots?"

"Well, that certainly makes dollar and cents sense," admitted a nodding Woz.

"These Germans are very professional, especially with their Prussian military tradition and history," remarked George with a hint of admiration in his voice.

THE SEICHEPREY TERRAIN

By the end of the next week, George and Woz had taken turns scanning the horizon with field glasses to check out the near lay of the land and educating each other. They also talked with a couple of pilots who had to force land nearby with damaged aeroplanes. George and Woz joked about doing Officers work and deserving Officers pay. But it eased their boredom and would help them survive if they ever got isolated or stuck out in no man's land. With the binoculars and consulting maps, they noticed that Seicheprey is at the foot of the slope just beneath Beaumont. And Beaumont is on a high, but not a very steep ridge, which runs for miles from Pont-a-Mousson to Flirey and Rambeaucourt. From Seicheprey north, they noticed a broad, rolling valley, dotted with towns formerly held by the Boche, St. Baussant, Lahayville, Richecourt, Nonsard and Pannes. From almost any point along the Beaumont Ridge a great panoramic view is visable. The countryside spreads out, beginning West where the valley narrows noticably toward St. Mihiel, and opening wider as you look East, in the opposite direction.

Since they were briefed upon being assigned to the Toul-Boucq area, they knew that looming up high and commanding a fantastic view for miles in all directions is the previously mentioned great Fort of Mont Sec, which the French once took at so great a casualty cost that they immediately abandoned it. On the far side of the wide valley was a long ridge similar to Beaumont Ridge. Vigneulles is at the bottom of this ridge, and Hattonville, near where their line is, rests at the top of the ridge. From the heights, the valley deceptively seems even and level, but, in fact, is really broken up by many smaller valleys and hills, streams and woods.

In the course of his various duties, Captain Hawkins asked for volunteers to undertake a dangerous task. Among the volunteers, he selected George, Private Flannery, and a Private Bill Buckman, a German-American who spoke and understood German. He and Lieutenant Malone took them to the map room and briefed them on their mission. They were to crawl out under the cover of darkness to set up a listening post as close to the Boche front line as they could safely get. This would involve a judgment on their part. They were also to take with them a telescoped series of pipe sections, where one was smaller and fitted inside the succeeding section. They were to form a hollow tube when fully extended, and that could make an excellent evesdropping pipeline. If they could get close enough to the Boche line to avoid using the pipe sections, so much the better. Otherwise, they were to try to insert the extended and locked pipe sections into the dirt or mud, and push them towards the Boche line to hear so much the better.

The pipe sections locked together by twisting the extended sections and locking them into a notch, which would hold the sections in place. It went without saying that they should be on the lookout for German units coming the other way and possibly attempting the same or a similar mission. If they ran into a raiding party, or a tunnel, they were to radio back immediately using their large and somewhat unweildy trench radio. In any event, in such a situation, they were to abort the mission and get back to their own lines as best as they could. They were not to stay at the post beyond two or three hours at the most, because the longer they remained in no man's land, the greater the chance they would be discovered, and captured or killed.

They were also made aware that the Boche called these daring missionaries, "pipe dreamers." They had similar missions executed by their own dare-devils. The Boche conducted what they called short raids to make these quick nettings. Capturing these "pipe dreamers" was considered by them to be a prized prisoner-catch and successes were amply rewarded. Once fully informed of the mission and its risks, they were given a final opportunity to stand down, but each one declined. They were to move out the next evening, just after midnight, under a quarter-moon.

The troika moved out at midnight as planned. They would leapfrog along going from one shell hole to another, each one alternatively covering for the other. They had covered their helmets with canvas cloth to absorb any reflection from the moonlight. They also covered the metal portions of their rifles with dirt and mud so there would be no glint to give them away. Their bayonets stayed sheathed. They had their compasses to help keep them headed in the right direction. They crossed into the enemy lines and headed for the protective cover of the Remieres Wood. They were to go as far as the Rupt de Mad River, appropriately named, to the east of Mont Sec. They were conscious of the lookout field glasses sweeping the area and their being looked down upon from the commanding heights of this modest mountain. There's was basically a reconnasiance operation to determine if this is still a defensive trenchline area or whether the Boche were also gearing up for an offensive against this area this far south from all the noise up along the British-French frontlines.

The constant refrain the American doughboy heard that angered them and triggered many a brawl in the local drinking establishments was that sooner or later, the Germans would seek out and go after the amateur Americans. The Boche wanted American blood. Their cautious introduction into the frontlines made the German High Command contemptuous of the fighting abilitiy of the American cowboys. German prisoners scoffed whenever the American Army was mentioned. "Where are they?" They scorned. Earlier, the British and French were asking the same question.

After a few hours out, George was beginning to think this was going to be another Argonne Forest ghost chase. But his rumination was jolted when he saw a sudden movement ahead and to the right from the corner of his eye. He picked up a rock and threw it at Flannery ahead of him to his left. He pointed anxiously in the direction of the sighting. Similarly, Flannery caught Buckman's attention. All three now moved forward in a low crouch following behind George. It looked to be about seventy meters ahead. Buckman and Flannery circled around opposite sides of George's flanks as they stealthily darted forward hesitantly. They also checked behind to their rear, so as not to be hit from behind.

George's intuitive sense told him there was something out there. Burned out campsites they had already encountered told him that there had been enemy in the area. This was enemy territory afterall. Focusing ahead, he startled himself when he could see bushes shaking in a clump. He again signaled Flannery excitedly with a confirming nod of his head. He had closed to within thirty meters and, though crouched, he had his rifle cocked and ready to fire. When the bush shuddered again George fired.

Bam! The shot echoed through the woods. He heard a sudden, piercing squeal! George instinctively threw himself on the ground. Then he heard a series of painful yelps. Rising to get a better look, he was startled to see a black wide-bodied animal with horned tusks through his nose burst out of the bushes screeching, and charging right at him. When the reality hit George that he was being attacked, he pulled up his rifle and fired a second time at almost point blank range. The wild animal hurled himself at George and knocked him and his rifle to the ground. George yelled as a pointed horn stabbed him in the thigh, spurting blood. George leaped for his scattered rifle and turned to face the animal that crashed and skidded along the ground. But the beast lay there twitching and squealing. Hurt and angry, George limped over and drove the butt of the rifle again and again against the wild snapping of the huge, blood splattered head. After repeatedly clubbing the beserk beast with a surge of adrenalin, George dropped to his knees exhausted, breathing heavily, and gasping. The beast stopped moving and went silent, a bloody mess.

Buckman beat Flannery to the scene as they ran up and skidded to a halt. Both stared speechless and stunned at the two bloodied combatants. After an awkward silence in which everyone took in the startling scene, Buckman was the first to speak,

"A wild boar! Can you imagine that?"

"I'm not imagining anything. I'm seeing it. A wild boar? He looks like an oversized pig with a bone through his nose," said an amazed Flannery.

"Damn! Damn! Damn!" George cursed as he ripped off the rest of his torn and bloody pant leg. He then attemped to tie off his leg with a tourniquet to stop the bleeding, but fell backwards from losing his balance. Help me, help me close it off!" He sputtered.

Flannery jumped over and grabbed the bloody pant leg and tightened it until the bleeding stopped flowing. George fell back, but had to turn sideways because he vomited from the sudden loss of blood and dizziness.

"My head is spinning," George gasped.

Buckman said, "We've got to get him back before he goes into shock. George, we're going to have to move you, dizzy or not. A Doc needs to look at this."

"That's ok. Let's go," agreed George.

"Wait a minute," said Flannery. "Let me pour some of this sulfur on the wound. It might help prevent an infection. This might sting for a second, George."

Then they stood George up and had him sit on Buckman's rifle, while George rapped his arms around their necks and they moved out. It was awkward walking and they had to stop periodically to rest. They had no choice, they agreed, but to abort the mission, short of the Rupt de Mad River. Not just because of George's injury, but because the sound of George's two shots may well have been heard.

"Even though the trees and the dense woods may have muted the sound of the rifle shots, we can't take that chance. Besides, these woods look to be regularly patrolled by the Boche," commented Flannery.

"And with George down, we can't take a chance that this temporary tourniquet will hold," added Buckman.

"How you doing, George? We'll get you back," reassured Flannery.

"I'm ok. The dizziness is gone. Don't worry about me."

"Hey, I wonder if this entitles you to a medal, George? Is a wild boar an enemy?" Asked Flannery.

"Well, it happened in enemy territory, didn't it?" Volunteered Buckman.

"That was one strong beast," said George. "I hit him twice. And fast, too. He was on me before I knew it."

"In our training, we discussed horses, mules, donkeys and pigeons, but never wild boers. Who would have thought of it?" Continued George, in an afterthought.

"If it wasn't for your injury, George, this would be funny, or at least ridiculous. It certainly is a unique experience," added Buckman. "But maybe not for the Frenchman or German, because boar hunting is fairly common in the forests of Germany and France."

Fortunately, they were not detected or impeded getting back to their lines. And they were able to get back before dawn broke. George couldn't have been in too much pain, because he was sleeping when they crossed back. They were met by stretcher-bearers and medics once safely back. George went straight to the rear Medic tent to have his wound looked at and dressed. It turned out to be a deep puncture wound that didn't require many sutures. And they were removed in a week. The sulfur powder must have helped, because it did not get infected, but George was not allowed back in the line for ten days to avoid a possible infection from the dirt, water and mud concentrated there. No medal was forthcoming. When told, George just laughed,

"Since when do they award medals for being stupid?"

CHAPTER THIRTY SIX

APREMONT

George was forewarned and participated in a number of special assignments regarding detachment duty for rolling sniper work. Therefore, when he was assigned to report to Apremont at the other end of their ten-mile front, he thought little of it. The terrain at Apremont was similar to Seicheprey, but both were much different than the Chemin des Dames sector. The only thing they had in common was mud. For nearly the whole ten-mile front line, a low, marshy, swampland faced them. Because of this, the trenches had to be built up battlements in many spots, rather than trenches below ground level. George preferred the built up battlements, because shooting down at an enemy was more effective, though it afforded less protection than a ground trench. It was a tradeoff that was advantageous or disadvantageous depending on the activity.

The nearby Village of Apremont was actually up on top of some hills behind enemy lines and occupied by the Germans. To keep them at bay, the 103rd Artillery with its prized 155 millimeter sniper gun was moved behind a hill that frequently and accurately keep the Germans in Apremont pinned down, even though the Germans had the higher ground and continually tried to knock out this gun. In addition, there was a roving 75 millimeter artillery piece, supplemented by a vest pocket 37 millimeter gun that was so accurate that it drove the Germans to great efforts to knock it out, equally without success, because the baby gun would fire away for half an hour and then hastily move away before the Boche could fix its position. But it bothered the American infantry in the area, because then they would get the shells fired back by the angry Germans. Because the American guns were more accurate that the Germans, it favored the Americans. To negate this advantage, the Germans decided to do something about it.

When the 26th Division was settled in, the adjacent French Corps Commander advised General Edwards that their left flank was a problem area because of the poor terrain for defense and suggested he might want to build it up. General Edwards agreed; but before he could get the engineers to complete rebuilding the area defenses, the Germans attacked at night with their own artillery on April 5th. This turned out to be a prelude to a ground attack by eighty men, with the Boche deciding to get under the deadly guns of the artillery. It was a relatively short battle, less than an hour, and more of a probing attack, and the Boche quickly withdrew, taking their wounded with them. George happened to be in a ready position and brought down one of the attackers and wounded another. Three other Boche attackers were found dead. One doughboy suffered a crease wound to the head, but not seriously.

The Germans attacked again on April 7th with a larger force, but still less than a hundred men. Because of the darkness and wild shooting, relatively few casualties were incurred. George thought he wounded two Germans and Woz, who came up to the front trench line with a reserve unit thinking the Germans had a larger force, swore that he made a kill, but the body was dragged away, he claimed. Only a couple of Boche bodies could be found the next morning. George thought they were being tested.

There was a third attack three days later on April 10th with a yet still larger force, near to two hundred. The stutter bursts of the French Hotchkiss machine guns used by the Americans cut them down in large numbers, too large for them to drag all of them back to their lines, and many bodies and injured were left behind. This battle went most of the evening. George was sighting a German officer when his rifle was suddenly shot out of his arms. The wooden stock was shattered and George got a splinter in his eye. He retired to the rear to have a medic look at it, cursing his luck. Back at the aid station, a small sliver of wood was washed out of his left eye and a temporary patch was put over it to protect the scratch from further damage.

After the Germans were repulsed once again, Phil Dodger and Dewey Akers came back to see how George was doing. Phil picked up George's rifle with the wooden stock shot off and asked a rhetorical question,

"Will this thing shoot?"

Sargent Klick going buy grabbed it from Phil's hand and shot it off in the air.

Bam!

"There's your answer," said Sargent Klick, as he kept on walking and threw it back at Phil without breaking stride.

"I can shoot it, but I can't aim it very well, or snipe with it. With the stock gone, the balance is off. I'll go to the ammo and supply tent and get it replaced," remarked George.

"With that patch on your eye, you won't draw a sniper assignment very soon," commented Dewey Akers.

"What difference will a patch make? Don't you squint before you squeeze off a shot, anyway?" Asked Dave Cochrane.

"Yeah, I squint, but I don't close my eye, so the patch is a hindrance," replied George.

Three days later on April 13th, the Germans attacked once again with a similar size force, only this time it was 2:00 am. George had taken some instruction on the Hotchkiss with Flannery as a precaution in the interim. They jumped up, cleared the sleep from their eyes and ran to the machine gun post. George took the trigger and Flannery fed the ammo into the machine gun. George sprayed his area to enfilade with another Hotchkiss from another mounting station fifty meters to his right. George felt awkward with this unfamiliar weapon and saw dirt kick up and trees splinter but couldn't tell if he had hit anyone or they just threw themselves on the ground to return fire. The gun jammed and George cursed uncharacteristically, while clearing the jam. Flannery picked up his Springfield and fired individually until George signaled that

he was ready to go again. George wasn't into half a clip, when a
Boche threw a potato masher, their long stem hand grenade, that
landed to Flannery's right causing an explosive mushroom to throw
dirt and debris over them. Flannery yelled:
"Aaarrgg! My eye! My eye!" At the same time he covered his
right eye.
"Shrapnel?" He asked himself. Then he answered his own
question as he pulled his hand away from his eye.
"Jesus! It's not shrapnel! It's my thumb! My thumb's gone!"
Flannery was staring at his bloody hand with his thumb missing.
"Frank, your own thumb hit you in your eye. Your eye's ok,
it's your thumb. Here, I found it. Let's go back. Medic! Medic!"
Yelled George.
"Let me tie off your thumb, Frank. It'll stem the flow. Take it
easy. We'll get you out of here. Medic! Oh, here you are. Here's his
thumb, in my handkerchef."
"Ok, soldier. Easy does it. We're outta here," said the Medic,
as he guided a stunned Flannery, looking stunned by his odd injury,
and saying nothing.
George then took up a Springfield rifle and returned fire. If
they're close enough to throw hand grenades, he's got to be
especially alert, he thought. How did he not hear the tin cans
they hung from the perimeter wire, George wondered. Then,
just as soon as the assault began, it ended. This battle didn't last
half an hour. The Boche withdrew and disappeared into the night.
Again, George saw quite a few bodies in front of the trenches.
The rest of the night was quiet. He would hear the report in the
morning.
Flannery was taken back to the Division surgeon and was said
to be doing ok. They had to stop the bleeding, ice the wound, and
cut away the dead skin and tissue. They didn't know if they could
re-attach the thumb. But his infantry days were said to be over.
How could he pull a trigger with no use of a trigger thumb? Was
this injury sufficiently serious to have him invalided home? That
was to be determined.

The tin can dilemna was solved easily enough when they found blankets thrown over the tin cans to smother any noise. Simple enough, he thought.

The next day, the body count was obtained. The four-battles-in-eight-days total count gave the Americans over a four to one favorable casualty ratio. They felt pretty good that they repulsed all four attacks, though they were not considered major battles. Their casualties were relatively light. George was saddened to hear that Sargent Gonzalez was killed, shot through the head, and Roddy O'Byrne had a knee cap injury. George had a scratched eyeball, a nothing injury. Flannery's injury was much more serious. George thanked the heavens once again. Somebody upstairs is looking after me, he thought to himself, with gratitude once again.

When an American observation balloon reported that the Germans had drawn back to the other side of Apremont, the Division and Brigade Commanders approved Company H's return to the Seicheprey end of the line. There was some concern that the Germans will try that area next. Back they went, blooded and a little seasoned, though cautioned by their Divisional Commander, Major General Clarence Edwards, that the fighting there was not considered major encounters. Nevertheless, he congratulated the doughboys on successfully repelling the attacks. He thought they were probing and testing attacks.

During the month of April in the Seicheprey area, it was commonplace for enemy patrols to cross and confront each other in small-scale skirmishes in No Mans land. They sometimes would suffer some casualties, mostly minor, but eventually made their way back to their lines without further incident. The Boche didn't seem to want to engage in a large or extended shoot out. One night George and Woz's squads were out on patrol when George got his foot caught in something. When he jerked it free, he yelled involuntarily when his boot picked up a skull! Woz and Dave Cochrane heard him, turned back and jumped into his foxhole with fixed bayonets in front of them. George had just kicked the hollow skull away.

"Damn thing scared the hell out of me," snapped an irritated George.

"George, look behind you," said an alarmed Woz. With that said, Woz thrust his bayonet into the side of the shell hole and pulled out the ribs of a skeleton.

"Hell, that looks to be a couple of years old," remarked Cochrane.

"Probably, a shell burst victim," said a now composed George.

"Is it German or French?" Wondered Cochrane.

"Who cares," quiped Woz. "Lets get moving. This neutral zone is a grave yard."

With that, they made it safely back to their trench line, having completed their patrol with nothing else of any note to report. It was ghoulish enough that No Man's land was a former battle scene hiding buried skeletons. It gave the rest of Company H the creeps. The following day Company H was pulled back into a reserve position for a period of rest after their four-battle defense over an eight-day period. The guys were in the Company mess and the subject of General Pershings hand gestures came up.

"Hey, Guys. Did you ever notice Pershings hand gestures? He likes to smash his right fist into his left palm for emphasis. Another favorite hand habit of his is to fling his fingers open and then closing them, like he's throwing something on the ground," said Dewey Akers.

"Why do you care what Pershing does with his hands?" Asked Phil Dodger.

"I just think it's odd, that's all."

"It's not odd, it's just Pershing being Pershing. That's his personality. He's being himself, that's all," replied George.

"So Akers, you run your hand through your hair. You might end up pulling your hair out; is that odd, too?" Asked Woz.

"I didn't know it bothered you?" Retorted Akers.

"It doesn't. I'm just saying you have a nervous habit and so doesn't Pershing. So what's the big deal?" Riposted Woz.

"Big deal? Big deal is right. What's the purpose of this stupid conversation?" Intervened Davy Cochrane.

"I just wanted to raise the intelligence level of this group, that's all," said a sarcastic Akers.

"Ok Guys," interrupted a Lieutenant Malone, who just walked over; "now that you've reached the level of intelligence you deserve, knock it off. Akers, check the duty roster. I think you've been assigned to a listening post. Then you won't have to talk, just listen."

"With pleasure," remarked a defiant Akers, as he grabbed his rifle and walked away.

George laughed and shook his head at the absurdity of the matter, and the rest of the group tittered and reacted with their own mirth.

"Speaking of hands, the Medics said Frank Flannery is being sent to Chaumont to the AEF Surgeon General to see if they can reattach his thumb to his hand," mentioned the Lieutenant.

"For that kind of surgery, they'll probably have to send him stateside. The war is over for him, is my bet," said Woz.

"He may have lost a thumb, but it also may have saved his life," remarked George.

"That's probably the way he should look at it, anyway," claimed Lieutenant Malone, who had joined the conversation.

"I'm going to miss Flannery; he got on my nerves sometimes, but he was a good soldier," commented Sargent Sardonis.

"Oh, yeah, well maybe you got on his nerves, too. Did you ever consider that, you regular Army lifer," taunted Woz.

Sargent Sardonis, another Border man, merely smiled, didn't rise to the bait and merely mentioned that,

"As you all know, most of our injured are never returned to their original unit. General Edwards agrees with our complaints that this practice hurts our cohesiveness and morale, but he says the Corps Commanders believe it is wasteful and inefficient tracking down old outfits for the recovered injured to return to. Except for a specialist, they simply assign him to the nearest suitable unit, knowing that he has already been replaced by another soldier, generally speaking."

"Yeah, *generally* speaking, because the *Generals* believe that, we don't," complained Sargent Sardonis.

"But, on the other hand," said George, "casualties and deaths always affect the cohesion and morale of its unit members. For this reason, many units go forward understrength. If there are too few survivors to continue to fight effectively, and their unit can no longer operate as originally designed, then these splinter or remnant units can be attached to other allied units. That's war."

"There you go again, George, arguing both sides of an issue. You should get the book learning to become a lawyer," commented Woz.

"I'm just airing different angles, that's all," said George. "Its common sense."

"Incidently, that's why we call General Edwards 'Daddy Edwards,' because he genuinely cares for the soldiers under his command. However, his superiors think he has become too conservative. Pershing wants daring and results, so he frequently finds fault with Edwards field generalship," lamented Woz.

It was an unnerving experience to face four battles within a little over a week's time at early morning hours. It raises havoc with normal sleep patterns, but then again that was the very reason why the Boche did it, pondered George. He was also learning that the Germans liked to attack at the extremities of lines or sectors, or at the end of a unit or at the joint between units, because they believed those points to be the weakest and easiest to exploit. And the buried skeleton or skeletons in No Man's land couldn't help but make them wonder and shudder at their possible futures.

In the meantime, the German High Command had to put down persistent Allied publicity about ship-loads of arriving doughboys and the failure of the German U-boats to sink a single troop ship. Among the rank and file of the German Army, rumors persisted that the Americans were crossing the Atlantic Ocean with millions of soldiers. The Kaiser's sneering disparagement of the fighting ability of the amateur American army was wearing thin, though no major engagements against them had yet occurred, despite the willingness and champing at the bit of each to take the others measure.

"Look at the millions of Russians the Czar threw against us; the largest Army in the world. We hurled them back to Petrograd! The civilian army of cowboys will suffer the same fate!" Roared Kaiser Wilhelm.

To buttress their contempt for the field army of the late-arriving Americans, the German propagandists felt they needed to prove the battlefield unworthiness of the Americans. The full might of their considerable propaganda organization waited with bated breath the first German victory to trumpet their superior military skills. The German High Command searched the American sector for a target. They wanted a very public and quick success. The Seicheprey sector was selected. And they waited for the temporary confusion that invariably accompanied a change in the line, when one Division of troops would replace another, when they would be most vulnerable to an attack. They saw their opportunity when the 26th Division of the US Army replaced the 1st Division, the already noted tough, "Big Red One," who were being pulled out and sent to the red hot zone of the Soissons sector.

To disguise their planned large raid at Seicheprey, they initiated a series of skirmishes against the American line at Apremont. When the Americans rushed troop detachments to Apremont this further weakened the Seicheprey Sector. This surprise was somewhat reduced by the Yanks rushing its bruised detachments back to Seicheprey. The Germans would attack the now weary defenders, anyway.

As they scornfully and smugly remarked, "Fritz will drop a calling card on the Americans, by smashing them a bloody nose, and to teach them a lesson." They had been angling toward this for a few weeks at Apremont and the past week at Seicheprey, by instigating many, but small night engagements to keep the Americans off balance, disturb their sleep and to lull them into a false sense of security at non-attacked sectors. In the process they also wanted to test their fighting ability with a surprise, sneak attack with an overwhelming force. It would be the first large scale

German trench raid on the Americans. By this time the earlier French warning that this would likely happen was apparently forgotten by the American defenders in the whirlwind of war.

What was more difficult to fathom was the fact that the American Intelligence Bureau had advised the Command Headquarters that a German attack seemed imminent, because of the large number of German troops concentrating behind their lines. A run up to the coming raid may also have been indicated by the softening up by artillery barrages aimed at the Sibille trench area, particularly. No special precautions were taken to counter these warnings. Near the Sebille trench, the 26th Battalion Headquarters was located in the village of Seicheprey itself, as was a medical unit.

At 3 a.m. a sudden and ferocious artillery barrage opened up on the 26th Yankee Division and exploded over a two-mile front along the area including the tiny village of Seicheprey. George was knocked out of his dugout bunk bed and thrown onto the wooden plank floor. The force of the concussion blew the wooden door off its hinges and its splintered pieces sailed over George's head, now prone on the floor with the rest of his horizontal body. George gritted his teeth and shielded his eyes from the flying dirt and debris, as he jumped up to grab his steel helmet to protect his head. He then dove under the lower bunk-bed and curled up in a fetal position for maximun protection. The ground shook with tremendous shudders as the Boche guns rained down their high explosive shells, shattering the area with tremendous roars that pained Georges ears. He reflexively put his hands up to his ears to prevent suffering punctured ear-drums. Nevertheless, George felt the throbbing, dull pain of an instant headache. Shouting and yelling could be heard between shell bursts.

"Take cover! Take cover!" Howled Captain Hawkins.

George knew that the minute the shelling stopped he, and everyone else in Company H, had to run up and to man the front lines, because invariably the German infantry would be close on the heels of the rolling barrage and attacking right behind it. They knew something was coming because their telephone lines had been cut, destroying their communications to summon in help or call up reserves, if needed. Runners and carrier pigeons would have to be relied on as a fallback communication system. A rolling barrage in front and back of their position was also supposed to prevent the Americans from evacuating their wounded and dead, as well as isolating the front trench-line, by preventing reinforcements or replacements. Back at Apremont they had endured a box barrage, whose purpose was to box-in the defenders; the box barrage is generally used in smaller attacks.

The ground trembled with shock tremors from the whistling and whining shells. The German gunners were as accurate here and now as the American cannoneers were at Apremont. George could also hear the American gunners returning fire. George had learned to distinguish the enemy shells from the Allies and American pieces, since the AEF were using French made shells for the most part. As the shelling moved down the line away from George, he turned outward, uncovered his head, and glanced out of the blown out door. The concussions and and dirt sprays flying through the open door of his dugout shelter settled to the floor, and through the residual dust he was able to see the return fire of American trench mortars. It was designed to be manned by five men to handle the heavy shells, loading, sighting, lookout with field glasses and the lanyard pullers in this crude baby artillery gun. George could see only four, but they were handling things with brisk, urgent efficiency. George reveled with the welcome sight that the doughboys were giving them back a bit of their own.

He couldn't help expressing a slight smile at the return fire, as he saw the eruption of orange colored flames, accompanying a deafening roar. A thundering thrust soared through the air reigning death and destruction on the receiving end. A crash of rendered steel, followed by clouds of blue-green smoke tailed off into a yellow mist. The distant cry of the suddenly injured was frightening and comforting at the same time. Only in war does such a contradiction make sense, thought George. This barrage continued for the next two hours. At 5 a.m. the shelling suddenly stopped. But the deafening silence was quickly followed by odd sounding whistles. George knew they weren't American whistles. He leaped to his feet and ran out of the debris-strewn dugout to man the trench line for the assault he knew was coming. He was joined by the rest of his Company that survived the barrage. They jumped up onto the fire step and commenced firing almost immediately, as the enemy was closing in rapidly. Their training instinctively kicked in.

The Boche came out of the mist and fog caused by the early morning dew and shell smoke, yelling and screaming. Unknown to George, the German raiders concentrated their attack on the end trenches to his left, including the Sibille trench. George focused on the field of fire in front of him. With death whizzing by his head and bullets zipping and thudding into sandbags all around him, he fired back at dark, darting special German assault troops who had blackened their faces and bayonets with mud, and had their helmets covered in burlap to dull any glare. George found himself grunting with each pull of the trigger and gasping for breath. But his prior experience under fire helped him to stay focused.

"Oh-h-h!" Cried out a doughboy. It was Davy Cochrane! "Dave, you're hit! Medic! Medic!" George hollered. But then George had to ignore him, if only temporarily. He couldn't chance being overrun, while looking at a wounded man. He saw a Cochran spin out from the wall and crumble at his feet. Cochrane fell down into the black abyss. He landed with a thud onto the wooden duckboard at the bottom of the trench. The moonlight sliced across the trench top half, leaving the bottom black as ink. He couldn't see Davy, but he could hear him. Reloading a clip, George glanced down and flashes of light from exploding shells gave fleeting views of Davy's body writhing and twitching in spasms of pain. He was opening his mouth, but nothing was coming out, but gushes of his own blood.

The Sibille trench shortly thereafter looked like it was being overrun. Hand to hand combat was resorted to by the suddenly swamped doughboys. George turned his fire in their direction to apply flank pressure. The Boche broke through and headed for the

Village of Seicheprey. The village would be isolated and cut off, with many casualties, and some Americans fighting to the death. One cook took his meat cleaver and split the head open of an attacking German soldier. Despite the breakthrough, the rest of the line seemed to be holding.

"Medic! Medic!" George screamed again on Cochranes behalf, surrounded by the chaos and the insanity. Just then a medic grabbed Cochrane and pulled him into a dugout. Now George heard the distinctive sounds of trench mortar shells whining down. This interrupted his fire until he ducked down and the shell landed and shrapnel blasted its peripheral damage and collapsed a dugout shelter, burying doughboys inside, trying to work a radio. George ran over instinctively, with others joining him, and helped dig them out, and helped up those that were alive. Leaving the ghastly scene when the medics arrived, George ran back, jumped up onto the fire step and resumed firing.

The battle was raging when George saw to his horror doughboy discipline breakdown further down the line with the 104th Infantry Regiment, when doughboys went over the top after a mortor shell direct-hit their trench. Enemy guns had gotten their range and they panicked and fled the protection of the trench for the open field. They were met with German machine gun fire and flamethrowers. The flamethrowers were intended to drive them out of their dugouts and the trenches. Before that, the German maxims mowed them down right in front of their own trench line. The Company Lieutenant was screaming and pulling them back into the trenches.

American return shellfire was finding the range of the Boche guns and knocking them out, but the panicked soldiers couldn't wait. It was a terrible massacre that never should have happened. The bodies had to be left there in front of the trench line, until there was a break in the battle, which raged without let up for the next hour. In combat, that's an eternity. By 6 p.m. the Boche fell back, taking with them their many prisoners from the Sibille trench. With varying levels of intensity, the fighting resumed from fixed positions for the rest the morning. The cries of the wounded were disheartening, but watched with caution. American speaking Germans would fake crying for help to draw out would be rescuers, only to be picked off by waiting German snipers. Some bodies were booby-trapped. Those wounded that could be pulled back with some chance of safety, were pulled back by overworked medics and volunteers. Smoke screens sent up by the Americans were of some help in rescuing the fallen. Nevertheless, George noticed with disgust and frustration, that at least one volunteer was cut down by a sniper. At this stage of the war, old conventions disappeared, and the Boche now shot at any Red Cross insignia, as well as snipers targeting Officers. Pick off the rescuers and the leaders, seemed to be their rationale, though no German prisoner ever admitted this, as far as George knew.

Firing down both sides of George's trench line could be heard as the result of additional rear guard actions, but dissipated as the afternoon wore on. Then, at mid-afternoon, a different sounding shell was shot at and over the American lines. American flares went up of a pre-determined color. Gas flares! The Gas guards yelled out the warning that went all along the line,

"Gas! Gas! Masks on! Masks on!"

The surprise was that gas attacks usually precede an attack, not come after one. Nothing was happening in this raid according to expectations. George, having previously suffered burn and blister injuries as the result of a mustard gas attack, grabbed for his gas mask from his hip belt, but it was gone. It had been shot off during the day! At first, smoke shells were fired over the American lines, but no infantry attack followed, as expected. Instead, artillery and cannister shells of gas started falling and exploding all along the line. The shells burst open and yellow-green smoke drifted up and spread throughout the area. George ran back to the nearest dugout looking for a gas mask. He stumbled and fell in his rush. He grabbed some canvas from his canteen and covered his mouth and nose to keep from inhaling the poison. His eyes stung and smarted. He cried out for a gas mask, but no one had an extra one.

"Find a body, George! Take one from a body! Shouted Woz!"

George grabbed his eyes, now starting to burn, as Woz pulled him out of the trench and dragged him away. Others were also choking and crying out for help. Panic ensued as doughboys without gas masks fled the trenches and ran back hoping to outrun the gas clouds. But a wind was blowing their way and carrying the poisonous fumes with them. Some doughboys fell to their knees overcome, coughing, retching and clawing at their eyes. Gasping for breath only accelerated the ingestion of the poison gasious, tiny air pellets. The previously designated Gas Guards yelled out,

"Chlorine! Chlorine gas!"

When George heard that it was Chorine gas and not Mustard gas, as before, he pushed a surprised Woz away and said,

"Let me be, Woz. Leave me alone!"

Then an astonished Woz watched as George hurriedly unbuttoned the front of his pants, pulled out his penis, and urinated on the piece of canvas. Woz was too stunned to do anything but stare in disbelief. Then through his mask, he spontaneously sputtered in a muffled voice,

"George, what the hell are you doing?"

George continued to cough as he then raised the urine soaked canvas cloth to his face and covered his mouth, nose and eyes. He inhaled with deep breaths and it seemed to calm George. His breathing gradually leveled out; he coughed less violently and noticably began to breathe easier, even as he continued to stagger forward. Woz looked on from behind his gas mask and his smothered voice uttered an exclamation that George could hear, but not understand. George waved back at Woz that he was ok. But now Woz wasn't. His own labored breathing accumulated moisture that became mucus and water causing Woz to pull off his mask to clear the mucus mess. He had to hold his breath while frantically doing this. A nearby shell explosion knocked him off his feet, and his mask out of his hand. He automatically gasped and inhaled more poisonous gas, choking him. Desperately and blindly he clawed and reached around in the mud and chaos. Somehow he grabbed the mask and covered his face. It helped, but caused him to feel dizzy. George had stumbled on not knowing Woz had been knocked off his feet.

At this time, the wind shifted and the gas cloud started to blow back the other way. It was returning toward the German lines! Woz hurried forward and resumed guiding George away and to the nearest Medical unit for assistence. George had been knocked to his knees by the same shell explosion as Woz, but not to the ground, Woz having blocked some of the concussion with his big body. They took a still coughing, but steadier George for treatment. The medical orderly explained to a still puzzled Woz that urine was a temporary home remedy that served in an emergency to protect against the effects of chlorine gas. George was apprised of this home remedy when he was previously treated for mustard gas, a more serious and poisonous chemical pollutant.

Woz was treated and later released back to his post. Though released himself, Woz had to leave George with the medics for overnight observation. He returned to his unit, anxious at the chaos and casualties around him. By late afternoon, another artillery barrage was thrown at them. As it turned out, this was a German cover for their troops to withdraw from the field of battle. As dark came, only sporadic shots could be heard. A few of the nervous or trigger-happy doughboys were shooting at crazed, fleeing animals, shadows or ghosts. Some shot at birds picking at dead bodies. Burial details and medics retrieved the wounded and the bodies of the dead. The corpses had to have their dog tags pulled, logged by the Grave Registration people and quickly buried to avoid the spread of disease. Divisional Command, of course, wanted a casualty count. It wasn't pretty.

CHAPTER THIRTY SEVEN

PERSHING FURIOUS

The casualty count was upsetting to General Pershing, in particular. There were many reasons, besides the casualties themselves. That was bad enough, because it was the largest number of casualties the Americans had suffered to date on the Western Front. Specifically, the doughboys lost 80 dead, and 130 prisoners were taken back to the German lines. The American prisoners were forced to carry back some of the German wounded and dead. And some of those were forced to go back a number of times for this dangerous type work. All told the 26th Division had 634 casualties, composed of the wounded, missing, prisoners and the dead.

The Germans attacked through favorable fog and mist conditions that gave then cover until they were almost on top of the US Troops. The total German attack force numbred 3300 men, of which half were casualties. This was later confirmed by an American Officer who escaped being a prisoner from the Sibille trench. The Doughboys had only 350 men in the Sibille trench, and were thus outnumbered 9 to 1.

General Pershing was especially enraged with the poor defense in that section because its weakness was forewarned by both American and French Intelligence and no remedial action was taken facilitating the disaster. It was the first time American troops fought the Germans without the help of the French, and its failure to hold the middle of the line made the Division, Pershing and the American Army look bad. The 102nd Infantry Regiment of the 26th Division was taken by surprise and mauled. It would furnish

France's Marshall Foch and Britains Field Marshall Douglas Haig a basis to claim that the Americans couldn't go it alone and thus should not have an independent Army. Pershing blamed General Edwards for not having the Division ready. Edwards was the only National Guard General, as opposed to Regular Army General, to command a Division on the Western Front. The National Guard was widely viewed by the Regular Army as composed of politically connected parlor patriots or weekend warriors, as they derisively called them, who were not nearly as effective as the Regular Professional Army.

In some cases they were right and in other cases they were wrong. For an example of the latter, there is the stellar performance of a National Guard Battery D, of the 129th Field Artillery in the 35th Division fighting in the American front, above Belleau Wood and east of Verdun. These 194 spirited men, firing four guns, distinguished themselves consistently with effective fire, and were led by a Captain Harry Truman, later President of the United States.

And the capture of so many US prisoners at Seichprey didn't include the potential tactical disadvantage of having so many prisoners that might be tricked of forced to divulge compromising information to the detriment of its fighting forces remaining on the line. Pershing made a mental note that he would remove Edwards from command at the opportune time.

It was especially humiliating to Pershing to have the German propagandists making banner headlines that the German Army had beaten the Americans badly, though it neglected to mention that the Germans suffered nearly three times the number of casualties. They also abandoned Seicheprey before the American counterattack reached the village. They got what they came for, prisoners and a successful sneak attack, before withdrawing. They trumpeted it as a public relations coup, if nothing else.

Pershing would have sacked Edwards on the spot, but hesitated to do so for a number of reasons. One was Edwards being politically connected in Washington D. C. and his dismissal now might disrupt Pershing's command. Another reason was that General

Passaga, the commander of the French corps under which the 26th Division was technically serving, though tactically it was on its own, had decorated the regimental colors of the 104th Infantry for its courage and fortitude at Apremont. This was the first time in history that a foreign power ever decorated the flag of an American Regiment. It had tremendous significance to American-French relations in that it recognized French acceptence of Americans as a fighting partner. The famous red and green Croix de Guerre medal was awarded to 116 doughboys before a military band that played the "Star Spangled Banner" and the "Marseillaise," each the National Anthem of America and France. Pershing could hardly remove Edwards from commanding the Division at the same time that a French General was decorating it. To prevent this from happening again, Pershing issued a standing order that no award from any other country was to be conferred on a US Army officer, soldier or unit in the future, unless and until he personally aproved it beforehand.

In the meantime, Edwards went along with thinking that the troops under his command performed admirably under overwhelming and trying circumstances, which was recognized and awarded the highest medal of France by the French High Command. He believed that he and his fellow West Point graduate Pershing's professional relationship was polluted by personal dislike.

George was treated for poison gas injuries for the second time and, after being put on medical leave and confined to quarters for a few days, released to return to regular duties. He was told he would be put in for the purple heart medal for being injured in battle, but he shrugged it off and paid it scarce attention, as was his way. Not surprisingly, after a battle has ended, a period of quiet descended on the sector, while both sides licked their wounds and planned their next moves.

George took advantage of his medical stand down to read his mail from home. His parents didn't have too much to say, they said, giving him details of their daily life. But this was important to George because it connected him to his family and normalcy,

EDDIE BRADY

which he needed as a lifeline to a yearned for home life and a better future. It gave him hope and helped him maintain his balance in this crazy war. He sometimes teased himself by opening Angelika's letters last, but most often he tore hers open first.

Dearest George,

I hope this letter finds you safe and well. I pray for you every day. We keep sending soldiers over there all the time, so we must be going to win. But the only soldier I dream about is you. You must come to my fitting room, so I can make you the best-dressed man in Boston. You are already the handsomest. I know you don't like me to say that, but you are. All the girls are jealous of me, because I have already found my man.

I have just the outfit in mind for you. Dark browns and blues should go well with your eyes and raven hair. You will be the fashion plate at church. I am still having trouble getting the cloths and dyes I want, because of the war shortages. I drive your car on Sundays to church and to the country for picnics. I always set a place on the blanket for you, a place of honor. Some friends make fun of me for doing this; they think I'm still playing with imaginary people like I did when I was young. They just don't understand. My imagination is all I have, while you are over there and I'm here. I'm sending you some cookies I made for you. It's terrible that they only feed you twice a day. No wonder you are hungry all the time. How can you win a war without enough food? Don't those Generals know anything? I hope these cookies don't get crushed, but if they do, eat the crumbs. They'll help fatten you up and give you energy. I kissed each cookie, so be sure you eat them top-side up.

Your brothers and sisters use your motor car the rest of the week, and often take it back and forth to Nashua. They say it's good for the engine, but apparently not for the tires, because they keep going flat when they hit a hole in the ground. The trolley cars around here are so frequent, that I only need a car to drive to the country.

My pillow is no substitute for you. So hurry-up and end the
war. Our wedding and our future children are waiting for you,
so we can start the rest of our lives.

Love you dearly,
Angelika

George was frequently amused by Angelika's perky and petulent nature. She writes like she talks. It's almost like she is right here talking to me, George mused. He would often read and reread her letters. It was like a breath of fresh air from home. Mail from home; it's the best morale booster, he thought.

"You keep smiling like that, George, and they'll put you away with the shell shocked boys," said Woz.

"These letters are my island of sanity. They remind me of how wonderful life can be."

"I hope it remains that way," said Woz. "You heard what happened last week to Martignetti from the 104th Regiment, didn't you? He remained chaste to save himself for his sweetheart at home, and he got a *'Dear John letter'* for his faithfulness. Life isn't fair, is it?"

"This whole war isn't fair. An Archduke's driver makes a wrong turn and twenty two million men take up arms and march into this World War that results in the mass slaughter of millions," mourned George.

"Enough on death. What's the status on our leave, so we can live a little?" Asked Woz?

"Captain Hawkins tells me that, unless all hell breaks out, we should go into a support unit, then into reserve and then leave. Leave, can you believe it?" "I'll believe it when I have the pass in my hand," remarked a cautious Woz.

In the middle of May, General Pershing ordered the Ist Division to move northwest of the Toul Sector, and to take part in an offensive to capture the ruined village of Cantigny that the Germans controlled. The Germans were using Cantigny as the furthest point of their third drive of the spring. Pershing wanted to erase the public relations coup the Germans made of the captured Americans at Seicheprey, that they blared from radio stations in Berlin and dropped leaflets over Allied lines trumpeting their alleged victory over the Americans. Though the body count at Seicheprey was three to one in favor of the Americans, and the Germans withdrew, they purposively didn't mention this fact. The surprise attack and American prisoners captured was enough of a victory and what the German propagandists were waiting for. One company of the 26th was specially assigned to attach itself to the Ist Division. The attack would prominently feature artillery.

"Artillery conquers, infantry occupies," was the byword of the American Commanders.

At the same time as this special assignment, George's Company H and Company K were the first to be taken out of rotation and given an unusual five day double-leave of 48 hours each and a travel day in recognition of their long service in the line, highlighted by their five battles within a two week period.

"A day for each battle?" Queried a jubilant George.

"Who cares? As long as we go." Countered Woz.

"Go. Where?" Asked George. "You're the party-hearty guy."

"Nancy. It's about twenty-five miles from here. I feel it calling me. The booze, the broads and the music, in that order."

"Let's see if there are any transports going there. The trains have delays and we don't have all the time in the world," suggested George.

And this was how they reached Nancy, a primary city in the Lorraine Province. They were able to get beds in a barracks on the edge of town, dropped their duffle bags, and got a ride into town. They weren't wasting any time. They headed for the nearest live looking bar, with the music and the gaiety blaring from the opened windows and front doors. French soldiers and American doughboys were everywhere to be seen. The local population, however, had many German speaking people, and had since 1871, given the history of the Province. They had been warned to be careful of German spies.

They walked briskly into the crowded bar, the *Maid of Honore*, presumably named after Jeanne D'Arc. It was mobbed with a buzzing crowd, with many animated converstions ongoing, punctuated with lively hand gestures, music and a singer well into song, with a few crap games going on and more card games. A section of the floor was set aside for dancing. A loud, festive atmosphere prevailed. George and Woz worked their way through to the bar and ordered local beer. They meandered around and when they saw a rare few empty seats at a table they sat down. Since there was eight seats at the round table, people came and went. While sitting there, chug-a-lugging their beer, a woman approached George,

"Handsome doughboy buy Georgette a drink, Ja?"

"George, she's got the same name as you, only she's female. Buy her a drink; she can tell us what's going on locally. If you won't, I will."

"Ya frauline, sit down." Said George.

With that, Georgette surprises George, and whistles at a waiter that she obviously knows.

"Pierre! Cognac for ve and da doughboy."

"Are you German or French?" George asks her. She is small framed, with bright blue eyes, and strawberry blonde hair, but a little tough looking, George thought.

"Georgette, she is both." She says in her distinct accent.

"Oh, you mean you're half French and half German."

"Ya. Is so." Mr. doughboy."

"George, they call me George."

"Ya, is George. I compree."

"You work here long?"

"Ya. Much months. Is better than last place Georgette work."

"This place can be dangerous with all these drunken soldiers, don't you think?"

"I no worry. I carry."

"Carry what, if you don't mind me asking?"

She pulled up her full skirt and slipped a small derringer from her garter. George looked at the snub-nosed revolver and smiled.

"It looks like a toy," he said.

"No toy. Bad bang, bang. My boyfriend, monsieur, he give Georgette."

She then, just as unobtrusively, slid the heavy little revolver back under her red garter.

The waiter returned with their cognac, and George paid him.

"Merci, monsieur," responded the waiter, as he rushed off to answer another call for

"Pierre! Mon ami!"

"It sure would be a shame to get blood on your beautiful clothes, wouldn't it?" asked Woz, who had been following the conversation with interest.

Georgette took her drink, tossed it down in one gulp, and turned toward Woz and said with a disgusted sigh,

"Monsieur, when it comes to dat, Georgette vill not vorry about staining my dress."

The obvious common sense of her answer caused George to feel stupid. So he sipped his cognac.

"Monsieur George need a place tonight?"

"Oh, I'm all set, merci beau coup."

With a wave of her hand and a resigned look on her worn face, she rose and without saying another word disappeared into the crowd, looking for business.

"George, she was propositioning you. Why didn't she ask me?"

"Because she came to me and I bought her a drink, you didn't."

"Well, she didn't look like the type I'd want to get too close too, anyway; not with her bang, bang toy gun," said a suddenly sober Woz.

The combination of travel and booze caught up to both of them, and they left Joan of Arc's place to get back to their billet before they ran out of money too early in their leave time. The following lazy days of late sleeping on cots was a welcome relief. Bouncing up and hitting the bars, dance halls, picture shows, live entertainment, even though they didn't fully understand the French or German songs and didn't recognize some of the English songs, was a tonic for their souls. Woz tried the crap and card games, but lost early and often enough to chase him away at George's urging, and while he had any money left. They never knew for sure when or where their next payday would be, or if they would be in an area where they could spend it.

"We better head back. I can't believe our leave is almost over. These days just flew by," lamented George.

"Always does when you're having fun. That's the way of it," affirmed Woz. Whatever, let's hit the road. General Pershing is waiting for us to win the war for him."

George and Woz joined many in the two companies making their way back to Seicheprey. Their expressed feelings were a mixture of restfulness as the result of the pleasant change and the freedom to do whatever they wanted, and go where they wanted, within given boundaries, and anxiety and wonder of what was next on their horizon. Often, when coming back from leave, there were new orders waiting for them.

"Belleau Wood?" Akers repeated back to Lieutenant Malone.

"The Marines have had a real donneybrook with the Germans at Chateau Thierry, and even more so just six miles away at Belleau Wood. The month of June has been a real hellhole for them. They took fearful casualties, though they did stop the Boche on six separate attacks at Belleau Wood. The Boche were trying to breakthrough to Paris," said the always serious Malone.

"This time he was dead-on accurate and not exaggerating," confirmed a sullen Captain Hawkins. "The Marines lost so many men, they need the Army to replace their decimated manpower. That's us."

In a slightly hushed tone of voice, the Captain continued,

"I heard that when Pershing read the report of the terrible losses in Marine dead, injured and captured at Belleau Wood, he took the report, stiff necked, disciplined, and composed, read it in front of his aides, stared into space and muttered,

'All these men lost their legs, arms, and lives following my orders.'

"He then turned away, walked into his office and shut the door so hard, it bounced slightly open, and sitting down, burst into tears, buried his bowed head into his hands, his body racking with grunts."

"THE WOOD"

The 26th Division was loaded onto trucks, then trains, and back to trucks again in a stop and go, hurry up and wait type trip to the Chateau Thierry-Bellau Wood Salient. This salient was a large protuberance that was dug into the Allied lines as the result of the June drive of the Germans that would, back and forth, tail into and peter out into the first week of July. The Marne River ran close by the area, which was along the main road from Metz to Paris. Anticipating their final drive on Paris, Ludendorf had Big Bertha, the largest German gun, firing its giant shells on Paris since March 21, with the first German offensive of the 1918 spring season. By the summer a million Parisians had fled the capital city in a panic and the French government was planning to move to Bordeaux, the provincial capital in the southwest of France. French morale was as low as it had ever been in the war.

The French Premier, Georges Clemenceau, the aging "Tiger of France," tried to reach the front lines near the German breakthrough to make his own assessment of the American Front, but was blocked at a massive traffic jam caused by doughboys moving to the front. He turned back in a rage. Back in Paris he telegraphed a fiery rant at President Wilson and tried to get Pershing sacked. But Wilson brushed him aside and stood by his General.

The German troops in this breakthrough thrust were composed of their best, the elite Prussian Guards, and the crack Bavarian Storm Troopers under Prince Rupprecht. They had knocked the French off of the Chemin des Dames Ridge, where the 26th Division had recently occupied for six weeks in February and March. The Boche continued their penetration for twenty miles into the Allied lines and twenty miles wide. The French had fallen back from

Chateau Thierry, disorganized and withdrew helter skelter to a rear line of defense.

"Go back! Go back! The Boche! The Boche are coming!"

They so warned the advancing American Marines who took their places in the line. The Marines reportedly responded with:

"Retreat Hell! We just got here!"

"This is as good a place to die as any," and

"It's kill or be killed."

Telephone communication reports reached the 26th Division of the heroic stand of the Marines they were going to join. The disjointed transportation system had everyone grumbling and complaining. While stopped at a siding and spread out along the track, smoking and eating their food rations, some one yelled,

"Look!" He was pointing up in the sky at a developing dogfight between a couple of dozen aeroplanes. They were circling around each other and getting in position to attack. The doughboys were all pointing up and trying to identify the type of aeroplanes. Gunfire was sporadic and light at first. George and Woz stretched their necks watching the action.

"It's American pilots flying French Nieuports and the new Spads against German Fokkers and Pfalzs," shouted Captain Hawkins.

"Those red nose planes are the Fokkers from Von Richthofen's squadron," added Lieutenant Malone.

"Who the hell is Von Richthofen?" Asked Woz.

"He's the 'Red Baron,' Germany's greatest air ace. He was shot down by ground fire, of all things, back in April. But many of the members of his squadron are aces," continued the Captain.

The aeroplanes kept trying to get behind and under each other for tactical advantages. Originally, five Allied planes went after seven German machines. Then twelve more German aeroplanes jumped into the melee. Up and down, round and round they went, as the fascinated doughboys watched in awe and excitement. Then two planes crashed in mid-air!

"Oh my God, a head on collision!"

"A furball, it's called," exclaimed the Lieutenant.

"Ooh! Look at those sharp turns!" Yelled Akers.

"The fighter pilots have to take short, sharp turns because of the short range of their guns," shouted Captain Hawkins.

Comments and hand and arm gestures shot up toward the wild fight in the sky. Planes caught fire, smoke followed them down as they plummeted to the ground and crashed. Because of the smoke and flames, it was sometimes difficult to tell whose planes were shot down. Another plane, a red nosed Fokker had its wing shot off and spun crazily as it plunged toward the ground. A Nieuport burst into flames and dove down. The planes spread out, and furious pursuits took place. More smoke and more downings. The surviving planes gradually disengaged and flew back toward their own lines, their fuel running low after a long battle.

Captain Hawkins walked over to a group of doughboys still gesturing excitedly about what they saw and said,

"All you guys who think the flyboys get all the glory, hot meals and warm beds every night, take note. Two American fighter pilots were shot down just now, and five Germans. That was better than they usually do in this sector, because they are usually outnumbered by Fritz Pfalz, single seater fighters. In their early training, almost seven out of ten American fighter pilots never survive with their lives pilot school. And our Captain Eddie Rickenbacker has been lobbying for pilot parachutes. Some of the German pilots have them. Think about that and count your blessings."

The Captain then motioned at Lieutenant Malone and Sargent Sardonis, the latter then shouting,

"Ok, you dogfaces, get back on the train. We got a war to win. Let's go! Let's go. Move it! All aboard!"

Meanwhile, back of the German lines at Chateau Thierry, a German scout in early June reported to General Von Boehm, at his headquarters. The proud PrussianVon Boehm commanded forty German Divisions in the area.

"Mon Gen-er-al, the French have withdrawn and Americans are now in the line and dug in. They're Marines and a prisoner we took claims we are in for it. Our artillery, mortor launchers, machine guns and aeroplanes are inflicting devastating injuries on these Marines, but they fight on. They are as tough on defense as the Brits. We can't move them just now."

"Madness. It's madness. They don't know when they are licked. Our losses are also terrible. Hindenburg is all over me. And they are not our equal; they are just fresh troops. Go around them, you swine! Why do I have knuckleheads for Field Commanders? Go around them!"

The German Field Commanders ordered a flanking movement through Belleau Wood, about six miles away. They had brought along 200 Maxim machine gun teams and positioned them throughout Belleau Wood, which, at one square mile, was about half the size of Central Park, in New York City. Its true size was one and a half miles long and one-half mile wide. The Boche would later refer to it as "Hellwood." But the Marines also anticipated the same movement and eventually stopped it, fighting on doggedly, though suffering appalling casualties.

The battles raged back and forth throughout June. It was wild hand to hand fighting, with the Germans calling the American Marines "Devil dogs" because of their Indian style of fighting. By this they meant they were undisciplined hordes, yelling while attacking, shooting from the hip, directly attacking machine guns, leaping over parapets and diving into trenches, slashing with bayonets and knives. To them it was madness and mayhem, with everyman for himself. Despite their unorthodoxy, the Marines finally drove the Germans out of Belleau Wood by June 26th. But their losses were so high that it necessitated the need for an urgent call for the US Army to be brought in to relieve the Marines at Belleau Wood as soon as they could get there.

Effective American artillery fire helped keep the Germans behind the "*Wood*" and buried in their shelters, but not for long. During this interval the Boche were rebuilting their forces, and secretly, gradually working their way back into the wood. A final attack and push to Paris would be made. The 2nd Division, including the Marines, would be relieved. The 26th Yankee Division was selected to replace the Marines. For their own defense, expecting the Americans to attack again, the Germans again filled the Wood with an exceptional number of machine gun emplacements, which were well disguised by the deep foliage, dense trees and heavy underbrush of this old hunting preserve. Although the wood was a relatively small area, it was a killing field. Kidney shaped, its thick, tall trees had occasional open areas that offered no cover and invited death to anyone who dared to cross it.

CHAPTER THIRTY EIGHT

BELLEAU WOOD

The 26th Division was brought up west of Chateau Thierry between Bouresches and Lucy-le-Bocage, both heavily damaged villages, and marched to the Belleau Wood area to give them a sense of the lay of the land. They had been more fully briefed on the way in. They didn't know that the Germans were quietly planning and plotting to re-enter the Wood and getting ready to launch another attack in a final desperate attempt to break through the American lines and capture the war-winning prize of Paris.

While marching toward the Wood, Akers passed on some scuttlebutt he had heard when they stopped near Bouresches.

"Hey Woz. Remember that Nieuport we saw shot down East of here? The American fighter pilot of that downed plane was Quentin Roosevelt!"

"So, who's he?"

"Hell and damnation, Woz. You don't know the name of former President Theodore Roosevelt's son?"

"He's got a bunch of sons, hasn't he? How am I supposed to know them all? Anyway, that's awful. It'll probably kill his old war commander of a father."

"What about his mother," said a saddened George. "What a shame."

"Yeah. And I heard he was well liked, a good pilot, but too much of a daredevil. He flew off on his own to attack a squadron of late-arriving Fokkers and got isolated and surrounded. A big loss for us."

EDDIE BRADY

"And I heard that the artillery saved the Marines at Belleau Wood. They decimated the tree-tops with saturation shelling. The falling tree limbs acted like shrapnel slivers cutting and clubbing the Heinie trapped troops below. It also knocked down most of their tree forts. They had machine guns as well as snipers up there. The saturation shelling savaged them and inflicted so many casualties that they had to pull out of the Wood," remarked Sargent Sardonis.

"But even on our side, manning an artillery team can be dangerous. If a bad shell explodes inside the cannon, it can wipe out a whole team. And every other team, seeing that happen, and ready to fire next, has to wonder if they got a bad shell in their supply, too. That's got to be nerve wracking," said George. "Yet, courageously, they stand by their guns."

"And they have to be accurate also. If they fire short or long and hit their own soldiers, that's got to rip them up morale wise, added Woz."

Captain Hawkins, not liking the conversation, changed the subject,

"Heinies, Sarge? The French call the Germans Boche, the Russians call them Fritz, the Brits call them Huns. And I've heard Prussian, Teutonic, and Heinies. Did I miss any?"

"Yes, bastards. The Germans have more nicknames than we have cuss words. So that one is good enough," said Akers. "And who cares, anyway."

"It's a better subject for our morale than our own planes crashing, shelling our own men, or bad shells blowing up our own men," snapped back the Captain.

With that cue, George started singing the popular Army refrain, *"How you gonna keep 'em down on the farm, after they're seen Paris."*

The others joined in and sung a full chorus.

"Even though da Paris is-a offa da limits to us-a, damn it all-la!" Complained Private Pasquale DiGregorio.

Then Woz, not to be outdone by his best friend, continued the singing with a tuneful, risque song the British had dedicated to the good time, painted ladies of Armentieres in Northwestern

France early in the war, and the Yanks adopted, "*The Madamoiselle from Armentieres, parlez-vous!*" was changed to "*The Madamoiselle from Bar-Le-Duc, parlez-vous! Inky Dinky Parlez-vous!*" Woz's discordant voice, however, scarcely gave it justice. His spirited rendition, or joire de vivre, as the French would say, nevertheless, was contagious, as the other doughboys picked up on it and the air vibrated with their chorus.

Their marching steps picked up and they sauntered along the road with a bounce in their step and a rare bouyancy in their hearts.

"See what you started, George?" Cracked Akers.

"Guilty on all charges," smiled George.

"How we doing now, Captain; our morale officer?" Sargent Sardonis inquired.

Captain Hawkins just smiled, and nodded, nothing needing to be said.

———————————

The 26th Division approached Belleau Wood as usual at night and away from the Marne River where they would be more readily detectable, because the half moon deflected light off the water. They also took advantage of whatever ravines or gulleys the land provided to give them natural cover, proceeded single file, and kept reminding themselves not to bunch up, with no talking. Scouts were sent out ahead, to cover their flanks, and had a rear guard cover their tail. Their French guide suggested they use the stealth of the Native American Indian on their way in, to watch for trip wires, land mines and booby traps. They were also reminded to leave souvenirs alone, after one doughboy picked up a Boche helmet and out fell a head!

George smiled at the irony of being told to use these stealth tactics and the French and European fascination with the Native American Indian. Woz's second squad followed behind George's first squad. Because of George's recent unconventional experience, he was also uniquely alert to the possible presence of animals, especially wild boars. After a typical long night march of stop and go, they arrived at their destination, about a mile short of Belleau Wood. They settled in a day ahead of schedule.

The doughboys dug only narrow rifle pits, or "graves" as their deadpan humor called it, for some cover. And they had to dig with bayonets, tin cups and spoons, and the short handled shovels they had, because the engineers had not yet arrived with entrenching tools. They were also hungry because they had eaten through their emergency rations and moved too far ahead of their rolling kitchens. Some French meat they had became spoiled and inedible. They smoked inside their blankets to quell their hunger. But the best cure for hunger was sleep, and they slept where they fell. The Marines planned to pull out the next night under cover of darkness. They looked, haggard, wasted and worn out. It was the tenth of July, 1918, hot during the day and warm throughout the night.

The 101st Army Engineers were brought up to dig a trench line and to bury the dead. The 2nd Division did not have the time to dig graves, before it was pulled out of the line and sent off to a different sector. As it turned out they had no time to dig much of a trench line either, as the terrain was flat and open. Besides, priority was given to burying the many bodies of Marines and Germans that littered the landscape. Some of bodies had been there for a month and the air reeked with an awful, gagging stench. The burial-detail groups, volunteers, had to wear gas masks to stifle the foul smell. George and other volunteer doughboys from Company H went forward into the Wood to help the Engineers bury the dead. With suicide snipers still around, one doughboy said that entering Belleau Wood was like entering a dark hall full of assassins.

In the middle of the Wood stood the ruined remnants of a hunting lodge. American shellfire had been so heavy and destructive that the trees were burnt bare of leaves and the shattered tree trunks blackened from fires. Then a most ghoulish of sights sickened a startled Woz,

"Oh, my God," murmured Woz, from the inside of his gas mask. "Look up, George!"

Body parts and fragments of clothing were hanging from the bare branches of blackened trees. George looked up at the birds of prey that were circling around and picking at what was left of human beings. He turned away in disgust. Then he entered the hunting lodge, what was left of it. Now it was George's turn to inadvertently summon Woz.

"Hell and damnation! What is this!"

Woz hurried in through the blown out front door, saw George pointing at a table, and looked.

"Can you believe it? Look at this dead German sitting up straight in a chair, eyes open, with three cards still left in his hand," exclaimed George.

His hands were lying on a tilted, broken three legged table. A second German was slumped onto the slanted table, with the side of his head lying against it. A third German was sprawled on the floor clutching a card, the jack of clubs, reaching toward the front of a crumbled fireplace.

"Where's the fourth German? Four people play cards, not three." Said George.

Woz shrugged and walked around. George circled the other way, but also saw no one else. They both exited out the front door frame, stepping over broken glass, stones and dusty debris.

"There he is!" Snapped Woz.

Half buried under a splintered front door to the side, on the right, was a fourth German soldier, holding a Luger pistol in his hand and spilled cards in the other. It portrayed macabre sudden death or permanently interrupted life, however it struck you, shuddered George. They left the Wood later that day, thinking it nothing but an uninhabitable desolate graveyard.

The next morning the Signal Corps checked the telephone and communication wiring of the sector, and wire patrols checked the barbed wires for any cuts. It didn't take the Boche long to welcome the newly arrived Army. Shelling commenced at mid-day. The Germans were using 77 millimeter guns called "Whiz bangs" for the sound they made and the larger 88 millimeter guns known as "quick dicks" because of the low trajectory of the shells it fired, resulting in quicker arrivals and explosions. At first it seemed to be just probing to gauge the US Army's return fire capability. Gas sentries were also set up, because of the heavy gas shells fired by the Boche on the Marines. The Marines accelerated their departure to thin out the number of Americans in the target area. The doughboys set up their machine gun stations, trench mortors and field artillery emplacements. Two of the Divisions field artillery units were detached and assigned to the 2nd Division that was headed into a hot zone further north. Chateau Thierry and Belleau Wood, part of the *Pas Fini Sector*, became a quiet sector, if only because of the deafening silence following the German withdrawal, after a horrendous six-week period of ferocious battles.

For the first few days it indeed was a relatively quiet sector. While things were slowed down, and George had the time, he wrote Angelika,

> *Dear Angel,*
>
> *I'm firing off this letter to let you know I'm fine. I've convinced all the bullets heading my way go around me on your orders. So you see, my darling, your indominatable spirit and charm is irrestible.*
>
> *And, of course, charm, is your middle name, I don't care what your parents say. From harm to charm is my future. I mean, our future. It's written in the stars that we can both see above in our common sky. Also, I want to order two children right now. You are not the only one who can give orders in this family-to-be. I would like to have a son to carry on the Dilboy family name, but he can have your personality. Then we can have a girl, who will have your beauty and my personality. How's that for the well-rounded family?*
>
> *And speaking of family, tell my brothers not to burn out my car. I've got big plans for that chariot. I thought that maybe*

we could take a honeymoon trip to Texas. Gas will be more available by then. The dusty Texas terrain and sunny weather remind me of Alatsata and Smyrna. Maybe we could even visit El Paso and the Rio Grande River or the port city of Brownsville. Think on it.

Also, save some blue and pink cloth for our boy and girl. You can make their clothes. Whether a girl or a boy comes first, doesn't matter. We'll have fun picking out the names together.

I know my silliness irks you at times. Sometimes I do it on purpose, because you're so pretty when you're cross with me. Besides, you become taller when you're mad, but not as tall as me. Hee, hee. Know also and please understand that clowning around helps me vent. Comic relief relieves my tension and hides my nervousness or awkwardness.

God, how I miss you, Angel. Apart, I feel our love can be whispered from heart to heart. I will hold you in my heart until I can hold you in my arms. Your presence in my heart remains as warm as the sun kissed wind, fresh as a sighing breeze, your hot, caressing breath covering my lips. I dream of you all the time, my lips brushing your hair, your breath warming my face, your breasts holdling my heart, our two selves merged into one passionate embrace.

My beloved Angelika, be assured I find sublime comfort in my belief, that if I don't make it, and I am denied our tomorrows, my last vision of you will be to hold you in my arms, hearing your voice in the wind, seeing your face in the stars, and feeling your soft, summoning lips blending with mine, to the end of my breath.

Loving you forever, I will always be
Georgie, Your Georgie

A sigh of satisfaction spread through George on finishing, sealing and dropping the letter off for mailing. "It gets me from here to her," George thought, "my lifeline to whatever will be. Now that my priorities are set, let's get on with this war so I can go home."

On July 15, 1918, the German's, led by a desperate General Von Boehn, and his prized Prussian Guards and Bavarian storm troopers, launched a fifth offensive on the Western Front. It began with a furious artillery barrage pouring out of that desolate, graveyard called Belleau Wood, stripped bare of foilage, reaking of leafless, lifeless, dying trees, with the putrid, foul smelling stench of some hurried, half buried bodies, rotting in the baking sun. With a down wind blowing toward the dug-in doughboys, the air was suffocating, making breathing difficult, and causing the men in the trenches to violently turn their heads away. There, George, Woz and the doughboys waited in curled up bodies, instinctively ducking and cringing away from the shellfire bursting all around them.

They waited impatiently for the American guns to return fire. But first the American guns had to locate and target the Boche guns. It could be difficult because the Gemans cleverly fired two or three guns at a time, so that it would be tougher to detect which guns were zeroing in on their position. The trapped Americans anxiously waited for the gas guards to shout their warning, or send up their gas flares. And they wouldn't know if it would be mustard or chorline poison gas that was incoming. They dreaded the gas shells and cannisters splatting on the ground to burst out of their shells and to suck the breath out of their lungs. Thereafter a German infantry charge was sure to follow the relentless barrages. It was the Marine nightmare all over again, only this was the seventh battle of Belleau Wood.

For three hours the barrage thundered overhead. The doughboy Army had only a rough wire in front of them. The open, flat terrain in front of wheat fields, where they were less than a mile from the Wood, allowed them only to be able to hastily build up some parapets. And they didn't have enough time to build many of those. The whining, whistling roar of the exploding shells sent geysers of dirt flying in arched sprays, murderous mountains of shrapnel, steel fragments cutting into and tearing human flesh, inflicting gruesome injuries and death.

The Germans were saturation-shelling the American Army, in the same way the Marines had shelled the Boche the prior month.

But at least the Boche had the shelter and initial protection of the Wood. It was payback time. George saw a doughboy blown up. When the smoke cleared, the doughboy disappeared; he was blown into oblivion. As the creeping shells exploded down the line, hands, arms and heads were blown off bodies, littering the area with raw bloody body parts. Dead horses and mules dotted the scarred ground, stone stiff, with one whose legs stuck up in the air. The grisley scene and stench was so revolting, some doughboys vomited on the spot. Even among the survivors, some bodies lifted right off their feet by the shell concussions. It was a sickening, frightful, helpless feeling. One could only hold on and endure.

Then George hair stood on end, as he heard a hideous scream cry out,

"Aaarrggghhh! Aaarrrgghhh! Aaaggghhh!

He turned and saw Woz bent over in the next trench screaming! Reflexively, George lunged for the trench ladder and speed-climbed it, leaping over the top, running down the line and threw himself across the dirt parapet. He slid down the side of the log reinforced earthworks, pushed aside some doughboys, grabbed the still yelling Woz, shook him and shouted,

"Woz! Woz! What's the matter? What's wrong? Are you hit? Where? Where?"

Stunned to see George, Woz suddenly stopped yelling and shouted,

"Hit? No. No. I can't stand the noise. I'm screaming to relieve the pressure, the pressure in my ears. God! When will it stop?"

"Woz, cover your ears! I said, cover your ear-r-rs!"

George shoved Woz down on the fire step, took Woz's hands and placed them on each side of his head and covered his ears.

"Keep them there!" Shouted George. Then George fell back, and sat himself down on the fire step, breathing heavy and trying to regain his composure. Fortunately, the shelling started to slow down. After a few minutes went by, George looked up and saw the green gas flare go up, followed by the vocal warning of the gas sentries,

"Masks on! Masks on! Incoming gas! Incoming gas!"

George immediately pulled his mask off his hip and placed it over his face. He then went across and grabbed Woz, who was fumbling to get his mask on. He helped him finish putting it on, and when all set, they mumbled their muffled ok's through the masks. They then both joined the other doughboys mounting the fire step and watched through lifting, irregular clouds of smoke, advancing German infantry. It wasn't too long until the first front line orders were given,

"Hold your fire! Hold your fire!"

Then still later, as the smoke continued to rise, the field became clearer still, and the creeping enemy soldiers could be seen getting into rifle range, the shouted orders changed to,

"Fire at will! Make it count! Fire at will!"

George and Woz and the front line of doughboys opened fire. Some riflemen, unfocusing, fired in panic at an encroaching enemy, but most fired with discipline, using their sight, aim and fire training before pulling the trigger.

Some of the German artillery fell short and was exploding on their own infantry. This miscalculation helped pile up Boche bodies as close as forty meters in front of the American lead front line. This unusual mistake threw this ground assault into confusion and inadvertantly blunted it. The Boche attacked sputtered to an uneven stop. Slowly, and then more rapidly, the Germans pulled back. Some doughboys immediately jumped up to pursue, but were called back by their officers.

"What the hell's going on? We're got them on the run," ranted one doughboy.

"Let our line mortors and rifle-fire chase them back. How do we know the fall back isn't a trap to suck us into the Wood and their waiting machine guns?" Barked Major Mulholland, who was personally checking the line, and moved on, growling, "Discipline! Discipline!"

"Medics! Medics! Over here! Over here! Shouted Lieutenant Malone. George and Woz ran around the bend in the line, where a hastily built earth-log shelter caught a rare direct hit and buried those within. A doughboy staggered out, coughing, choking and clearing debris away from his blocked path.

"Inside, Inside. Captain Hawkins is hit, hit bad," he sputtered. Then he collapsed.

A medic helped him along. George and Woz threw broken logs aside and avoided fallen corrugated tin roof pieces that could cut them severely. Many rescuers were about the devastated shelter pulling scrap out of the way. Cries of pain and heavy groaning helped them locate the injured. But no Captain Hawkins could be found.

"Where's Captain Hawkins?" yelled George.

"Outside! Outside! He's on a stretcher. We pulled him out of the rubble," spoke a medic, pushing Woz out of the way.

Rushing back, they found him on the ground, bleeding from the head and mumbling incoherently. He was on his side, having rolled off the stretcher.

"Woz, help me pick him up," said George, with some urgency.

George had his feet and Woz grabbed his shoulders. As they lifted Captain Hawkins to the stretcher, George was jolted to see the Captain's left arm fall off!"

"My God!" spit out George. Woz said nothing, but his mouth was open in disbelief.

Recovering from the shock, George yelled,

"Medics! Medics! We've got to get him out of here! Ice! Put the arm in ice."

"Where the hell we going to get ice in July?" Sputtered Woz.

"Just get him to a medical tent. He needs a doctor!" said a distraught George.

A medic ran over, calmly told George to put the severed arm on the Captain's body and told Woz to take the head end of the stretcher. They hurried and stutter-stepped the stretcher out of the ruins. They disappeared back to the rear, while George slumped down on the ground and stared blankly ahead, trying to get his bearings. Lieutenant Malone came over and reassuredly tapped his shoulder.

"They'll do what they can for the Captain, George. Let's hope for the best."

George nodded his head in silent understanding, then went along with the Lieutenant to see how the surviving-well could help those in need. The area looked like hell on earth, with fires flickering, smoke all around, the air reeking with the acrid smell of cordite, some doughboys striding around with purpose, others staggering around in a daze, and still others just looking about registering the reality of the horror. The rest of the day and the next one was spent treating the injured, assessing the damage, and bringing in manpower replacements from the support and reserve troops. In this environment, strangers became friends fast, having shared a common tragedy. Despite surface friendships, one learned not to become too close to any new replacement, in case they went "west" the next battle, and so the blows of further deaths wouldn't hurt them as much, emotionally and mentally, that is.

Assessing the damage, the artillery suffered three destroyed guns from the 101st, 103rd and 51st artillery units, as the Boche concentrated their fire on destroying the American guns and their supply dumps. Even undamaged guns can't hurt the enemy if they have no shells. Now the 26th Division's artillery firepower was seriously diminished. They would have to use their trench mortars and get close enough to the enemy to use rifle grenades and hand thrown grenades, which will increase the casualty rate, inevitably.

Two days post-battle, Company H was saddened to hear that Captain Hawkins, West Point graduate and revered commander, died on the operating table from loss of blood and shock. With things quieted down, the survivors of Company H were allowed to attend this one of many burials in the rear. There he was put in an individual grave with the full military honors available in the sector. Bill Buckman and Pasquale DeGregorio also suffered injuries, and were treated for shell fire and gas wounds, though they returned to the line.

CHAPTER THIRTY NINE

AISNE-MARNE OFFENSIVE

The Germans, with admirable discipline, were consolidating their forces, and they kept the Americans away with sparse and disjointed shellings. With studied whimsicality, and at odd, unexpected times, they alternated the shelling. They launched high explosive shells that announced their coming by their screaming shrieks, and alternated those with chlorine and mustard gas shells. The doughboys hunkered down, hoping to survive the barrage. Eventually, the shelling ceased, more surprisingly, the expected folow-up attack did not happen. The Germans used the shelling to consolidate their lines.

Meanwhile, Marshall Foch and General Pershing finalized plans to counterattack at Belleau Wood and other fronts. It would be called the Aisne-Marne Offensive, named after the two rivers serving as north and south boundaries of the attack. Closer to Chateau Thierry and Belleau Wood and the Marne River, it was also called the Second Battle of the Marne. The first was the famous "Miracle of the Marne," in which the Germans made their mighty drive into France toward Paris in 1914 in an early attempt to end the war. It was stopped only when the desperate French rushed thousands of soldiers to the front lines in hundreds of taxi's it commandeered from Paris to stop the Germans from overrunning Paris.

At last the Americans would take the offensive at this furthest point of German penetration, the Chateau Thierry-Belleau Wood salient. Because of the element of surprise, secrecy was paramount and no advance shelling would precede the attack. The local commanders requested this because the Division's artillery capability had been so depleted, that its inclusion would only announce to the Boche how weakened it was. Beforehand, only haphazard shelling answered the equally limited Boche fire.

Adding to the misery, it started to rain late into the night of July 17th. At 10 p.m. the troops were assembled in Company-strength under various covers back of the lines. The details and objectives of the attack were announced to the troops, who had sensed during the day that something was up. Watching their Officers scoot around with stern and serious faces told them what no words could. Something big was in the wind. Anxiety and anticipation levels rose up.

They were to re-assemble at designated points in the front line at 3:00 a.m. They were given extra bandoleers and told to be ready to fix bayonets.

"Are we going to get close enough to use our bayonets?" Asked a wondering Woz.

"That and our trench knives. Bullets run out and rifles aren't as useful in hand to hand fighting," answered a chuckling George.

"Damn it, George. What the hell is so funny!"

"Nothing. I'm nervous and tense, like you. Maybe more so. With all my war experience, I still tighten up with nerves at these times. I always will. So I joke; it breaks the tension. It works for me; I'm sorry it bothers you, Woz."

"Aww, forget it. It's individual, I guess."

"3:00 a.m., note 3:00 a.m. we move out, fix your watches!" Lieutenant Malone, loudly whispered, as he moved down the line. He was now Captain Malone, taking the deceased Hawkins place with a field promotion.

"Fix bayonets! Fix Bayonets! Came the hissed cry down the line at thirty minutes before "go."

Clicking his bayonet into place, George suddenly plunged it into the side enbankment and rubbed dirt on the blade to take away any glint. He removed his helmet and did the same. Without saying a word, Woz did likewise. At 3:00 a.m., however, they were told to stand down and stand by. They were waiting for additional artillery to be moved up. The tension was nerve wracking; the men were fidgety, restless and irritable. They cursed the air blue, chewed tobacco, and munched on hardtack candy, with George alternately joking and feigning sleep. George's antics entertained some, distracted others and a few turned and moved away in disgust to do their own thing.

Finally, fearing that the primed soldiers would lose their edge, and unable to wait any longer, the Commanders decided to attack without the hoped for artillery. At 4:25 a.m. the word came, "Five minutes! At Four thirty we go!"

"George, you got a watch. Reset it."

"I don't have to. It was set at 3:00 a.m. and is still accurate now," replied George absentmindedly. Staring ahead blankly for a few minutes, he suddenly shuddered and snapped out of it, glanced tensely at his watch and stiffened up to a rigid alertness.

"Fix Bayonets! At the ready!" ran down the line. A moment of pause and then finally, verbal commands,

"Let's go! Move out! Let's go!" So came the harsh whispers and the rustle of mass movement, as the doughboys got moving into the black abyss of No-Mans-land. Their pent up energies poured out as they spread out across the open fields in single, vertical files, not horizintal, following in a crouch the uneven, pockmarked ground, scarred by shellholes, and debris ridden wasteland. A single, vertical file gave less killing power to a machine gun that moved horizontally. George could hear his own breath as he gasped and grunted his way ahead. After a quarter mile, he heard a laboring Woz say,

"Ease up, George!" Warned Woz. "Careful, crouch speed doesn't mean jumping ahead. You'll isolate yourself."

"Only a quarter moon for light. That's a help." Answered George, after looking up at the dark sky, blinking with a few stars.

The rain was lightening up, but it made little difference, as George was soaked through his now heavier woolen uniform. The coarse fabric actually itched less, even though the lice still bit and hid in his hair. Scratching his head was a useful distraction during this advance. By 5:30 a.m. they were suddenly met with enemy flares turning the sky into instant day and exposing their advance. Shortly thereafter the enemy artillery opened up. The whining and whistling bomb shells exploded amongst the doughboys, scattering them into vulnerable bunches, eliciting commands of, "Don't bunch up! Spread out! Spread out!" yelled Captain Malone.

They were approaching their first objective, a raised railroad embankment to the right of the Wood somewhere near the small village of Vaux. Well hidden were two German machine gun nests, alongside an abandoned, ruined railroad station that was roofless. The machine guns were concealed by debris and scrub-brush, but not for long. The stutter-starts and rat-a-tat staccato rhythm of the deadly Boche maxims announced their arrival by the piercing screams of the suddenly spinning and falling doughboys. The air became fouled with "aaarrgggs!" "Oh-h-h!" "I'm hit! I'm hit! Medic! Medic!" "Damn!" "Uh!" "Bastards!" "Get those guns!" Crazy chaos and abrupt screams rent the air.

The twin terrors of the shellings and the machine gun fire took a terrible toll on the advancing Americans. The doughboys, in an odd contempt for their lethal destruction, irreverently referred to the machine guns as "typewriters." Though barely noticed on the ground, overhead air battles were starting to roar with the first arrival of dawn. The German Aeroplanes were far superior in number to the American French-made Nieuport fighters.

Back on the ground, the shelling now included gas. The condensed acid of the poisonous gas cannisters splat and the cracked cannisters split open and blinded and burned its victims. At the same time the high explosive shells caused instant death and covered the American lines with smoke. It was a cruel torture to wear a gas mask in the suffocating, sultry heat. Heavy breathing, condensed moisture build up and mucus filled the grotesque mask. Doughboys could not breathe inside or outside the mask; they were damned either way. One doughboy choked to death on his vomit. In the July heat, perspiration pooled in armpits and in groin areas, causing blistering and stinging burns from mustard gas. One doughboy had poured water from his canteen to his genitals to stop the burning, and having failed, he took a discarded, tank fuel-can and poured it's contents on his private parts to kill the lice. A bullet knocked the can out of his hands, sparking a fire. He burst into flames, and screaming, was burned to death. A doughboy witnessing this horrible tragedy, lost it and ran ahead in a blind rage, firing his rifle wildly, until he was cut down and killed by German machine gun fire.

The emphasized orders to the doughboys were to keep moving, don't look back, don't stop, not even for a buddy, because the medics will get there and are more qualified to help the hurt. Get to your objective! More lives will be saved by first taking out the enemy.

George and Woz continued zig zagging ahead, ignoring the bullets kicking up all around them. They tripped over some of their fallen doughboys, both alive and dead. They sought the cover of some four feet high wheat fields, aided by a ground rain mist. After the rain stopped, they even stumbled over revolting, grisly, bloated corpses. The tall wheat stalks, wilted by lack of rain all summer until then, and bullets that cut the stems, also brought them within the shorter range of nearby mortors with their higher trajectory. The Germans were following the doughboys as they moved along by the ripples they made in the yellow wheat field. Realizing this, the doughboys stopped to hide their whereabouts and to catch their breath. The doughboys talked, but not loud. They conversed in horse whispering, just audible enough to know who was near. George could hear Captain Malones voice telling them to stop and stay still. When George reached for his canteen to swig some water, he found that a bullet had pierced the bottom and it was empty. But what he thankfully found on his leg were water stains, not blood.

This wholesale killing of human beings by machine guns was mind numbing to George. Modern machine guns, artillery, mortors, automatic rifles, poison gases, tanks, submarines and aeroplanes, were all new to this total, world war. How did the Marines do it, wondered George. They drove the well-hidden and well dug-in German infantry out of Belleau Wood. As weird as it was, George found himself flashing back to the shoreline at Alatsata and Boston's Charles River with Angelika. He was yearning for a safe past, if only for a fleeting second, in this field of wheat and death. This close to death, he treasured life. War makes no sense; even the winners lose, he thought. Then George whispered out loud,

"This madness has got to end."

Then George heard Captain Malone give the order to move out. He regained his feet, but continued on in a very low crouch. He had to get around those machine guns. They were killing machines, mowing down doughboys. What the Americans didn't realize was that the Germans had the same idea as the Americans and were quickly and quiety heading straight for them. Each enemy was headed for each other in the night not knowing of the others presence, until the recent flares.

The Germans had snuck into the back of the tiny village of Vaux and set up the machine guns along a railroad line with a roofless station house beside it. George and Company H was facing the two machine gun teams hiding behind the railroad threstle. To the Americans right was Vaux, to their left was Belleau Wood. George heard Captain Malone shout out,

"We've got to take out those machine guns!"

George decided on his own to circle around to the left, though he had to get by some machine gun nests to his extreme left from Belleau Wood. Since dawn was coming up soon, he had to move right away. He was able to zig zag ahead with short bursts across open areas, grabbing what cover he could behind tree stumps, piled wheat stacks, tall grass clusters and some drainage ditches. He finally got to the railroad trestle, went behind the ruins of the train station and went for the far machine gun team. He carefully threw himself onto the ground and took aim. He used a stick under the barrel to steady his rifle and squessed off a shot. Bullseye! The German triggerman fell forward over the gun. The ammunition feeder pulled his luger, and spun the gun around looking for George. George fired off a second shot and winged the Boche, and knocked the pistol out of his shooting hand. The German yelled in pain, then fled. He ran toward the seond machine gun. The startled second machine gunner turned and fired, mistaking the running comrade as an American and shot him through. Seeing what he had done, and responding to another shot by George that missed, but came so close, that the twosome grabbed their gun and retreated into the roofless station to join the third machine gun team.

At this time the American artillery got the range and a barrage hit both ends of the train station house, collapsing the walls and exposing them to hostile rifle fire. By then, Sargent Klick and a contingent of H Company attacked the station house. An artillery shell landed beside the third machine gun and instantly killed both Germans. George threw a hand grenade at the second crew that had jumped up and fled. One was cut down by the grenade blast and killed instantly, but the other escaped. George was the first to burst over the station rubble. He was turning the dead Germans over with his rifle, checking to make sure they were dead and not faking it, when the other Americans arrived.

"Good shooting, George. You got here first!"

"Sarge, thanks for the backup," said a smiling and relieved George. While they were slapping each other in congratulations for reaching their initial objective, a serious Captain Malone came up and cut them off with the warning,

"Watch out guys, Boche snipers about. They're part of their rear guard. They're looking for careless pursuers. Take a five minute blow. Let me check the casualties." He then went out and Woz and Buckman came in, and joined them for a quick cigarette, now that the sun was out.

Moments later, however, a runner came bounding into the train station with a hand written order from Colonel Hume to the highest ranking officer. At the moment it was Sargent Klick. He took the handwriten note, which curtly said,

Move to your left flank. Machine guns in Belleau Wood.
Take them out. Now!

By Order of,
Colonel Frank Hume
103rd Infantry

Captain Malone ran in, Sargent Klick handed him the handwritten order, he read it and barked,

"Let's go! To the Wood. New objective. Single file, machine guns!"

Back through the wheat fields they ran, slowing down and crouching low when they hit the wheat. Some protection was afforded by the cover, but not against the diving Boche Fokker fighter aeroplanes strafing the area. They also faced artillery, mortor fire, rifle grenades and gas shelling, though the gas was over to their far left. It was crazy with firing and fighting, blown dirt, explosions in their midst, but the worst damage was being inflicted by the Boche "typewriters." There were screams and cries of "I'm hit, medic!" "Help me!" "Water." "My leg! My leg!" These desperate cries could be heard everywhere. It was unnerving and insane. They were bogged down near the villages of Torcy and Givry that were so small they didn't even appear on most maps of the area.

Ahead of George was the edge of the yellow wheat field that was mostly crushed from prior shellings, mortors and the killing gases that ruined vegation like wheat, as well as lives. The scene was further obscured by ground morning mist from below, and sky mist from the prior nights rainfall from above. Adding to the soup was the smoke from the high explosive shells raining down. The northeast corner of Belleau Wood reigned over this morass of miasma, sloping down to the devastated Village of Belleau, which, ironically, means "beautiful water" in French. To the far left, or west of the Village of Belleau one could see the top of the ruined church of the tiny, abandoned slip of a community named Torcy. In the opposite direction, but not within view, was another miniscue hamlet called Bouresches, once a whistle stop on the local trunk of the passing railroad. This was the same trunk line that ran along the busted and shattered earthwork embankment that carried a few miles of unused, old broken tracks. The tracks ran through the Bouresches to Belleau to Torcy route going along a valley that paralleled the 26th Yankee Division attack line.

Captain Malone could be heard ordering out two flanking movements to get the machine gun nests at the beginning of the

Wood near the enbankment causing terrible casualties. American bodies were piling up at an alarming rate. Guys were falling all around George. Something had to be done! They were sitting ducks! A doughboy to George's right screamed out and fell forward, blood gushing from his mouth, dying instantly. On the other side, George heard Woz cry out, "I'm hit! My knee! My knee!"

George took his bayonet out and snapped it back on with steely determination. As Sargent Klick was crawling past, he looked at George and asked,

"George, what are you doing?"

"I'm going to get that gun!"

Having said that, George jumped to his feet and ran forward, leaving an opened mouthed Sargent Klick wondering if he had lost his senses. George ran zig zag through the low lying wheat field. Bullets kicked up wheat stalks and filled the air with a golden haze. The thud and whizzes of passing bullets whipped past his face and gyrating body. The mist and smoke provided some cover, but the sun was burning through and adding its heat.

"Cover! Cover him! Hollered Sargent Klick.

He rose to his feet so the troops could hear him. "Commence firing! Commence firing!" At the same time Klick was emptying his semi-automatic rifle. But with the roar and din of battle, not too many heard him, but more saw him. George was about one hundred yards away from the nearest machine gun team when he bolted forward. He fell after about fifty yards, tripping over a broken wagon wheel. He fired a few rounds from his semi-automatic rifle, regained his feet and now was fully exposed to enemy fire. He lunged forward weaving and bobbing from left to right and back the other way. He ran on adrenaline and instinct. At seventy five yards he went down, hit by enfilading fire from two machine guns that criscrossed each other. George was hit and hurt. He lifted his rifle and took careful aim. He fired off a round and immediately killed the trigger man of one machine gun. When the feeder took over the machine gun and fed himself with one hand and fired with the other, George's steady aim shot him dead and that gun was silenced.

Now George picked himself up and staggered forward again, firing from the hip as he ran. Sargent Klick and a contingent of H company was now within fifty yards of the edge of the woods, moving up to support George. Klick could see the German second machine gun team pointing excitedly at George and turning the gun directly on him and firing away. Wheat pieces and dirt kicked up all around George. He went down a second time within twenty yards of the machine gun, point blang range! He was hit again and again. He raised his rifle and, bleeding profusely, slowly aimed and pulled the trigger, knocking the trigger man backwards with a bullet through his right temple. Two intrepid Germans attacked George! George slowly raised his rifle and pulled the trigger on his beloved springfield rifle and killed the first German and then the second. Three dead Germans lie between George and the German machine gun. The last German who was awkwardly feeding his machine gun, leapt up and fled. Seeing this and hearing the advancing American infantry yelling and screaming like mad Indians, a fourth maxim gun crew pulled out awkwardly carrying their heavy machine gun and withdrew to the rear. A final Boche machine gun emplacement just abandoned their gun on the ridge of the enbankment, and withdrew into the interior of the woods.

The flanking platoons from the right and left converged on the ridge securing the area. Sargeny Klick and Captain Malone ran back to George. He was alive, but gushing blood from his mouth and sweating heavily, gasping for breath, but trying to say something. Woz staggered up with the help of another doughboy. He threw himself to the ground and held George's bloody head propped up in his lap, and clearing blood from his face, cried out,

"George! George! Hang on buddy. Hang on. We'll get you out of here." "Help is on the way. Hang on, George. Hang on. You'll be ok. Stay with us, buddy."

"What's he saying?" Asked Sargent Klick.

"He's not saying anything. He's singing." Said a sobbing Woz, rocking George back and forth.

"Medic! Medic! Blubbered Woz.

A medic inserted himself between Woz and George. It was then that Woz noted the bullet holes across George's chest like a line of stitches. As they lifted him into a stretcher, Woz saw the bloody pulp of a smashed leg. It was almost severed.

"Oh, my God! Look at all the holes! I can't count them!" Spluttered Woz.

George's eyes were open, but he was staring blankly, and breathing in gasps, but also talking funny.

"What's he saying?" Asked Klick.

"He's not saying, he's singing."

"Singing what?"

"A song named 'Empty Arms.'"

"Woz, let go. Let go. He's losing a lot of blood. We've got to get him back," pleaded Captain Malone.

Woz let go, but before he did, he pulled from George's hand, bloody papers that turned out to be letters from Angelika.

They whisked George away. Woz couldn't get up. He grabbed his bloody knee, blubbering like a baby, rocking back and forth, mumbling "George, George."

"Klick, you and Hollowway, put Woz across your rifle and carry him back. His knee is a mess." So ordered Captain Malone. "I've got to go on."

Later, while Sargent Klick was sitting down, contemplating the day's cataclysmic events, and Dilboy's charge, he was heard muttering to himself,

"That was one of the greatest feats of personal bravery in the world war."

Woz was carried back to the rear for a medical tent. He went numb, not so much mentally, as emotionally, and not so you would notice, with all the craziness of the surrounding war running amok; it made things look surreal. As George lay on a cot staring at the tent ceiling, sedated from pain, the talk among the wounded was about George Dilboy's amazing charge.

"Maybe his promotions will come through, for all the good it will do him now. He's been put in twice for promotions, but they say upstairs is holding them up because Pershing doesn't favor

General Edwards recommendations," remarked one injured doughboy, his head wrapped in bandages.

"Just what the hell was Dilboy trying to prove anyway? A rifle against machine guns? And alone? What did he prove?" Asked another doughboy, who raised his arm in wonderment, the other in a sling.

Woz rose slowly from his cot, careful of the knee. He turned to the questioning doughboy and said,

"What did he prove? That one man with courage makes a majority."

George's thigh was such a bloody pulp and he was so shot up, they evacuated him all the way back to the Division Surgeon. They had to give him a massive transfusion of blood to replace its loss, and to avoid him going into shock. His condition was critical, but he was still alive. It was 9:30 a.m., July 18, 1918.

While Woz's injuries were being treated, he went into a drug masked depression, which they didn't realize until later, after his initial surgery. Woz stonewalled a young psychiatrist brought in on a consult. Back at a hospital near the Atlantic coast, after a few more fruitless sessions with another psychiatrist, Woz blurted out in frustration,

"I wasn't there. You don't understand, Doc, I wasn't there."

"Wasn't where?" Asked Doctor Feinstein.

"George—my best friend in all the world, always seemed to be there for me. But when he needed me, I wasn't there! I just wasn't there! Now he's a cripple, maimed for life, if he lives."

Then Woz cracked. He burst into tears, weeping uncontrollably. He hid his head in shame and humiliation, but he couldn't stem the flow. The dam ruptured and he couldn't stop it. It was a long time coming. The doctor let it happen, then had Woz sedated so he could sleep. He knew now that Woz would recover.

"Why do I feel so guilty?" Asked a still later distraught Woz. "By all that's right in this world, George should have lived a healthy life and I should be the cripple or have died. It's not fair," Woz lamented.

"War isn't fair, Mr. Wozlowski. It never has been. You're just expressing your humanity. Survivors guilt is common in war. That may not make you feel any better, but at least you know you are not alone."

"When will it go away? When will the nightmares stop?"

"Grief takes time. And time is a healer. If you are not patient, you'll become one," said the doctor.

"Ha, ha, laughed Woz. I'm already a patient. That's just great. If I'm not careful, I'll become what I am."

Doctor Feinstein couldn't help smiling. The incongruity humbled him. A distraught patient was making more sense that him.

"Mr Wozlowski, let's assume that you were there for George. He might have been injured or died anyway, or you both might have died. Would that make you feel any better?"

"No. I might feel even worse."

"Exactly. One has to be realistic, Mr. Wozlowski. Horrible things happen, especially in war. It's not your fault. People get severely hurt, live and die, whether there's a war or not. What makes you or I think we are God, able to save another's life? We are lucky if we can save our own."

"I know, I know, but it still hurts."

"And hurting is healing. It may never go away, not completely. Nor should it."

Never?"

"Grieving is a vital life process. It defines us as human beings. We should never forget out heroes. In this sense, the dead consecrate the living. He has touched your life. Honor his life or death by living the rest of your life as best you can. A long or healthy life is a gift that is guaranteed to no one, as you now know."

"But he was so young, so full of life. I know he's going to die. I just know it. A beautiful fiance and family waiting at home. George had such a bright future. Where's the sense?"

"You can make the sense. A life is measured by its deeds, not its length. By carrying on his memory, you honor it, and by telling his story it can reach generations yet unborn. In that sense, he lives on. And so can you. Wouldn't he do the same for you?"

Woz stopped and thought about that for a moment. Then he slowly, almost imperceptibly, nodded his head and said,

"Yeah, he would. If the situation was reversed, I know he would."

———————————

The doughboy drive continued through Belleau Wood and beyond in the days to follow. In the near term, the Boche would be driven back another twenty miles, closing off the salient and flattening out the line. Thereafter, the Germans would be pushed back one hundred miles to Verdun to the north of the salient, and south of the salient beyond St. Mihiel toward the German border. In the end, the Germans five desperate offensives in March, April, May, June and July of 1918 failed to push through to Paris. The American soldier was at the point of the big thrust to stop the Boche, and then helped the Allies drive them back all along the Western Front.

The vaunted German Army, self-described as the best in the world, would back up and spend the rest of the war on the defensive. The German High Command now knew that they could not win the war. In the nearly four months remaining in the war, they would try to make the best peace terms they could negotiate. But they would have little bargaining leverage and the Armistice terms would be such a humiliation, that it would be tantamount to a German surrender.

CHAPTER FORTY

THE END

Woz had surgery to clean up and repair his left knee back at the Division headquarters medical unit. But he would also need reconstructive surgery. So he would be invalided back to the States for this sophisticated procedure. This injury ended the war for Woz. While still in France, he kept inquiring about George. The last he heard during the late afternoon of July 18th, George was in still serious condition, and was being rushed into surgery. He was still alive, and the doctors were fighting to save his life. Beyond that the confusion of the war prevented him from getting a clear update.

In mid-August Woz progressed well enough to be shipped back to the states with other medical cases to receive continued treatment and surgery. In September, he was released to go home to Brickbottom, with outpatient followup in Boston. With help, he healed physically, emotionally, mentally and spiritually with the help of his doctors and family, and friends like Angelika. He went from a wheelchair to crutches to a cane, and eventually he could ambulate, but with an obvious limp. But he was alive and had a future. He had heard that the wounded at Chateau Thierry and Belleu Wood would be coming back through Boston. He told a frantic Angelika what he heard and she couldn't get any information from the Army because she wasn't family.

Family members were advised by the Army that the Red Cross were having communication problems due to broken lines, confusion and chaos, and the run up to the closing months of the war. Telegrams, notices and mail all were experiencing back-up due to war priorities and they would be notified as soon as possible. Some few notices fell through the cracks due to bureau inefficiences. George's, apparently, was one of them. Woz was involved in his own treatment and recovery to mount other than periodic inquiries. Government reassurances were forthcoming, but little information.

The Red Cross and a Government agency confirmed that, yes, it was true that many of the wounded from Chateau Thierry and Belleau Wood were scheduled to go through Boston on a certain date, but the passenger and injury list was incomplete at the moment and that family would be notified as soon as possible. That was enough for Angelika. She was encouraged as much as discouraged by the lack of formal notice, and insisted on going down to Commomwealth Pier to meet the troop ship, even if George wasn't on that particular one. She wanted to see the happy faces of the families of returning veterans. Whatever their injuries, at least thet were alive. And Woz himself should be grateful that he survived, she lectured him, as was her way. She even asked to push Woz around in his wheelchair in Brickbottom to help her practice for George, should he need that. It made her think of George and fed her hopes. Woz was treated like a returning hero in the neighborhood and city, which he surely was, thought Angelika.

The big day arrived and Angelika rushed down to the Commonwealth Pier early to see the preparations being made for receiving the war heros home. She dressed in her best finery, highlighted by her broad laced and feathered hat, and full skirted long white laced embroided dress. Her neck, sleeves and bodice had frilly lace all along its borders. She felt so special! Her man was coming home, hurt but alive. The rest of her life was about to begin.

She even drove George's car into Boston, something she wouldn't ordinarily do and didn't like to do. But she thought it would please George. She had threatened all kinds of bad tidings if George's brothers didn't drive that car down from Keene, New Hampshire. They made it, and in time for the whole crew of them to clean and polish up the motor car to a lusty sheen. Then they all piled in for the short drive to the Boston landing wharf. Antonios, however, fell sick with the flu raging all around and had to stay home, with Marianthe. Woz was going to stop by the house to check on Antonios and Marianthe, before going himself to the port of entry and the welcoming throngs.

At the Commonwealth Pier, everyone was waiting with excited anticipation. The people brought fruit to eat while they were waiting and made like they were having a light picnic. The atmosphere was festive, with smiles and squeals all about. They joked and clowned around to burn off extra energy. They kept checking with the British Cunard Shipping line clerk to see that the ship was on time and proceeding as scheduled. Yes, it had left New York harbor and yes, it was scheduled to arrive on schedule, barring any unseen circumstances, an irritated clerk re-assured them. Any change in the arrival time, rest assured he would announce it as soon as it came in.

Beaming with expectation, Angelika sought affirmation from her pocket glass mirror and others, who kept telling her she looked fine, the wind hadn't mussed up her hair and her expensive perfume smelled divine. She sat when she felt like it, which wasn't often, because she was restless and kept jumping up. Others smoked and occasionally pulled out a round, chained watch from a vest pocket.

Finally, they heard the announcement that the giant steamship, the Leviathan, was entering the outer harbor and would be approaching the dock soon. The escorting tugboats seemed puny next to the huge, four-funneled steamship. The Leviathan was the largest passenger ship in the world in 1917. Owned by Germany, it was seized as a war prize when America declared war on Germany, and converted to military passenger use transporting American troops. The announcer also asked the dockworkers to clear the docking area until the ship was secure, and reminded the now swelling, throngs of waiting people to remain behind the fence for everyones safety. An electric buzz seemed to go through the waiting crowd. Angelika couldn't contain herself with the thrill of it all, gigling and trembling with excitement. She frequently rose up and stood on top of her toes to get a better view. She strained her neck, while holding her hat on, because the massive ship brought in a wind with its wake and shadow, adding to the breathless frenzy.

Unseen to Angelika was the slow figure of a big man, getting bigger and bigger, as he neared her. He was lurching, and limping toward her, hobbling along on a cane, with a pained expression on his face. He carried a telegram in the closed fist of his free hand. It whipped back and forth, menacingly. He said nothing, but gave Angelika the opened telegram. Spotting woz, Angelika shouted a gleeful greeting, as she took the telegram. Steadying her hand, she struggled to keep the telegran still, as she read it,

> To: *Antonios Dilboy*
> *71 Linwood Street*
> *Somerville, Massachusetts*
>
> *"The Secretary of War desires to express his deep regret that your son has been killed in action at Belleau Wood, France, in the service of his country."*
> *Our thoughts and prayers go out to you and your family for your loss.*
> *You will receive every courtesy and cooperation from this Office with respect to this matter. Further information will be furnished you as soon as it becomes available.*
>
> *Sincerely,*
> *Secretary of War*

Cutting short the reading, Angelika screamed out a blood curdling, piercing yell that was drowned out by a blasting horn from the just arriving steamship. Between the ship's happy horn blasts, her screaming was initially heard by some as a hysterically happy spouse spotting her husband on board the ship. Angelika dropped to her knees howling helplessly in disbelief. Her frantic wailing soon startled those around her, who gave her wide berth and strange looks. Woz reached down to comfort her, but she pushed him away and cried out uncontrollably, her body heaving and wracked with deep, gasping sobs. The telegram was whipped away from her tiny fist, as it fluttered furiously in the wind, flying away.

The family gathered around reaching out to touch her. A policeman rushed over to see about the loud commotion. Quickly informed, he turned around and told the gathering curious to move away, that everything was under control. He suggested to the family that they take her inside to the medical station. John and Kostas Dilboy carried Angelika, still crying out in overwhelming grief, inside. There she was too distraught to take any aspirin. An ambulance was called and she was hustled out to a nearby hospital and put under sedation to calm her hysterics. The family followed in George's car.

In the days that followed Uncle Kostas contacted the Government for more details. The family was still stunned and felt confused and grief stricken. Antonios sent a telegram to Yiasemi and followed it up with a long letter. George was buried initially near Belleau Wood and then later transferred to a common American graveyard near the Argonne Forest.

Angelika was so depressed she refused to talk to anyone, and her family worried about her emotional stability. She needed professional help to cope with this life-shattering blow. In one of the few comments she made in the following months, she told Woz that she knew death in war was always possible, but she didn't think it would happen to George. She simply refused to believe it would happen, and when it did, she was totally shattered. Her family and friends prayed for her recovery and for her mental health. It was touch and go for months. She was too overwrought to work. Gradually, her parents got her to do simple errands, go to church, and talk to Woz, when she suddenly decided she wanted to know what went on over there. She was bitter and angry, but opening up to life, little by little.

One surprise she discovered was Woz telling her that George and he weren't drafted, they both enlisted, because it meant they could serve together. They both thought they would be shortly drafted anyway, especially as both were veterans. And they figured the sooner they enlisted, the sooner they would get out and get on with their lives. Angelika was not angry at this well-intentioned deception, because she believed George was getting restless again and would have volunteered anyway, eventually. She didn't agree with that, but knew George would be miserable if he didn't go "over there," and others thought him a slacker or draft dodger. She loved him for the person he was, and wouldn't fault him now.

What did upset her was Woz revealing that as George lay bleeding and seriously injured from countless bullet wounds from the deadly German machine guns, he held her letters and was singing.

"At first I thought he was talking. But I instantly realized he was singing, as best he could, a song entitled 'Empty Arms.'"

"Whose arms was he singing about, his or mine?"

"Both, I imagine. He was grasping your letters and singing to you, Angelika, with his last breaths."

Angelika burst into tears again, sputtering in frustration,

"If I didn't have my faith and belief in in eternal life, I think I would lose my mind."

"He will always be with us, in spirit," said Woz. "He enriched our lives while he was amongst us. Life is for the living, Angelika. We must move on if we are to honor his memory. He would want that, wouldn't he?"

"Yes, I suppose. I have to believe that, or I couldn't go on."

She still had her life, such as it was, Angelika mused. And slowly, she was starting to get spirit and spark back again. In great relief to her parents and many supportive friends, she resumed work part-time, and then full time. She was still trying to find out how this horrible experience fit into God's plan for her. At church, they told her to have faith. God would reveal to her his plan for her in the fullness of time. She soldiered on, hoping for a better future. It could only go up, she reasoned philosophically.

POSTSCRIPT

Five years later, in 1923, after making what peace they could with the past, Woz and Angelika buried their grief and passion into each other and married.

AFTERWORD

After the parade in Boston in April, 1919, featuring the march-past by the survivors of the 26th Yankee Division, Antonios wanted to re-unite with Yiasemi in Chios. The Turks had surrendered to British Forces, along with a contingent of American Forces in Constantinople, and the aging Sultan, Mehmet V, was put under House Arrest, on November 11, 1918. The Greek Army was encouraged and allowed by the British to recross the Aegean Sea and land at Smyrna to reclaim their properties and to recolonize the area. Antonios wrote Yiasemi that maybe now they could get their illegally confiscated property back, in Alatsata. Besides, with George's death, he had less reason to stay in Boston and he wanted to see the rest of his family. So he took a steamship back to Greece and on to Chios.

For the next three years the Greek Army succeeded in slowly pushing the Turkish Army four hundred miles inland, back all the way to the capital of Ankara. After Antonios's return to Asia Minor, and at his request, the body of George Dilboy was dug up from the Argonne Forest and transferred to Alatsata for reburial in the town of his birth. A James Testa of East Boston, representing the United States, accompanied the body back to Alatsata. There his casket, with the American flag draped across it, was marched through the town, lined by 17,000 mourners among the local citizenry. A large framed photograph of Dilboy was carried before the casket. Next to the oversized image of the hero, a large American flag was prominently displayed. Leading the way was a Greek military honor guard. The funeral cortege marched along the lined streets to the local Greek Church of St. Constantine, where his body lay in state in an open casket, as the townsfolk filed by to honor the "hero" Dilboy.

However, by this time, in September, 1922, a patriotic Turkish General named Mustafa Kemal Ataturk had rallied his Army and stopped the Greeks at Ankara, the Turkish capital city. Ataturk was an extraordinarily intelligent, handsome, brilliant military leader, with a long-term vision to modernize Turkey, along Western lines, having studied French history, in particular. This was the same General that led the Turks to drive off the British from its shores at the nine-month battle at Gallipoli in the Dardanelles Straits in 1915.

Back in 1922, relentlessly, the Turks pushed the Greek Army back to Smyrna, with the Greeks destroying each town through which it retreated, following a scorched earth policy to leave nothing of value to the counterattacking Turks. At Smynra, the Turks in full revenge, lost all pretense of discipline and savaged the town, burning Smyrna to the ground. In the process, they massacred thousands of Greeks indiscriminately, and drove up to a hundred thousand other fleeing Greeks off that coast to a motley assortment of Greek and other Nation's boats. The Greeks fled to various offshore islands, back to mainland Greece, and any place that would give them refuge.

During their rampage, the Turks attacked and invaded the Church of St. Constantine in Alatsata, and desecrated the remains of the "Greek hero" Dilboy. They also terrorized the villagers and committed unspeakable atrocities, including seizing and murdering a local Greek priest by nailing him to a barn door, in mock crucifixion of a Christian martyr. Other priests were lynched.

Fifty miles away, Antonios and Yiasemi and their family were among the desperate, fleeing refugees. They left the nearby island of Chios for Samos, another offshore Island further out in the Aegean Sea and South of Chios. Safely away, Antonios mailed a letter to his son, Kostas, of 4 Poplar St., Somerville, State of Massachusetts, in America. The letter from an exhausted and upset Antonios said:

I want to tell you that the casket containing the remains of your brother George was in the church of St. Constantine, and the Turks went in there, broke the casket open, scattered the bones all

over the floor, tramped on them, and also on the American flag
that covered the casket. Then with their swords, they struck them in
the bones, and tried to make the people who were seeking refuge in
the church eat them.

Please have someone get in touch with the American consul
about what has happened to your brother's remains.

This letter was taken to political, military and veterans
authorities and caused an international uproar. US Secrtary of State
Hughes telegraphed the American Consul at Smynra demanding
an immediate and thorough investigation and a report back to
him personally. Congressman Underhill of Massachusetts was most
active in pressing for a speedy investigation, and if possible, the
return of the remains to this country for a proper and fitting burial.
Massachusetts US Senators Lodge and Walsh added their protests
to the chorus. Authorities at the Capital in Washington D.C.
reassured the outraged Veterans Organizations in general and the
George Dilboy, Veterans of Foreign War Post, in Somerville, in
particular, that they regarded the incident as internationally serious.
The State Department and the U. S. Navy located the body and
demanded an apology and reparations from the Turkish government.

Still later, Antonios and the family would leave the Island of
Samos and resettle in the largest Greek Island of Crete, further out
in the Aegean, southwest of Samos, to get further away from the
maurauding Turks. Ultimately, other Dilboy family and relatives
scattered in various directions, including Athens, on the Greek
mainland, and to America.

Back in Turkey, the reaction of the Turks was quite different
from the Americans. Ataturk was concerned, not because a lowly,
Private Greek-American soldier's grave was disturbed, but because,
having driven all foreigners out of Turkey, he didn't want to give
the Americans any excuse to re-enter their country. He sent a
personal emissary to investigate, well knowing that regretably,

thousands of atrocities were committed that were far worse that a senseless grave incident that occurred in the process of driving the Greeks off the coast of Turkey.

Ataturk's personal emissary, at a private meeting met, Nurettin Pasa, Commanding General of the Turk First Army, a noted hothead, and sometime rival of Ataturk. Ataturk, however, tolerated his excesses because he needed him in the field. The ruthless rogue General was the military commandant of Smyrna, now renamed Izmir. He was incensed at the thought of any American coming on Turkish soil uninvited. He ranted:

If the Americans dare to enter Turkish territory, we will drive them into the Sea, as we did the Greeks, massacre them as we did the Armenians, or push them out of Turkey, as we did the British, and the French. What is America, anyway? The British flushed out their sewers and all their criminals and malcontents wash up on the shores of America and Australia. It's a country of castoffs, a garbage heap! The British and the French beat Germany. The Americans arrived late, held the shortest front, suffered the fewest casualties, and they want all the glory. They better not try to land on Turkish territory or I will personally see them die on the beaches, like the trapped 250,000 British troops and their Colonial lackies at Gallipoli.

A month later, waiting at the port of Cesme, across from Chios, and near Alatsata, General Nurettin Pasa, and the Chief Aide of Ataturk met the Commander of the American Warship, *USS Litchfield*, and his Navy bluejackets, after the Turkish Government offered their sincere regrets that the incident happened. The Turkish Army was lined up in salute formation in a reception line. The Turkish Army Band burst out with a stirring rendition of the American National Anthem, followed by the Turkish National Anthem. The body of Private George Dilboy of the American Army had been retrieved, put in a beautiful wooden casket and covered with an American flag, ready to be surrendered to American authorities. The formalities were brief and cordial.

Turkey welcomes the distinguished representatives of the American Government. We are only too pleased to return to you the honored remains of this American patriot and hero. The perpetrators of this unfortunate incident have been apprehended and punished severely. They will not overindulge in Greek liquor again, we assure you. He returns to his adopted homeland with our apologies and best wishes.

General Nurettin Pasa, on behalf of the American Government, I thank you for your co-operation. We look forward to a future of good relations between our two countries. We have every confidence that under the leadership of your esteemed General Mustafa Kemal Ataturk, you will succeed in restoring your country to a prosperous future.

In explaining the turn around in his attitude to his own astonished aide, the seething, contemptuous, General Nurettin Pasa, fumed that Ataturk mandated that the easiest way to get rid of the Americans was to give them what they wanted. *Besides,* he spat, *who cares about the bones of a dead Greek?*

Back in America, the body was unloaded at the Brooklyn Navy yard and entrained to Washington D.C. There, the Authorities initiated discussions with the City of Somerville as to whether he should be finally buried in Arlington National Cemetery or in the Boston area. Antonios Dilboy, the hero's father, decided the issue by selecting the Arlington National Cemetary because,

George belongs to America.

THE POWER OF EXAMPLE

As an interesting aside to George Dilboy's witnessed heroism, an amazing companion-incident occurred concerning the witness, Sargent Klick. Perhaps this should not be wondered at, given the power of example. The U.S. Army issued the following citation,

"General Orders 26, War Department, Washington D.C., February 14, 1919. Albert W. Klick, Sergent, Company H, 103rd Infantry. For extraordinary heroism in action near Bois de St. Remy, France, September 12, 1918. With the aid of six comrades Sargent Klick attacked and put out of commission a machine gun, which was checking the advance of his company. Later, he captured without aid twenty prisoners, and while advancing against another nest, he was twice wounded. Although in severe pain, he declined the use of a litter, walking three kilometers to a dressing station."

WORLD WIDE TRIBUTES

Sargent Albert W. Klick of Company H, remembers Dilboy as short and dark complexioned, and a jolly, good fellow. He remembered George as always willing and smiling, with a happy-go-lucky personality. He was a good mixer and generous hearted. Because he danced and clowned around, entertaining the troops against boredom, especially on the Mexican front, he was called "Kike," a Jewish reference, referring to his clownish and fun loving ways. The troops would frequently encourage him to entertain them. He was good for Company morale. Klick served continuously with Dilboy and met him frequently up to the time of his death. In France, Klick remembers Dilboy as always one of the first to step forward at the request for volunteers in the lines, or for exceptionally dangerous duties out in No-Man's Land. He served with George Dilboy in Company H, and was an eyewitness to his charge. He claimed that *"It was one of the greatest feats of personal bravery in the World War."*

Colonel S. M. Shumway, was Battalion Commander of Company H, and also an eyewitness to Dilboy's charge. He asserted, "It was one of the most impressive sights I experienced in the war. . . . . He was a fine a soldier as ever served under the Stars and Stripes."

General Clarence Edwards, Commander of the 26th Yankee Division, said that, "George Dilboy's charge was one of the war's epic's . . . . George Dilboy was one of the outstanding heroes of the war."

Across the U.S. and in Europe there are memorials to George Dilboy. In France, there is the Belleau Wood Memorial Park, maintained by a French Association, where there is a monument dedicated to the Marines of the U.S. Navy (then specially attached to the U.S. Army) and to the soldier George Dilboy of the 103rd Infantry of the 26th (Yankee) Division. The bronze plaque shows a slight young man, bayonet fixed, charging towards the woods.

At least four American Legion and Veterans of Foreign Wars Posts have been chartered and named after George Dilboy in Somerville, MA, New York City, Chicago, and Keene, New Hampshire, where he first enlisted. The Veterans of Foreign Wars chartered the first George Dilboy Post in Somerville, MA, on October 14, 1920. Officially, George Dilboy was awarded the then called Congressional Medal of Honor by the War Department, by order of the President of the U.S., in June, 1921.

A statute of Dilboy is located in Nea Erithrea, near Athens, Greece. As reported in the Greek newspaper *The National Herald,* and a noted cinematographer, James Chimbidis, a three-quarter length bust of Dilboy stands in Mason City, Iowa.

The "Hero Dilboy," as the Greeks refer to him, was buried for the fourth time and finally put to rest on November 12, 1922 in Arlington National Cemetary with unparalleled government ceremonies, celebrations and celebrities. With full military honors, he was buried before President Calvin Coolidge, the former Governor of Massachusetts, U.S. Senators and Congressmen, and a delegation from the City of Somerville's Dilboy Post: Commander Gene Driscoll, Joe Filadora, John Borges, Gene Carver, John Keating, Johnny Dickerman, Chet Hobbs, Hugh Turner, J. Gilman and Chuck Robinson. Military and Naval Commanders of the highest rank, Cabinet members, Senators, Diplomats Governors of States and leaders of every veterans organization in the country attended the tribute.

But perhaps the most memorable speech given at the impressive ceremonies for the burial of a Private in the U.S. Army was that given by a Vasilco I. Chebethes, Commander of the American Veterans of Hellenic Descent:

May we who have been spared to enjoy the blessings of the victory he died to win, recognize the exacting obligation of living in an age of light whose silvery arrows have been forged upon the anvils of death. May we here highly resolve to carry on the fight; and may we receive courage and inspiration to follow the dictates of duty, even though it may mean the loss of our fortunes and lives. Then we shall have built him a monument more lasting than brass and more enduring than the crumbling magnificence of the Pyramids. Then we shall have paid him a tribute sweeter than the songs of the Angels.

At Somerville City Hall, a statue of Private Dilboy was dedicated on August 26, 1930 after a huge parade before thousands of people. A memorial bronze tablet at the *Masachusetts State House in Boston* bears his name and soldierly figure.

On July 10, 1938, the main road leading into Camp Edwards, Bourne, MA was formally dedicated as Dilboy Road in honor of the World War I Medal of Honor winner.

There is a large memorial statute of George Dilboy in Illinois, dedicated in 1942 by a group of Greek-American World War I veterans. It is maintained by the veteran's administration outside the Edward Hines, Jr. Hospital, the largest veteran's hospital in the world.

In 1944, during World War II, the Nazi's invaded the largest Greek Island of Crete, raided the Dilboy family home and stole the Medal of Honor, posthumously awarded to George Dilboy as a war souvenir. It was never returned. The Medal had been given to relatives of the hero by Antonios Dilboy, father of the hero.

Fifty five years later, in June, 1999, Nicholas Burns, the US Ambassador to Greece, during a large, moving ceremony and reception, formally restored the Medal of Honor to Georghios Rosakis of Athens, second cousin of George Dilboy. He accepted the medal on behalf of all of Private George Dilboy's relatives, USA and Greek Veteran Groups, Greeks and Greek-Americans world-wide.

On July 24, 2000, the United States Flag was raised and lowered from the flagpole of the battleship USS Arizona resting in 38 feet of water at the bottom of Pearl Harbor, Hawaii in memory of George Dilboy, awarded the Congressional Medal of Honor, World War I. This Certificate of Flag Presentation was signed and authenticated on May 3, 2001 by Robert T. Conway, Jr. Rear Admiral, U.S. Navy, Commander, Navy Region, Hawaii, and Kathleen J. Billings, National Park Service Superintendent, USS Arizona Memorial.

To put matters into a fuller perspective from a broader overview, there have been approximately 40 million men and women called to the colors in our country's history. Of that number, less than 3,500 have been awarded the Medal of Honor.

In 2005, an eight million dollar renovation is scheduled to be completed at the George Dilboy football and soccer Stadium in Somerville, MA. This structure is believed to be the largest monument in the world dedicated to the Greek "hero."

Looking back at a final view, George Dilboy died fighting *"Over there"* so that we at home could live in peace and freedom over here. He gave the last full measure of his devotion, and his and other veteran's sacrifices will live on forever.

OLD COLOSSUS MEETS NEW COLOSSUS

In a marvelous and stirring quirk of history that touches many aspects of this story, there stands the Colossus of Rhodes, a lighthouse on the Island of Rhodes in southeastern Greece. Rhodes is the largest of the Dodecanese Islands in the Aegean Sea, off the southwest coast of Turkey. As with all lighthouses, its purpose is to be a beacon of hope to the troubled at sea, beckoning them to its safe shore. The saga of George Dilboy and his family is illustrative of millions of others seeking safety on the shores of America. The thrill of hope and a new beginning is the reality experienced in being welcomed by the light of freedom eminating from the outstretched arm of our Statute of Liberty. It's history coming back to meet itself, and is an amazing confluence of what you give, you get.

Could anyone have captured the spirit better than the Poetess, Emma Lazurus, in her forever famous poem, *The New Colossus*:

> *Give me your tired, your poor,*
> *Your huddled masses yearning to breathe free,*
> *The wretched refuse of your teeming shore.*
>
> *Send these, the homeless, tempest-tost to me,*
> *I lift my lamp beside the golden door!*

Lest we forget, America is a nation of immigrants, who contribute, indeed.

BIBLIOGRAPHY

BOOKS

In addition to the books and oral histories cited in the Foreword, I acknowledge and include the following references:

The Greek War of Independence, by David Brewer, 2001, The Overlook Press, Woodstock and New York, NY.

Balkan Ghosts, A Journey Through History, by Robert Kaplan, 1993, St. Martins Press, Ist Ed., New York.

The Balkans, A Short History, by Mark Mazower, 2000, The Modern Library, New York, NY.

The Balkan Wars, by Andre Gerolymatos, 2002, Basic Books, a member of the Perseus Books Group, New York.

The Balkans, From Constantinople to Communism, by Dennis Hupchick, 2001, 2002, Palgrave Publishers Ltd. (formerly Macmillan Press Ltd.). Palgrave is the new global publishing imprint of St. Martins Press LLC, Scholarly and Reference Division.

A Travelers History of Greece, 4th edition, by Timothy Boatswain and Colin Nicolson, Interlink Books, an imprint of Interlink Publishing Group, Inc., Northhampton, New York.

Greece, Land of light, Picture Book, by Nicholas Gage and Barry Brukoff, 1998, a Bulfinch Press Book/Little Brown and Company, Boston, New York and London.

Blood on the Border, by Clarence Clendenen, 1969, Macmillan Co., Inc., Collier-Macmillan Canada Ltd., Toronto, Ontario, Canada.

Pancho Villa, A Biography, by Jean Rouverd, 1972, Doubleday and Co., Inc., Garden City, New York.

The Great Pursuit, by Herbert Molloy Mason, Jr., 1970, Random House, New York.

Pershing, General of the Armies, by Donald Smythe, 1986, Indiana University Press, Bloomington, Indiana.

Until the Last Trumpet Sounds, by Gene Smith, 1998, John Wiley and Sons, Inc., New York.

World War I, by Gail B. Stewart, 1991, America's War Series, Lucent Books, P.O. Box 289011, San Diego, CA.

The First World War, An Illustrated History, by John Keegan, 2001, Alfred A. Knopf, New York.

The Battle of Belleau Wood, by Richard Suskind, 1969, The Macmillan Company, New York, NY, Collier-Macmillan Ltd., London, England.

Make the Kaiser Dance, Living Memories of a Forgotten War, The American Experience in World War I, by Henry Berry, 1978, Doubleday and Company, Garden City, New York.

The Great War, by Cyril Falls, 1959, G. P. Putnam's and Sons, New York, NY.

Atlas of the First World War, by Martin Gilbert, 1970, Dorset Press, London, England.

The Great War, Perspectives of the First World War, Edited by Robert Cowley, 2003, Random House Trade Paperbacks, New York.

The Last Days of Innocence, by Meirion and Susie Harries, 1997, Random House, New York.

The Irish Guards in the Great War, The First Battalion, by Rudyard Kipling, 1923, 1997, Spellmount Ltd., The Old Rectory, Staplehurst, Kent, England.

The First World War, by Michael Howard, 2002, Oxford University Press, England.

The First World War, by Martin Gilbert, 1994, Henry Holt and Company, New York.

11th Month, 11th Day, 11th Hour, by Joseph E. Persico, 2004, Random House, New York.

The Doughboys, America and the First World War, by Gary Mead, 2000, The Overlook Press, Peter Mayer Publishers, Inc., Woodstock, New York.

Ataturk, the Biography of the Founder of Modern Turkey, by Andrew Mango, 1999, The Overlook Press, Peter Mayer Publishers, Inc., Woodstock, New York.

NEWSPAPERS AND PERIODICALS

U.S. Embassy Newsletter, May, 1999, Athens, Greece regarding George Dilboy article and re-issuance of Medal of Honor.

Somerville Journal, Somerville, MA, currently part of The Community Newspaper Company, Needham, MA, many and various articles regarding George Dilboy published from 1920's through the present time, 2005.

George Dilboy Memorial Foundation Publications, George Dilboy Chapter No. 13, Disabled American Veterans of the World War, Chicago, Illinois.

Greek Epirus Army, 1ˢᵗ Balkan War, 1912-1913, Military Collection by Alex Mehtidis, source: Greek Army Historical Service, '1912-1913 War' Volume B; B'Army Corps, 'Battles of the Greek Army for the liberation of Epirus', June 1965, and Mission Militaire Francaise en Greece, 'Rapport du Lt. Colonel Crosson-Duplessix au sujet du siege de Jannina', Athenes: 30 Acril 1913 (Reprinted in Ioannina by IMIAX in 2000).

The Hellenic Chronicle, America's largest newspaper for Greek-Americans, Thursday, July 24, 1986, article on Brickbottom section of East Somerville.

The Hellenic Chronicle, Wednesday, June 16, 1999, Article on re-issuance of Medal of Honor, posthumously, to George Dilboy, through his second cousin, George Rosakis, of Athens, Greece by U.S. Ambassador to Greece, Nicholas Burns, in Athens, Greece.

Hellenic Chronicles, Illustrated Monthly Magazine, English Section, New York, August, 1944, Main Office, Chicago, Illinois, picture and article showing burial of sealed box of all the historic letters of George Dilboy at the base of the statute of the Dilboy Memorial at Hines Hospital, Illinois.